**Oxford Applied Mathematics and Computing Science Series**

*General Editors*

J. Crank, H. G. Martin, D. M. Melluish

R. G. GARSIDE
*University of Lancaster*

---

# The architecture of digital computers

CLARENDON PRESS · OXFORD
1980

*Oxford University Press, Walton Street, Oxford* OX2 6DP

OXFORD LONDON GLASGOW
NEW YORK TORONTO MELBOURNE WELLINGTON
KUALA LUMPUR SINGAPORE JAKARTA HONG KONG TOKYO
DELHI BOMBAY CALCUTTA MADRAS KARACHI
NAIROBI DAR ES SALAAM CAPE TOWN



Published in the United States by Oxford University Press, New York



**British Library Cataloguing in Publication Data**

Garside, R G
The architecture of digital computers.-(Oxford applied mathematics and computing science series).
1. Electronic digital computers — Design and construction
I. Title II. Series
621.3819′58′2 TK7888.3 79-41148

ISBN 0-19-859627-8
ISBN 0-19-859638-3 Pbk



Printed and bound in Great Britain by Morrison & Gibb Ltd, Edinburgh.

## Preface

WHEN I learnt my *second* machine-level language, I became fascinated by the possible variations in computers at this level. My fascination resulted in this book, which is designed to give a comprehensive survey of computers from 1946 to the present, and which should be of interest to anyone involved in computing. In particular it should appeal to those who are interested in the differences between computers at an architectural level, for example programmers who would like to know more than is revealed in their assembler language manuals. It is suitable as a textbook for courses on computer architecture for second- and third-year undergraduate students, who have done some programming at the machine level.

The book describes the different features seen by a machine-level programmer, after all the supportive software is stripped away. It does not attempt to describe this software itself. Nor does it describe the technology and design of the combinatorial and sequential circuits out of which the hardware is built. A number of excellent books are available which describe these two levels. The computers discussed are always general-purpose, stored-program digital computers, except for a brief excursion to analog and hybrid computers in Chapter 7.

An attempt has been made to adhere to a common terminology throughout, despite the use by computer manufacturers of different terms for the same thing (or the same term for different things). In several cases, of course, terms introduced by IBM have become de facto standards.

I would like to thank the many computer manufacturers and others who have supplied information, my colleagues and students at the University of Lancaster on whom I tried out a number of these ideas, and my wife for continual encouragement.

*Lancaster, October 1979* *R.G.G.*

## Contents

## Acknowledgements

Details of the Data General Nova are taken from *How to use the Nova computers* (Copyright 1970, 1971 by Data General Corporation). Figure 3.22(a) is reprinted from *User's manual: programmer's reference: S/130 micro programming WCS feature* (Copyright 1977 by Data General Corporation. Reproduced with permission of Data General Corporation.)

Details of the DEC PDP-8 are taken from *PDP8/e and PDP8/m small computer handbook* (Copyright 1971 by Digital Equipment Corporation). Details of the DEC PDP-10 are taken from *DECsystem 10 assembly language handbook* (Copyright 1967, 1968, 1969, 1970, 1971, 1972 by Digital Equipment Corporation). Details of the PDP-11 are taken from *PDP11/45 processor handbook* (Copyright 1971 by Digital Equipment Corporation. Reproduced with permission of Digital Equipment Corporation.)

Details of the IBM 360 and 370 ranges are taken from *IBM system/360 principles of operation* (Copyright 1964 by IBM Corporation) and *IBM system/370 principles of operation* (Copyright 1970, 1972, 1973 by IBM Corporation. Reproduced with permission of IBM Corporation.)

Figure 1.5 is derived from *John Von Neumann: collected works,* Volume 5 edited by A. H. Taub. (Copyright 1961 by Pergamon Press Ltd. Reproduced with permission of the publisher.)

Figure 2.19 is reprinted from *A guide to IBM 1401 programming* by D. D. McCracken. (Copyright 1961 by IBM Corporation. Reproduced with permission of IBM Corporation.)

Figure 2.21 is reprinted from *Communication networks for computers* by D. W. Davies and D. L. A. Barber. (Copyright 1973 by John Wiley & Sons Ltd. Reproduced with permission of the publisher.)

Figure 3.22(b) is reprinted with some revision from *Burroughs B1700 systems reference manual.* (Copyright 1972 by Burroughs Corporation. Reproduced with permission of Burroughs Corporation.)

Figure 5.10 is reprinted from *Operating systems* by S. E. Madnick and J. J. Donovan. (Copyright 1974 by McGraw-Hill Book Company. Reproduced with permission of the publisher.)

Figure 6.15 is reprinted with some revision from *Control Data 6000 series computer systems reference manual.* (Copyright 1966, 1967, 1968, 1969, 1970, 1971, 1972, 1973 by Control Data Corporation. Reproduced with permission of Control Data Corporation.)

Figure 6.19 is reprinted with some revision from 'Distributed computer networks' by P. T. Kirstein in *Nature* for 16th October 1975. (Copyright 1975 by MacMillan Journals Ltd. Reproduced with permission of the author and publisher.)

# 1 Introduction

## 1.1. The Classic Von Neumann Computer

THE TYPICAL programmer sees a modern computer in terms of one or more high-level languages, together with a command language which he must use to communicate with the operating system. His only contact with its hardware may be with an interactive terminal (if he is lucky), or with a series of error messages couched in terms of the internal structure of the computer (if he is unlucky). Even the assembler-language programmer is protected from some of the worst idiosyncrasies of the computer's hardware by the ministrations of the operating system (typically in the control of peripheral devices). The aim of this book, however, is to look beneath this superstructure, and to describe computers and their variation at a basic hardware level, below the operating system but above the detailed electronics; we discuss further the nature of this level in § 1.3.

We first consider a very simple computer, with which we can introduce the basic concepts and terminology required for the remainder of the book. We choose to do this in terms of a simplified version of the computer described in the paper 'Preliminary discussion of the logical design of an electronic computing instrument' by Burks, Goldstine, and Von Neumann (1946), for reasons which will be mentioned later. This computer, shown in Figure 1.1, consists of four sections: the store; the data manipulation unit; the input and output units; and the control unit. We review the salient points of these sections in turn.

(a) *The store*

The *store* is a collection of store locations or *words,* into each of which the computer can place a piece of information, to be retained for later extraction and use. A word is a group of electronic components, each of which can be set into either of two states. Thus a word can store any information that can be coded in the form of an appropriate number of binary bits: such a piece of information might be a numeric value, a group of one or more characters, or (as we shall see later) an instruction for controlling the computer.

The number of bits of information which a store word can hold is its

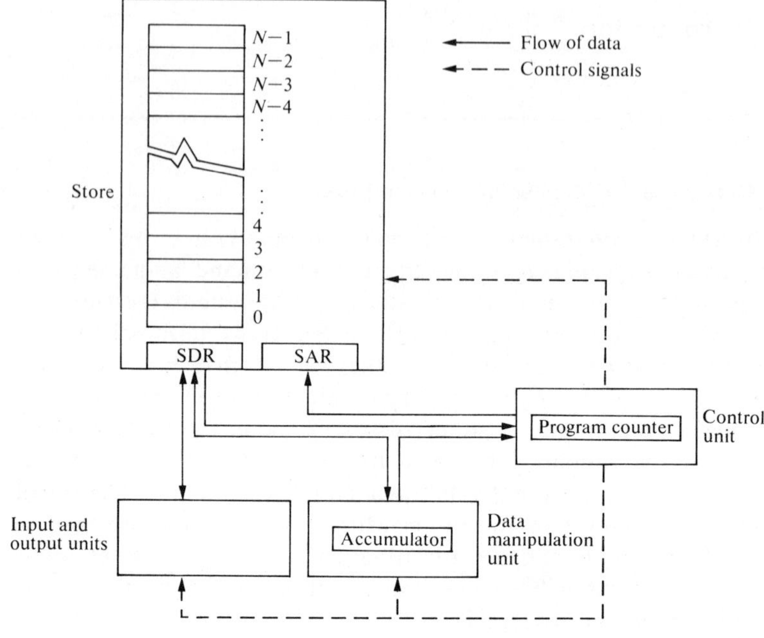


FIG. 1.1

*word length,* and is the same for all words in the store. The word length for the store of a particular computer is chosen to hold a maximal numeric value or number of characters appropriate to the application area and cost to which the computer is designed. Word lengths vary from 12 or less to 64 or more bits, typical lengths being 16 and 32 bits.

In order to store or retrieve information we must have some means by which the computer can refer to any location. Since a store is constructed as a vector or linear sequence of words, we specify each one by its position in the sequence. Thus if we have a set of $N$ words or store locations, each has an associated numeric value in the range zero to $N$–1, the *store address,* by which it is uniquely specified. Such a store address is a new type of information that we might want to deposit as the contents of a word.

Two special storage devices or registers form part of the store, the *store address register* (SAR) and the *store data register* (SDR), or store buffer register. In order to store a piece of information, it is placed in the SDR; the address at which it is to be stored is placed in the SAR, and the control unit of the computer sends a 'write' signal to the store. After some delay depending on the technology involved, the operation is complete; the specified location contains the new information, its previous contents having been overwritten and lost. In order to retrieve a piece of information, its address is placed in the SAR and a 'read' signal sent to the store; after some delay, the information is available in the SDR, for routing to some other part of the computer. Note that the store location accessed still contains a copy of the information read.

We assume that the store is randomly accessible; that is, the time taken to access a store location in order to store or retrieve information is constant and (in particular) is independent of the particular location being accessed and of the location previously accessed.

Notice that we avoid the (anthropomorphic) term memory, and the term core store, which presupposes a particular store technology (although it is often used generically); when we wish to distinguish among several levels of storage on a computer, we will refer to this basic level as *main* or *primary* store. Furthermore the term *register* is sometimes used to refer to any device which holds a group of one or more bits of information, and which is capable of being accessed at electronic speeds: in this book we use it only for storage devices provided for some special purpose (such as the SAR), and do not apply it to a general store location.

(b) *The data manipulation unit*

The *data manipulation unit* is capable of performing any of a fixed set of *operations* as signalled by the control unit. A typical operation requires two pieces of data or *operands* upon which to operate; one is extracted from an appropriate location in store, and one is found in a special storage device or register within the data manipulation unit, the *accumulator*. The result of the operation is placed in the accumulator, destroying its previous contents. In a computer oriented towards numerical calculation, the operations must include provision for addition and subtraction, and probably multiplication and division as well; on a computer oriented towards character manipulation there would be various operations for moving and scanning character strings.

We have chosen a name for this unit which does not presuppose numerical calculation; other terms for this unit are the arithmetic unit, the arithmetic and logical unit (ALU), and the mill (a term introduced by Babbage, and used in some British computers).

(c) *Input and output units*

Any computer has a number of input/output or peripheral devices attached to it, both for communication with the outside world (card readers, line printers, terminals, etc.) and for augmenting the computer's information storage capacity (magnetic discs, magnetic tape, etc.). As with the data manipulation unit, these units are able to carry out any one of an appropriate set of operations when signalled by the control unit; for example, to read a digit punched on paper tape and store it in a specified store location or to retrieve a digit from a specified store location and print it on an electric typewriter.

At present we assume that the computer does only one thing at a time. If a read or write operation is started on a peripheral device, the computer awaits the completion of this operation before continuing with the next. When we consider that a typical input/output operation is thousands or millions of times slower than a typical internal operation (such as the addition of two numbers), and that there may be other tasks to which the computer could turn its attention while such an operation is going on, then we can see scope for redesigning the computer in this area.

We introduce the term *transput* from the Algol 68 language to cover both input and output: thus for instance we will talk of a transput device instead of a peripheral device, and a transput operation instead of an input/output operation.

(d) *The control unit*

The *control unit* supervises the operation of the other three sections of the computer discussed above. It does this by initiating the transfer of data between units, and by sending appropriate control signals, in accordance with a schedule or *program* of *instructions*. Each instruction is encoded in such a way that it can be held in a store location, so that the store contains both the data being operated on and the program of instructions specifying the operations to be performed. The control unit contains a special storage device or register, the *program counter,* which contains the address of the store location holding the next instruction to be executed or obeyed. Other names in common use for this register are the instruction counter, next instruction address register (or NIAR), sequence register, and current order register.

While the computer is running, the control unit is executing a basic cycle divided into two phases, *fetch* and *execute*. The *fetch* phase involves extracting the contents of the store location referred to by the program counter, and decoding it into an operation code portion, specifying an operation to be carried out, and an operand portion, specifying a store address (whose numeric value we will indicate as $X$). The program counter is then incremented by one, to point to the next store location in sequence, since this normally holds the next instruction to be executed. The control unit then enters the *execute* phase, to carry out the operation decoded in the fetch phase. There are three cases.

(a) An operation of the data manipulation unit is called for; for example, transfer the numeric value held at store address $X$ to the data manipulation unit, and add it to the value in the accumulator, or transfer the value in the accumulator to the store and deposit it at address $X$.

(b) An input/output operation is called for; for example, transfer the character at store address $X$ to the typewriter and print it, or read the next character punched on a piece of paper tape and transfer it to the store, to be deposited at address $X$.

(c) The sequence of instructions being executed is to be changed, so that the next instruction to be executed is not the one stored immediately after the instruction currently being executed. The store address $X$ extracted from the current instruction is placed by the control unit in the program counter (destroying its previous contents), so that the next fetch extracts an instruction from store address $X$ (and then from store addresses $X+1$, $X+2$, etc., until a further such 'jump' instruction is encountered).

We require two types of jump instruction; one (the *unconditional jump)* which always changes the program counter, and one (the *conditional jump)* which changes the program counter only if a certain condition is true (such as that the accumulator contains a non-negative value); if the condition is false, the next instruction to be executed is the one stored immediately after the jump instruction. Thus the computer selects a course of action dependent on the data values it encounters.

To illustrate these concepts, Figure 1.2 gives a section of program to compare the contents of locations 100 and 101, and store the larger value in location 102.

Load into accumulator contents of location 100
Subtract from accumulator contents of location 101
If contents of accumulator non-negative, jump to
Load into accumulator contents of location 101
Jump to
Load into accumulator contents of location 100
Store accumulator in location 102
•
•
•
•

FIG. 1.2

***The stored program concept***

One of the consequences of holding instructions in store locations is that they can be treated as data, and manipulated as such by the computer. This allows us to write programs which incorporate instruction modification. Suppose, for example, that we wish to write a program in which the computer has to sum $N$ values held in successive store locations, perhaps with store addresses 100, 101, 102, and so on. $N$ may be too large for there to be room for that number of add instructions to be held economically in the store, or the value of $N$ may not be known when the program is being prepared (for example it might be read in as a piece of data). On the simple computer described above we would have to do something like the following:

We write an add instruction which initially refers to store address 99, and arrange to have it executed $N$ times by appropriate use of a conditional jump instruction. Then, before each execution of the add instruction, we arrange to manipulate it as data in such a way that one is added to the address portion of the instruction; thus the add instruction refers successively to store addresses 100, 101, 102, and so on. A skeleton program for this is shown in Figure 1.3.

Set accumulator to zero
Set loop counter to N
Add one to operand field of 'add' instruction below
Add into accumulator contents of location 99
Subtract one from loop counter
If loop counter > 0, jump to

FIG. 1.3

There are major difficulties with the use of this technique, since it is likely to result in programs whose structure is extremely opaque, and which are therefore very difficult to understand and debug. Furthermore the lack of any rigid demarcation between the (unchanging) program and the (changing) data means that the computer hardware cannot be used to protect the program from corrupting itself, nor can a single copy of a program be shared simultaneously by several users. For these reasons the basic form of instruction modification described above is no longer used; instead its effect is achieved by the use of index registers, as described in the next section.

The stored program concept, the realization that instructions can be encoded and held in the store of the computer together with the data being operated on, is an important one for two reasons. First, as mentioned above, it introduced the idea of instruction modification, for which better mechanisms could then be found. Second, a program as a whole could be treated as data by a supervisory program; a loader, an assembler or compiler, or an operating system. Since this is such a vital concept, all the computers discussed in this book are stored program computers. We are thus ignoring two classes of externally programmed device, common in the early days of computing:

(a) Computers whose programs were held on such external media as paper tape or punched cards. Examples of this class are the Harvard Mark I (Aiken and Hopper 1946) and Babbage's analytical engine (Bowden 1953, Appendix 1).
(b) Devices where the program resides in a plugboard, such as the early ENIAC computer (Goldstine and Goldstine 1946).

We could envisage computers with two main stores, one for the program and one for data, but these would be very inflexible. Instead we assume that each store location in main store can hold either an instruction or a piece of data; this does not, of course, preclude the possibility of distinguishing these two cases at any particular time, either by segregating instruction areas from data areas, or by marking store locations in some way.

***The general-purpose electronic digital computer***

Let us now try and define rather more precisely the type of device that we are considering. We have introduced the term *computer,* and by this we mean a device which can process substantial quantities of data without detailed human intervention.

We have limited the field to stored-program computers, and we further limit the field to *general-purpose* computers; that is, to computers with an instruction set rich enough to perform a wide variety of tasks. This concept is rather vague because it can be shown that a computer with a very basic instruction set can simulate a Turing machine and therefore can, in theory, perform any 'computable' task, so that such a computer is (again in theory) completely general-purpose (see for example Minsky 1967).

We will not normally discuss the technology out of which the architectures that we describe are to be implemented. However, we will from time to time assume that we are discussing *electronic* computers, implemented by the routing and gating of electrical signals. This does not preclude the theoretical possibility of implementation in other technologies, such as fluidics (see for example Gluskin, Jacoby, and Reader 1964), although historically this has not been the case.

Finally, we will be considering *digital* computers, where data is stored and manipulated by devices that can assume one of only a finite number of states, rather than by devices which can assume any state in a prescribed continuous range (as in analog computers).

### *Von Neumann's computer*

There are many possible computers which could have been used to exemplify the terms we have introduced. For example we could have used a simple computer such as the DEC PDP-8, or a suitable hypothetical computer such as that presented for didactic purposes by Knuth (1968). However, these have assimilated some of the developments in computer design which we will discuss later. Instead, we choose to use the Von Neumann, Princeton, or IAS (Institute of Advanced Studies) computer introduced in Von Neumann's paper. We take this paper to mark the beginning of the era of modern computing, since it was the 'first widely circulated document about high speed computers' (Knuth 1970).

The paper proposed a computer with a store of 4096 40-bit words stored on the faces of a number of 'Selectrons' or electrostatic storage tubes, this being a device able to provide random-access storage before the introduction of the ferrite core store (first used on the Whirlwind computer at MIT in 1953). Although such a device matches the modern conception of main store, most early computers (such as EDVAC (Knuth 1970) and EDSAC (Wiles and Renwick 1949)) had a serial store, implemented as a magnetic drum or set of delay lines (as discussed in §5.6).

The word length of 40 bits was chosen to give suitable accuracy for the type of fixed-point binary calculations for which the computer was designed (hardware floating-point arithmetic having been rejected). Instructions of such a length would have been wasteful of storage, so instructions were 20 bits long (6 for an operation code, 12 for a store address, and 2 unused) and held two to a store word, as shown in Figure 1.4. The control unit executed first the left-hand instruction, then the right-instruction, of each word in the program. Pairs of jump instructions were provided to transfer control to the left- or right-hand instruction of a specified store location.

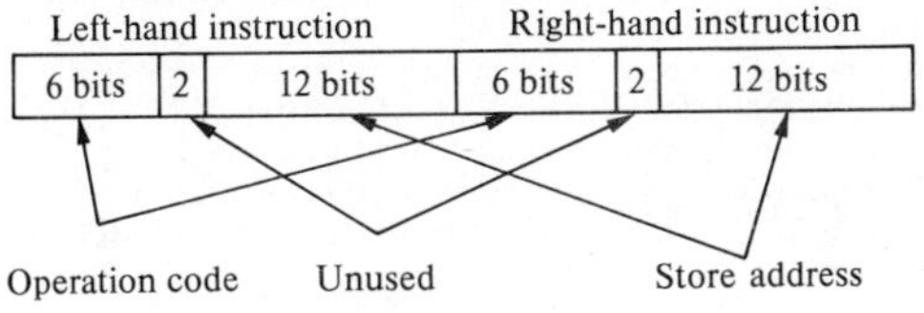


FIG. 1.4

The internal operations proposed in this paper are shown in Figure 1.5. Notice the 'partial substitution' orders (18 and 19), provided for instruction modification and subsequently altered to provide certain shifting facilities as well. Apart from the storage of two instructions to a word, the only extension to our rudimentary computer is in the provision of a second storage device or register in the data manipulation unit, the arithmetic register AR, used in conjunction with the accumulator for multiplication and division; the need for such a register is discussed in §2.1. Figure 1.6 shows how the section of program in Figure 1.2 would appear encoded for the Von Neumann computer, to occupy locations 50 to 53.

Input/output operations were not specified in detail in this paper, but three devices were proposed: an electric typewriter for the transfer of small quantities of data, a display unit for graphical presentation of results, and several magnetic wire or tape units to provide a secondary storage medium and for all normal input and output. It was expected that input data would be transcribed to the magnetic wire by a process which did not involve the computer, and similarly for output.

### *Word-oriented single-address binary computers*

Some basic features of the Von Neumann computer do not carry over to all the other designs we will study, for it can be characterized as a word-oriented, single-address binary computer.

| Operation code | Operation |
|---|---|
| 1 | Load Acc with $C(X)$ |
| 2 | Load Acc with $-C(X)$ |
| 3 | Load Acc with absolute value of $C(X)$ |
| 4 | Load Acc with − absolute value of $C(X)$ |
| 5 | Add $C(X)$ to Acc |
| 6 | Subtract $C(X)$ from Acc |
| 7 | Add absolute value of $C(X)$ to Acc |
| 8 | Subtract absolute value of $C(X)$ from Acc |
| 9 | Load AR with $C(X)$ |
| 10 | Load Acc with $C(AR)$ |
| 11 | Multiply $C$(AR) by $C(X)$, leaving most significant part of product in Acc, least significant part in AR |
| 12 | Divide $C$(Acc) by $C(X)$, leaving quotient in AR and remainder in Acc |
| 13 | Jump to instruction in left half of location $X$ |
| 14 | Jump to instruction in right half of location $X$ |
| 15 | If $C(\text{Acc}) \geqslant 0$, jump to instruction in left half of location $X$ |
| 16 | If $C(\text{Acc}) \geqslant 0$, jump to instruction in right half of location $X$ |
| 17 | Store $C$(Acc) at location $X$ |
| 18† | Move the left-most twelve bits of Acc to the operand field of the instruction in the left half of location $X$ |
| 19† | Move the left-most twelve bits of Acc to the operand field of the instruction in the right half of location $X$ |
| 20† | Perform a one-bit left arithmetic shift of $C$(Acc) |
| 21† | Perform a one-bit right arithmetic shift of $C$(Acc) |

$X$ Numeric value of operand field of instruction
Acc Accumulator
AR Arithmetic register
$C(X)$, $C$(Acc), $C$(AR), contents of store location $X$, of accumulator, of Arithmetic register respectively
† The effect of these instructions was modified in later papers by Goldstine and Von Neumann (1947, 1948).

FIG. 1.5

| Location | | |
|---|---|---|
| 50 | 00000100000000001100100 | 00011000000000001100101 |
| 51 | 01000000000000000110100 | 00000100000000001100101 |
| 52 | 00110100000000000110101 | 00000100000000001100100 |
| 53 | 01000100000000001100110 | • • • • • |

FIG. 1.6

(a) To say a computer is *word-oriented* means that the basic unit of storage is a word, of from twelve to sixty-four or more bits, able to hold a complete numeric value or (usually) at least one instruction; in §2.5 we will meet the character- or byte-oriented computer, where the basic unit of storage is 6 to 8 bits long.

(b) A *single-address* or *one-address* computer holds only one store address per instruction. The other common instruction format is the *two-address* format, where each instruction holds the addresses of two operands, and one of these addresses is further used to hold the result. These and other possible arrangements are discussed in §3.2.

(c) Finally, this computer is oriented towards the performance of arithmetic on values held in a binary format (that is, to base two). In §2.5 we discuss the possibility of performing arithmetic directly on values held in decimal format (that is, to base ten). Strictly speaking all modern digital computers are binary, in the sense that the basic electronic units out of which they are built can assume either of exactly two stable values (thus representing one binary bit). Devices where the units can assume any one of three or ten states have been proposed but rarely implemented: for the ternary (3-state) case see Knuth (1969, pp. 173–5). We thus use the term *binary* for computers which manipulate numeric values expressed directly in a binary format, and *decimal* for those where binary patterns are interpreted as decimal digits.

## 1.2. The Development of the Computer

Since the introduction of the stored program concept, there have been many developments in the design of general-purpose digital computers, but only two can be described as vital omissions from the computer described in the previous section.

### *The index register*

The first of these is the index register, introduced on the Manchester University Mark I computer in the late 1940s (Kilburn, Toothill, Edwards, and Pollard 1953).

Let us consider again the problem of adding together $N$ values held in store locations 100, 101, 102, and so on. It would be convenient to be able to write an instruction to add into the accumulator the contents of store address 99, and to have some automatic means for modifying the instruction just prior to its execution, so that it refers successively to addresses 100, 101, 102, and so on. This can be done by providing a storage device in the control unit, called the *index register* (or B-line on the Manchester computer). We then arrange for the contents of this register to be added to the store address in each instruction before it is used to access a particular location in the store. Our 'add' instruction now has the effect

> add into the accumulator the contents of the store location with address (99 + contents of index register).

Thus when the index register holds a value (say) 4, the 'add' instruction will have the effect 'add into the accumulator the contents of store location (99+4) or 103'.

By controlling the value held in the index register, we can make the add instruction refer to a different element each time it is executed. Notice, however, that the instruction itself, coded as a binary pattern in a particular store location, does not change between executions.

We now need instructions to insert a value into the index register, or to modify the value held (for example, by adding one). In this example we initialize the index register to zero and, on each iteration of the loop, we add one to the value held by the index register before executing the add instruction. A skeleton program is given in Figure 1.7. Sometimes we will wish to use the add instruction without modification by the index register, so we need an extra bit set aside in all such instructions, to specify whether or not the modification of the operand field by means of the index register is to take place.

```
Set accumulator to zero
Set index register to zero
Set loop counter to N
Add one to index register←────────────────────────────────┐
Add into accumulator contents of location (99 + index register)│
Subtract one from loop counter                                 │
If loop counter > 0, jump to ──────────────────────────────────┘
```

FIG. 1.7

A common extension to this technique is to provided several such index registers. Now a larger field is required in the instruction to specify, not only that indexing is to be performed, but also which index register is to be used. We may also have further instructions to manipulate the index register or registers. Index registers are discussed further in §4.2.

### *Interrupts*

The second major development in computer design is the interrupt facility, which seems to have appeared first on the Univac 1103 computer (Bell and Newell 1971, p. 48) in the early 1950s.

In early computers, as mentioned above, input/output (or transput) operations were treated in the same way as internal operations (such as addition); once the operation had been started, the control unit awaited its completion, before continuing with the extraction, decoding, and execution of the next instruction. This was an inefficient system, since there would often be other processing that the computer could be doing while a transput operation was being completed.

We therefore modify each transput instruction so that it merely initiates an operation (such as to print a digit on the electric typewriter), and allow the control unit immediately to continue with the next and subsequent instructions while the transput operation is being carried out.

The program must have some way of establishing when a transput operation is complete, so that a further operation can be initiated or (in the input case) so that the input character can be processed. To this end each transput device has an associated one-bit register, which is cleared as an operation starts and is set to one when it terminates; an instruction is provided to read this register, and thus the programmer can establish when a transput operation is complete. Such a one-bit register holding information as to the status of a transput unit is called a *flag*; more generally, we use the term *flag* to refer to any one-bit field holding status information (whether in a special register or in a portion of a store location).

Such a solution has the disadvantage that, if the transput units are to be driven at anything like their full speed, the programmer must scatter test instructions through his program. A better solution (common to all modern computers) is to allow the control unit to continue with subsequent instructions as before, but to allow any transput unit to interrupt the control unit when an operation is complete. This interruption, or *interrupt,* takes the form of automatically switching the control unit from its current sequence of instructions to a separate sequence of instructions, whose task is to deal with the completion of the transput operation (and perhaps to initiate a further such operation). There must of course be provision for retaining information about the interrupted sequence of instructions, so that processing can continue from the point at which the interruption took place.

A simple interrupt system might operate as follows. Suppose an interrupt signal is sent to the control unit by a transput device while the instruction at location $n$ is being executed. The execution of the current instruction is completed, the current contents of the program counter ($n+1$) are stored in some fixed location (perhaps zero), and the program counter is loaded with a fixed address (say one). Thus the control unit proceeds to execute instructions from locations 1, 2, 3, . . . etc., and these constitute the interrupt service routine to deal with the interrupt. When this routine has completed its operation, it returns to the interrupted program by using the old program counter contents stored in location zero. The interrupted program therefore proceeds with the execution of the instructions at locations $n+1$, $n+2$, . . ., etc. as if nothing had happened, until the next interrupt signal is received.

As we shall see in §6.3, the interrupt facility can be expanded to switch instruction sequences on the occurrence of many different events; further we will see the need for a means of ensuring that at critical times the computer is able to ignore all but a subset of these events.

### *The effects of changing technology*

It is traditional in the computer field (insofar as the term 'traditional' has a meaning for a subject only thirty years old) to refer to four *generations* of computers, according to the electronic technology out of which the control and data manipulation units are constructed. This is shown in the first three columns of Figure 1.8.

The most obvious result of the evolving technology is increased speed, from a few thousand instructions per second to several millions or tens of millions of instructions per second. Other important aspects, however, are the reduced cost per functional unit, reduced power requirement, and increased reliability and flexibility in use.

Main storage technologies have similarly evolved, as shown in the fourth column of Figure 1.8. Again we have an increasing speed but, equally important, a decreasing cost per bit, and therefore a capacity increase from a few tens of words to several million characters of main storage.

We tend nowadays to see these generations not merely in terms of

| Generation | Approximate dates | Processor technologies | Main store technologies |
|---|---|---|---|
| 1 | War years to early-1950s | Valves | Delay lines, Cathode ray tubes |
| 2 | To mid-1960s | Transistors | Magnetic cores |
| 3 | To early-1970s | Integrated circuits | Magnetic cores, Plated wire, etc. |
| 4 | To the present | Large-scale integration | Semiconductors |

FIG. 1.8

the underlying electronic technology, but also in terms of the organization of the hardware and software involved in a computer system; thus the transition to the fourth generation can be seen more as a change in the way that computer systems are organized (with the use of such techniques as virtual storage and distributed intelligence), than as a change in the underlying technology.

A major problem with early computers was the question of reliability; pessimistic forecasts were made of the mean time to failure of assemblies of several thousand valves, and a prime consideration in designing a computer was to make it as simple as possible. With the improving reliability and flexibility and reducing cost of electronic components, it is possible to build more complex hardware systems to simplify the requirements on the computer programs. Thus we have already seen that the provision of (hardware) index registers provides a facility (instruction modification) which previously had to be provided by software, and the interrupt facility is the hardware equivalent of scattering transput test instructions through a program. Throughout this book we will see examples of situations where a facility (for example stacks in §3.2, store protection in §5.1, and sophisticated transput operations in §6.2) could be provided by means of a piece of software, but is nowadays provided by extra hardware.

It is interesting to note that certain problems which have been solved by technological improvements reappear as the technology continues to evolve. Thus the problem of splitting a program between two storage media, one fast but small and the other large but slow, has reappeared at different times and at different storage levels. As with the history of the automobile, several radically different early designs were tried out before the main stream of development settled on the Von Neumann model; some of these ideas have reappeared as specialized computers or as variations on the basic model (for example parallel operation of components of the data manipulation unit).

Because of this we will not attempt in this book to trace a historical sequence from early, simple computers to later, complex ones. Instead we will discuss together all design variations in each particular field; within a field it should not be assumed that the more complex facilities are the later ones, since evolution has often been towards simplifying systems from the programmer's viewpoint. The history of computers is discussed in Serrell, Astrahan, Patterson, and Pyne (1962), Rosen (1969), and Randell (1975).

### *Application areas*

In the early development of computers there was a split between computers designed for scientific calculations and computers designed for commercial or business data processing. Scientific computers would carry out calculations on numeric values held (on the earliest computers) in binary fixed-point format or (more typically) in binary floating-point format; the transput facilities, particularly in the first generation of computers, would be rudimentary. Computers for business use, on the other hand, were oriented towards operations on strings of characters and would require much more extensive transput facilities; arithmetic would normally be in decimal rather than binary, to avoid the time taken in conversion.

Nowadays it is clear that this distinction is illusory; scientific applications of computers often require character string manipulation and need many of the transput facilities of business data-processing, while business applications increasingly need sophisticated arithmetic calculation. Thus many third and fourth generation computers provide a range of facilities (such as several data-types) in an attempt to cover the whole spectrum of applications in one design.

Another important application area for computers is in real-time control. Once reliability was adequate, computers could be used to control chemical plants, scientific experiments, missiles in flight, and the like. Such computers have, of course, to stand up to more extreme environmental conditions than in the application areas described above. Architecturally they are likely to have a short-word length (most commonly 16 bits), to perform arithmetic in fixed-point binary format, and to be provided with sophisticated transput and interrupt facilities.

Recently such *minicomputers* have become more similar to computers in the mainstream, with extensive data-types and with larger addressing ranges, and are entering the fields of more conventional scientific and business computing (see for example the early DEC PDP-8, and the more recent PDP-11, Data General Nova, and GEC 4000 series). We see, therefore, that a number of specializations have appeared since computers were introduced, but typically these have been reabsorbed into the mainstream of computing.

### *Microprocessors*

With each generation of computer technology, the physical space taken up by the electronic components has become smaller and smaller, until with the introduction of large-scale integration (LSI) it became possible to fit thousands of components onto a silicon chip less than a quarter of an inch square. This allowed a complete processor, consisting of data manipulation unit and control unit, to be fitted onto a chip. The first such *microprocessor* was the Intel 4004, which used a basic 4-bit unit of data and appeared in 1971. A wide range of 8-bit and 16-bit microprocessors is now available. If we add some storage on a second chip, we obtain a complete microcomputer at an extremely low cost and small physical size, and this can economically replace hardwired logic. We can use these microcomputers to build 'intelligence' into appropriate parts of a computer system (such as the transput devices), but they are increasingly finding applications outside conventional computing, for example in controlling washing machines and the ignition systems of cars. The physical implementation and application areas of microcomputers are thus different from mainstream computers, but at the instruction set level which we discuss in this book they can be treated as variations on the central Von Neumann model. Microprocessors are discussed in more detail in Aspinall and Dagless (1977).

As an example of microprocessor architecture, we briefly discuss the Intel 8080, a well-known microprocessor which has been widely copied. Physically the Intel 8080 is a package approximately two inches long by half an inch wide by a fifth of an inch deep. It has 40 pins for communication with other chips and the outside world, 8 to pass an 8-bit data word or *byte,* 16 to pass an address, 4 for power supply, and 12 for control signals (6 for input to the 8080 chip, 6 for output from it). In order to complete the processor, a chip containing a clock, and some electronics to provide the power supply, are necessary. Store chips come in two forms; normal read/write store (usually called RAM, for random-access memory) and read-only store or ROM (for read-only memory), where the contents of individual words can be read but not written. Since a microcomputer is usually dedicated to controlling some fixed task, the program of instructions can be permanently built into the ROM so that it cannot be corrupted. A typical microcomputer system therefore consists of a microprocessor chip, one or more ROM chips, one or more RAM chips (to hold variable data), and a further chip to decode the top few bits of the 16-bit address coming from the microprocessor, in order to direct it to the appropriate store chip. Further chips provide standard types of communication path between the microprocessor and transput devices.

The basic unit of data in the Intel 8080 is the 8-bit byte, and instructions are provided to perform fixed-point binary arithmetic between 8-bit values. Because of the low precision of 8-bit arithmetic, facilities are provided for propagating a carry bit from one arithmetic operation to the next, so that multiple-precision arithmetic operations can be programmed. Because of the expected application areas of this microprocessor (including pocket calculators), facilities are also provided for performing arithmetic on bytes interpreted as two 4-bit decimal digits.

As on the Von Neumann computer, the Intel 8080 has an (8-bit) accumulator, on which most arithmetic operations take place, and a (16-bit) program counter, to hold the address of the next instruction to be executed. There are also six 8-bit registers called B, C, D, E, H, and L, which can be used individually or in pairs (BC, DE, and HL) to hold intermediate values during a computation. A register pair can also be used to hold an address; in fact, one form of addressing mode used by instructions expects to find the operand address in the HL register pair. There is also a 16-bit stack pointer register, which holds the address of the top of a stack or last-in-first-out list of store locations (see Chapter 3).

Three instruction formats are used; a 1-byte format with just an operation code (for example 'clear accumulator'), a 2-byte format with an operation code and a 1-byte operand field (for example 'load into accumulator the value in the second byte of the instruction'), and a 3-byte format with an operation code and a 2-byte operand field (for example 'load into accumulator the contents of the byte whose address is given by the second and third bytes of the instruction').

### *Ranges of computers and optional features*

When we discuss computer design variations in the ensuing chapters, we will tend to make two assumptions which it is as well to clarify; first, that each computer is designed independently for a particular application area and to purely technical criteria; and second, that a computer design is implemented as a fixed set of facilities for all customers.

In fact, a computer manufacturer normally designs a number of compatible models rather than a single computer, and these cover a range of speeds, capacities, and costs. The models will be architecturally very similar, usually with all (or most of) an instruction set in common; further, transput devices and main storage may be transferable between models. This makes it easier for the customer to move to a larger model in the range as his requirements increase, and eases the manufacturer's problem of providing software for a number of different computers. Examples of this are the ICL 1900 and 2900 ranges of computer. However, this is at the expense of a new problem of economically providing, on the lowest model in the range, all the hardware facilities needed on models at the upper end of the range.

Furthermore, manufacturers wish to transfer their customers to their new ranges of computers from earlier models, and therefore want to minimize the problems of transition. This can be done by making the new range of computers architecturally similar to earlier models, and by making improvements only in the technological implementation of this architecture; alternatively we can use microprogrammed emulation, as discussed in §3.6.

To the technical criteria for designing a particular computer will therefore be added criteria of compatibility with earlier models or with other models in the same range. This is, of course, part of the technological solution of the computer manufacturer's general marketing problem of capturing and retaining a customer base.

First generation computers were designed with a fixed instruction set and store size, and with a fixed complement of transput devices. It soon became apparent that customers had different requirements for the number and type of transput devices to be attached to their computer. It is usual today therefore to provide a number of general electronic interfaces to which a range of transput devices can be attached, and a set of general instructions which can be used to control any transput device available at present or in the future, from the computer manufacturer or elsewhere.

When larger quantities of main store became available, customers would not always want the maximum quantity addressable by the control unit. So most computer models are now made available with a range of different storage sizes.

Finally, we mentioned above that many third generation computers have a range of facilities to cover a number of application areas; if some of these facilities are optional, we may particularize our computer for an application area by selecting from these options. For example, models in the IBM 370 range have a basic instruction set for general data manipulation and transput control, an optional floating-point instruction set for scientific calculation, and an optional decimal digit string instruction set for business data-processing. Thus a computer model is tailored for a customer by a choice of optional features, main store capacity, and number and type of transput devices.

## 1.3. Computer architecture

In this book we are concerned with those internal design aspects of a computer which directly affect the way in which it processes data; we therefore exclude such external aspects as the packaging of electronic components and units, the supply of power, or the conditions under which the computer is capable of operating, important though these are.

As we suggested earlier, most users (and even most programmers) see the computer at a level remote from the hardware, shielded as it is behind layers of operating system and compiler software. As illustrated in Figure 1.9, we can make out a number of levels more basic than this; the electronic circuits themselves, the logical fuctions (such as gates and flipflops), and the functional units (such as adders and registers).

In this book we will be looking at the level at which facilities are provided in electronic hardware, as they might be seen by a system programmer about to implement the most basic software on the computer. We choose to consider a system programmer's view rather than that of an application programmer (even at the assembler language level), because the latter would expect to use facilities provided by supervisory software to mask the hardware treatment of such things as transput control.

We term this the level of *computer architecture,* at which a set of logically integrated hardware functions are programmed to carry out

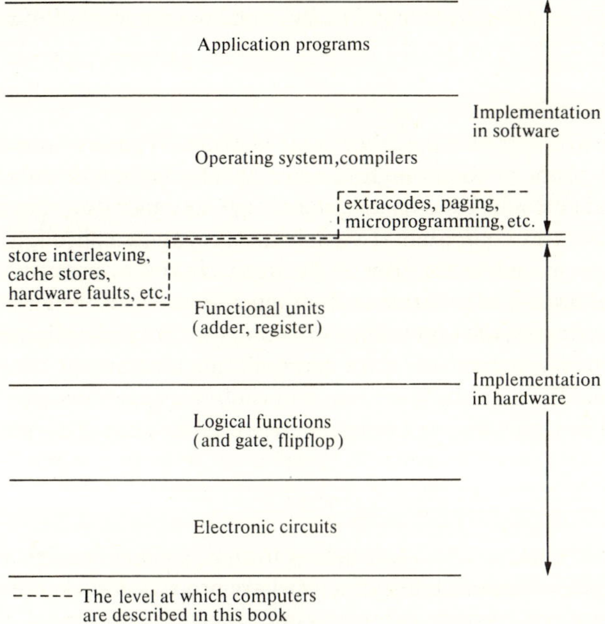


FIG. 1.9

the processing of data. It is to be distinguished from the *implementation,* in which electronic circuits are designed to realize an architecture. We could implement the same architecture in a number of ways, and some ranges of computers (such as the IBM 370 range) are designed to a common architecture but with a radically different physical implementation for each model. Books which describe this architectural level, and which are recommended for further reading, are Bell and Newell (1971), Stone (1975), Tanenbaum (1976), and Foster (1976a).

In practice certain aspects of an implementation may be discernible at an architectural level, most noticeably in coping with hardware faults and in the possibilities for enhancing program performance. We drop below the level of computer architecture to discuss these in Chapter 8. Furthermore, we discuss certain concepts in computer design which could be treated as implementational, their use being transparent to the architecture; the cache stores of §5.4 usually fall into this class.

There are a number of important implementational design decisions which we mention here only briefly, as below the level of our current interest:

(a) *Synchronous and asynchronous operation.* If control and data signals are propagated through the circuits of a computer only at time instants controlled by a master 'clock' or pulse generator, then we have a *synchronous* computer. If signals are propagated through the circuits at a rate governed only by the delays in the circuits themselves, then we have an *asynchronous* computer. Because of the greater simplicity of design, the major units in a computer are generally synchronous. Thus the control and data manipulation units might be timed by one clock, the store by a second, and each transput device by its own clock. Thus each unit is internally synchronous, but is asynchronous with respect to other units; we therefore require synchronizing hardware at the interface between each pair of units.

(b) *Serial and parallel data manipulation.* In data manipulation on a *parallel* computer all bits of a word are processed at the same time, while on a *serial* computer the bits of a word are processed one after another. Thus if addition takes $t$ time units per bit position, a serial computer with $n$ bits per word will take $nt$ time units to add two words, whereas a parallel computer will take $t$ time units (plus some time for the carry propagation). A serial computer requires less logic in the data manipulation unit than a parallel computer, but the control unit may be more complicated. Many early computers were serial, since they were built round serial storage media such as delay lines. Nowadays store technologies are inherently parallel, and the majority of computers are parallel in operation. The choice of a serial implementation for a computer would affect the architecture to the extent that we must choose a representation for negative numbers that can economically be processed in a serial manner.

(c) *Improved data manipulation algorithms.* Finally, the speed at which arithmetic operations can be carried out is one of the limiting factors to the internal processing speed of a computer. We are led to consider ways of speeding up these operations, for a given fixed technology and for a given fixed representation for numbers (which determines the results of these operations at an architectural level). Thus we are led to consider such topics as carry-lookahead for addition,

Booth's algorithm for multiplication, and non-restoring methods for division. Details of such topics can be found in books on computer hardware design such as Hill and Peterson (1973), Hellerman (1973), or Townsend (1975).

In early computers, in particular those of the first generation, little distinction was made between architecture and implementation; the architecture was whatever could reliably and economically be implemented in hardware. Today there is a growing tendency to define a computer architecture some way above the basic hardware level, to be implemented in a mixture of hardware and software, whose proportions may vary with the evolution of computer technology and with different models in a range. When an architecture is implemented partly in hardware and partly in software we require such concepts as extracodes and microprogramming, and these are discussed in Chapter 3. We will thus discuss features above the hardware architecture level from time to time, to complete the picture of a facility implemented only partly in hardware.

### *Plan of the book*

In Figure 1.1 we showed a typical computer divided into four sections: the store; the data manipulation unit; the control unit; and a number of transput units. In practice we may find it difficult to separate the hardware of the data manipulation unit from that of the control unit. We therefore treat these two sections as one, the central processing unit or processor, and we redraw our typical computer as shown in Figure 1.10 with three sections: the store; the processor; and the transput units.

The processor contains circuitry to request the next instruction from the store, and to receive, decode, and execute it; the latter may require further read or write accesses to the store, or interaction with a transput unit. It contains a number of processor storage registers, among them the accumulator, the program counter, and one or more index registers.

Starting from Figure 1.10 we consider design variations in each of the three sections. In chapters 2 and 3 we consider design variations in the processor. In Chapter 2 we consider the formats in which data might be held for manipulation by the computer, and the types of operations appropriate to each format. In Chapter 3 we consider other

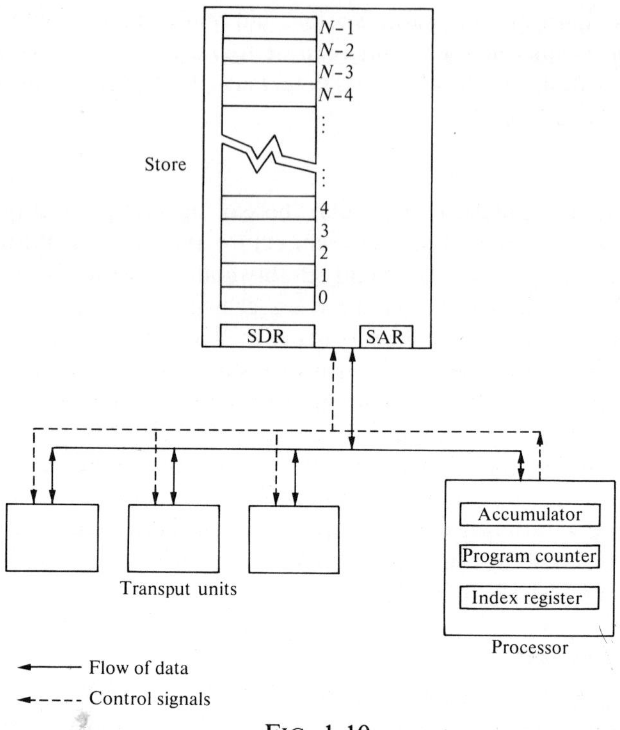


FIG. 1.10

aspects of processor design; the layout of instructions and how operands may be accessed by an instruction, control and other instructions not dealt with in Chapter 2, provision for supervisory software, and the concept of microprogramming.

Chapters 4 and 5 discuss design aspects of the store. Chapter 4 considers addressing modes; that is, the range of ways (commencing with index registers) in which an instruction can specify a location in the store. Chapter 5 considers other aspects of the store; protection of store areas from being inadvertently overwritten, the use of particular store locations for special purposes, means by which the store's apparent capacity and speed can be increased, and the use of associative and cyclic stores.

When we turn to the third section of Figure 1.10, we see a wide range of devices for receiving information from the outside world, for transmitting information to the outside world, and for expanding the storage capacity of the computer. Because of this wide range, most computer designs are not tied to the details of individual devices, but provide generalized transput control features and instructions, to which any selected input, output, or backing storage device may be interfaced. Chapter 6 therefore begins with a description of such general transput systems. Because of the mismatch between processor and transput device speeds, we are led to consider uncoupling the devices from direct processor control and providing them with some degree of autonomy. Chapter 6 therefore deals with the possible degrees of autonomy provided for transput control systems. This begins with the concept of interrupts introduced in §1.2, and leads on to the idea of interconnecting a number of processors.

All the computers we consider are general-purpose, at least in theory, although they may be oriented towards particular application areas. In Chapter 7 we consider computers whose orientation has resulted in an architecture radically different from those in the rest of the book, although they have a sufficiently general instruction set to lay claim to universality. Finally, in Chapter 8 we consider some topics on the border between architecture and implementation; dealing with faults in the hardware of the computer, ways of speeding up the processor, and the interface between computer and operator.

There is a problem in analysing computer designs in this way, in that a computer is an integrated system, and decisions in the design of one section of the computer will have effects in other sections. We must therefore expect certain aspects of computer design to reappear throughout the book, to be seen from a slightly different angle each time. One particularly important design decision is the choice of word length, since this affects how instructions are stored, the number of bits which are used to specify operation codes and addressing modes, and what data formats can or must be provided (for example, double-length working may be a necessity, if a short word length is chosen). If the word length is short, consideration must be given to methods for achieving an adequate address range with a short operand field.

In order to provide specific illustrations of the ideas and techniques discussed in the book, we use a number of well-known conventional computers as running examples throughout the text. These are as follows:

(a) The DEC PDP-8 (Bell and Newell 1971, pp. 120–36; DEC 1972a), an early minicomputer with a 12-bit word, appearing in 1965.

(b) The DEC PDP-11 (Bell, Cady, McFarland, Delagi, O'Laughlin, Noonan, and Wulf 1970; DEC 1972b) and Data General Nova (Data General 1971; Townsend 1975, Chapter 8), more recent 16-bit mini-computers, both appearing in the period 1970–1.

(c) The IBM 360 and 370 ranges of medium and large computers, based on a common 'byte-orientated' architecture (see §2.5). For most purposes the architecture of models in the IBM 360 range (appearing in 1964–5; Amdahl, Blaauw, and Brooks 1964; Blaauw and Brooks 1964; IBM 1964; Bell and Newell 1971, pp. 561–87) is the same as that in the IBM 370 range (appearing in 1970–1; IBM 1970; Katzan 1971a; Case and Padegs 1978). However, we usually refer to the latter in the text, as it has a number of additional features of interest, such as paging and segmentation.

(d) The DEC PDP-10 (appearing in the late 1960s: DEC 1972c; Bell, Kotok, Hastings, and Hill 1978), a typical medium-sized, word-oriented computer.

(e) The Burroughs range of medium and large computers comprising the B5000 (appearing in about 1961), the B5500, B6500, and B7500 (appearing in the late 1960s), and the more recent B5700, B6700, and B7700. These all use an architecture based on stacks and segmentation, and oriented towards high-level language usage; its fully-developed form is described in Hauck and Dent (1968), Creech (1970), and Organick (1973). In the text we refer to this architecture as the 'B6700 computer' for brevity.

(f) The CDC 6600 'super-computer' (appearing in 1964; Thornton 1964, 1970; CDC 1966), an architecture oriented to very high speed operation on scientific problems. The CDC 7600 has a similar but extended architecture.

(g) The ICL 2900 range of medium and large computers (announced in 1974; Huxtable and Pinkerton 1977; Buckle 1978) and the University of Manchester MU5 (Kilburn, Morris, Rohl, and Sumner 1968; Sumner 1974; Ibbett and Capon 1978) on which it is based, as examples of more recent architectural practice.

***The instruction set***

We will usually be treating individual instructions or groups of instructions in terms of the facilities that they control, so it is worth saying a few words here about the instruction set as a whole. It has been shown that a single instruction is sufficient (in theory) for a general-purpose computer (Van der Poel 1956); however, instead of a theoretically sufficient instruction set, what we require is an instruction set which provides a practical set of operations in which applications can be programmed.

The DEC PDP-8 computer has the instructions shown in Figure 1.11, and this must be near the lower practical limit. The IBM 370 range of computers has more than 180 different instructions, but some of these provide the same operation (such as 'add') on different data types; we could reduce this number by using a tagged architecture, as described in §2.6.

Furthermore, an instruction set could provide an arbitrary collec-

| Operation code | Mnemonic | Operation |
|---|---|---|
| 0 | AND | Logical and $C(X)$ with $C$(Acc), leaving result in Acc |
| 1 | TAD | Add $C(X)$ to Acc |
| 2 | ISZ | Add 1 to $C(X)$; skip next instruction if $C(X)$ is now zero |
| 3 | DCA | Store $C$(Acc) at location $X$, and clear Acc |
| 4 | JMS | Store $C$(PC) at $X$; jump to instruction at location $X+1$ |
| 5 | JMP | Jump to instruction at location $X$ |
| 6 | | Perform transput operation (with details of device and operation encoded in the remainder of the instruction) |
| 7 | | Perform operation not involving a store location, so the operand field $X$ specifies the specific operation in one of three groups (discussed further in Chapter 3);<br>group 1: clear Acc (CLA), increment Acc (IAC), negate Acc (CIA), etc.<br>group 2: skip next instruction on positive Acc (SPA), on zero Acc (SZA), etc.<br>group 3: perform operation on (optional) extended arithmetic element, for example multiplication |

$X$ Numeric value of operand field of instruction
Acc Accumulator
PC Program counter
C($X$), $C$(Acc), $C$(PC) contents of store location $X$, of accumulator, of program counter, respectively.

FIG. 1.11

tion of operations which seem likely to be convenient, or we can attempt to group the operations and provide some structure in the set of instructions provided; the instruction set of the Pegasus (Elliott, Owen, Devonald, and Maudsley 1956) is a good example of the latter.

### *Describing the Architecture*

The architecture of a computer is usually defined in terms of the format and effect of machine-level instructions. This description is given, partly verbally and partly in a more formal way (by tables and diagrams), in the computer system reference manual, or in a programmer's guide to the computer's assembler language; the latter tends to subsume the effect of some of the computer's more basic software in the description.

There have been a number of attempts to define languages at the assembler level which would be portable from one computer to another; the compatible computer ranges of the previous section are, of course, one such attempt. Conway (1958) suggested a Universal Computer-Oriented Language or UNCOL, which would be a common assembler language for all computers. However, a sufficiently general language would have all the disadvantages of not being able to deal with the idiosyncrasies of a particular computer, with none of the advantages of a high-level language. Another solution is the so-called 'high-level assembler language', or 'machine-oriented high-level language' (Van der Poel and Maarssen 1974), for example BCPL (Richards 1969) and PL360 (Wirth 1968) which provides such high-level facilities as block structure and loop control, but with some concessions to the type of manipulations required at the machine level.

Alternatively we can start at the level of registers and transfers between registers, and describe our architecture in terms of these primitives; a microinstruction set would be an example here. Iverson (1962) designed the APL language to describe hardware at this level, although the language is general enough for use in other areas; Falkoff, Iverson, and Sussenguth (1964) give a description of the IBM 360 architecture using this language. Bell and Newell (1971, Chapter 2) suggest a pair of notations for describing computers; ISP (Instruction Set Processor) for descriptions at the instruction level, and PMS (Processor–Memory–Switch) for an over-all view of hardware components making up a complete computer system. The ISP notation has been used to describe the appropriate parts of the DEC PDP-11 computer (DEC 1972b).

In this book we will be using verbal, informal descriptions rather than such a formal language for two reasons; (a) these languages define more detail than we usually wish to consider; and (b) they describe complete computers, whereas we wish to look at any stage at a particular aspect of a number of computers.

One further means of describing a computer should be mentioned for completeness; this is the use of some numeric value or values to indicate computer performance. In early computers the add or store cycle time would be quoted; even today raw computer power may be expressed in terms of the number of instructions executed per second, using a weighted average over some standard instruction mix. This of course says more about the technology than the architecture of a computer. A more realistic performance measurement, which takes into account the effectiveness of an architecture, is the resources (including time) required for processing a set of standard benchmark programs, which cover the expected areas and types of use of the computer. For a survey of this area see Lucas (1971) and Stone (1975, Chapter 11).

**Problems**

**1.1.** Describe in detail the sequence of steps carried out by the store, data manipulation unit, and control unit of the Von Neumann computer when executing the sequence of instructions given in Figure 1.6.

**1.2.** How does the Von Neumann computer distinguish between a location holding a pair of instructions and a location holding a numeric value?

**1.3.** A set of fifty numbers is held in the store of a Von Neumann computer, say in locations 100 to 149. Write a program, using the instruction set given in Figure 1.5, to find the largest number and put it in location 150. Comment on any difficulties caused by (a) the lack of index registers, (b) the presence of two instructions per word, and (c) the provision of only a single conditional jump instruction.

**1.4.** Two index registers are to be added to the Von Neumann computer. How would you modify the instruction format and add to the instruction set? Reprogram problem 1.3 using this new facility.

**1.5.** Using your extensions to the Von Neumann computer for problem 1.4, write a program to sort into ascending order 100 numbers starting at, say, location 200.

**1.6** Suppose the Von Neumann computer had $n$ input devices, the $i$th device having a device flag register $DF_i$ and a device buffer register $DB_i$. We add the following instructions:

| | | |
|---|---|---|
| Start Input Device *i* | : | set $DF_i$ to 0, and start reading the next character into $DB_i$; on completion, set $DF_i$ to 1. |
| Read *i* | : | transfer into the Accumulator the contents of $DB_i$, and set $DF_i$ to 0. |
| Test *i* | : | if $DF_i$ is set to 1, skip the following instruction. |
| Interrupt On | : | switch the interrupt system on. |
| Interrupt Off | : | switch the interrupt system off. |

When the interrupt system is on, and any device flag register is set to 1, then the computer finishes the current instruction, switches the interrupt system off, stores the contents of the program counter in the left-most twelve bits of store location 0, and continues to execute instructions starting at location 1. Write an interrupt routine to service input device one.

**1.7.** Extend your answer to problem 1.6 so that it deals with any number of input devices. Why should the 'Interrupt On' instruction have a delay of one instruction before taking effect?

**1.8.** Suggest instructions to control a set of output devices, and extend your interrupt service routine accordingly. What are the problems of allowing a high-priority device to interrupt the servicing of a low-priority device?

**1.9.** Obtain a manual describing the instruction set of a medium or large computer. Attempt to place the features described in the following categories:

(a) Features provided by the assembler program.
(b) Features provided by the supervisory software.
(c) Features provided by the instructions at the architectural level.
(d) Features caused by the implementation.
(e) Features of particular transput devices.

Do the same for a mini- or micro-computer. Are the categories more or less clearly distinguished?

**1.10.** Write a program to simulate the architecture of a computer of your choice (such as the Von Neumann Computer). Do you have to make assumptions about details of the implementation of the computer in order to complete your program? Is there any way to distinguish the running of a program on your simulator from its running on the original computer (apart from speed)?

**1.11.** Write a program, for a computer to which you have access, to clear all of main store (including that occupied by the program). If this is not possible on your computer, what is the minimum number of uncleared locations?

# 2 Data-types and operations

## 2.1. Fixed-point binary arithmetic

IN THIS chapter we describe various formats in which data may be stored and manipulated within the computer. Historically the computer has been seen as a device for performing calculations (as evidenced by the term 'computer'), and for this reason we commence our discussion of data-types with the fixed-point binary format. Not only is this format the simplest and earliest means of storing numeric data in the computer, it is also used for store addresses and forms the basis for encoding the individual subportions of more complicated arithmetic data-types, such as the fraction and exponent of the floating-point format described in §2.2. For further reading on computer arithmetic see Richards (1955), Flores (1963), Knuth (1969), or Stein and Munro (1971).

It should be noted that, despite the historical primacy of arithmetic calculation as the *raison d'être* for computers, we ought perhaps to see them instead as symbol-processing devices. This would lead us to begin with the logical and data transfer operations of §2.3 and §2.4. We would then treat arithmetic as a set of manipulations which (in theory) could be built up from these more primitive operations, but which in practice are supplied as basic computer instructions for efficiency.

A computer word holds a fixed number of bits, in a range from about 12 to 64, and we number these bit positions consecutively, starting at zero at the right-hand or least-significant end. Then, in the fixed-point binary format, the presence or absence of a bit at the $i$th bit position indicates the presence or absence of the $i$th power of two in the numeric value held. Thus in a 16-bit word, the fixed-point binary value 0010101101110001 represents $2^{13}+2^{11}+2^{9}+2^{8}+2^{6}+2^{5}+2^{4}+2^{0}$, or 11, 121 in decimal.

Here we assume that the right-hand bit position represents $2^0$ or one, so that numeric values lie in the range zero to $2^n-1$, where $n$ is the word length. We could instead scale all numeric values held in the computer by agreeing that this bit position shall represent some other positive or negative power of two. Indeed, we can use different scaling factors for different pieces of data, as long as we align the binary points appropriately when performing arithmetic. The position of the binary point affects the basic arithmetic operations only when performing multiplication and division. It is usual to consider fixed-point binary values either as integral (as described above), or as proper fractions with absolute values lying in the range zero to one; we use the former convention for the rest of this section.

### *Negative numbers*

In some circumstances, the numeric values we wish to represent and manipulate take on only non-negative values. This is usually the case when fixed-point binary format is used to represent store addresses, for example. However, for normal fixed-point binary arithmetic, we wish to have a range of positive and negative values.

In order to represent signed numeric values, we divide the range of available binary patterns into two nearly-equal sections, and use one to represent the positive, and one the negative, values. Conventionally, those patterns whose left-hand or most significant bit position contains a zero represent positive values, and those where it contains a one

| | Representation of $-a$ as an $n$-bit number ($a \geqslant 0$) | Example ($-455$ as a 16-bit number) | Representations of zero | Maximum negative number |
|---|---|---|---|---|
| Sign-and-magnitude | $2^{n-1}+a$ | Sign bit ←magnitude→ 1 : 000000111000111 | 00...00<br>10...00 | 11...11<br>$-(2^{n-1}-1)$ |
| | | ↓ invert all bits | | |
| One's complement (Diminished radix complement) | $(2^n-1)-a$ | Sign bit 1 : 111111000111000 | 00...00<br>11...11 | 10...00<br>$-(2^{n-1}-1)$ |
| | | ↓ add one | | |
| Two's complement (Radix complement) | $2^n-a$ | Sign bit 1 : 111111000111001 | 00...00 | 10...00<br>$-2^{n-1}$ |

We consider numbers to be integral (so $0 \leqslant a < 2^{n-1}$, and +455 is held as 0000000111000111 in a 16-bit word).

FIG. 2.1

represent negative values. Thus this left-hand bit position is a sign bit, set to zero for positive, and one for negative, values. A technique of representing signed numbers for which this is not the case, the excess-value representation, is described in §2.2.

There are three standard methods for representing signed numbers, as shown in Figure 2.1. These vary in the way that the set of binary patterns is mapped onto the negative numbers; the positive numbers are represented in the same way in all three methods. In the *sign-and-magnitude* method, the sign bit is used as described above, while the remainder of the word holds the absolute value of the number in the normal unsigned form. In the *one's complement* method, any pattern whose sign bit is one represents the negative of a number obtained by replacing one by zero and zero by one in each bit position. A difficulty with both these methods is that two different binary patterns represent zero, so that testing for zero becomes slightly more complicated. In the third method, *two's complement,* any pattern whose sign bit is one represents the negative of a number obtained by inverting all bits and adding one. There is now only one representation for zero, but there is now a negative number whose absolute value cannot be represented in the computer word.

All three methods have been widely used, with two's complement as the most common on current computers; we use this convention for the rest of the section, unless stated otherwise.

### *A basic set of operations*

The most common computer organization for arithmetic operations is the one-address system introduced in the Von Neumann computer in Chapter 1. Thus we have a processor register called the accumulator, the same length as a word of computer storage. All binary arithmetic operations take place between a value in the accumulator and a value read from the store, and the result is left in the accumulator. We discuss the various arithmetic operations required for this type of system; modifications for the other systems described in §3.2 should be obvious.

A comprehensive set of basic arithmetic operations to manipulate fixed-point binary numbers consists of the following:

(a) Add contents of a store location to contents of the accumulator, leaving the result in the accumulator.
(b) Subtract contents of a store location from contents of the accu-

mulator, leaving the result in the accumulator.
(c) Load the contents of a store location into the accumulator, overwriting the accumulator's previous contents.
(d) Store the contents of the accumulator in a store location, overwriting the location's previous contents.
(e) Negate the contents of the accumulator in accordance with the appropriate method of representing negative numbers.
(f) Take the absolute value of the contents of the accumulator, leaving the result in the accumulator.
(g) Clear (i.e. set to zero) the accumulator.

We can, of course, manage with a much smaller set of operations. The basic instruction set of the DEC PDP-8 computer (Figure 1.11) provides TAD, DCA, CIA, and CLA which are (a), (d), (e), and (g), with (d) in a form which clears the accumulator after storing its contents. To obtain the effect of the load operation (c), we add into an accumulator already cleared either explicitly by CLA or implicitly by DCA. The normal store operation is obtained by following DCA by a TAD from the same location. The subtract operation (*A*-*B*) can be obtained by

CLA
TAD *B*
CIA
TAD *A*

and the absolute value of *A* can be obtained by:

CLA
TAD *A*
SPA
CIA

Conversely, we may combine two or more of these operations in one more powerful instruction. The Von Neumann computer, for example, has a range of load instructions to load the accumulator with the contents, negated contents, absolute value of the contents, or negated absolute value of the contents of a store location. A similar set of variations is provided for add and subtract.

An instruction to clear a store location is occasionally provided, but more general manipulation of store locations (such as 'negate contents of store location') is rare. A number of early computers had an instruction to extract a square root, but nowadays this operation is achieved by software.

### *Shifting*

Since we are considering a binary computer, multiplication and division of the contents of the accumulator by a power of two can be accomplished by shifting the contents to the left or right an appropriate number of positions. A store address is not required by a shift instruction, so it is normal to use this portion of the instruction to specify the number of bit positions to be shifted.

In a shift operation, a decision has to be taken as to what is to happen at each end of the shifted pattern. Consider Figure 2.2 where we illustrate the shifting by one bit position of a six-bit binary number using two's complement representation. Rows (b) and (c) show the simplest form of shift, where zeros are shifted into the vacated end of the pattern, and bits shifted out of the pattern are lost. This is adequate for left shift, at least as long as the bits shifted out are the same as the sign bit. However, this form of shift does not work for right shift, and we need *arithmetic* right shift, shown in row (d). In this form of shift, we 'propagate the sign bit'; that is, the value shifted into the left-hand bit position is a copy of the sign bit. Notice that the right shift truncates the result; some computers provide a version of arithmetic right shift which adds to the right-hand bit position of the result the value of the last bit shifted out. This is shown in row (e) of Figure 2.2; it will be seen that this gives a rounded value as the result of a division by two.

| | Binary pattern 1 | Decimal equivalent | Binary pattern 2 | Decimal equivalent (2's complement) |
|---|---|---|---|---|
| (a) Original pattern | 001111 | 15 | 110001 | −15 |
| (b) Basic left shift of (a) | 011110 | 30 | 100010 | −30 |
| (c) Basic right shift of (a) | 000111 | 7 | 011000 | 24 |
| (d) Propagating the sign bit on right shift of (a) | 000111 | 7 | 111000 | −8 |
| (e) Adding in the last bit shifted out on right shift of (a) | 001000 | 8 | 111001 | −7 |

FIG. 2.2

Whatever the method of representing negative numbers, most computers provide the appropriate arithmetic shifts to preserve the numerical validity of the shifted results. In one's complement format, the basic left shift of Figure 2.2 is inadequate; instead a copy of the sign bit must be shifted into the right-hand bit position (why?). In sign-and-magnitude format, the basic left and right shifts must be used, but with the sign bit not participating in the shift.

### *Multiplication and division*

There are several possible approaches to multiplication and division in fixed-point binary, all of which have been used at some time. We could provide no hardware for these operations, so that they must be programmed when required out of the basic steps of addition, subtraction, and shifting. Alternatively, we could provide multiplication and division only of non-negative numbers, or multiplication but not division, or multiplication together with the operation of taking the reciprocal (as on the Cray-1 super-computer). However, we will consider the provision of hardware for both operations, the usual situation on modern medium and large computers. For definiteness we consider multiplication and division of integral numbers held in two's complement format in an $n$-bit word (so that the numeric value of a word lies in the range $-2^{n-1}$ to $2^{n-1}-1$).

The hardware to perform multiplication requires two $n$-bit registers to hold the multiplier and multiplicand, and a $2n$-bit register to hold the product, since it may have up to ($2n$-1) significant bits. The basic algorithm shown in Figure 2.3 is the normal pencil-and-paper method, with modifications to deal with negative numbers held in two's complement form. Initially the partial product is zero. The multiplier is then scanned from right to left, and each multiplier bit is examined in turn. If the examined bit is a one, the multiplicand is added to the partial product. The partial product is then shifted to the right, the sign bit of the multiplicand is copied into the vacated position, and the next bit of the multiplier is examined. Finally, a correction is required if the multiplier is negative; in this case the multiplicand is subtracted from the partial product to form the final product.

It will be seen from Figure 2.3 that separate registers for partial product and multiplier are unnecessary. Instead they can occupy the left- and right-hand portions of a single $2n$-bit register. After a multiplier bit has been examined, it is dropped by shifting the partial product and multiplier together one position to the right.

Multiplication for $n=4$: PP = partial product;
MR = multiplier; ↑ marks the multiplier bit being examined.

(a)
Multiplier = +5 = 0101
Multiplicand = +6 = 0110

```
       PP        MR
       0000      0101
add    0110         ↑
       ----
       0110
shift  00110     0101
                   ↑
shift  000110    0101
                  ↑
add    0110
       ----
       011110
shift  0011110   0101
                 ↑
shift  00011110
Result = +30
```

(b)
Multiplier = + 5 = 0101
Multiplicand = −6 = 1010

```
       PP        MR
       0000      0101
add    1010         ↑
       ----
       1010
shift  11010     0101
                   ↑
shift  111010    0101
                  ↑
add    1010
       ----
       100010
shift  1100010   0101
                 ↑
shift  11100010
Result = −30
```

(c)
Multiplier = −5 = 1011
Multiplicand = 6 = 0110

```
            PP         MR
            0000       1011
add         0110          ↑
            ----
            0110
shift       00110      1011
                         ↑
add         0110
            ----
            10010
shift       010010     1011
                        ↑
shift       0010010    1011
                       ↑
add         0110
            ----
            1000010
shift       01000010
correction  1010
            ----
            11100010
Result = −30
```

FIG. 2.3

Notice also how all the additions take place in the left-hand half of this $2n$-bit register. For this reason the $2n$-bit register has in the past usually been implemented as an $n$-bit accumulator extended on the right by a special $n$-bit register for multiplication (and division, as we shall see). On the Von Neumann computer this was called the arithmetic register (AR); but it is more commonly referred to as the multiplier–quotient (MQ) or quotient (Q) register.

To multiply two numbers, say $A$ and $B$, the following sequence of instructions would be performed:

Move $A$ to MQ register (load MQ with multiplier)
Clear Accumulator (set first partial product, if not done automatically by 'multiply')
Multiply by $B$

The final instruction brings $B$ to a multiplicand register and performs the multiplication, leaving the left-hand portion of the product in the accumulator and the right-hand portion in the MQ register. It will be seen that extra instructions are now required to load and store the MQ register, either directly from or to a store location, or via the accumulator; see for example instructions 9 and 10 on the Von Neumann computer (Figure 1.5).

As discussed in §3.2, many modern computers have an array of accumulators. In this situation the multiply instruction finds the multiplier in one accumulator, the multiplicand in a second accumulator or in a store location, and the resultant product occupies a pair of adjacent accumulators. The full power of the instruction set is now available for manipulating each half of the product.

Suppose that, in multiplying $A$ by $B$, the initial partial product is some non-zero value $C$. Then the final result of using the above multiplication algorithm is $A \times B + C$. So the same hardware can provide both a 'multiply' and a 'multiply-and-add' instruction, depending upon whether or not the initial partial product is zero.

The programmer usually requires an $n$-bit result after multiplication, so an appropriate portion of the product must be extracted for further processing; with the above (integral) convention, the right-hand $n$ bits would be taken. Some computers have a variation on the multiply instruction which delivers an $n$-bit result for operands limited in size, or which rounds a $2n$-bit result to $n$ bits.

In division we have a dividend $N$ and a divisor $D$, and require a quotient $Q$ and remainder $R$ such that

$$N = D \times Q + R, \qquad 0 \leqslant R < D$$

The divisor, quotient, and remainder are $n$ bits long, and the dividend is $2n$ bits long. It will be seen that this is a form of inverse to the 'multiply-and-add' operation.

We consider for the moment only the case where $N$ is non-negative and $D$ is positive, and assume they are of such a size that overflow does not occur (see problem 2.4). Then a basic algorithm for division is shown in Figure 2.4, again derived from the normal pencil-and-paper method. Initially $N$ is taken as the first partial remainder. Then there are $n$ stages, each of which generates one quotient bit and a new partial remainder. For each stage, the partial remainder is shifted left, and the divisor is subtracted from it to form a new tentative remainder. If the result is positive, it is the new partial remainder and the new quotient bit is one; otherwise the quotient bit is zero, and we 'restore' the previous remainder by adding the divisor to the tentative remainder.

Figure 2.4 has been drawn to show that, as the partial remainder is shifted left, the vacated positions can be used to hold the bits of the quotient. Thus the $2n$-bit register initially holding the dividend will,

Division for $n=4$: PR = partial remainder;
Q = quotient; ↑ marks the quotient bit being generated.

```
            Dividend = 34 = 00100010
            Divisor = 5 = 0101
            Complement of Divisor = 1011

              PR          Q
            00100010
shift       0100010     ????
                        ↑
Subtract    1011
            -------
            1111010     0???
                        ↑
Restore     0101
            -------
            0100010     0???
                        ↑
shift       100010     0???
                        ↑
Subtract    1011
            ------
            001110     01??
                        ↑
shift       01110     01??
                        ↑
Subtract    1011
            -----
            00100     011?
                        ↑
shift       0100     011?
                        ↑
Subtract    1011
            ----
            1111     0110
                        ↑
Restore     0101
            ----
            0100

            Q = 6, Remainder = 4
```

FIG. 2.4

after division, hold $R$ in the left-hand $n$ bits and $Q$ in the right-hand $n$ bits. This dividend register will be the register which holds the product in multiplication, made up of the accumulator extended on the right by an MQ register (on a computer with a single accumulator) or a pair of adjacent accumulators (on a computer with an array of accumulators).

A second divide instruction may be provided which automatically rounds the quotient according to the value of the remainder, or accepts an $n$-bit (instead of a $2n$-bit) dividend.

### *Arithmetic tests*

So far we have discussed instructions for manipulating numeric values to obtain a new value. A further requirement is to be able to select for execution one out of two or more sequences of instructions depending on a previously calculated numeric value. On the Von Neumann computer the only conditional jump instruction was one which tested for a non-negative value in the accumulator. It is difficult to program naturally with such a restricted set of conditional jumps, so it is usual to provide the ability to jump on any of four accumulator conditions—zero, non-zero, positive (including zero), and negative—and perhaps on combinations of these conditions.

The only other conditional jump instructions based on arithmetic tests that are at all common are

(a) Jump if the contents of a specified store location is zero, usually forming part of an 'increment and jump if zero' instruction (see §3.3).
(b) Tests on the equality or otherwise of two values, held either in two store locations, or in an accumulator and a store location.

### *Overflow*

*Overflow* is the condition in arithmetic calculation when the result of an operation cannot be correctly represented within the computer, without changing the form of representation. It occurs under the fol-

Examples of overflow (for a 4-bit word, using integral two's complement representation).

```
(a) Addition
                +4 = 0100
                +5 = 0101+
                     ----
                     1001    = −7
                Note: carry into sign bit = 1
                      carry out of sign bit = 0

(b) Negation −2^(n−1) = −8 = 1000
               Invert bits      0111
               Add one          1000 = −8

(c) Left shift + 5 =            0101
               Shift one bit    1010 = −6
               left

(d) Division    Dividend =  34 = 00100010
                Divisor  =   2 = 0010
                Quotient =  17 = 10001 (too big for 4-bit word)
```

FIG. 2.5

lowing conditions for two's complement arithmetic, illustrated in Figure 2.5.

(a) For addition and subtraction, when the carry into the sign bit and the carry out of the sign bit are different.
(b) On negation of the maximum negative number ($-2^{n-1}$ in an $n$-bit word).
(c) For left arithmetic shift, when the sign bit is changed; rounding errors in right arithmetic shift are not usually considered to be a case of overflow.
(d) Overflow cannot occur on multiplication if the values are assumed to be integral, but multiplication of two operands both of which are the maximum negative number causes overflow under the fractional convention.
(e) For division, when $|N| \geqslant 2^{n-1}|D|$, $N$ being the dividend and $D$ the divisor (see problem 2.4). This includes the case of division by zero.

For sign-and-magnitude and one's complement, there are equivalent conditions for overflow to (a) and (c), condition (e) is the same, and conditions (b) and (d) do not cause overflow.

On some computers, no automatic tests are made for overflow, and the programmer has to incorporate into his program explicit checks for overflow as required. On early computers which included automatic tests for overflow, a detected overflow condition caused a halt. On more recent machines, overflow causes a special overflow flag to be set (for later testing by the program) or generates an interrupt, causing entry to an overflow recovery routine.

### *Multiple-length arithmetic*

We have already seen how the operations of multiplication and division introduce the use of double-length operands. Often the programmer rounds these to single-length values, but in order to retain precision he may wish to manipulate double-length operands (particularly if the word-length is short). For this reason, some computers have further instructions to deal with such operands, held either in a 'double-length' accumulator (the combined accumulator and MQ register, or a pair of adjacent accumulators) or in two consecutive store locations.

Typical double-length instructions are to load and store the double-length accumulator, addition and subtraction; less common are double-length compare and negate. Double-length shifts are usually provided, where bits shifted out of one register of the double-length accumulator are shifted into the other. Double-length multiplication and division are rarely provided, as these would involve quadruple-length operands.

There may be a requirement for precision greater than that obtained from double-length arithmetic, or double-length arithmetic may not be provided, and in this situation it is necessary to program the basic multiple-length arithmetic operations out of simpler operations. A multiple-length value is held in a number of consecutive store locations; the left-most bit of all words but the first (which holds the sign bit) may either be used arithmetically or may be ignored.

The hardware designer can simplify the programmer's job in several ways. The basic requirement is for a *carry flag,* a one-bit processor register which is set according to whether or not carry occurs out of the accumulator during an arithmetic operation; the carry is out of the left-hand or next to the left-hand bit position, depending on whether the left-hand bit position participates in multiple-length arithmetic or not. Notice the difference between overflow and carry; overflow indicates that the result of an arithmetic operation is invalid, while carry always occurs (for example) when adding two negative numbers together.

Given a conditional jump instruction which can test the value of the carry flag, the processing of multiple-length operands can be programmed. Triple-length addition is illustrated in Figure 2.6.

Multiple-length addition using three 4-bit words.

```
  601 = 0010         0101          1001
 -161 = 1111         0101          1111
                                  ----
                           carry
                        1    ←     1000
                     ----
               no
           0   ←     1011
        ----  carry
  carry
     ← 0001
  ignored

  Result 0001        1011          1000 = 440
```

FIG. 2.6

## 2.2. Floating-point arithmetic

In the previous section we mentioned that the programmer using fixed-point binary format could consider the binary point to be at an appropriate position in the word for each item of data. Operands must then be aligned for arithmetic calculation (where necessary) by shifting. If the programmer stores, with each item of data, a scaling factor indicating the position of its binary point, then an automatic system could perform this alignment. On early computers sets of subroutines to perform these manipulations were provided, but the task was soon taken over by hardware. Thus, on most medium and large modern computers, hardware is available (perhaps as an optional extra) to manipulate arithmetic quantities consisting of a numeric value together with a scaling factor, and this is known as *floating-point* arithmetic.

Floating-point format, then, represents arithmetic quantities in the form $f \times b^e$, where $b$ is a fixed number known as the *base* or *radix;* it is often two, but other values have been used, such as 8 and 16 (for example on the Burroughs B6700 and IBM 370 range respectively). The numeric value $f$ is called the *fraction* or *mantissa,* and the scaling factor $e$ is called the *exponent*. To hold a number in this form, the computer word is divided into two unequal portions, the larger to hold the fraction and the smaller to hold the exponent. These two values are represented in fixed-point binary format, the exponent as an integer and the fraction with the binary point to the left of its left-hand or most significant bit (although, as we shall see, the latter convention is not invariable).

As an example, Figure 2.7 shows the value 6.25 held in floating-point format with base 2 in a 16-bit word, divided into 10 bits for the

Representation of 6.25 in floating-point format (base = 2; positive fraction and exponent only).

| | exponent | fraction |
|---|---|---|
| $0.78125 \times 2^3$ | 000011 | 1100100000 |
| $0.390625 \times 2^4$ | 000100 | 0110010000 |
| $0.1953125 \times 2^5$ | 000101 | 0011001000 |

FIG. 2.7

fraction and 6 bits for the exponent. Notice that there are several possible representations of the same value. For definiteness, and to maximize the number of significant digits in the fraction, we require all non-zero floating-point numbers to be held in *normalized* form. This means that the fraction and exponent are adjusted until the fraction (considered as a sequence of digits in the base used by the floating-point system) has a non-zero left-hand or most-significant digit. Thus, for a floating-point system with a base of two, the fraction must have a non-zero most-significant bit, and lies in the range $\frac{1}{2} \leqslant f < 1$. If the base is 16, then the most significant hexadecimal digit must be non-zero; i.e. at least one of the four most-significant bits must be non-zero. In general for a base $b$, the fraction of a normalized non-zero floating-point number is in the range $1/b \leqslant f < 1$.

So far we have assumed that the fraction and exponent are positive. However, both must be allowed to take on negative values, so that we can represent negative numbers and normalized numbers with absolute value less than $1/b$. The fraction can be represented as a signed number by any of the methods discussed in the previous section.

The most common method of representing the exponent is the *excess-value* or *biased* representation, where a fixed value of $2^{k-1}$ (where the exponent field has $k$ bits) is added to the exponent. The result is a positive number (sometimes called the *characteristic*), which is then represented as an unsigned fixed-point binary number. For example, for a 6-bit exponent, we use an 'excess-32' representa-

A floating-point format in a 16-bit word.

| | Sign | exponent | fraction |
|---|---|---|---|
| $6.25 = 0.78125 \times 2^3$ | 0 | 100011 | 110010000 |
| $-6.25$ | 1 | 100011 | 110010000 |
| 0.0625 (unnormalized) | 0 | 100000 | 000100000 |
| 0.0625 (normalized) | 0 | 011101 | 100000000 |
| Zero (unnormalized) | 1 | 000011 | 000000000 |
| Zero (true) | 0 | 000000 | 000000000 |

FIG. 2.8

tion; the exponent is in the range −32 to +31, and to obtain the characteristic we add 32 to give a number in the range 0 to 63.

Any floating-point number with a zero fraction represents zero. However, the standard or normalized representation of zero (*true zero*) has a (positive) zero fraction and the smallest possible exponent. For an exponent held in excess-value representation, this means that true zero is represented by a word with all bits set to zero.

Figure 2.8 illustrates a complete (hypothetical) floating-point format with base 2 in a 16-bit word. One bit holds the sign, 6 bits hold the exponent in excess-32 representation, and 9 bits hold the fraction in sign-and-magnitude representation. For further discussion of floating-point arithmetic see Knuth (1969) and Stein and Munro (1971).

### *Floating-point operations*

The instruction set for operating on floating-point numbers includes the four arithmetic operations of addition, subtraction, multiplication, and division (usually without remainder); negate and clear (set to zero) operations may also be provided. If the floating-point accumulator is separate from the fixed-point accumulator, then there will be appropriate load and store instructions; otherwise the fixed-point load and store instructions are used. In the former case there may, as with fixed-point arithmetic, be instructions to load the negated contents, absolute value of contents, or negated absolute value of contents of a store location into the accumulator.

We need to be able to test for floating-point zero, or for a positive or negative value, and change the instruction sequence accordingly. There is a problem here of the multiplicity of representations of zero, so such a test is usually only for true zero. It has been suggested (Knuth 1969, pp. 199–201) that testing for floating-point zero is not appropriate, and that a more suitable test would be for any value in a small range about zero, the size of which could be set by the programmer. Similarly, if a floating-point compare instruction is provided, it should test not for equality but for an absolute difference lying within this range.

Standard floating-point instructions normalize the result of each arithmetic operation; this is known as *post-normalization.* An additional set of floating-point instructions is sometimes provided which does not post-normalize the result of an operation. Use of such a set of unnormalized operations may give a better indication of the accuracy of an arithmetic calculation.

### *Overflow and underflow*

As with fixed-point arithmetic, the results of some floating-point operations cannot be represented in the standard format. We define the two conditions of (exponent) *overflow* and *underflow*, when the exponent becomes respectively too large or too small to be represented in floating-point format. These conditions usually result in a flag being set, or an interrupt to a recovery routine being taken. In some computers underflow in an operation forces a true zero result with no error indication.

A separate floating-point error condition may be signalled on loss of significance (i.e. a zero fraction) in addition or subtraction.

On the CDC 6600 computer certain values of the floating-point exponent are set aside to represent zero, infinite, and 'indefinite' operand values, and rules are given for arithmetic operations on these quantities (for example, the difference of two infinite operands is indefinite).

### *Variations on Floating-point format*

We have assumed that the exponent and fraction are packed into one computer word. In this case the programmer is forgoing some of the precision of single-length fixed-point arithmetic in exchange for an

Floating-Point formats on the IBM 370 range (base = 16; exponent held in excess-64 representation; fraction held in sign-and-magnitude representation).

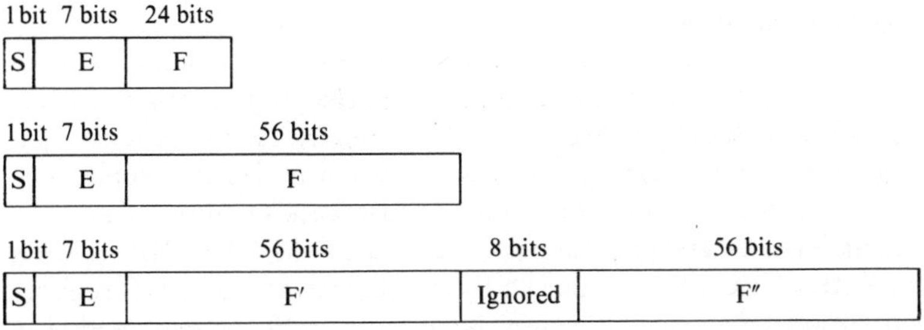

| 1 bit | 7 bits | 24 bits |
|---|---|---|
| S | E | F |

| 1 bit | 7 bits | 56 bits |
|---|---|---|
| S | E | F |

| 1 bit | 7 bits | 56 bits | 8 bits | 56 bits |
|---|---|---|---|---|
| S | E | F′ | Ignored | F″ |

S = sign of number.
E = exponent.
F = fraction.
(F′, F″) = most and least significant half of fraction.

FIG. 2.9

increased range of values. However, it is common (especially on computers with short word-lengths) for a pair of consecutive store locations to be allocated to each floating-point value, to allow increased precision. The floating-point accumulator must now be double-length, and operands are specified by the address of the first store location in the pair. In some computers both a short and a long floating-point format and instruction set are provided, so that the programmer can trade precision against storage space. Indeed the IBM 370 range of computers has three different formats for floating-point operands, as illustrated in Figure 2.9. It is usual for the extra length in the long format to be used to extend the precision of the fraction, while the range of exponents is the same in all formats.

In all the above we have assumed that the numeric value $f$ of a floating-point quantity is a fraction, in the range $1/b \leq |f| < 1$ when normalized. This is by far the most common technique, but on some computers $f$ is considered to be an integer with a binary point on the extreme right; in this case we use the term mantissa, rather than fraction, for $f$.

Perhaps the most interesting example of this is on the Burroughs B6700, illustrated in Figure 2.10. On this computer there is no fixed-point arithmetic, and all arithmetic is done in short or long floating-point format. In short floating-point format the mantissa $f$ is integral; since both exponent and mantissa are held in sign-and-magnitude form, integers are simply short floating-point values with an exponent of zero. In long floating-point format the binary point lies between the portion of the mantissa in the first word and the portion of the mantissa in the second word.

If floating-point hardware is not provided on a computer, then instructions may be provided to help with the programming of floating-point arithmetic subroutines. This usually takes the form of a special left shift instruction to simplify normalization, sometimes called 'shift and count' or (more unfortunately) 'normalize'. For example the extended arithmetic element on the DEC PDP-8 has a 'normalize' instruction which shifts the accumulator and MQ register left (inserting zeros at the right-hand end), until the most and next most significant bits of the accumulator are different. The number of shifts performed is placed in an accessible register called the step counter. Figure 2.11 illustrates the action of this instruction.

The Burroughs B6700 floating-point formats (base = 8)

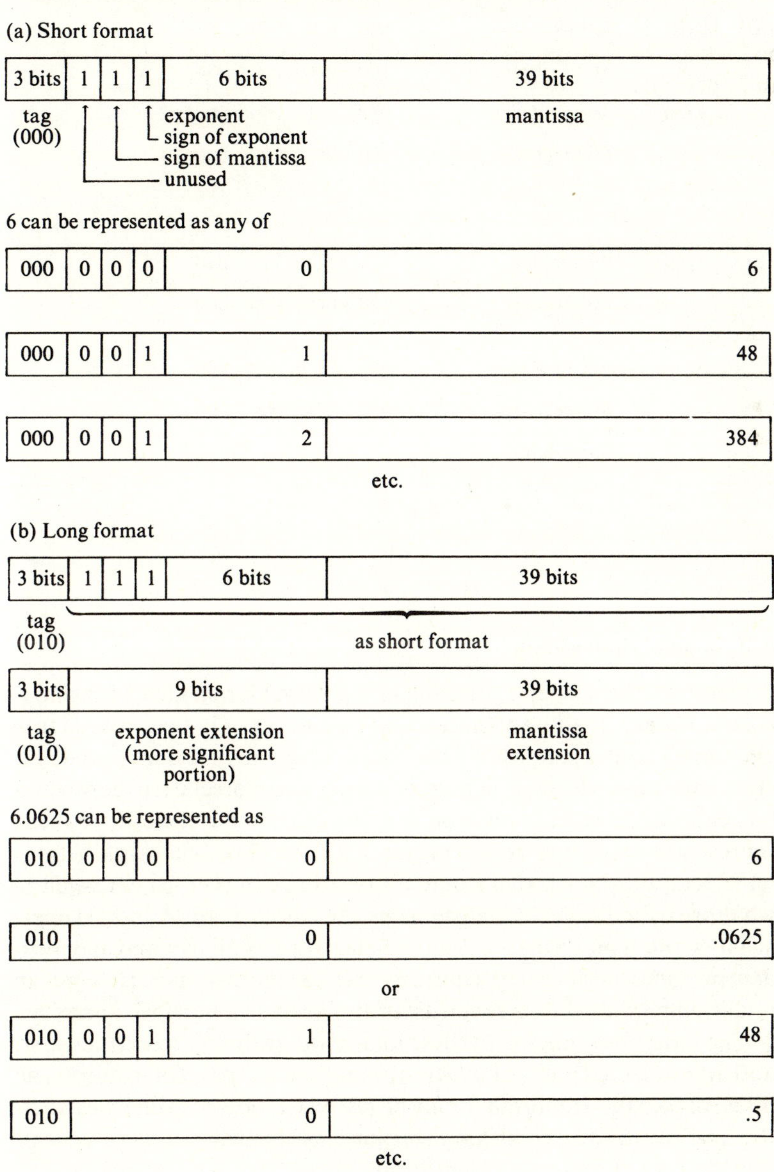


FIG. 2.10

Action of the DEC PDP-8 'Normalize' instruction

| | | | |
|---|---|---|---|
| (a) | Before | Accumulator | 000 000 000 101 |
| | | MQ register | 100 000 000 000 |
| | After | Accumulator | 010 110 000 000 |
| | | MQ register | 000 000 000 000 |
| | | Step counter | 8 |
| (b) | Before | Accumulator | 111 111 111 010 |
| | | MQ register | 100 000 000 000 |
| | After | Accumulator | 101 010 000 000 |
| | | MQ register | 000 000 000 000 |
| | | Step counter | 8 |

FIG. 2.11

### 2.3. Logical operations

Consider the concept, common in high-level languages, of the *boolean variable;* that is, a variable which can take only two values (true and false) and upon which the usual boolean functions—and, or, etc.—can be performed. There is an obvious correlation between a boolean variable and a single bit position in a computer word, with one representing true and zero representing false. The boolean functions which can be applied to a single bit position can then be extended to what are called *logical operations* on the whole word. A logical operation is one which treats all bits of the word similarly and independently; there is no carry from one bit to another, nor is there an underlying implied interpretation of the word as a numeric quantity.

The most common use of these logical operations is to extract, test, and alter selected parts of words of other data-types; for example, an integral fixed-point number may be tested for odd or even by extracting and testing the right-hand bit (at least in two's complement or sign-and-magnitude representation). They can, of course, also be used to manipulate boolean variables.

### *Basic logical operations*

It is most common to find the following three logical operations between the contents of the accumulator and the contents of a store location. They are illustrated in Figure 2.12 for a 16-bit word.

(a) *And* or *logical conjunction.* Here each result bit is set to one only if the corresponding bits in the two operands are both one. This operation can be used for extracting fields of interest from a word by 'masking'. For example, Figure 2.12 (a′) illustrates the extraction of the bottom four bits of a word for further processing. This operation can also be used to clear a specified bit of a word to zero, as shown in Figure 2.12 (a″).

(b) *Inclusive Or* or *logical disjunction* (sometimes referred to simply as Or). Here each result bit is set to one if either (or both) of the corresponding bits in the two operands are one. This operation can be used to set a specified bit of a word to one, as shown in Figure 2.12 (b′).

(c) *Exclusive Or* or *non-equivalence.* Here each result bit is set to one if either (but not both) of the corresponding bits in the two operands are one. Exclusive Or can be used to invert a specified bit of a word, as shown in Figure 2.12 (c′).

We also need the operation of *logical complement* or *Not,* by which each zero bit becomes a one and each one a zero. Notice that this is the same as negate or arithmetic complement under the one's complement representation.

Since logical values are manipulated in the accumulator used for fixed-point binary arithmetic, no separate load and store instructions are required.

There are 16 possible boolean functions of two variables. As shown in Figure 2.13, these range from trivial ones such as merely copying the first operand to the more useful ones discussed above. Sometimes a logical instruction is provided which allows specification (in a sub-operation field) of any of these 16 operations, to be performed on the two operands of the instruction. However, it is only rarely that the more esoteric operations are ever used, particularly in programs compiled from high-level languages.

## Logical operations

(a) And

| | |
|---|---|
| Operand *a* | 0010 0011 0100 0101 |
| Operand *b* | 0011 0100 0101 0110 |
| Result | 0010 0000 0100 0100 |

(a′) Use of And for masking

| | |
|---|---|
| Operand | 0010 0011 0100 0101 |
| Mask | 0000 0000 0000 1111 |
| Result | 0000 0000 0000 0101 |

(a″) Use of And for clearing *i*th bit

| | |
|---|---|
| Operand | 0010 0011 0100 0101 |
| | 1111 1101 1111 1111 |
| Result | 0010 0001 0100 0101 |

(b) Inclusive Or

| | |
|---|---|
| Operand *a* | 0010 0011 0100 0101 |
| Operand *b* | 0011 0100 0101 0110 |
| Result | 0011 0111 0101 0111 |

(b′) Use of Inclusive Or for setting *i*th bit

| | |
|---|---|
| Operand | 0010 0011 0100 0101 |
| | 0000 0100 0000 0000 |
| Result | 0010 0111 0100 0101 |

(c) Exclusive Or

| | |
|---|---|
| Operand *a* | 0010 0011 0100 0101 |
| Operand *b* | 0011 0100 0101 0110 |
| Result | 0001 0111 0001 0011 |

(c′) Use of Exclusive Or for inverting *i*th bit

| | |
|---|---|
| Operand | 0010 0011 0100 0101 |
| | 0000 0010 0000 0000 |
| Result | 0010 0001 0100 0101 |

(d) Not

| | |
|---|---|
| Operand | 0010 0011 0100 0101 |
| Result | 1101 1100 1011 1010 |

FIG. 2.12

Boolean Functions of Two Variables

| | |
|---|---|
| *A* | FFTT |
| *B* | FTFT |
| False | FFFF |
| And (*A*, *B*) | FFFT |
| | FFTF |
| *A* | FFTT |
| | FTFF |
| *B* | FTFT |
| Exclusive Or (*A*, *B*) | FTTF |
| Inclusive Or (*A*, *B*) | FTTT |
| Nor (*A*, *B*) | TFFF |
| Equivalent (*A*, *B*) | TFFT |
| Not (*B*) | TFTF |
| Implies (*B*, *A*) | TFTT |
| Not (*A*) | TTFF |
| Implies (*A*, *B*) | TTFT |
| Nand (*A*, *B*) | TTTF |
| True | TTTT |

FIG. 2.13

### *Masking*

Masking is such a common operation that many computers provide at least one arithmetic or logical instruction which can specify a mask as well as the primary operands. Only those bit positions corresponding to a one in the mask are involved in the primary operation. The mask may be held in an implied processor register (for example accumulator zero in a computer with an array of accumulators) or in a store

Load accumulator under mask from store location X

| | | | | |
|---|---|---|---|---|
| Store location X | 0101 | 0101 | 0101 | 0101 |
| Mask | 0011 | 0011 | 0011 | 0011 |
| Accumulator | 0000 | 1111 | 0000 | 1111 |
| Result | | | | |
| (a) Leaving unmasked bits | 0001 | 1101 | 0001 | 1101 |
| (b) Clearing unmasked bits | 0001 | 0001 | 0001 | 0001 |

FIG. 2.14

location specified in the instruction. The most common instructions in this area are load, store, and move under mask, where bits are copied from the source to the destination location only for those positions corresponding to a one in the mask. The remaining bit positions in the destination are either all left unchanged or all set to zero (the latter being equivalent to logical 'And'). The two possible forms of operation are shown in Figure 2.14.

***Logical shifts***

A common logical operation is logical shift left or right. As with arithmetic shift, each bit is moved a number of positions to the left or right. However, all bits participate equally, and there is no overflow testing or rounding correction.

There are two forms of logical shift, which differ in what happens at each end of the binary pattern. In the basic form (shown in rows (b) and (c) of Figure 2.2), zeros are shifted in at one end while bits are lost at the other; in the second form (called *rotate* or *circular* shift) bits shifted out of one end of the pattern are shifted in at the other. These are shown in Figure 2.15.

Some computers provide both logical and circular shifts, together with the appropriate arithmetic shifts. Others provide only logical or only circular shifts, and arithmetic shifts must be constructed from these basic operations. For example, the DEC PDP-8 computer provides only one- and two-bit circular shifts. As before, further shift instructions may be provided for double-length operands.

Logical and Circular Shifts

| | | |
|---|---|---|
| (a) | Original Pattern | 0010 0011 0100 0101 |
| (b) | Circular Shift 4 left of (a) | 0011 0100 0101 0010 |
| (c) | Circular Shift 6 right of (b) | 0100 1000 1101 0001 |
| (d) | Logical Shift 4 left of (c) | 1000 1101 0001 0000 |
| (e) | Logical Shift 6 right of (d) | 0000 0010 0011 0100 |

FIG. 2.15

***Logical tests***

Many computers have an instruction which is a variation on the operation of scanning the bit positions of a computer word. In the simplest case an instruction tests for all, some or none of the bits being set to one. This could be extended by the incorporation of a mask. An example of such an instruction is TM (test under mask) on the IBM 370 range, which sets the condition code (see §3.3) to indicate the presence of none, some, or all bits set to one in a masked portion of a byte.

An alternative approach is for the instruction to scan from (usually) the most-significant to the least-significant end of the word, searching for the first bit set to one, and placing the number of that bit position in a suitable register. Notice the similarity between this operation and the 'shift and count' instruction discussed in the last section.

A further possibility is an instruction to count the number of one bits in a computer word, and place the result in a suitable register; this is useful in the calculation of parity.

Strictly, the only possible logical comparison between two operands is for equality or inequality. However, some computers (such as the IBM 370 range) have what are called logical comparison instructions, which turn out to be unsigned fixed-point binary comparisons.

## 2.4. Data transfer, part-word, and multiple-word operations

In the first three sections of this chapter we considered a word-oriented, single-address computer with one accumulator. We studied the operations required by those dominant data-types which act on a complete word: fixed and floating-point binary arithmetic, and logical values. Among these operations we can distinguish several examples of data transfer operations, such as loading and storing the accumulator.

It is possible to envisage a general data transfer instruction (or set of instructions) which would move a word, a portion of a word, or several words from a source to a destination (either processor registers or store locations). In fact, however, it is not economic to provide such generality, and the situation described in the earlier part of this chapter is typical. A small number of data transfer instructions will be provided, integrated with the computer's dominant data-types, and making available only those transfer paths which are expected to be heavily used. Other paths can be programmed out of sequences of those provided, together with logical operations where necessary for masking, etc.

In this section we briefly discuss the forms of data transfer instruction commonly found on word-oriented computers: first for whole-word transfers, then for the larger subdivisions of the word (such as the half-word), and finally for multiple-word transfers. We omit discussion in this section of the subdivision of a word into the smaller units of those other dominant data-types, the character and the decimal digit. Consideration of those data-types, in the next section, leads us to introduce a different form of computer architecture, the character- or byte-oriented computer, where the basic storage unit is much shorter than the word (typically eight bits long) and all data-types are multiples of this unit.

### *Single word transfers*

The instructions provided in this category depend heavily on the major data-types available and the addressing structure of the computer.

(a) On a single-address computer with one accumulator we find load and store instructions, perhaps with variations which interpret the value being transferred (for example, load absolute value).
(b) If the computer has more than one processor register, then instructions are necessary to transfer values to and from these registers, the source or destination of the value being either another processor register or a store location. Instructions 9 and 10 on the Von Neumann com-

puter (Figure 1.5) are examples of such instructions.

Notice that, if a computer has an array of accumulators, as discussed in §3.2, then the two instructions:

Load accumulator *n* from store location *X*
and;
Store accumulator *n* in store location *X*

are logically sufficient. But this means that data transfer between processor registers is slowed down to the speed of store access. Hence an instruction of the form:

Load accumulator *n* from accumulator *m*

is usually provided.

(c) To transfer a value from one store location to another in a one-address computer, the programmer uses a pair of load and store instructions, with an accumulator as an intermediate location. On a two-address computer a 'move' instruction which specified the address of both store locations would be available.

(d) Interchanging the contents of two words (whether processor registers or store locations) requires a temporary location *T*, and the sequence of instructions;

Move *A* to *T*
Move *B* to *A*
Move *T* to *B*

For this reason some computers provide an instruction to exchange the values, either in an accumulator and a store location (for example the DEC PDP-10), or in two processor registers.

***Part-word operations***

We now consider how provision may be made for manipulating subdivisions of a word.

(a) First, notice that explicit part-word instructions are not logically necessary. The programmer can always extract the relevant portion of a computer word by masking, using either an 'And' instruction or a 'Load under Mask' instruction if available. However, there are obviously time overheads for this packing and unpacking.

(b) Certain portions of a computer word have special significance for particular data-types: for example the exponent field of a floating-point number, and the operand field of an instruction. A computer will occasionally have an instruction which extracts a value from, or inserts a value in, that part of a specified computer word. An example of the latter is instructions 18 and 19 on the Von Neumann computer (Figure 1.5).

(c) On a computer with a long word-length, it is wasteful to store small fixed-point binary numbers one to a word. Instead, the programmer can store two such numbers in a word, each in a *half-word*. Instructions may therefore be provided to facilitate the manipulation of such a data-type.

Figure 2.16 lists the instructions provided on the IBM 370 range of computers to manipulate half-word values. In each instruction but

IBM 370 Half-Word Instructions

| | |
|---|---|
| AH | Add half-word *X* to accumulator *n* |
| CH | Compare half-word *X* with accumulator *n*, setting a condition code (see § 3.3) to indicate the result. |
| LH | Load half-word *X* into accumulator *n* |
| MH | Multiply half-word *X* by accumulator *n*, leaving the least significant 32 bits in the accumulator. |
| SH | Subtract half-word *X* from accumulator *n* |
| STH | Store half-word from accumulator *n* at *X* |

*X:* specified store location.

*n:* specified accumulator.

FIG. 2.16

STH, the source is a specified half-word (16 bits) in the store, considered as a fixed-point binary value. This value is converted to a full-word (32 bits) by extending the sign bit to the left, since two's complement representation is used. The resultant value is then manipulated in the appropriate way: for example, AH causes the 32-bit value to be added to the appropriate 32-bit accumulator. For STH the least significant half of the specified accumulator is deposited in the specified half-word location in store. Since the IBM 370 is a byte-oriented computer, the half-word store locations are specified by their byte address, as described in the next section.

Figure 2.17 illustrates the half-word data transfer operations on the DEC PDP-10 computer, together with the variations which specify what action is to be performed on the other half of the destination word. Each operation can be used with the source as a store location and the destination as an accumulator (i.e. as a load instruction) or the converse (i.e. as a store instruction). Notice that, since the PDP-10 is a (36-bit) word-oriented computer, the operand field specifies a word, and the half-word is specified in the operation code. On this computer the right-hand half of each instruction is occupied by a store address, so that these instructions provide a generalized version of the facility

DEC PDP-10 Half-Word Transfer Instructions

| | |
|---|---|
| HLL | Transfer left half of source to left half of destination |
| HRL | Transfer right half of source to left half of destination |
| HRR | Transfer right half of source to right half of destination |
| HLR | Transfer left half of source to right half of destination |

Treatment of other half of destination:

(a) Unchanged

(b) Insert all 0's

(c) Insert all 1's

(d) Extend sign of transferred half-word

FIG. 2.17

mentioned in (b) above. The PDP-10 also has an instruction which interchanges the two halves of a word during transmission, and one which adds one simultaneously to both halves of an accumulator.

(d) We could, of course, extend our subdivision of computer words even further. On the Univac 1108 computer, for instance, a 36-bit word can be subdivided into halves, thirds, quarters, or sixths, and a selection field in the instruction specifies which portion of the store location is involved in any arithmetic operation. The selected portion is aligned with the least-significant portion of the other operand (held in a processor register), and sign extension may or may not be applied (depending on the size of the portion and the value in the selection field). On this computer simultaneous addition or subtraction may also be performed on corresponding halves or thirds of two words, one in a processor register and one in a store location.

A few computers have provided instructions to operate on any single bit, or on any contiguous group of bits, in a word. A problem with such instructions is the number of bits required to select a word, a bit within the word, and (in the latter case) the length of the bit group. For this reason, and because of the limited use for such general data-types, the only data-types smaller than a word which are at all commonly provided for in the instruction set are half-words, characters, and decimal digits. Any other subdivisions can be accessed and manipulated by the logical operations of § 2.3.

***Multiple-word operations***

Sometimes the programmer wishes to manipulate a group of contiguous words as a single unit. The only common instructions provided to help are:

(a) *The double- or multiple-length arithmetic operations* discussed in §§ 2.1 and 2.2.

(b) *The block transfer instruction.* This instruction specifies a number of words to be moved *n*, a source, and a destination address. Then the *n* words beginning at the source address are transferred to an area beginning at the destination address. This obviously allows speedier movement of blocks of data than a programmed loop containing a single-word move instruction (or a load and store pair). In computers fitted with mass store (see § 5.4), such a block transfer instruction may be the only means of moving data between it and the main store.

(c) *The multiple accumulator load and store instructions.* These load or store a set of processor registers (typically a sequence of accumulators in a computer with an array of accumulators) from or to a consecutive sequence of store locations. They are used for rapid saving and restoring of the 'process context' on entry to and exit from a subroutine, or in processor mode changes (see § 3.5).

## 2.5. Decimal Arithmetic and Character Handling

In §§ 2.1 and 2.2 all arithmetic calculation is performed with operands in binary format; that is , to base two. However, outside the computer, numerical data is generally held in decimal format, for obvious anatomical reasons (although there have been suggestions from time to time that manual calculation should be done in binary or octal, for example, Phillips 1936).

There are two ways of coping with this disparity. Either the computer converts the initial data from decimal to binary and the final results from binary to decimal, performing all internal calculations in binary, or a data-type and instruction set is provided to perform arithmetic operations directly in decimal. The first method is appropriate if large amounts of calculation are to be performed on the input data, since the cost of conversion is more than out-weighed by the increased speed and compactness of binary arithmetic. The second method is appropriate when only a small number of arithmetic operations are to be performed on each of a large number of initial items of data. Generally the first method is used for scientific, and the second for commercial, data-processing.

### *Word-oriented decimal arithmetic*

A few (mainly early) computers provide word-oriented decimal arithmetic operations. Each operand is a computer word (either in the accumulator or a store location), made up of a fixed number of decimal digits. The basic hardware of such a computer is still binary, so that each computer word is, in fact, divided into a fixed number of equal length fields of bits, each representing one decimal digit.

There are a number of methods of encoding a field of bits to represent the ten decimal digits, four of which are shown in Figure 2.18; for

| Decimal digit | BCD | Excess-3 | Biquinary | 2-out-of-5 |
|---|---|---|---|---|
| 0 | 0000 | 0011 | 0100001 | 11000 |
| 1 | 0001 | 0100 | 0100010 | 00011 |
| 2 | 0010 | 0101 | 0100100 | 00101 |
| 3 | 0011 | 0110 | 0101000 | 00110 |
| 4 | 0100 | 0111 | 0110000 | 01001 |
| 5 | 0101 | 1000 | 1000001 | 01010 |
| 6 | 0110 | 1001 | 1000010 | 01100 |
| 7 | 0111 | 1010 | 1000100 | 10001 |
| 8 | 1000 | 1011 | 1001000 | 10010 |
| 9 | 1001 | 1100 | 1010000 | 10100 |
| unused | 1010 | 0000 | | |
| | 1011 | 0001 | | |
| | 1100 | 0010 | | |
| | 1101 | 1101 | | |
| | 1110 | 1110 | | |
| | 1111 | 1111 | | |

FIG.2.18

further discussion see Richards (1955). The most common is the binary-coded decimal representation (BCD). Here 10 of the 16 possible bit patterns of a 4 bit field are used to represent the decimal digits 0 to 9, the remaining 6 being unused. Any of the 3 representations for negative numbers could be used, sign-and-magnitude being most common.

All the usual arithmetic operations of addition, subtraction, multiplication, division, and comparison are provided, as in § 2.1. Only decimal arithmetic may be provided, or separate instruction sets might treat each computer word as either a binary or a decimal value.

A few of these computers also have a decimal floating-point format. Here the fraction is held as a series of decimal digits, with a floating-point base of ten rather than a power of two; normally the exponent is still held in binary format.

Few modern large or medium-sized computers have such word-oriented decimal arithmetic. It is more usual nowadays to provide decimal arithmetic (if at all) on a data-type derived from character string handling. It is to such character string formats that we now turn.

### *Character-oriented computers and the IBM 1401*

The word-oriented architecture derives from viewing computers as calculating devices. Large numbers of calculations are to be done, so that the design aim is to choose a word size which gives suitable precision, and to do all arithmetic in the most efficient way, using fixed or floating-point binary format. On this view transput will be relatively infrequent, so that the cost of converting to and from decimal format is acceptable. However, in commercial applications the emphasis is different, as a glance at the Cobol language indicates. The basic unit is the (variable-length) string of characters. The manipulations performed may include arithmetic operations on some of these character strings, but we will probably wish to do them directly on the decimal digits, rather than convert to and from binary for each arithmetic operation.

We therefore consider building an architecture round character string manipulation, rather than round word manipulation. The first common computer using this character-oriented architecture was the (second-generation) IBM 1401 (McCracken 1962, Bell and Newell 1971, pp. 225–34).

The basic addressable unit of storage on the IBM 1401 computer is the character, which holds eight bits. Six data bits encode a character set consisting of the digits 0 to 9, the letters A to Z, and a number of special symbols (such as blank and comma), as shown in Figure 2.19. The seventh bit is a parity bit, and the eighth is known as the word mark bit; by the usual definition, this computer therefore has a 7-bit word. Each operand is a string of one or more consecutive characters. In order to facilitate arithmetic, an operand is specified by the address of its right-hand (least-significant) character, and the left-hand (most-significant) character of the operand is indicated by having its word mark bit set to one.

Because operands may be very long, no accumulator is provided on this computer; all operations take place between operands in the store. The most basic instruction is the move, which copies characters from a source field to a destination, until a character with the word mark bit set is encountered in one of the two fields.

For example, suppose we had two fields (or character strings) in the store at addresses 300 and 350, as shown in Figure 2.20 (a); the addresses are those of the right-hand characters of the fields, and the characters whose word mark bits are set are indicated by underlining. Then if the computer executes the instruction,

Move Characters to Word Mark: Source Address 300: Destination Address 350

the result will be as shown in Figure 2.20 (b). Characters have been

## IBM 1401 Character Codes

| Binary Code | Character | Card Code |
|---|---|---|
| 00 0000 | blank | |
| 00 0001 | 1 | 1 |
| 00 0010 | 2 | 2 |
| 00 0011 | 3 | 3 |
| 00 0100 | 4 | 4 |
| 00 0101 | 5 | 5 |
| 00 0110 | 6 | 6 |
| 00 0111 | 7 | 7 |
| 00 1000 | 8 | 8 |
| 00 1001 | 9 | 9 |
| 00 1010 | 0 | 0 |
| 00 1011 | # | 3-8 |
| 00 1100 | @ | 4-8 |
| 01 0001 | / | 0-1 |
| 01 0010 | S | 0-2 |
| 01 0011 | T | 0-3 |
| 01 0100 | U | 0-4 |
| 01 0101 | V | 0-5 |
| 01 0110 | W | 0-6 |
| 01 0111 | X | 0-7 |
| 01 1000 | Y | 0-8 |
| 01 1001 | Z | 0-9 |
| 01 1011 | , | 0-3-8 |
| 01 1100 | % | 0-4-8 |
| 10 0000 | − | 11 |
| 10 0001 | J | 11-1 |
| 10 0010 | K | 11-2 |
| 10 0011 | L | 11-3 |
| 10 0100 | M | 11-4 |
| 10 0101 | N | 11-5 |
| 10 0110 | O | 11-6 |
| 10 0111 | P | 11-7 |
| 10 1000 | Q | 11-8 |
| 10 1001 | R | 11-9 |
| 10 1011 | $ | 11-3-8 |
| 10 1100 | * | 11-4-8 |
| 11 0000 | & | 12 |
| 11 0001 | A | 12-1 |
| 11 0010 | B | 12-2 |
| 11 0011 | C | 12-3 |
| 11 0100 | D | 12-4 |
| 11 0101 | E | 12-5 |
| 11 0110 | F | 12-6 |
| 11 0111 | G | 12-7 |
| 11 1000 | H | 12-8 |
| 11 1001 | I | 12-9 |
| 11 1011 | • | 12-3-8 |
| 11 1100 | ◊ | 12-4-8 |

FIG. 2.19

The Move Instruction on the IBM 1401 Computer

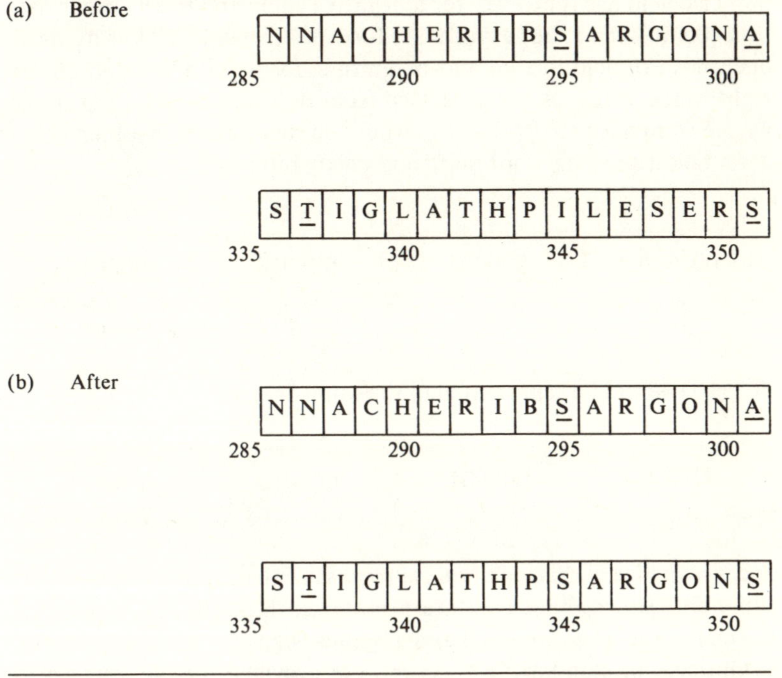


FIG. 2.20

copied from the first field to the second, until a word mark (here in the source field) is encountered.

This instruction does not affect the pattern of word marks in the destination field, but there are other instructions to set or clear the word mark bit in a designated character, to clear all word marks in a designated area, or to copy a source string and word mark to a designated area (ignoring and clearing any word mark bits in the destination field encountered in the process).

To describe how arithmetic is performed on the IBM 1401, we must look at the representation of characters a little more closely. The six data bits of a character are divided into two zone bits and four numeric bits. All six bits are used to represent most symbols in the character set, but it can be seen from Figure 2.19 that the digits 0 to 9 are represented by the four numeric digits, with the zone bits set to '00'. However, the zone bits of the right-hand (least significant) digit of a numeric field are set to '10' for a negative value and to any other pattern (00, 01, or 11, but usually 11) for a positive value. Thus numeric operands are held in sign-and-magnitude form, with the sign on the right, since operands are processed from right to left. As an example we see from figure 2.19 that 103 would be represented in a four-character field (ignoring word mark and parity bits) as

| 001010 | 000001 | 001010 | 000011 |
|---|---|---|---|
| 0 | 1 | 0 | 3 |

So −103 would be represented in the same field as

| 001010 | 000001 | 001010 | 100011 |
|---|---|---|---|

A consequence of this technique of representing negative values is that some bit patterns have two interpretations; thus '100011' represents the character 'L' as well as 3 and a 'minus' sign.

Optional or standard instructions are provided for the four arithmetic operations. For example, the 'add' instruction adds two numeric operands in the above format, leaving the result in place of the second operand. The operands may be of different lengths; if the first operand is shorter, the computer processes it as if it was extended on the left with zeros; if the second (destination) field is shorter, some of the more significant digits of the result are lost.

There is an instruction which compares two fields for equality or non-equality, and in the latter case it indicates which field is greater. There are further instructions to test a specified character for a set word mark bit, or for various combinations of zone bits.

The Honeywell H200/2000 range of computers (Honeywell 1965; Flores 1969, pp. 194-227), which was derived from the IBM 1401, provides similar but enhanced facilities. One enhancement is to provide two mark bits in each character, an 'item mark' and 'word mark' bit; if both bits are set this is called a 'record mark'. We can thus build up a hierarchical data structure in storage, of fields of characters (terminated by a word mark) grouped together in items or records. Most instructions operate on fields, but a special move instruction allows movement of a group of fields as an item, and the record is the unit of transfer in transput devices. Further data formats are also provided, for variable length fixed-point binary arithmetic and fixed-length floating-point binary arithmetic.

### *The Byte-Oriented Computer and the IBM 360/370 Architecture*

The two lines of computer development, represented by the word- and character-oriented architectures, have coalesced in the byte-oriented computer. Here we have a design based on the character, providing the character string handling requirements of the commercial application, with a word-oriented architecture superimposed upon it, to allow the more efficient binary arithmetic to be used when required. This type of computer is typified by the IBM 360 and 370 ranges, and a very similar architecture is used for the RCA Spectra 70 range and English-Electric (later ICL) System 4 range of computers.

The basic unit of storage is the 8-bit character or *byte;* unlike the IBM 1401, all eight bits are available for holding information, there being no word mark bit and the parity bit being a ninth (hidden) bit. Because there is no word mark bit, the length of each operand is specified or implied in the instructions which manipulate it, which means that there is an upper limit to the length of such operands.

There are two data types involving byte-string operands. The first treats the operand as a string of 8-bit characters (allowing a set of 256 characters, as shown in Figure 2.21), or a string of bytes of eight logical bits. There are instructions to move strings, to compare them, and to perform the usual logical operations.

However, arithmetic cannot be done on these byte strings as they stand; instead they must be converted to a different string data-type, known as packed decimal. It can be seen from Figure 2.21 that the bit patterns representing the digits 0 to 9 as characters all have binary '1111' in the left-hand four bits of the byte, with patterns '0000' for decimal 0 to '1001' for decimal 9 in the right-hand four bits. In order to convert a numeric character string to packed decimal format, the left-hand four bits (known as the zone bits) are stripped off each byte, and the remaining sets of four (BCD coded) numeric bits are packed two to a byte, to form the resultant packed decimal byte string. As on the IBM 1401 computer, the zone bits of the right-hand (least significant) digit of a numeric character string usually represent the sign

## The EBCDIC Character Codes

| EBCDIC | Bit Configuration | EBCDIC | Bit Configuration | EBCDIC | Bit Configuration | EBCDIC | Bit Configuration |
|---|---|---|---|---|---|---|---|
| NUL | 0000 0000 | SP | 0100 0000 | | 1000 0000 | PZ 7/11 | 1100 0000 |
| SOH | 0000 0001 | | 0100 0001 | a | 1000 0001 | A | 1100 0001 |
| STX | 0000 0010 | | 0100 0010 | b | 1000 0010 | B | 1100 0010 |
| ETX | 0000 0011 | | 0100 0011 | c | 1000 0011 | C | 1100 0011 |
| PF | 0000 0100 | | 0100 0100 | d | 1000 0100 | D | 1100 0100 |
| HT | 0000 0101 | | 0100 0101 | e | 1000 0101 | E | 1100 0101 |
| LC | 0000 0110 | | 0100 0110 | f | 1000 0110 | F | 1100 0110 |
| DEL | 0000 0111 | | 0100 0111 | g | 1000 0111 | G | 1100 0111 |
| | 0000 1000 | | 0100 1000 | h | 1000 1000 | H | 1100 1000 |
| RLF | 0000 1001 | | 0100 1001 | i | 1000 1001 | I | 1100 1001 |
| SMM | 0000 1010 | ¢[ | 0100 1010 | | 1000 1010 | | 1100 1010 |
| VT | 0000 1011 | . | 0100 1011 | | 1000 1011 | | 1100 1011 |
| FF | 0000 1100 | < | 0100 1100 | | 1000 1100 | | 1100 1100 |
| CR | 0000 1101 | ( | 0100 1101 | | 1000 1101 | | 1100 1101 |
| SO | 0000 1110 | + | 0100 1110 | | 1000 1110 | | 1100 1110 |
| SI | 0000 1111 | \| | 0100 1111 | | 1000 1111 | | 1100 1111 |
| DLE | 0001 0000 | & | 0101 0000 | | 1001 0000 | MZ 7/13 | 1101 0000 |
| DC1 | 0001 0001 | | 0101 0001 | j | 1001 0001 | J | 1101 0001 |
| DC2 | 0001 0010 | | 0101 0010 | k | 1001 0010 | K | 1101 0010 |
| TM | 0001 0011 | | 0101 0011 | l | 1001 0011 | L | 1101 0011 |
| RES | 0001 0100 | | 0101 0100 | m | 1001 0100 | M | 1101 0100 |
| NL | 0001 0101 | | 0101 0101 | n | 1001 0101 | N | 1101 0101 |
| BS | 0001 0110 | | 0101 0110 | o | 1001 0110 | O | 1101 0110 |
| IL | 0001 0111 | | 0101 0111 | p | 1001 0111 | P | 1101 0111 |
| CAN | 0001 1000 | | 0101 1000 | q | 1001 1000 | Q | 1101 1000 |
| EM | 0001 1001 | | 0101 1001 | r | 1001 1001 | R | 1101 1001 |
| CC | 0001 1010 | ! ] | 0101 1010 | | 1001 1010 | | 1101 1010 |
| CU1 | 0001 1011 | $ | 0101 1011 | | 1001 1011 | | 1101 1011 |
| IFS | 0001 1100 | * | 0101 1100 | | 1001 1100 | | 1101 1100 |
| IGS | 0001 1101 | ) | 0101 1101 | | 1001 1101 | | 1101 1101 |
| IRS | 0001 1110 | ; | 0101 1110 | | 1001 1110 | | 1101 1110 |
| IUS | 0001 1111 | ¬ | 0101 1111 | | 1001 1111 | | 1101 1111 |
| DS | 0010 0000 | − | 0110 0000 | — | 1010 0000 | RM 5/12 | 1110 0000 |
| SOS | 0010 0001 | / | 0110 0001 | | 1010 0001 | | 1110 0001 |
| FS | 0010 0010 | | 0110 0010 | s | 1010 0010 | S | 1110 0010 |
| | 0010 0011 | | 0110 0011 | t | 1010 0011 | T | 1110 0011 |
| BYP | 0010 0100 | | 0110 0100 | u | 1010 0100 | U | 1110 0100 |
| LF | 0010 0101 | | 0110 0101 | v | 1010 0101 | V | 1110 0101 |
| ETB | 0010 0110 | | 0110 0110 | w | 1010 0110 | W | 1110 0110 |
| ESC | 0010 0111 | | 0110 0111 | x | 1010 0111 | X | 1110 0111 |
| | 0010 1000 | | 0110 1000 | y | 1010 1000 | Y | 1110 1000 |
| | 0010 1001 | | 0110 1001 | z | 1010 1001 | Z | 1110 1001 |
| SM | 0010 1010 | 7/12 | 0110 1010 | | 1010 1010 | | 1110 1010 |
| CU2 | 0010 1011 | , | 0110 1011 | | 1010 1011 | | 1110 1011 |
| | 0010 1100 | % | 0110 1100 | | 1010 1100 | | 1110 1100 |
| ENQ | 0010 1101 | — | 0110 1101 | | 1010 1101 | | 1110 1101 |
| ACK | 0010 1110 | > | 0110 1110 | | 1010 1110 | | 1110 1110 |
| BEL | 0010 1111 | ? | 0110 1111 | | 1010 1111 | | 1110 1111 |
| | 0011 0000 | | 0111 0000 | | 1011 0000 | 0 | 1111 0000 |
| | 0011 0001 | | 0111 0001 | | 1011 0001 | 1 | 1111 0001 |
| SYN | 0011 0010 | | 0111 0010 | | 1011 0010 | 2 | 1111 0010 |
| | 0011 0011 | | 0111 0011 | | 1011 0011 | 3 | 1111 0011 |
| PN | 0011 0100 | | 0111 0100 | | 1011 0100 | 4 | 1111 0100 |
| RS | 0011 0101 | | 0111 0101 | | 1011 0101 | 5 | 1111 0101 |
| UC | 0011 0110 | | 0111 0110 | | 1011 0110 | 6 | 1111 0110 |
| EOT | 0011 0111 | | 0111 0111 | | 1011 0111 | 7 | 1111 0111 |
| | 0011 1000 | | 0111 1000 | | 1011 1000 | 8 | 1111 1000 |
| | 0011 1001 | 6/0 | 0111 1001 | | 1011 1001 | 9 | 1111 1001 |
| | 0011 1010 | : | 0111 1010 | | 1011 1010 | | 1111 1010 |
| CU3 | 0011 1011 | # | 0111 1011 | | 1011 1011 | | 1111 1011 |
| DC4 | 0011 1100 | @ | 0111 1100 | | 1011 1100 | | 1111 1100 |
| NAK | 0011 1101 | ' | 0111 1101 | | 1011 1101 | | 1111 1101 |
| | 0011 1110 | = | 0111 1110 | | 1011 1110 | | 1111 1110 |
| SUB | 0011 1111 | " | 0111 1111 | | 1011 1111 | EO | 1111 1111 |

FIG. 2.21

('1101' for negative, '1111' or '1100' for positive, values). In packed decimal format the right-hand four bits of the least-significant byte do not hold a digit, but instead hold a pattern to represent the sign of the number. This is illustrated in Figure 2.22.

Instructions are provided for addition, subtraction, multiplication, division (with a remainder), and comparison of such packed decimal operands. Provision is made for dealing with operands of different lengths (up to a maximum of 31 digits), the shorter operand being conceptually extended on the left with zeros. Although most processing of arithmetic fields is from right to left, the operand is specified by the address of its left-hand byte; since the instruction specifies the length of each packed decimal operand, the address of the right-hand byte is easily obtained.

A word on these computers is defined to be a set of four consecutive bytes (32 bits), and is specified by the store address of its left-hand byte. As on a normal word-oriented computer, 32-bit accumulators are provided. The instructions for binary arithmetic refer to these accumulators and to the contents of a 32-bit word whose left-hand byte is specified in the instruction.

Notice that a set of four consecutive bytes could be treated as a word containing a 32-bit binary pattern upon which word instructions can operate, or as a byte string to be operated on by the byte string instruc-

Representation of Decimal numbers on the IBM 370 (using three bytes)

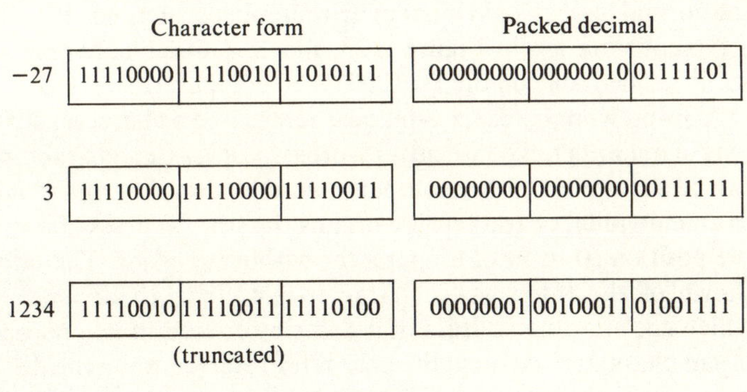


FIG. 2.22

tions, or (possibly) by the packed decimal instructions. In fact there are on these computers at least four word-oriented data-types; instructions are provided for fixed-point binary arithmetic on 16-bit half-words (2 consecutive bytes) as well as 32-bit words (or full-words), and for floating-point arithmetic on 32-bit words and 64-bit double words (8 consecutive bytes). Floating-point arithmetic on quadruple words (16 consecutive bytes) is also available on some models.

On the IBM 360 range restrictions are placed on which sets of consecutive bytes may be considered to form a word-oriented unit; thus the left-hand byte of a half-word must be at an even address, that of a full-word must be at an address divisible by four, and so on. These alignment rules mean that such computers do not in fact operate as pure byte-oriented machines, and are a consequence of a way in which the architecture of the computers has been inplemented. These restrictions have been removed on the IBM 370 range, but operand alignment at appropriate addresses is still recommended for efficiency.

### *Character handling on word-oriented computers*

Most modern computers attempt to provide facilities for manipulating strings of characters and possibly decimal digits. We have already seen how this is done on a byte-oriented computer. On a word-oriented computer the word is interpreted as an integral number of characters, and facilities are usually provided for transferring an individual character between a string and an accumulator, where it can be manipulated (for example, as one or more decimal digits), by the normal logical and (binary) arithmetic instructions. We illustrate a typical situation in Figure 2.23; this is a simplified version of the facilities available on the DEC PDP-10 computer.

A 36-bit word holds six 6-bit characters, and a character string consists of a number of consecutive words. In order that character strings can be accessed, another computer word holds a *descriptor* or pointer to an individual character: it contains the store address of a word and the position (0 to 5) of a character within the word. The effects are shown of the three basic character-handling instructions, each of which specifies the address of a descriptor word in its operand field. 'Load character' extracts the character referred to by the descriptor, placing it in the least-significant end of the accumulator (clearing the rest of the accumulator); 'Deposit character' stores the character from the least-significant end of the accumulator at the position referred to by the descriptor (leaving the rest of the string unaffected). 'Increment

## Character Handling on a Word-oriented Computer

Accumulator 287 300 301 302

| Accumulator | 287 | | | 300 | | | | | | 301 | | | | | | 302 | | | |
|---|---|---|---|---|---|---|---|---|---|---|---|---|---|---|---|---|---|---|---|
| | 4 | | 300 | T | I | G | L | A | T | H | P | I | L | E | S | E | R | | |

(a) Load into accumulator character whose descriptor is at 287

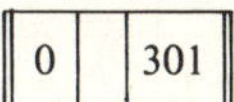


(b) Increment descriptor at 287

| 5 | | 300 |
|---|---|---|

(c) Deposit character at position whose descriptor is at 287

| 300 | | | | | | 301 | | | | | | 302 | | | |
|---|---|---|---|---|---|---|---|---|---|---|---|---|---|---|---|
| T | I | G | L | A | A | H | P | I | L | E | S | E | R | | |

(d) Increment descriptor at 287

| 0 | | 301 |
|---|---|---|

FIG. 2.23

descriptor' makes the descriptor refer to the next character in the string.

In this example we have assumed a character size of 6 bits. In fact on the PDP-10 the descriptor contains a field specifying the character length, allowing it to be anything from one to 36 bits long. Some computers provide an extra field in the descriptor to specify the number of characters in the string still to be processed, and this would be decremented by the 'Increment descriptor' instruction.

We have implied a clear distinction between word- and character-oriented computers, as is the case for large and medium-sized computers. But in minicomputers, with short word lengths, the distinction is not so clear. For example the DEC PDP-11 minicomputer has a 16-bit word and array of accumulators: however the basic store unit is the half-word or (8-bit) byte, and there is a set of byte-oriented instructions. On several microprocessors (such as the Intel 8080) the basic unit of storage and manipulation is the 8-bit byte.

Two operations on characters strings which are particularly common are translation and editing. Many computers therefore provide instructions to execute these operations on character strings, whether they are implemented as bytes or as subdivisions of words.

### *The translate operation*

The translate operation is used to convert a string from one character set to another. There are three operands, a source and a destination character string, and a translation table with one entry for each possible binary bit pattern that a character can hold. The characters of the source string are examined one-by-one. If the $i$th character has binary value $v_i$, then the $i$th character position in the destination string is loaded with the $v_i$th entry in the translation table. This is illustrated in Figure 2.24, which shows the translation of an (8-bit) character

Translation Table for Conversion from IBM 1401 Character Code to IBM 370 Character Code

| 64 | 241 | 242 | 243 | 244 | 245 | 246 | 247 | 248 | 249 | 240 | 123 |
|---|---|---|---|---|---|---|---|---|---|---|---|
| 0 | 1 | 2 | 3 | 4 | 5 | 6 | 7 | 8 | 9 | 10 | 11 |

| 124 | 0 | 0 | 0 | 0 | 97 | 226 | 227 | 228 | 229 | 230 | 231 |
|---|---|---|---|---|---|---|---|---|---|---|---|
| 12 | 13 | 14 | 15 | 16 | 17 | 18 | 19 | 20 | 21 | 22 | 23 |

| 232 | 233 | 0 | 107 | 108 | 0 | 0 | 0 | 96 | 209 | 210 | 211 |
|---|---|---|---|---|---|---|---|---|---|---|---|
| 24 | 25 | 26 | 27 | 28 | 29 | 30 | 31 | 32 | 33 | 34 | 35 |

| 212 | 213 | 214 | 215 | 216 | 217 | 0 | 91 | 92 | 0 | 0 | 0 |
|---|---|---|---|---|---|---|---|---|---|---|---|
| 36 | 37 | 38 | 39 | 40 | 41 | 42 | 43 | 44 | 45 | 46 | 47 |

| 80 | 193 | 194 | 195 | 196 | 197 | 198 | 199 | 200 | 201 | 0 | 75 |
|---|---|---|---|---|---|---|---|---|---|---|---|
| 48 | 49 | 50 | 51 | 52 | 53 | 54 | 55 | 56 | 57 | 58 | 59 |

| 0 | 0 | 0 | 0 |
|---|---|---|---|
| 60 | 61 | 62 | 63 |

Example: source string

| I | B | M | | 3 | 7 | 0 | — | 1 | 6 | 5 | • |
|---|---|---|---|---|---|---|---|---|---|---|---|
| 57 | 50 | 36 | 0 | 3 | 7 | 10 | 32 | 1 | 6 | 5 | 59 |

Destination string

| 201 | 194 | 212 | 64 | 243 | 247 | 240 | 96 | 241 | 246 | 245 | 75 |
|---|---|---|---|---|---|---|---|---|---|---|---|

FIG. 2.24

string from the IBM 1401 code (see Figure 2.19) to the IBM 370 code (see Figure 2.21).

As it stands, this operation requires three addresses, but it can be made into a two-address operation by making the source and the destination strings the same; thus the $v_i$th entry in the table replaces the $i$th character in the source string. A variation on this is to hold in each entry in the translation table, not only the value to be placed in the destination string, but also the address of a new translation table to be used for the next source character. If the address of the current translation table is always specified, we have the simple translate operation described above; however, now a new table can be selected (for example) after meeting a shift character.

***The edit operation***

The edit operation is used to prepare a numeric value for printed output. A numeric value stored inside a computer (after conversion if appropriate) consists of a series of decimal digits. There are several things we would like to do to improve the readability of this value:

(a) Leading zeros should be suppressed and replaced by blanks. Occasionally we wish to replace leading zeros by some other character, usually an asterisk, to guard against manual alteration of the value; this is known as 'cheque protection'.
(b) Commas, decimal points, or other separators may be inserted.
(c) A sign character (or some other character, such as a currency symbol) may be inserted immediately before the first significant digit of the value, or some sign indication (such as 'DR' and 'CR') may be placed immediately after the value.

Some or all of these operations are performed by the edit operation, which has three operands; the location of the numeric value to be edited (a string of decimal digits), the destination string to hold the final edited characters, and an editing pattern giving details of the editing to be performed.

The editing pattern consists of one entry per character position in the destination string: each of these specifies insertion either of a designated character or of the next character from the source string, and this may depend on the sign of the value being converted or on whether the first significant digit has yet been reached.

Figure 2.25 describes and illustrates the IBM 370 edit instruction.

| Conditions | | | | Results | |
|---|---|---|---|---|---|
| Pattern entry | Current state of significance (initially off) | Source digit | Next digit a plus sign | Result character | New state of significance |
| DS | Off | 0 | — | Fill character | Off |
| | | 1–9 | No | Source digit | On |
| | | | Yes | Source digit | Off |
| | On | 0–9 | No | Source digit | On |
| | | | Yes | Source digit | Off |
| SS | Off | 0 | No | Fill character | On |
| | | | Yes | Fill character | Off |
| | | 1–9 | No | Source digit | On |
| | | | Yes | Source digit | Off |
| | On | 0–9 | No | Source digit | On |
| | | | Yes | Source digit | Off |
| FS | — | — | — | Fill character | Off |
| MC | Off | — | — | Fill character | Off |
| | On | — | — | Message character | On |

Editing pattern

| SP | DS | DS | , | DS | SS | DS | • | DS | DS | D | R |
|---|---|---|---|---|---|---|---|---|---|---|---|

(a) Source string (packed decimal)

| 01 | 23 | 45 | 6+ |
|---|---|---|---|

Destination string

| SP | SP | 1 | , | 2 | 3 | 4 | • | 5 | 6 | SP | SP |
|---|---|---|---|---|---|---|---|---|---|---|---|

(b) Source string (packed decimal)

| 00 | 00 | 01 | 2+ |
|---|---|---|---|

Destination string

| SP | SP | SP | SP | SP | SP | 0 | • | 1 | 2 | SP | SP |
|---|---|---|---|---|---|---|---|---|---|---|---|

(c) Source string (packed decimal)

| 00 | 00 | 12 | 3− |
|---|---|---|---|

(d) Destination string

| SP | SP | SP | SP | SP | SP | 1 | • | 2 | 3 | D | R |
|---|---|---|---|---|---|---|---|---|---|---|---|

'SP' represents the space character

FIG. 2.25

The source, destination, and editing pattern are all byte strings, and the editing pattern has four possible entries: digit selector (DS: binary 00100000), significance starter (SS: binary 00100001), field separator (FS: binary 00100010), and message character (MC: any other binary pattern). The fill character is the first entry in the editing pattern.

This operation may be put in two-address form by placing the editing pattern in the destination string (where it will be overwritten), or inserting it as a string of 'micro-operations' in the instruction stream. The edit operation may also provide the address of the first significant digit, to facilitate insertion of a special character immediately before this digit, as mentioned in (c) above.

### 2.6. A multiplicity of data-types

Most computers have at least two representations for numeric data, for example a fixed-point binary format in which arithmetic is performed, and a character string format used by transput devices. Some computers have a large number of different numeric data-types. For example, the IBM 370 range has up to seven: character string and packed decimal; half- and full-word fixed-point binary; and short, long, and extended floating-point binary. It is possible to write subroutines which convert any numeric value from one format to another, but all but the smallest computers provide instructions to facilitate the conversion between at least some of their data-types. For example the IBM 370 range has instructions to convert between (numeric) character strings and packed decimal strings, and between packed decimal strings and 32-bit binary numbers; the edit instruction described earlier is also a form of conversion instruction. The PDP-10 computer has instructions for conversion between fixed and floating-point binary.

When a computer has a number of data-types, many operation codes are used up in providing the same arithmetic operation for operands with different formats. Thus, on the IBM 370 range, 6 different 'add' instructions are required, one for each data format except character string; in fact 15 different 'adds' are provided, including those for unnormalized floating-point and unsigned fixed-point arithmetic, and those for the case where both operands are held in accumulators. This may restrict the set of operations that can be provided for some or all of the data-types; it also makes it easy for the programmer to use an instruction on an operand with the wrong format, although assemble-time checks may help to reduce the number of errors of this sort.

One obvious way to minimize this problem is to reduce the number of different data formats. Thus the Burroughs B6700 computer provides no fixed-point arithmetic and uses (short or long) floating-point arithmetic instead, as discussed in § 2.2. Alternatively, a single set of arithmetic instructions can be provided, and a processor mode register specifies what format the operands can be expected to be in. This is an acceptable solution if we expect to concentrate on one form of arithemetic for a number of instructions, but if we are using several forms (for example, floating-point calculations with address computation in fixed-point format) then we have to change the contents of the mode register continually. A few computers use variations on this method.

***Tagged architecture***

The use of a mode register reduces the number of operation codes required, but it does not eliminate the problem of an instruction being given operands of one format when it expects another format. This problem can be solved by storing an indication of the data format in a special 'tag field' along with each item of data. Then only one instruction is provided for each arithmetic operation. If an 'add' instruction is being executed, the hardware of the computer examines the tag fields of the two operands, and selects the correct form of 'add', whether the fixed-point, short or long floating-point, decimal digit string, or some other data-type. If the operand formats are different, or one operand is unsuitable for arithmetic manipulation, then the hardware can automatically invoke a conversion operation or (more likely) signal an error condition for treatment by software.

Such a tagged computer architecture (Iliffe 1968; Feustel 1973) can obviously be extended. A simple extension is to provide a particular value of the tag field which does not specify a data format, and which always causes an error condition to be signalled whenever an operand is accessed with this value in the tag field. This facility can be used to indicate individual items in a set of data that have to be treated in a special way, different from the majority of items in the set; a special case is 'undefined' items, which have not as yet been assigned a value.

We can further extend the scheme into the non-numeric parts of the computer, by providing tag field values for all data formats, for instructions, and for descriptors; that is, computer words holding information about areas of the store (we have already met these in § 2.5). This would form the basis of a scheme for protecting all words of store from being manipulated by instructions which are not defined for the relevant data format.

Two disadvantages of such techniques are that each word has to have a tag field added to it (and this may need to be quite long to hold a suitable range of values), and execution of each instruction becomes more complicated (and therefore possibly slower). However, these disadvantages are unlikely to be great in the light of current developments in technology. The use of tagged architecture is limited to research projects at present, although the Burroughs B6700 computer makes some use of tagging.

## Problems

**2.1.** Show how the following numbers would be held in a 16-bit word in the sign-and-magnitude, one's complement, two's complement, and excess-value representations: 0, ±1, ±2, ±257, ±32 767, ±32 768.
**2.2.** Suppose that the right-hand bit of a 16-bit word represents $2^{-15}$ instead of $2^0$, so that there is an implied binary point immediately to the right of the sign bit. If the two's complement representation is used, show how the following numbers would be held: 0, ±1, ±0.25, ±0.171875.
**2.3.** On page 37 an algorithm is given for the signed multiplication of integral two's complement $n$-bit numbers. Rewrite this as a procedure in a suitable high-level language. How would the algorithm need to be altered if numbers were stored in fractional form (as in problem 2.2)?
**2.4.** The division algorithm described in §2.1 is restricted to the case of a non-negative dividend, a positive divisor, and no overflow. Extend the algorithm to deal with a general dividend and divisor, and include a test for overflow (i.e. when the quotient cannot be represented in $n$ bits). Assume the dividend and divisor are integral, in two's complement representation. For definiteness, assume that the remainder is zero or has the same sign as the dividend (see Stein and Munro 1971, Chapter 6 for more details).
**2.5.** Devise a suitable representation for signed multiple-length binary integers for a computer to which you have access, and write subroutines to negate, add, and subtract such operands. Write further subroutines to implement any other operations which you consider would be useful (for example multiplication and division).
**2.6.** Make a list of conditions causing overflow under the sign-and-magnitude and one's complement representations, in a similar form to the list on page 42.

**2.7.** Show how the following numbers would be held in normalized form in the floating-point format given in Figure 2.8: 0, $\pm 1$, $\pm 128$, $\pm 0.171875$.

**2.8.** Why may unnormalized floating-point arithmetic give a better indication of accuracy than normalized arithmetic? (Hint: consider the operation $A-B$, where $A$ and $B$ are nearly equal). The IBM 7030 Stretch computer (Buchholz, 1962) has a 'noisy' mode of floating-point arithmetic as well as the standard mode. In noisy mode the final bit shifted in on normalization is one (instead of zero, as in the standard mode). How could this be used to assess the accuracy of a floating-point calculation?

**2.9.** Show how the 'normalize' instruction described on page 48 would be used to convert a two's complement binary number to a fraction and exponent for use in floating-point arithmetic.

**2.10.** Show how the Exclusive Or operation can be used to (a) clear a word, (b) interchange two words without using an intermediate location, and (c) add two binary numbers (And and shift may be used in this last part, but not of course any arithmetic operations).

**2.11.** Suppose we have a store word which describes the status of a number of conditions, with each of which a subroutine is associated. Thus if bit $i$ is set to one, condition $i$ is true and subroutine $i$ is to be entered. In §2.3 an instruction is described which establishes the position of the most-significant bit set to one in a word. Show how this can be used (with a jump table) to cause entry to the appropriate subroutine in the above situation. Rewrite the code if the instruction jumps to address $X+i$, where $i$ is the position of the most-significant bit set, and $X$ is the contents of the operand field of the instruction. What assumptions have you made about the relative priority of the various conditions? (After reading §6.3) How might these instructions be used to speed interrupt handling?

**2.12.** How could a double-length rotate instruction operating on a pair of processor registers be used to interchange their values?

**2.13.** In §2.4 several methods are mentioned for specifying a particular subportion of a computer word. List these methods, and try to suggest the factors involved in selecting a particular one for a computer design.

**2.14.** Estimate the speed increase in using a (hypothetical or actual) block transfer instruction on a computer to which you have access, over the best alternative way of performing the move. State any assumptions you make.

**2.15.** You have to design a character set for a computer with an 8-bit character. Leaving aside considerations of compatibility with other computers, in what ways could the allocation of binary patterns to graphic symbols simplify the processing of character strings? (Consider, for example, putting character strings in dictionary order, or testing character strings for validity). How good is the character set in Figure 2.21 from this point of view?

**2.16.** This chapter mentioned several ways in which the end of a character string may be indicated. Describe their advantages and disadvantages (and those of any other methods you can think of).

**2.17.** The compare instruction on the IBM 1401 computer

Compare *A* *B*

sets an equality indicator if the character string in the field at address *A* is exactly the same as the character string in the field at address *B*, and sets a high or low indicator appropriately if they are unequal (using the collating sequence shown in Figure 2.19). What problems would arise if this instruction is used to compare numeric fields?

**2.18.** Design a translation table to translate from the IBM 370 character code to the IBM 1401 character code. This will be the inverse of the translation table given in Figure 2.24.

**2.19.** On the IBM 370 range of computers, the three operands of the translate instruction are all strings of 8-bit bytes. Suppose we wish to permute the order of the bytes in a string. For example, the string:

| byte 0 | byte 1 | byte 2 | byte 3 | byte 4 | byte 5 |
|---|---|---|---|---|---|

is to become

| byte 5 | byte 4 | byte 2 | byte 0 | byte 1 | byte 3 |
|---|---|---|---|---|---|

How can this be done with the translate instruction? (Hint: let the translation table hold the string to be reordered.)

**2.20.** Consider a translate instruction in which

(a) The source and destination strings are scanned from right to left;
(b) Each entry in the translation table contains both a value to be inserted in the destination string, and the address of a new translation table for the next source character.

Suppose further that we have an instruction which, given two character strings, perform a binary addition on corresponding pairs of characters. For example, if we have strings of four 6-bit characters:

| 000001 | 000010 | 000011 | 000100 |
|---|---|---|---|

and

| 000111 | 000110 | 001001 | 000110 |
|---|---|---|---|

the result should be:

| 001000 | 001000 | 001100 | 001010 |
|---|---|---|---|

Show how the above translate instruction could process this result string to make it a digit-by-digit sum to a non-binary base. For example, to a base of ten, the result should be:

| 001000 | 001001 | 000011 | 000000 |
|---|---|---|---|

What restrictions are there on the choice of base? (This translate instruction is a version of one found on the IBM 7090 computer, and used for implementing decimal arithmetic).

**2.21.** Follow in detail the sequence of events illustrated by each of the editing examples in Figure 2.25. How must the editing pattern be altered to insert asterisks in place of high-order zeros in these examples?

**2.22.** Write subroutines, for a computer to which you have access, to convert between a numeric character string and a format in which numeric calculations can be carried out. In the most general case, this might convert between strings of the form:

$$\pm dd...d.dd...d\uparrow\pm dd...d$$

and binary floating-point ($d$ is any decimal digit, and ↑ means 'times ten to the power').

# 3 The instruction set

## 3.1. Instructions as a data-type

IN A STORED-PROGRAM computer the instruction set is one of the most important data-types to be held in the computer store. What operations then do we need on this data-type? On early computers it was necessary to provide facilities to manipulate the operand fields of instructions. In §1.1, for example, we showed a sequence of instructions to add one to the operand field of an 'add' instruction, so that when executed it referred to successive locations in store. Several early computers therefore provided an instruction to manipulate the operand field of another instruction; instructions 18 and 19 on the Von Neumann computer (Figure 1.5) are an example. Modern computer architecture makes this type of instruction modification undesirable and, since the introduction of index registers, it has become unnecessary. Therefore the only operations nowadays provided on this data-type are to jump to or execute an instruction; we deal with these operations in §§3.3 and 3.4.

Here we discuss possible variations in the format of instructions, and the matching of instruction length to computer word size. Such variations may be irrelevant to the programmer, even when writing a program in a low-level language, since the assembler deals with the detailed representation in the computer store of the sequence of instruction fields specified by the programmer.

### *Basic instruction formats*

Figure 3.1 illustrates some typical instruction formats. Figure 3.1(a) shows the basic instruction format for a single-address computer. It has an *operation code* or *function field,* specifying what operation the computer is to perform, and an *operand* field, which specifies an operand (usually as a store address) or the location for a result.

Nowadays most computers have several methods by which an operand may be specified: we have met direct addressing and indexing in Chapter 1, and the other methods are discussed in Chapter 4. The operand field may therefore be divided into two portions, as shown in

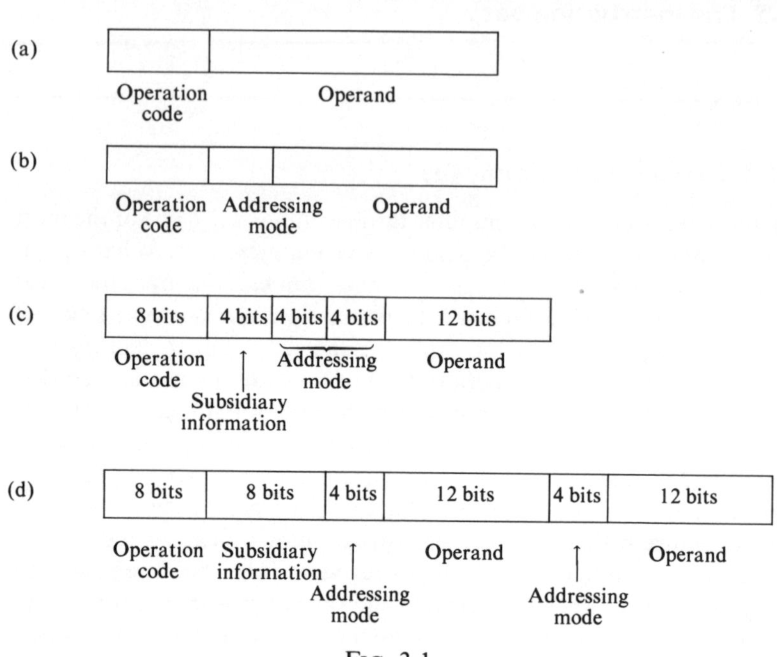


FIG. 3.1

Figure 3.1(b). The larger portion holds a numeric value, and the smaller, the *addressing mode field,* specifies how the numeric value is to be interpreted; for example, as a numeric quantity for direct use (see the next section), as a store address, or as a numeric quantity to be added to the contents of an index register to form a store address. Often this field simply encodes the number of the index register to be used, with one value implying 'no indexing': any other addressing methods available would then be specified as part of the operation code field.

Many computers have a further field in the instruction, to specify subsidiary information required by an operation. This is illustrated by Figure 3.1(c), which shows one of the five formats of IBM 370 instructions, the RX or 'register and indexed storage' format. The subsidiary information field specifies which one of 16 accumulators is to participate in the instruction, a common use for this field. The addressing mode field is divided into two subfields, each of which specifies one of the 16 accumulators whose contents is to be added to the operand (or 'displacement') field to give an effective address: a value of zero in either subfield means no indexing by this field.

Figure 3.1(d) illustrates a typical two-address instruction: this is another format of instruction from the IBM 370 range, the SS or 'storage to storage' format. Here the subsidiary information field specifies the length or lengths (in bytes) of the operands. The addressing mode fields (one per operand) each specify an accumulator (or none) whose contents are to be added to the appropriate operand (or 'displacement') field to generate an effective address.

Certain operations do not require the specification of a store address; an example is shifting the accumulator left or right. There are several possible ways of representing such instructions in the computer store.

(a) The operand and addressing mode fields are simply ignored. Thus the number of bits to be shifted is specified in the subsidiary information field, or encoded as part of the operation code field.

(b) A second possibility, which makes better use of the instruction length, is to calculate an effective store address from the operand and addressing mode fields in the instruction in the normal way (for example, by adding the contents of an index register). But the effective address is then used, not to specify a store location, but as subsidiary information for the operation to be performed (such as the number of bits to be shifted). This allows the subsidiary information for an operation to be modified (for example, by manipulating an index register) without modifying the instruction itself. This method is used for shift instructions on, for example, the IBM 370 range.

(c) A third approach is to divide the instruction set into a number of groups, and provide a different instruction format for each group.

For example, (on a one-address computer) we might have a group of data-manipulation instructions with an operation code field, a small subsidiary information field to specify an accumulator, and addressing mode and operand fields. Then a second group comprises those data-manipulation instructions not requiring a store address, which have an operation code field and a large subsidiary information field. A third is transput instructions, requiring a field to specify one from a range of peripheral devices. Jump instructions could be a fourth group, if the layout of the addressing mode and operand fields differs from that of the first group. For examples see the Data General Nova (discussed later in this section) and the DEC PDP-11.

Thus the operation code field is decoded to specify, not only what operation is to be performed, but also how the bit pattern of the remainder of the instruction is to be interpreted.

***The operation code field***

We have assumed in the above that the operation code field is fixed in length, but we may be able to make better use of the instruction length by having a variable-length operation code field.

If we have a fixed-length instruction word with one of the formats shown in Figure 3.1(a)–(c), then the number of bits required to specify such secondary information as an operand address limits the size of the operation code field, and therefore limits the maximum number of different operations with this amount of secondary information. However, if there are further operations requiring less secondary information, then another instruction format can be provided with a longer operation code field. Typically one value of the short operation code field marks an 'escape' into the format with the longer operation code field. For example, the IBM 370 range has several instruction formats, all with 8-bit operation code fields occupying the first byte (two formats are shown in Figure 3.1(c) and (d)). But if the first byte has a (hexadecimal) value of 9C, 9D, 9E, 9F, or B2, then a 4-byte 'S' format instruction is indicated, and in this format the operation code field occupies the first two bytes.

This can obviously be extended to allow a range of different sizes of operation code field, so that we can provide more operation codes for less secondary information (such as operand fields) in a fixed instruction length. The assignment of binary bit patterns to operation codes, and of portions of the operation code field to positions in the instruction format, must be done in such a way that the hardware of the computer can decode the instruction; thus it must be possible to extract an initial portion of the operation code from a fixed position in the instruction and decide, from the bit pattern found there, whether an operation is now specified (in which case the rest of the instruction can be interpreted as secondary fields) or whether a further portion of instruction has to be decoded, and so on. Usually only a small number of different

Instruction Formats on the Data General Nova Computer

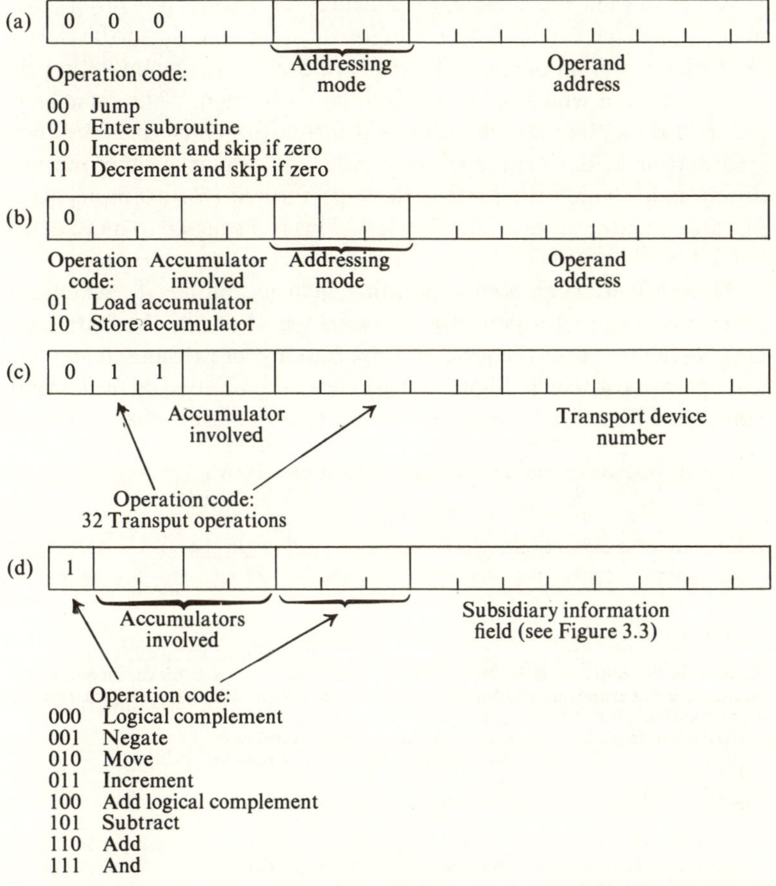


FIG. 3.2

operation code field sizes are used, rather than a completely variable field size. Figure 3.2 illustrates the various instruction formats available on the Data General Nova computer.

Notice that we have mentioned two ways of specifying an operation to be performed: by having various lengths of operation code field, or by having a fixed length operation code field together with some form of subsidiary information field. In a real situation, such as on the Data General Nova, it may be difficult to distinguish between the two.

### *The subsidiary information field*

We have seen the subsidiary information field as providing parameters needed by an operation, such as the number of bits to be shifted or the length of an operand. Instead we can see it as completing the specification of which operation is to be performed. Thus some computers use for the jump instruction a format in which the subsidiary information field is a sub-operation code field, which specifies the condition under which the jump is to be performed (for example, accumulator positive, or overflow flag set). This is discussed in more detail in §3.3.

Alternatively such a sub-operation field might specify secondary functions to be performed with the main operation. On the Data General Nova computer the group of instructions for arithmetic and logical operations (seen in Figure 3.2(d)) has an 8-bit sub-operation field, detailed in Figure 3.3. This specifies whether the result of an operation

The Sub-operation field on the Data General Nova

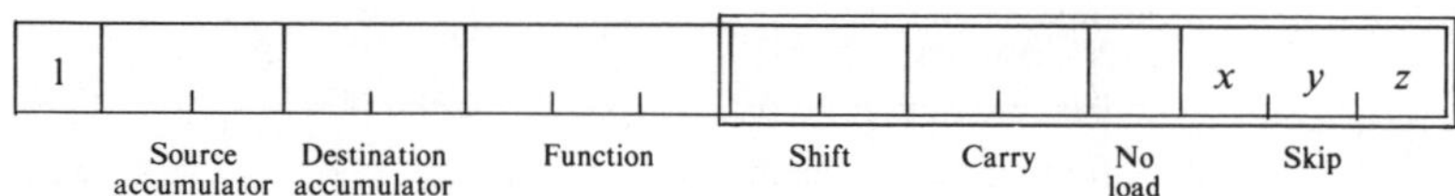


Execution sequence:

(a) Perform the primary operation, specified by the 'function' field, on the 16-bit operand in the source accumulator (logical complement, negate, move, increment) or on the 16-bit operands in the source and destination accumulators (add logical complement, subtract, add, and).

(b) Take a carry bit, specified by the 'carry' field as follows:

00 current state of carry register
01 zero
10 one
11 complement of current state of carry register

(c) For the non-logical primary operations (negate, increment, add logical complement, subtract, add), complement the result of (b) if there is a carry from the most-significant bit of the result of (a).

(d) Shift the 17-bit value obtained by concatenating the result of (c) on the left of the result of (a). The 'shift' field specifies what shift to perform:

00 none
01 left circular shift one bit
10 right circular shift one bit
11 swap the 8-bit halves of the result of (a), leaving the result of (c) unchanged

(e) If the 'No load' field is zero, store the result of (d) in the carry register and the destination accumulator. Otherwise do not store the result.

(f) Test the result of (d) according to the 'skip' field. Suppose $x$, $y$, and $z$ are the three bits of the 'skip' field, and $c$ and $r$ are the most significant bit and the least-significant 16 bits (respectively) of the result of (d). Then the next instruction is skipped if:

exclusive or ($z$, or (and ($x$, $r = 0$), and ($y$, $c = 0$))).

FIG. 3.3

is to be shifted, how any carry is to be dealt with, whether the storing of the result is to be suppressed, and under what conditions a skip is to be executed. The last two used together allow tests to be performed without affecting the operands.

### *Bit significance*

The allocation of operation code bit patterns to particular instructions may be arbitrary, within any constraints set by the use of variable length operation code fields.

However, an attempt may be made to allocate particular bits or groups of bits in the operation code field to particular features of the instruction; one bit, for example, might specify whether the result of an operation is to be placed in the accumulator, and another whether the fixed-point arithmetic unit is to be used by the operation. This is called *bit significance.* Since it results in long operation code fields, full bit significance is not used for operation code assignment, except at the microprogram level discussed in §3.6. Because of this connection, the term 'microprogrammed' is sometimes used to describe instructions with bit significance, such as the 'operate' instruction on the DEC PDP-8 computer (described on p. 88).

Some limited bit significance is provided by splitting the operation code field into two portions, one specifying the instruction group and one the particular instruction within the group. This is done, for example, in the operation code field of the IBM 370 range of computers, as shown in Figure 3.4.

IBM 370 Operation Code Field

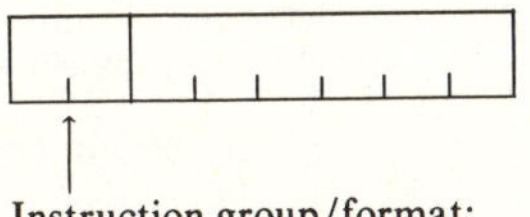

Instruction group/format:

00 'register-to-register' (RR) group—2 bytes long
01 'register-and-indexed-storage' (RX) group—4 bytes long
10 'register-and-storage' (RS) group } 4 bytes long
'storage-and-immediate' (SI) group }
On the IBM 370 range (but not the IBM 360) this group also includes one rather special RX instruction (Load Real Address) and the group of S format instructions
11 'storage-to-storage' (SS) group—6 bytes long

FIG. 3.4

It is more common to find bit significance in sub-operation fields. Thus on the DEC PDP-8 computer, there is a 3-bit operation code field; if the operation code is 7, then the 'operate' instruction group is indicated, and a particular function is specified by a sub-operation field consisting of the remaining nine bits (of the 12-bit word). If the left-hand bit of this field is zero, then a 'group 1 operate instruction' is indicated and the significance of the remaining eight bit positions is as shown in Figure 3.5. Several of these bits may be set in an instruction, in which case all the specified functions are carried out; the order in which functions are performed is fixed by having each function assigned to one of four timing points within the basic instruction cycle.

The Operate Instruction on the DEC PDP-8 computer

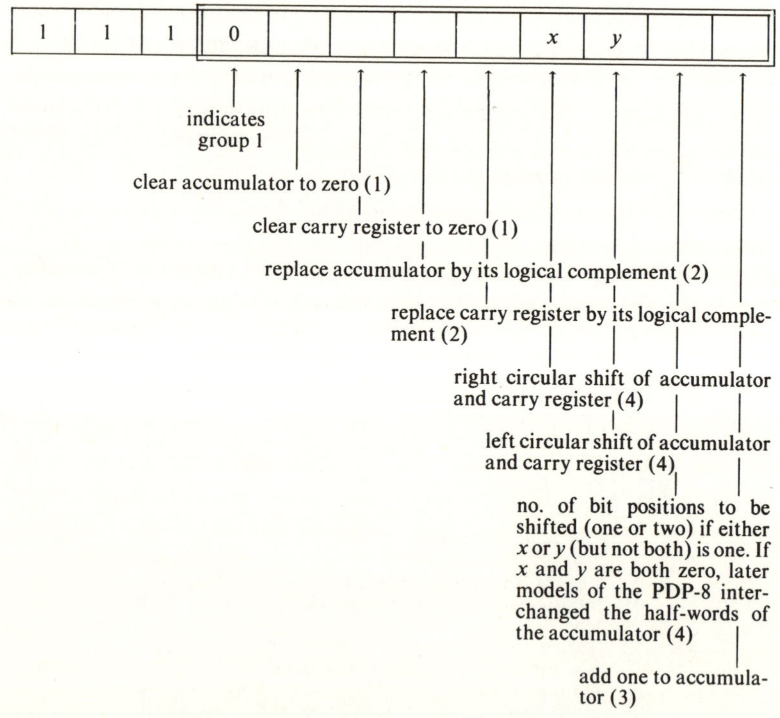


The numbers in brackets after the description of each bit refer to its timing point within the basic instruction cycle.

FIG. 3.5

For example, if the bits for 'logical complement of accumulator' and 'increment accumulator' are set, then the instruction 'complement and increment accumulator' (i.e. two's complement negate accumulator) is obtained.

If the left-hand bit of the sub-operation field is one, a different set of functions is indicated. These include tests on the accumulator and carry register (group 2) if the right-hand bit of the field is zero, and operations on an (optional) extended arithmetic element such as multiplication and division (group 3) if it is one.

### *Instruction length versus word length*

In the above discussion we have been considering a word-oriented computer where each instruction occupies one word. It will sometimes be the case that, for certain instruction groups, the number of bits required fully to specify an operation and all its associated information is less than the computer word length; so these groups are using the word inefficiently, and are candidates for occupying only a portion of a word. On the CDC 6600 computer (which uses a 60-bit word) instructions may be 15 or 30 bits long, according to the amount of information needing to be specified by the instruction.

In extreme cases all instructions have such unused fields, and then there may be room for two instructions to a word. An example of this is the Von Neumann computer, where arithmetic precision requirements forced a much longer word length than was required for instructions. An alternative solution is the provision of multiple-length arithmetic operations, of course.

Conversely, a group of complex instructions may require more bits than are available in a computer word, leading to a two-word format for instructions in this group. The instruction decoding process needs to recognize such double-length instructions and access a second instruction word.

The most common system on word-oriented computers is, of course, one instruction per word for all instructions.

### *Instruction syllables*

In the zero-address computers discussed in the next section, some instructions require only an operation code field while others require an operand specification as well, so considerable variation in instruction length is possible. The basic instruction unit is then the *syllable* (of perhaps 6 or 8 bits), instead of the word.

An instruction then consists of an initial operator syllable which specifies the operation to be performed, perhaps followed by one or more further syllables specifying a store address or subsidiary information. The operator syllable implies (or specifies in a subfield) how many syllables are required for the instruction. The syllables making up an instruction are placed immediately after the syllables of the previous instruction, without regard for the boundaries between words. Notice that the program counter has to indicate not only which word has been reached in a program, but also which syllable within the word.

### *Instruction addressing*

A problem in any word-oriented computer with instruction formats shorter than the word is how to address individual instructions. This reduces in practice to deciding how to specify the destination of a jump instruction, when this destination may be any part-word or syllable.

(a) One solution (which assumes such destinations are sparsely scattered within the instruction stream) is to force instructions which are jump destinations to be on word boundaries; this is the method used on the CDC 6600 computer.

(b) Another is to provide jump instructions with a field specifying a part-word or syllable address within the addressed word; this is the method used on the Burroughs B6700 computer.

On character- and byte-oriented computers we have the freedom to use these units of storage as instruction syllables, without any of the problems of syllable addressing mentioned above.

On the character-oriented IBM 1401 computer (McCracken 1962; Bell and Newell 1971, pp. 225–34) instructions are from one to eight characters long. Instead of coding the instruction length into the operation code, the word mark bit is set on the left-hand character of each instruction (which contains the operation code). Since instructions are processed from left to right on this computer (unlike data which is processed from right to left), the characters of an instruction are picked up until a word mark is reached (indicating the beginning of the next instruction); the instruction is then executed.

On the byte-oriented IBM 370 range, instructions can be two, four, or six bytes long. However on all models the basic instruction unit is the half-word, rather than the syllable or byte, and instructions must therefore start at even addresses.

## 3.2. The accessing of operands

Most of the arithmetic and logical operations discussed in the previous chapter are (or can be reorganized as) binary operations; that is, they require two operand values. An instruction for such an operation must therefore indicate three locations, two source locations for the two operands, and a destination location to hold the result.

### *Three-, Two-, and One-Address Instructions*

An instruction might therefore explicitly specify three store locations; an example of such a *three-address* instruction is

> Add the contents of store addresses *A* and *B*, depositing the result at store address *C*

In early computers such a technique was feasible, since store capacities (and therefore operand field lengths) were small, and addressing mode fields were often absent. An example of a three-address instruction format on an early computer is shown in Figure 3.6. However, with increasing store capacities and the presence of addressing mode fields, the use of three-address instructions makes for a very long instruction format, and the technique is not now used.

What the programmer wants in many cases is for the result of the operation to replace one of the operands. Hence we are led to consider a *two-address* instruction format, where one store address is the source of the first operand and the destination of the result, and the other store address is the source of the second operand. For example, the instruction

> Add *A* to *B*

specifies the addition of the contents of store addresses *A* and *B*, leaving the result in store address *B*. A typical two-address instruction format was illustrated in Figure 3.1(d). It could be implied in the operation code whether the first or second store address is to receive

| 6 bits | 12 bits | 12 bits | 12 bits |
|---|---|---|---|
| Operation code | Address of first operand | Address of second operand | Address of result |

FIG. 3.6

the result, but in practice any particular computer uses always the first address, or always the second address, as the destination: for example the SS (two address) format of the IBM 370 range uses the first address as the destination. If the effect of a three-address instruction is required, for example 'add *A* to *B* giving *C*', we need to use two two-address instructions,

Move *A* to *C*
Add *B* to *C* (giving *C*)

A two-address instruction format is usually still too long. We therefore take account of the fact that the programmer often wants (especially in scientific computing) to do further operations on the result of an operation, and consequently this result can be held in a storage register in the processor, the accumulator. Thus we have the conventional *one-address* instruction format (introduced in Chapter 1) where one of the operands and the result are held in the accumulator, and the store address of only the second operand has to be specified in the instruction. Typical one-address instruction formats were shown in Figure 3.1(b) and (c). Notice that holding the intermediate result of a calculation in the accumulator not only shortens the instruction length, but also increases the instruction execution speed, since the access time to a processor register is shorter than to a store location.

In this case the address of the first operand and result is implied since (for example) the 'add' instruction has the meaning

Add to the accumulator and leave the result in the accumulator

In fact, a two address format is really a 'two-explicit and one-implicit'-address format, and a one-address format is a 'one-explicit and two-implicit'-address format.

Computers designed for scientific calculation, where it is valid to assume that the result of one operation may be an operand of the next, have an accumulator and use the one-address format. Computers for commercial data-processing, where the assumption may be invalid and where an accumulator would have to be very long to deal with character string data formats, tend to use the two-address format and not provide an accumulator. Computers for use in both areas (such as the IBM 370 range) may provide two sets of instructions: a one-address set for word operands (using an accumulator), and a two-address set for character string operands.

### *An array of accumulators*

The provision of a single accumulator does not really correspond to the way in which most programs are written, since at any given point there are usually several intermediate values all of which are in the process of being manipulated. For this reason, a small array of accumulators (typically a power of two, such as 8 or 16) may be provided instead of a single accumulator.

Arithmetic and logical operations are now performed between operands both of which are in accumulators, or one in an accumulator and one in a store location. The instructions have to specify the accumulator to be used as well as the store address, giving some of the advantages of the two-address system without the long instruction format required to hold a second store address; this technique has therefore sometimes been called the '1½-address system'.

Such sets of accumulators seem to have appeared first in the Ferranti Pegasus computer (Bell and Newell 1971, p.170) and most modern computers are now designed with this feature. Since there are only a small number, it is economic to make the accumulators faster than the store elements, so that operations are performed at greater speed while all operands are held in accumulators. We therefore attempt to hold the current program 'context' in the fast accumulators as the program is executed; since it may be difficult for a programmer or compiler to establish such a current context at each point, it has been proposed that the accumulator array be replaced by an associative store, and this is discussed in §5.5.

As we have seen in the previous chapter, there may be several other processor registers accessible to the programmer apart from the accumulator, for example the MQ register. To achieve a more uniform instruction set, such specialized registers are replaced by the use of accumulators in the array. Thus on the IBM 370 range, double-length fixed point binary operands (such as for multiplication and division) are held in a pair of consecutive accumulators, and the instruction specifies the lower numbered accumulator of the pair; since the effective MQ register is an accumulator, we can use any of the computer's instruction set to manipulate it.

The most important such special register (after the accumulator) is the index register (or registers). At most points in a program there are several intermediate results and several index quantities; further, calculated results may later be used as index quantities. It is logical, therefore, to make provision for a subset of the accumulator array to be used as index registers, instead of providing separate index registers. In some computers all accumulators may be used as index registers, although an index specification of zero usually means no indexing rather than a specification of accumulator zero as index register: this is the case on the IBM 370 range. Thus the normal instruction set can be used on index quantities, without the need for a special index arithmetic set of instructions.

### *Instructions for an array of accumulators*

Let us now consider the types of instruction required by a computer with an array of accumulators. First we require normal 'load and store accumulator' instructions, as described earlier for computers with a single accumulator, except that now the instruction must specify the particular accumulator involved. Second, instructions to transfer data between a sequence of store locations and a sequence of accumulators, as described in §2.4, are useful for rapidly changing the processor context. Third, we require an instruction to move data from one accumulator to another, perhaps performing subsidiary operations on the data (such as negation) during the move.

For binary operations, on both one- and 1½-address computers, we have a number of possible ways of interpreting the explicit and implicit locations of operands and result. The following are possible:

(a) The first operand is in the (specified) accumulator, the second is in a store location, and the result replaces the contents of the original accumulator. This is the standard form, described in Chapter 2.

(b) The first operand is in the (specified) accumulator, the second is in a store location, and the result replaces the contents of the store location. A small number of instructions of this form is found in some, but not all, one- and 1½-address computers; a fairly common example is an 'add into storage' instruction.

(c) The first operand is in the (specified) accumulator, the second is in a store location, and the result replaces the contents both of the original accumulator and of the store location. This form is much rarer than (a) or (b). The peripheral control processor (PCP) of the CDC 6600 computer (see §6.5) has what is referred to as a 'replace add' instruction, where the result of adding the contents of the accumulator and a store location replaces both the accumulator and the store location. On the DEC PDP-10 computer most fixed point binary and logical operations (such as And and Add) have four modes, as shown in Figure 3.7.

Note that in the above discussion we have carefully distinguished the first from the second operand. In some operations, such as the logical operations, add and multiplication of equal-length operands, it is irrelevant which operand is considered as the first. However, certain operations are inherently asymmetrical, the most important being subtract and divide. If operand $A$ is in an accumulator and $B$ is in a store location, the above forms allow us to compute $(A-B)$ and $(A \div B)$, but not $(B-A)$ or $(B \div A)$ without further manipulation. To this end, some computers provide 'reverse' or 'inverted' subtract and divide, which (respectively) subtract the first from the second operand and divide the second by the first operand.

(d) Both operands are in accumulators and the result replaces the contents of one of the accumulators, whether the first or the second usually being fixed for a particular computer (as with two-address instruc-

Logical and Fixed Point Binary Operation Modes on the DEC PDP-10

(a) 'Basic', e.g. Add [Basic]:
C(accumulator) + C(store location) ▷ accumulator

(b) 'Immediate', e.g. Add Immediate:
C(accumulator) + immediate operand from instruction itself† ▷ accumulator

(c) 'Memory', e.g. Add to Memory:
C(accumulator) + C(store location) ▷ store location

(d) 'Both', e.g. Add to Both:
C(accumulator) + C(store location) ▷ accumulator, store location

† See p. 101.

FIG. 3.7

tions). This is illustrated by the RR format of instruction on the IBM 370 range, shown in Figure 3.8(a), where the result replaces the first operand.

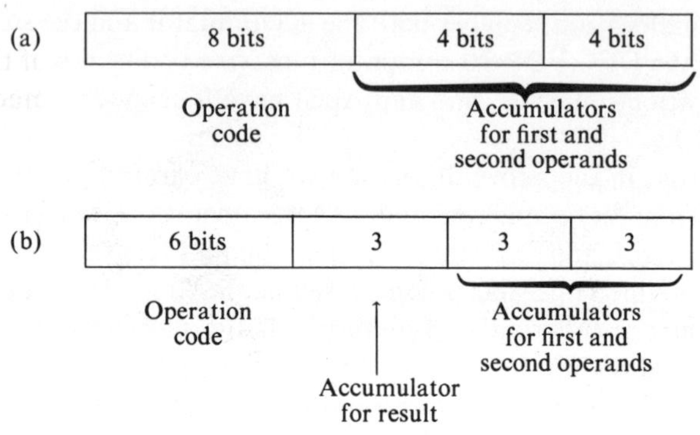


FIG. 3.8

Some computers have room in the instruction to specify a third accumulator to hold the result, giving the effect of a three-address instruction restricted to the accumulator array. For example Figure 3.8(b) illustrates one of the instruction formats on the CDC 6600.

Instructions with both operands in accumulators are shorter than those of forms (a), (b), and (c) above. In a computer with several instruction lengths this is, of course, no problem, but otherwise some of the instruction word may be unused. On the Data General Nova this problem is solved by the provision of a sub-operation field in the accumulator-to-accumulator format (see Figures 3.2 and 3.3); in fact, as these figures show, no accumulator-and-store operations are provided except load and store.

***Stacks and zero-address instructions***

Consider now an arithmetic expression written in a high-level language like Algol or Fortran, for example

$$(A+B)\times(C-D)$$

A compiler for a computer with an array of accumulators would translate it into a form such as

Load accumulator R1 from A
Add B to accumulator R1
Load accumulator R2 from C
Subtract D from accumulator R2
Multiply accumulator R1 by accumulator R2
Store accumulator R1 in result location

The compiler performs this translation by first transforming the original into reverse Polish notation, where each operator appears after its operands, in this case

$$AB+CD-\times$$

(see, for example, Randell and Russell 1964). It then uses this intermediate form to produce the final form above, allocating temporary results to accumulators (or to store locations if necessary). However, this intermediate form could be interpreted directly by a computer with a *stack* or last-in-first-out store.

The English-Electric KDF9 computer (Davis 1960; Haley 1962; ICL 1968) provided such a stack, implemented in hardware and referred to as a 'nesting store', instead of a conventional accumulator. This nesting store could hold up to sixteen operands, and is illustrated in Figure 3.9. New operands are always inserted at position one, and all operands already in the stack are moved down one position (or 'pushed'); only the most recently added operand could be removed (from position one) and the remaining operands are moved back (or 'popped'). An analogy can be made with the push-down stack of plates in a cafeteria or (as in the KDF9 manual) with the magazine of a Sten gun.

On such a stack-oriented computer an operand can be transferred from a store location to the top element of the stack (pushing down all previously entered operands), and the contents of the top element of the stack can be copied to a store location, the top element remaining on the stack or being deleted, moving up all earlier elements; the former is more akin to the conventional 'store' operation, although the latter is more common. All unary operations (such as negate) are performed on the top element of the stack, and binary operations are

The KDF9 stack.

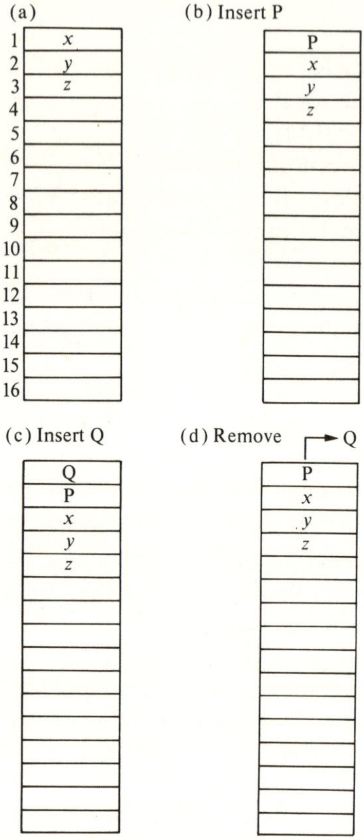

(a)

| | |
|---|---|
| 1 | $x$ |
| 2 | $y$ |
| 3 | $z$ |
| 4 | |
| 5 | |
| 6 | |
| 7 | |
| 8 | |
| 9 | |
| 10 | |
| 11 | |
| 12 | |
| 13 | |
| 14 | |
| 15 | |
| 16 | |

(b) Insert P

P
$x$
$y$
$z$

(c) Insert Q

Q
P
$x$
$y$
$z$

(d) Remove → Q

P
$x$
$y$
$z$

FIG. 3.9

performed on the top two elements of the stack (after which they are removed) and the result placed on the top of the stack.
The above example therefore becomes

Load from A
Load from B
Add
Load from C
Load from D
Subtract
Multiply
Store at result location

It will be seen that binary arithmetic and logical instructions need no explicit operands, and consist only of an operation code field; such an instruction therefore has a *zero-address* format. Instructions are required to jump to a specified store location conditional on the value in the top element of the stack (which may be removed by the jump instruction); an example is

Jump to location A if top of stack is positive

On the KDF9 computer various stack manipulation instructions were provided, such as to duplicate or erase the top element or to rearrange the top few elements.

There are two problems with the type of stack found in the KDF9 computer: (a) it is of fixed size, so that the programmer or compiler has to take care to keep within its bounds; and (b) in a multiprogramming environment the stack has to be emptied and refilled at each process switch; the latter could be done on the KDF9 only one element at a time (although suitable stack dump and restore instructions could be envisaged), and the problem was solved on that computer by providing multiple nesting stores.

The Burroughs B6700 computer gets round these problems by using a different form of stack, which is illustrated in Figure 3.10. Only the top two elements of the stack are (for speed) held in processor registers A and B. Operands are added to the top of the stack by being placed in A, whose contents (if any) are moved to B. The remainder of a process's stack is a vector of contiguous store locations. Three processor registers point to the bottom or base of the stack area (the BOS register), the top of the stack area (the LOS or limit of stack register), and the current position of the last element placed in the area (the stack register S). If an operand is 'pushed' out of B, the stack register is incremented and the operand placed at the resulting address. To remove an operand from the stack, that in A is removed, the contents of B moved to A, the contents of the store location referred to by the stack pointer are moved to B, and the stack pointer is decremented. This sequence is carried out by hardware, which also checks that the stack pointer remains pointing at a location within the stack area.

Because the stack is such a common programming device for retaining intermediate results in the right order (for arithmetic calculation, syntactic analysis, subroutine and interrupt entry and return, etc.), many modern computers provide facilities for manipulating a stack,

The stack on the Burroughs B6700 computer.

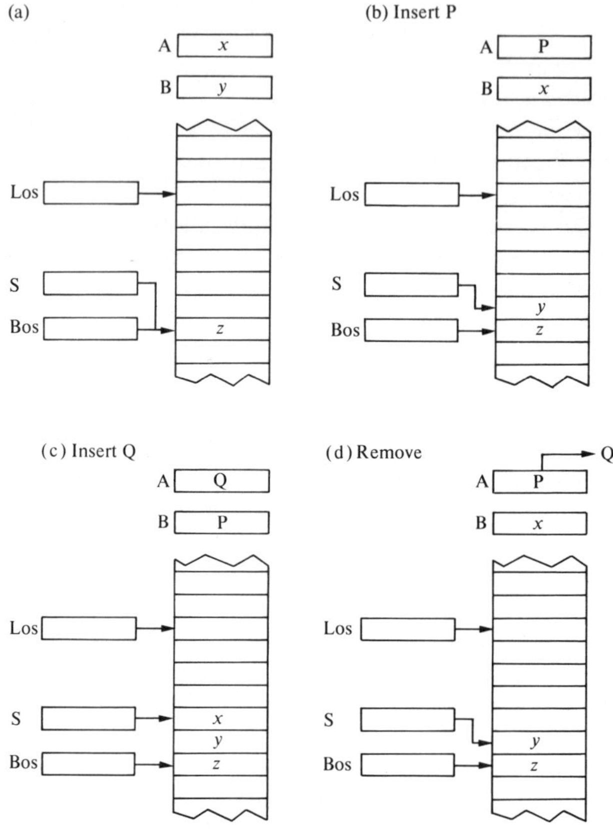


FIG. 3.10

even though they are basically one-address computers rather than zero-address like the KDF9 and Burroughs computers. A common technique (see for example the University of Manchester MU5 and ICL 2900 range, and many microprocessors) is to allow any contiguous block of store locations to hold a stack, and for a special processor register, the stack pointer, to hold the address of the location currently containing the top element of the stack. Provision is then made to manipulate the stack pointer and to transfer the data between the stack and an accumulator: this is discussed further in Wichmann (1974) and in the next section.

***Immediate operands***

We have seen that one implicit method of specifying an operand or result location is to imply the use of a processor register, such as the accumulator. Another way of implying an operand value (without giving a store address) is to include the value in the instruction stream. Such a value is known as an *immediate operand* or *literal*.

Most commonly certain instructions, or modes of instructions, interpret the contents of their operand field as a literal instead of an address.
Thus

Load 100

loads the accumulator with the contents of store address 100, while

Load literal 100

loads the value 100 from the operand field into the accumulator. Other operations (such as addition) could have similar literal modes: see, for example, the systematic sets of modes on the DEC PDP-10 shown in Figure 3.7. An implication of this is that the contents of the operand field may be modified in accordance with the addressing mode field before being used as a literal value; this allows some alteration of the value (for example, by adding the contents of an index register) without altering the instruction.

A second way of implying an operand is by encoding it as part of the operation code, although the range of values is very restricted as we do not wish to allocate many operation codes in this way. Notice that a clear accumulator instruction can be seen as such an instruction with an implied operand value of zero. Typical instructions in this class increment or decrement an accumulator; here the implied value is plus or minus one. Since the incremental value is encoded in the operation field, there is room to specify a store address in the instruction. This suggests an instruction to increment (or decrement) a specified store location by an implied value of one. This is a very popular instruction, since it allows counting without disturbing an accumulator; it is commonly made more useful by testing whether the count has reached zero after incrementing, and this is discussed again in the next section.

## 3.3. Control instructions

We have been considering, in the main, groups of instructions to perform operations on the different data formats held within the computer. We must now turn to those instructions which control the order in which these data-manipulation instructions are executed.

Normally the program counter holds the store address of the next instruction to be executed, and is incremented appropriately as each instruction is executed. In order to transfer control to a new sequence of instructions, a new value must be deposited in the program counter. This is done by a group of jump instructions, to be discussed in more detail in the remainder of this section.

The simplest transfer of control instruction is, of course, the unconditional jump or unconditional branch, after the execution of which the next instruction is taken from the store address specified in the jump instruction. Notice that the operand field of the jump instruction is not used to access a store location directly, but is loaded as an immediate value into the program counter (after any address modification, such as indexing); thus 'jump to location *x*' is equivalent to 'load program counter with literal *x*', rather than to 'load program counter from location *x*'.

### *Conditional jump instructions*

The unconditional jump is, of course, inadequate by itself to select a sequence of instructions to be executed, if the choice depends on results previously calculated by the program or read as input data (although instruction modification could be used). We therefore require a set of conditional jump or conditional branch instructions, which transfer control to the instruction at the specified store address only if a certain condition is met; if the condition is not met, the next instruction to be executed is that immediately following the jump instruction.

A typical set of jump instructions for a medium-sized, one-address computer might be those shown in Figure 3.11. The basic conditional jump instructions are (b) and (c); the condition may be encoded in the operation code field, or it may be specified in a subsidiary information field. The skip instructions (e), and the special jump instructions (f)

## Jump instructions on a typical one-address computer

(a) Jump unconditionally.

(b) Jump if accumulator zero,
non-zero,
positive ($\geqslant 0$),
negative ($< 0$).

(c) Jump if overflow flag is set,
clear.
Jump if carry flag is set,
clear.

(d) Jump if a specified transput condition is true (see § 6.2).

(e) Compare accumulator with store location and skip if equal,
unequal,
accumulator is greater,
accumulator is less.

(f) Modify index register and jump.

(g) Subroutine jump.

FIG. 3.11

and (g), are discussed later in this section.

If the jump conditions are specified by bits in a subsidiary information field, then we may be able to specify further conditions by setting combinations of bits. Consider a field of three bits $x$, $y$, and $z$, and let $r$ and $s$ be (respectively) the value of the contents of the accumulator and the value of the sign bit of the accumulator. Then suppose the jump condition is

exclusive or ($z$, or (and ($x$, $s$=1), and ($y$, $r$=0))).

This is a simplified version of a portion of the group 2 operate instruction of the DEC PDP-8 computer, and gives the list of jump conditions shown in Figure 3.12 (another example of this technique of combining jump conditions is given in Figure 3.3). Notice especially the first two. Jump on condition 'always' is an unconditional jump, so that we do not need a special operation code for this (although the assembler language may have a special mnemonic for it).

### *The null instruction*

Jump on condition 'never' is an instruction whose operation phase

Combined Jump Conditions

| Bit $x$ | Bit $y$ | Bit $z$ | Jump condition |
|---|---|---|---|
| 0 | 0 | 0 | always |
| 0 | 0 | 1 | never |
| 0 | 1 | 0 | $r \neq 0$ |
| 0 | 1 | 1 | $r = 0$ |
| 1 | 0 | 0 | $r \geqslant 0$ |
| 1 | 0 | 1 | $r < 0$ |
| 1 | 1 | 0 | $r > 0$ |
| 1 | 1 | 1 | $r \leqslant 0$ |

FIG. 3.12

does nothing (but presumably takes some fixed length of time to do it). It is a particular example of a *no-operation* or *dummy* instruction. On some computers such instructions are special cases of normal instructions, as in the example above; another example might be a multiple-length move instruction, with the number of words to be moved specified as zero. On other computers an operation code value (perhaps zero) is allocated to a special no-operation instruction.

This curious instruction may be used to pad out an instruction sequence so that it occupies a desired length of time or storage. Examples of the latter are for dummy entries in a table of instructions, or as an alignment filler in a computer with variable-length instruction formats.

***The skip instruction***

The jump instructions (b) and (c) in Figure 3.11 contain an operation code field (perhaps together with a subsidiary information field specifying the jump condition), and an operand field (perhaps together with an addressing mode field) to specify the location to which control is to be transferred if the condition is true (that is, if the jump is successful).

However, suppose that (in a single-address computer) we wish to provide a conditional jump instruction to test an operand which is not in an implied location such as an accumulator. For example, we might wish to test a specified store location to see if its contents are zero or non-zero, or to compare the contents of an accumulator with the contents of a specified store location as in Figure 3.11(e). There is then no room in the instruction to specify both a jump address and the address of the location to be tested. Further, on some small computers the subsidiary information field to specify a rich set of jump conditions may be so large that there is no room in the instruction for a jump address field.

A common solution is for the instruction to imply a jump address, the next location but one after the instruction. We thus have the typical 'skip' instruction;

> If the condition is true skip the next instruction; if it is false execute the next instruction

On a single-address computer (such as the DEC PDP-10) we may find conditional jumps on a test of the contents of an accumulator, or on a comparison of two accumulators, but conditional skips on a test of the contents of a store location, or on a comparison of an accumulator with a store location.

On a small computer (such as the DEC PDP-8) a minimal set of instructions is several conditional skips and an unconditional jump; thus 'jump to A if accumulator contents are zero' would be coded as:

> Skip if accumulator contents are non-zero
> Jump to location A

The skip technique may be extended in several ways:

(a) On several computers a subsidiary field specifies the direction and length of the skip with respect to the current instruction. Notice that such a skip instruction bears a close resemblance to a jump instruction using relative addressing (see §4.3).

(b) A multiway skip instruction has sometimes been provided. For example, a comparison instruction might execute the next instruction if the first operand is high, skip one instruction if the operands are equal, or skip two instructions if the second operand is high.

(c) An instruction may perform some data manipulation and skip the next instruction if an unusual condition occurs. A common example is an instruction to increment the contents of a specified store location and skip if the result is zero. Further examples are given in the search instructions in §3.4, and the transput instructions of §6.2.

### *Condition codes*

A second way of dealing with the amount of information to be specified in a conditional jump instruction is to separate the test and the jump into two different instructions, and to provide a short processor register to communicate between the two instructions. This register, the *condition code,* is set by the testing instruction to reflect the result. Then the only jump instruction that is logically necessary (though others may be provided for efficiency) is one to jump if the condition code is set to a specified binary bit pattern (or perhaps a specified group of patterns), and to drop through to the next instruction if the condition code is set to any other pattern. This technique is used in the IBM 370 range, which forms the basis of the examples which follow.

Suppose a comparison instruction sets a two-bit condition code, depending on a comparison of the contents of accumulator A with the contents of a store location B, as shown in Figure 3.13(a). Then, in order to jump to store address C if the contents of accumulator A are not less than the contents of store address B, we write

Compare Accumulator A to store address B
Jump to C if condition code is 00 or 10

The set of condition code patterns, any one of which is to cause a successful jump, is specified in the IBM 370 range by a four-bit subsidiary information field.

Setting of the (2-bit) Condition Code on the IBM 370 range

(a) by the 'Compare' instruction
00 $A = B$
01 $A < B$
10 $A > B$
11 never set by this instruction

(b) by the 'Add' instruction
00 result is zero
01 result is less than zero
10 result is greater than zero
11 overflow

FIG. 3.13

As with the skip technique, we can allow instructions other than tests and comparisons to set the condition code, with the added advantage over skipping that the setting of the condition code can be ignored where necessary. For example, Figure 3.13(b) shows how the add instruction on the IBM 370 sets the condition code. Notice how the overflow flag has been incorporated into the condition code.

Stack-oriented computers may set a condition code in the top element of the stack as a result of a test or comparison instruction; a jump instruction is then provided to jump conditional on the state of this top element (removing the element after testing).

### *The loop*

One of the most common programming devices is the *loop,* whereby a set of instructions is performed a specified number of times. Because of the frequency of occurrence of this device, most computers include instructions tailored to its use.

Such an 'increment count and jump' instruction specifies an accumulator, index register, or store location whose contents are to be used as a loop counter (and which will have been initialized by another instruction). When the instruction is executed it adds an increment value to the count, and tests whether the count has reached a limit value. If not (that is, further iterations of the loop are to be performed), a jump is made to a specified store address (presumably the beginning of the loop). If the limit has been reached, the next sequential instruction is executed.

The increment value and limit are commonly implied by the instruction as (respectively) plus or minus one and zero. If the jump address is also implied we have the 'increment count and skip' instruction described earlier.

### *Index register manipulation*

In many loops, the set of instructions manipulates successive elements from a vector in successive iterations. An index register normally holds the offset of the current element within the vector, and needs suitable modification between iterations of the loop.

A group of instructions is therefore needed to perform a suitable range of manipulations on the index register or registers. Typical operations are to load an index register from a store location, to deposit the contents of an index register in a store location, and to increment or decrement an index register (or to add the contents of a store location to an index register).

We may terminate the loop either by means of an 'increment (decrement) count and jump on zero' instruction, or when the contents of the index register reach a certain value (in which case we need an instruction to compare an index register with a store location).

The groups of instructions to manipulate index registers need to specify an index register and a store location. In the past the field which normally specified the addressing mode was often used in these instructions to specify the index register to be manipulated, thus reducing the available addressing modes. Nowadays index registers are commonly a subset of an accumulator array, so that the normal fixed-point arithmetic instructions are used to manipulate index quantities.

Because of the connection between looping and indexing, it is tempting to provide instructions which incorporate both loop counting and index modification. We briefly describe a number of variations on this idea below. However, while such techniques can be used effectively when programming in an assembler language, it is much more difficult for a compiler to recognize which constructions in a high-level language call for their use. Such compound instructions may therefore be less useful than appears at first sight.

(a) An index register is divided into a modifier field and a loop count field: the former holds the value to be added to the operand field of an instruction requiring indexed addressing. An instruction adds one to each field of a specified index register, and jumps to a specified address unless the loop count field has reached zero. This is available on the DEC PDP-10 computer.

(b) An index register is divided into a modifier field (as before) and an index limit field. An instruction adds one to the modifier field of a specified index register, and jumps to a specified address unless the two fields are equal. This is a simplified version of a facility provided on the IBM 370 range (but see below).

(c) In (a) and (b) we assume that the index register is large enough to hold both fields; for example, the DEC PDP-10 uses the two halves of a 36-bit accumulator. However, on the IBM 370, the fields are held in two separate accumulators specified by the instruction.

(d) In (a) and (b) we assume that the modifier field is always incremented by one, but other arrangements are possible. On the IBM 370 range the increment value is held in a third accumulator specified by the instruction.

An alternative method for dealing with vector elements of different lengths is for an increment value of one always to be used, but for the modifier field to be suitably manipulated when an element is accessed. Thus single-length elements require no manipulation; double-length elements require the index quantity to be shifted one bit position left before adding to the vector base address; half-length elements require a right shift, with the bit shifted out used to select the appropriate half-word. The type of manipulation required would be specified by the operation code of the accessing instruction, or by a descriptor referred to in the instruction. This technique of index scaling is used in the University of Manchester MU5 and the ICL 2900 range.

***Index registers and stacks***

One special use for an index register is to implement a stack in an area of store, by having the modifier field point to the current top element of the stack. The 'push' instruction performs the following sequence of operations:

Increment the modifier field
Store the new data at the address pointed to by the modifier field

The 'pop' instruction performs the following sequence of operations:

Extract the contents of the store location pointed to by the modifier field
Decrement the modifier field

This pair of instructions is available on the DEC PDP-10 computer, where the stack pointer is the modifier field of a specified accumulator, and the source of the data to be pushed or destination of the data to be popped is a specified store location. The push and pop instructions also increment or decrement the count field of the specified accumulator by one, and signal count over- and underflow. As was mentioned in the previous section, it is very common nowadays for such facilities to be provided with an implicit stack pointer register in the processor, rather than with an explicitly specified accumulator.

### *The subroutine*

The *subroutine* or *procedure* is another important programming device, whereby several pieces of similar program code are replaced by one piece of code to which control is passed as required. The problem here is to keep track of the point from which the subroutine is called, so that control can be returned to the correct place in the calling routine after the subroutine has been executed.

In the Von Neumann computer, control was returned to the calling routine by suitably modifying a jump instruction in the subroutine before entry. The method used in all modern computers is to provide a 'subroutine call' (or 'link') instruction, which jumps to a specified store location and saves the value of the program counter, to enable control to be returned from the subroutine.

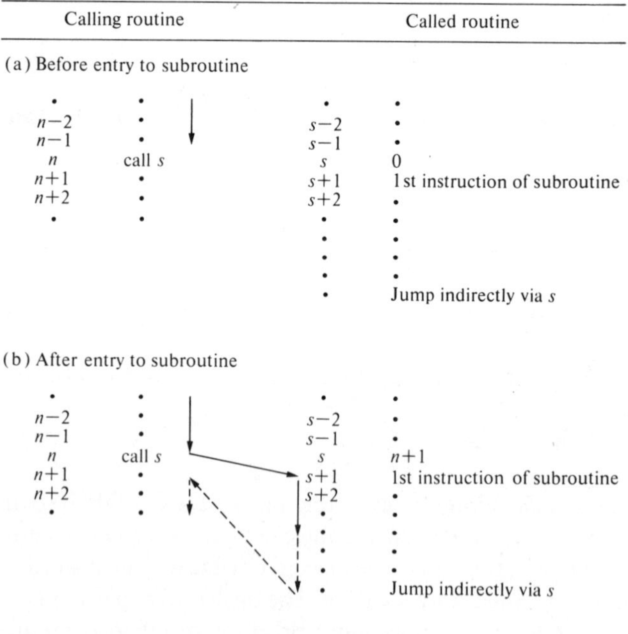


FIG. 3.14

A possible place to save the contents of the program counter (that is, the address of the instruction following the subroutine call) is in a suitable store location in the subroutine, typically its first location; the subroutine jump will then be to the second location of the subroutine. This method, illustrated in Figure 3.14, is used on the DEC PDP-8 computer. To return to the calling routine we perform a 'jump indirect' via the first location of the subroutine (see § 4.3). A slight variation (used by the CDC 6600 computer) is for the subroutine call to store a 'jump to location $(n+1)$'; to terminate the subroutine, we jump directly to this jump instruction.

This technique for calling subroutines has the disadvantage that locations are being modified in the instruction area, and that recursive subroutine calls are difficult. A more common system on modern computers is to store the return address in an index register. Thus a typical subroutine call instruction at location $n$ calling a subroutine at location $s$ places the address $(n+1)$ in the index register and jumps to location $s$. A particular index register could be implied for the return address, but usually the index register is specified in the call instruction. Parameters (or addresses of parameters) may be passed to a subroutine by placing them in locations following the subroutine call instruction, in which case the index register containing the return address can be used to access the parameter.

The return to the calling routine is by a jump using an address indexed by the appropriate index register. This is illustrated by Figure 3.15.

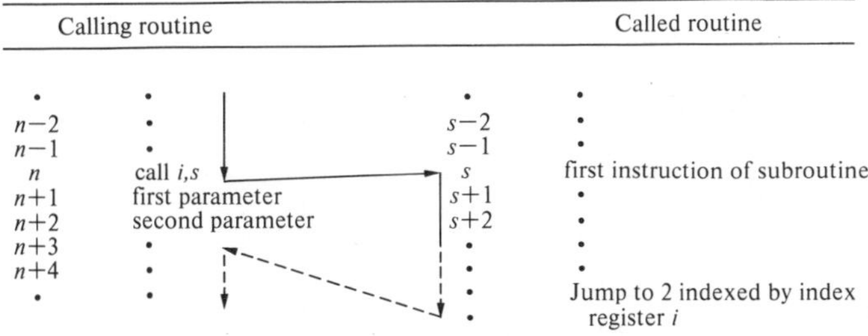


After the 'call', index register $i$ contains $n+1$

FIG. 3.15

### *Subroutine calls and stacks*

If subroutines call themselves recursively, a stack must be implemented to hold the return addresses. Because of this close association between stacks and subroutine linkage, some computers provide hardware stacks to deal with subroutine calls and returns.

The KDF9 computer (Davis 1960; Haley 1962; ICL 1968) provides a subroutine jump nesting store (or SJNS) of 16 elements. The subroutine call instruction places its address on the SJNS (pushing down all earlier entries) and jumps to the specified store address. The subroutine return instruction removes the top address from the SJNS (popping up all earlier entries), and jumps to it. Since $n$ rather than

| | Instruction executed | | After execution: Stack contents | After execution: Program counter contents |
|---|---|---|---|---|
| (a) | · | · | $n$ | $s$ |
| | $n-1$ | · | | |
| | $n$ | call $s$ | | |
| | $n+1$ | · | · | |
| | · | · | · | |
| (b) | · | · | $m$ | $t$ |
| | $m-1$ | · | $n$ | |
| | $m$ | call $t$ | | |
| | $m+1$ | · | · | |
| | · | · | · | |
| (c) | · | · | $n$ | $m+1$ |
| | $p-1$ | · | | |
| | $p$ | return +1 | | |
| | $p+1$ | · | · | |
| | · | · | · | |
| (d) | · | · | | $n+1$ |
| | $q-1$ | · | | |
| | $q$ | return +1 | | |
| | $q+1$ | · | · | |
| | · | · | · | |

FIG. 3.16

$(n+1)$ is stored on the stack, the address has to be adjusted by the length of the subroutine call instruction and any parameter list before jumping, and this length is specified in the operand field of the return instruction. This method is illustrated by Figure 3.16.

On the Burroughs B6700 computer the subroutine linkage stack is integrated with the operand stack described in the previous section and with the store addressing system; it is described in § 4.6.

On the DEC PDP-10 computer, subroutine call instructions are provided for saving the return address either in the first location of a subroutine or in an accumulator; but it also has call and return instructions which treat a specified area of store as a return address stack, in a manner similar to that described earlier in this section.

### *Subroutine transparency*

Subroutines are usually written to be 'transparent' to the calling routine; that is, the processor registers such as accumulators and condition codes can be assumed to be unaltered by the subroutine call, unless they are explicitly part of the subroutine linkage. This is achieved by saving information at the beginning of the subroutine if it is likely to be changed, and restoring it before the return.

The instructions to save and restore a set of accumulators, described in § 2.4, help here. However sometimes the subroutine linkage instructions themselves automatically save and restore some part of the required information (typically processor flags such as overflow).

### *The halt instruction*

Finally, mention should be made of the halt instruction. Most first and second generation computers had such an instruction to stop the computer, the instruction sometimes containing a store address at which execution was to be resumed upon suitable manual intervention. Further, some instructions halted the computer if an error occurred, such as attempted division by zero, whereas in a third generation computer this would be dealt with by setting a flag or generating an interrupt.

On a modern computer a halt instruction must be a privileged instruction (see § 3.5) if it is provided. Some modern computers (such as the IBM 370 range) do not have a halt intruction. Instead, the computer enters an idle or 'wait for interrupt' state; the full halt is then provided only by manual intervention.

## 3.4. Special groups of instructions

In this and the previous chapter we have discussed a number of groups of computer instructions, oriented to the principal data-types and operations for which the computer is designed. We will see further such groups in later chapters, particularly in Chapter 6 when we discuss transput and interrupt handling. In this section we attempt to provide a framework for discussion of a number of special instructions (or groups of instructions), provided in current computers or proposed for the future, which do not naturally fit into these groups. Notice that some instructions already discussed, such as 'edit' or 'shift and count', could be treated in this section as special-purpose instructions.

The computer's instruction set has evolved to provide the facilities required by the programmer, or to provide as one instruction a group of operations commonly found together. But the advent of almost universal programming in high-level languages alters the requirements of a computer's instruction set. What is now required is a simple instruction set without idiosyncrasies, since a compiler may be unable to recognize points in a program where it might use a sophisticated facility. The more complex instructions, described in this section for interest, are therefore tending to disappear from modern computers.

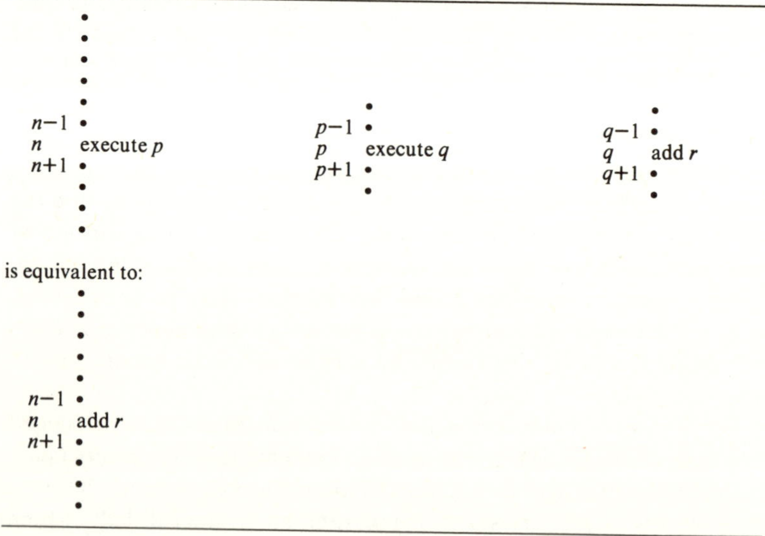


FIG. 3.17

### *The execute instruction*

A common instruction on the larger computers is *execute*, which causes execution of the instruction at the store location specified in the execute instruction. There may be restrictions on the type of instruction which can be executed in this way; for example, in the IBM 370 range it cannot be another execute. However, it could be a jump instruction, in which case control is transferred (assuming the condition is true, for a conditional jump instruction) to the jump address: otherwise, the next instruction executed is that immediately following the execute. Thus, the final result is as if the execute is replaced by the 'target' instruction; that is, by the instruction specified by the execute, or by the final non-execute instruction if a cascade of executes is allowed, as shown in Figure 3.17.

On the IBM 370 range it is possible to specify that the execute is to modify the second byte of the executed instruction. This technique

The Execute Instruction on the IBM 370

(a) Execute instruction:

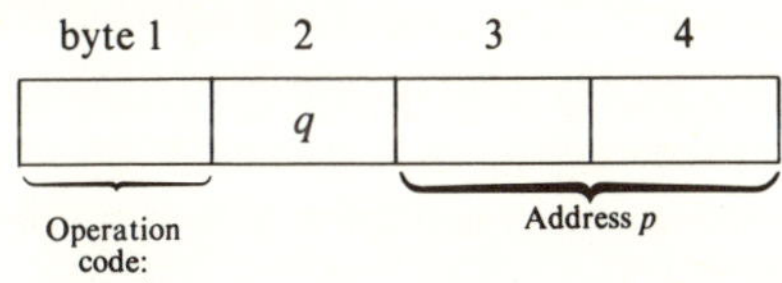


Execute instruction at store address $p$, with its second byte replaced by the bottom 8 bits of accumulator $q$

(b) Accumulator $q$ contents:
4

(c) 'Target' instruction at store address $p$

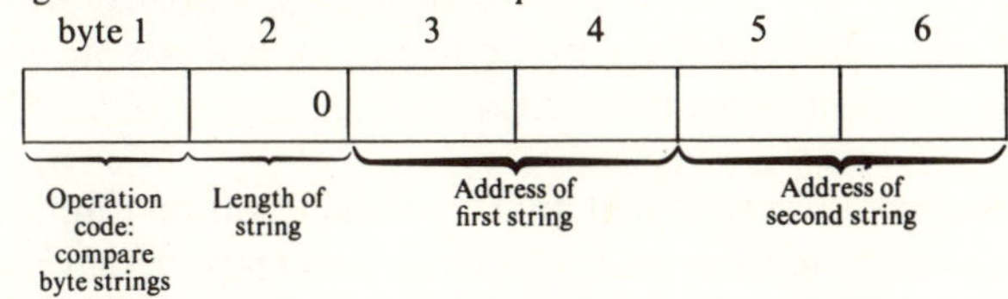


(d) Effective instruction
Compare two byte strings of length 5† (where this length can be adjusted merely by changing the contents of accumulator $q$)

† A length field value of $n$ means that the byte string length is $(n+1)$.

FIG. 3.18

gives us some of the advantages of instruction modification, while keeping instructions and data in separate areas. We can therefore use the execute to make up for some of the deficiencies of a computer's instruction set; examples might be the coding of jump tables where the computer does not have indexed jump instructions, or operations on dynamically variable-length data where the operand length is coded in the instruction format; the latter is illustrated in Figure 3.18.

***Iterated instructions***

We can envisage creating a new group of instructions by selecting one of the operations already met with, and producing an 'iterated' version of it. Thus, if we have a binary operation '*X*', we could produce an 'iterated *X* on addresses A and B' which would operate as follows:

Perform *X* between store locations A and B
Update the addresses A and B
Conditionally repeat

The updating of addresses A and B might take place in private registers within the processor hardware, or in program-accessible registers (such as the index registers).

Some examples (where the conditional repetition is based on a previously initialized counter) are:

(a) If *X* is 'move' and the updating is incrementation by one, we have the block transfer operations described in § 2.4.

(b) If the elements addressed by A and B are smaller than a word, we are in the realm of the character string operations of § 2.5.

(c) A fairly common example is 'sum', where *X* is 'add to accumulator' and A is updated by incrementing by one (B is not used). This sums in the accumulator the contents of a sequence of locations.

(d) If *X* ranges through the arithmetic and logical operations, we have the vector operations discussed later.

If *X* is some form of test instruction then the iteration might cease before the counter reached zero. For example, a 'compare for equality' between two vectors of store locations would cease as soon as an unequal pair was found.

A few computers allow the programmer to create his own iterated instructions by providing an 'iterated execute' or 'repeat' instruction, which operates as follows:

Execute the (perhaps modified) target instruction
Update an index register or the execute modification field
Conditionally repeat

Again the conditional repeat is based on a count set up by the repeat instruction, or on the setting of a flag by the target instruction.

***Search instructions***

An interesting type of instruction is the search or scan instruction, which may be seen as an iterated compare. A general search instruction has to specify several pieces of information; the address A and length L of a table to be searched, a comparison condition and a compared value (the former usually implied in the operation code or specified in a subsidiary information field, the latter in an implied location such as an accumulator). The instruction then operates as follows:

Load A and L into internal processor registers
Perform the comparison with the word at A
If the comparison is successful, terminate the instruction
Otherwise, decrement L and increment A
If L is zero, terminate the instruction
Otherwise, jump back to the second line

The instruction could set a condition code to indicate whether the search was terminated by a successful comparison or by L becoming zero; alternatively, one of these two results could cause a skip. If the comparison is successful, a program-accessible register is loaded with the address of the compared words; alternatively, A and L could be retained in program-accessible registers throughout the process, so that the programmer can interrogate them for the result of the search.

Examples of search instructions are the 'table look-up' (TALU) instruction on the University of Manchester MU5 computer, which performs a masked equality comparison between the contents of one store location and the contents of each of a vector of elements, the similar 'masked search for equal' (SRCH) instruction on the Burroughs B6700 computer, and the 'linked list look-up' (LLLU) instruction, also on the B6700, which performs a 'greater than or equal' comparison between an argument value and each of a linked list of elements.

A common type of search (called 'translate and test' on the IBM 370 range) is a variation on the translate instruction of § 2.5, and facilitates the scanning of character strings for delimiters. If the character currently scanned contains the value $v$, then the $v$th entry in a specified table is extracted; the scan terminates or continues depending on the value of this $v$th entry. On termination the extracted value and the address of the associated character in the string are made available to the programmer.

### *Unusual data-types and instructions*

In the last chapter we discussed a number of simple operations on two basic arithmetic data formats, fixed point and floating-point. We could envisage more complex operations (such as square root, logarithm, sine), but in conventional modern computers these are provided by software, though they are common in the programmable calculators of § 7.3.

We have seen pairs of words $(a, b)$ interpreted as double-precision arithmetic formats, with corresponding operations. A word pair $(a, b)$ could be interpreted as a complex number (representing $a+ib$), as a rational number (representing $a/b$ : see Knuth 1968, pp. 290–2), or as an arithmetic interval (representing the interval $[x;\ a \leqslant x \leqslant b]$ : see Knuth 1969, p. 207; Nickel 1968), but no conventional computers provide these data-types in hardware.

Computer instructions generally operate on individual scalar variables, although we have seen how the use of index registers allows us to interpret these scalars as elements of vectors or stacks. We can envisage providing arithmetic and logical operations on a vector as a single unit. Thus 'add vector $A$ to vector $B$' performs the iterated 'add $A[i]$ to $B[i]$' for all elements of the vectors, which would be referenced via descriptor words. This system has been implemented on several super-computers, since it provides scope for instruction overlapping (described in § 8.2). Examples are the CDC Star-100 (CDC 1971), the Texas Instruments ASC (Enslow 1974, pp. 274–89), and the Cray-1 (Yuval 1977; Russell 1978).

Other instructions are occasionally met with. Instructions to calculate check digits are fairly common on computers oriented towards communications. Further examples (mainly on older computers) are instructions to generate a random number (for example on the University of Manchester Mark I computer (Lavington 1975, p. 20)), to select the higher of two operands (for example on the KDF9 computer), or to sort a vector of values into ascending order.

## 3.5. Processor modes and process switching

There is a large discrepancy between the functions provided by the hardware of a computer (as described in this book), and the problem-solving device required by the user and the computer manager. Only a single user can access the computer at a time, and he has to write, debug, and run his programs in the most basic computer-oriented form. All but the smallest modern computers therefore have a layer of supervisory programs, the *operating system*, between the hardware and the problem programs, as shown in Figure 1.9. The tasks of the operating system are:

(a) To share between users the computer's resources (processor time, store, transput devices, and information — usually in the form of files of programs and data). In the simplest systems, where only one program is running at a time, this means merely expediting the change-over from one program to the next. Commonly it means at any instant having several partially-executed programs, among which the computer resources have to be shared in such a way that they interact (if at all) only in authorized ways.

(b) To make the hardware easier to use. This is done by having a *virtual computer* which more closely matches the user's requirements than the real computer, and implementing it partly by direct operations of the hardware and partly by operations of the operating system running on the hardware. A major aspect of the virtual computer is the provision of high-level languages, but the operating system is expected to provide other facilities, such as simple access to transput devices (in particular a filing system, and communication with the operator, and perhaps the user, at a terminal), the current date and time, etc.

For flexibility and economy the operating system is implemented as a set of programs, though in future more of its functions are likely to be taken over by hardware. For a more detailed discussion of operating systems see Hansen (1973), Madnick and Donovan (1974), or Lister (1975).

Since we wish to keep small the amount of main store occupied by the operating system, most of it is non-resident, being stored on magnetic disc or drum and brought into main store as required. However there must be a core of supervisory functions resident in main store at all times, which can bring in other functions as required. This is given various names, such as the *nucleus* or *executive*; we will use the term *supervisor* for this basic set of main-store-resident supervisory programs.

### *Supervisor mode and privileged instructions*

Because the problem program is under the control of the supervisor, it cannot be allowed unrestricted access to all the facilities provided by the computer. For this reason most computers run in two modes or states, the *supervisor* (or master) *mode* and the *problem* (or slave) *mode*; the current mode is signalled by a one-bit register in the processor. In supervisor mode all the facilities of the computer are available for use, while in the problem mode certain instructions (known as *privileged instructions*) are disallowed and cannot be executed. These privileged instructions include all instructions concerned with handling transput devices, the interrupt system, the store protection and virtual store mapping systems (if present), and usually facilities like the clocks and interval timers. Any use of these facilities by a problem program must be via a request to the supervisor, which can check the validity of the request and whether the problem program is authorized to use the facility.

Two points should be noted in connection with supervisor mode and privileged instructions.

(a) Large areas of an operating system (for example the compilers and the scheduling and accounting programs) do not require the use of privileged instructions, and therefore should not run in supervisor mode.
(b) Privileged instructions are not the only way of protecting critical facilities. If transput devices and processor facilities are controlled via store addresses (as discussed in § § 5.3 and 6.2), then the facilities can be protected by the store protection system, and privileged instructions can be dispensed with.

### *Mode-changing facilities*

The computer commences operation in supervisor mode after start-up. A privileged instruction is provided to pass from supervisor mode to problem mode, so that the instructions of a problem program can be executed. Any interrupt (such as that caused by the completion of a transput operation, or a floating-point overflow) causes a return from problem to supervisor mode, since it is the supervisor's task to process such conditions.

From time to time the problem program will wish to gain entry to the supervisor in a controlled manner, for example to request that a transput operation be performed. One way this could be done is to cause a program error of some kind, such as by trying to execute an invalid operation code (or a privileged instruction), since this of course causes an interrupt and entry to the supervisor. This is a risky method, since a program error might be interpreted as a supervisor request.

A better method is to provide a special supervisor call instruction, which causes a distinguishable interrupt into the supervisor to be generated. Such an instruction may have an operand whose value is passed to the supervisor as part of the interrupt. For example, the supervisor call instruction on the IBM 370 range passes a one-byte literal to the supervisor, to indicate the type of request being made: any further parameters are placed in accumulators.

### *Extracodes*

Another way in which controlled entry may be made to the supervisor is by means of *extracodes*, which were first used on the University of Manchester Atlas computer (Sumner, Haley, and Chen 1962).

It may be uneconomic or too inflexible to implement in hardware all of a computer's instruction set. This is especially the case where we have an instruction set defined for a compatible range of computers, since it will be difficult to implement economically at the lower (and cheaper) end of the range the complex facilities required at the upper end (though microprogramming may be an answer).

An extracode is an instruction which has a normal instruction format, but attempted execution of which causes an interrupt to be taken into the supervisor, instead of causing execution by the hardware. A subroutine within the supervisor performs the sequence of operations required by the instruction, and returns control to the instruction following the extracode.

Consider now a range of compatible computers. Some functions available to the problem program (such as transput operations, or program intercommunications facilities) will be implemented as extracodes on all models of the range. However some functions (for example, floating-point arithmetic) may be implemented by hardware on the larger, and by software on the smaller, models in the range. So the same instruction would, on one model, be executed directly by hardware and, on another, be recognized as an extracode and interpreted by a subroutine in the supervisor. Notice now that the range is compatible only at the virtual computer level and not at the hardware level.

Since extracodes are defined by the way in which they are handled by the supervisor, we could make the supervisor react in an 'extracode' fashion to any unallocated operation code. However, extracodes are usually distinguished by the fact that operation codes have been allocated to them at the computer hardware design level, either because they will be normal hardwired instructions in some models, or because an instruction requirement has been recognized that is uneconomic to implement in hardware. The invalid operation code interrupt and unimplemented instruction interrupt are thus distinguished at entry to the supervisor.

In the latter case the hardware may provide some assistance in interpreting the extracode. Thus it may perform the effective address calculation from the operand and addressing mode fields of the extracode, before entering the supervisor. Alternatively, assistance may be provided in the form of an 'analyse' instruction, which treats a specified store location as holding an instruction, unpacks its various fields, and calculates an effective store address.

### *Process-switching and the PSW*

Let us now consider the requirements of a multiprogramming system, where we have a number of programs occupying main storage and competing for an allocation of time on the processor.

We begin by introducing the term *process,* which is to be distinguished from the term *program.* A program (or procedure) is a static sequence of instructions, while a process is the dynamic execution of the instructions of a program. We must distinguish the two concepts since two processes may share a program of instructions (or, more generally, any set of computer words which are not altered, such as a table of constants). Thus, in a situation where five users are interactively editing files from their own terminals, there would be five processes but only one program, the editor being shared among the users. For further discussion of this concept see, for example, Lister (1975).

In a multiprogramming computer system, then, we have a number of processes competing for the resources of the computer, such as main storage areas, processor time, and access to transput devices. Most of these processes will be problem processes, but some may be operating system processes, such as one reading job descriptions from a card reader into a job queue on disc. It is a task of the supervisor to select (from time to time) the most suitable process to run, according to some strategy, and to switch between the process currently running and the new process.

While it is currently in execution, a process occupies certain registers within the processor, certain areas of main storage, and certain transput devices or parts of devices (such as disc storage areas). Now a process's occupation of main storage and transput devices changes relatively slowly. However, on each process switch we need to save the contents of all processor registers for the old process (the process *context*) and restore their contents for the new process.

What is needed, therefore, is a way of collecting together all the processor registers to allow rapid process switches. Now, the accumulators nowadays usually form an array, which can be rapidly saved and restored with the multiple accumulator instructions of §2.4. We then collect together all the remaining processor flags and registers into what is known as a *process state word* or PSW (some computer manufacturers say that the P stands for 'processor' or, incorrectly, for 'program'). The PSW thus contains the program counter, the condition code (if present), the processer mode register, and other miscellaneous processor flags, such as overflow.

An interrupt causes the current PSW to be stored (in main storage) and a new PSW to be loaded. This new PSW initiates the interrupt handling routine, a first task of which is to save the accumulator array. To switch to a problem process, the supervisor restores the contents of the accumulator array; it then issues a special privileged instruction to load a new PSW from a specified area of store, and the processor re-enters the problem process under control of this PSW.

### *Control registers*

The implication has been that the PSW is one or two computer words long, since (except for the program counter) it consists of a number of short processor registers. However, in many modern computers, we begin to require numbers of special processor registers to control store mapping and protection, and other sophisticated facilities, with new privileged instructions to manipulate them.

Rather than expand the PSW to hold such a set of miscellaneous registers, we can replace them by an array of control registers, just as we introduced an array of accumulators. Manipulation can be provided by store-and-control-register multiple-word move instructions (which are of course privileged), and the supervisor uses these to save and restore the control registers. Notice that, unlike the accumulator array, where each accumulator had generalized functions, each control register or portion of a register has a specific function, although it is accessed or manipulated by instructions in a general way. The IBM 370 range has a set of sixteen 32-bit control registers, which control various aspects of interrupt handling, multiprocessing, store-address mapping, process monitoring, and hardware-fault finding.

### *Multiple accumulator sets*

A way in which process switching may be speeded up is by the provision of multiple processor register sets. Thus a computer might have four or eight accumulator arrays, and a special processor register (or field in the PSW) specifies the particular array being used by the currently running process (although privileged processes may have some means of accessing other arrays than their own).

After a process switch, the new process can immediately use the accumulators without having to save the contents for the old process. Usually there will be more processes than accumulator arrays, in which case one array is allocated to all the low-priority processes (the contents being saved and restored as before), and the rest will be allocated one array to each high-priority process, to improve process switching time.

Some computers provide several so-called processor modes, distinguished by the allocation of a separate accumulator set to each mode; one mode (the problem mode) is further distinguished by having privileged instructions disabled, while the others are all supervisor modes entered under different interrupt conditions.

### *The processor mode revisited*

We introduced the processor mode register to distinguish two modes of running, the difference between the two modes being whether or not privileged instructions were enabled. Further differences may distinguish the two modes of running; thus supervisor mode might imply a particular accumulator array, no address mapping or protection, and all interrupts disabled, while problem mode implies a second accumulator array, use of address mapping and protection, and all interrupts enabled.

If such an all-or-nothing division into two modes is too restrictive, we can have several intermediate processor modes between the supervisor and problem modes. A fairly common system (such as on the DEC PDP-10 computer) is three processor modes; a problem mode, an intermediate mode with some restrictions in which much of the operating system is written, and an unrestricted mode for privileged manipulation of transput devices and processor facilities. This inner mode may be called the *kernel* mode, in which case the intermediate mode is called the supervisor mode.

More flexibility still is provided by separate processor registers in the PSW to indicate processor mode (with respect to privileged instructions), whether address mapping is required, how the store protection system is to operate (if this is separate from the address mapping), which accumulator array is to be used, and the state of the interrupt system.

### 3.6. Microprogramming

The instruction set of a computer includes a range of instructions, from simple ones such as to load an accumulator from a specified store location, to complex ones such as the edit and search instructions described earlier. However, in all cases the instructions can be broken down into a sequence of primitive operations on the various parts of the processor, such as the accumulators, the adder and the program counter; notice that some of these parts are not directly accessible to the programmer.

For example, the fetching and execution of a 'store accumulator' instruction can be broken down into a sequence of more primitive operations as shown in Figure 3.19. In practice this sequence would need to be expanded to include performing any specified address modification, and checking for pending interrupts before accessing the next instruction.

In a conventional computer design, the sequence of control signals to execute the instruction set is wired into the control unit of the processor. Instead we can design a computer which has as its instruction

Microprogram for 'Store Accumulator' Instruction

---

Send contents of program counter (PC) to store address register (SAR)
Send 'read' signal to store
After a delay, the next instruction appears in the store data register (SDR)
Send contents of PC to one side of adder
Send constant 'one' to other side of adder
Send adder output to the PC
Send the operation code portion of the SDR to the decoder
The decoder recognizes the instruction, causing the following steps:
  send the store address portion of the SDR to the SAR
  send the contents of the accumulator to the SDR
  send 'write' signal to store
Repeat

---

FIG. 3.19

set a set of primitive operations (or *micro-instructions*), to cause control signals to be sent to the various parts of the computer, and data to be transferred from one processor register to another. Then each instruction at the normal level of machine code (such as 'store accumulator') is implemented as a sequence or *microprogram* of such primitive operations or micro-instructions; the more complex instructions of course require looping and conditional jumping in the microprogram, just as in conventional programming.

The computer holds the microprograms in what is normally referred to as a *control store.* It is nearly always separate from the main store of the computer, since it is faster and more expensive, and is normally read-only, so that the microprograms cannot be inadvertently altered. Computers with control units implemented in this way are called *microprogrammed* computers. The concept was introduced by M. V. Wilkes in his paper 'The best way to design an automatic calculating machine' (Wilkes 1951), and was first used to implement the control unit of the Edsac II computer at the University of Cambridge (Wilkes, Renwick, and Wheeler 1958). For further reading on microprogramming see Rosin (1969), Husson (1970), Davies (1972), and Tanenbaum (1976).

Figure 3.20 gives a simplified layout for a microprogrammed computer. The control store, containing up to a few thousand words, is set up initially with bit patterns representing the microprograms for the instruction set to be implemented. Each micro-instruction is divided into two portions, the *control bits* and the *sequencing bits.* Each con-

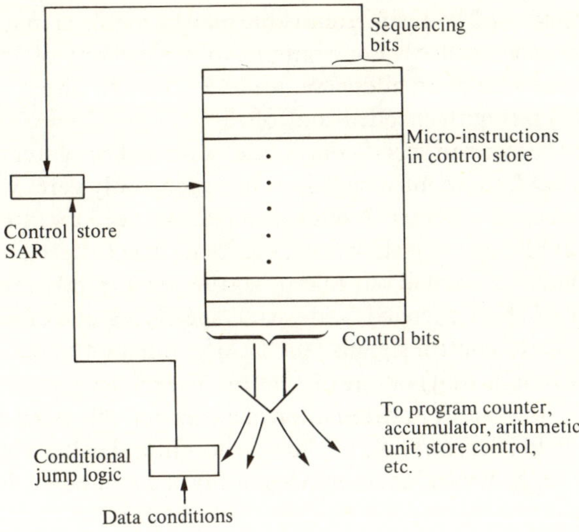


FIG. 3.20

trol bit position of the control store is connected to a unique control gate within the processor.

Thus the first two bits might be connected to the gates which control the data paths from the accumulator to each side of the adder, the next two to the gates which control the data paths from the SDR to each side of the adder, and the next one to the gate which controls the data path from the adder output to the accumulator. Then if a micro-instruction contains the control bits 10011 followed by zeros, the paths from the accumulator to the left-side of the adder, from the SDR to the right side of the adder, and from the result latches to the accumulator are opened; thus the contents of the accumulator and SDR are added together and placed in the accumulator.

### *Encoded control*

In a large computer there may be several hundred control gates in the processor, so it would be uneconomic to have a bit for each gate in the micro-instruction. Instead of *direct control* of each gate by a control bit, we can have *encoded control* in which a group of bits control a number of gates. Thus $N$ control bits could directly control $N$ independent control gates. However, if this group of $N$ bits is taken as one field, then we can encode a range of $2^N$ binary values; thus $2^N$ gates can be controlled (or $2^N-1$, since one value may be required to specify that no gate is to be opened). For example, to connect any of 16 accumulators to one side of an adder we need 16 bits with direct control, or $4(=\log_2 16)$ bits with encoded control.

Notice that we can specify only one at a time of the gates controlled by such a field, so we must encode as one group only gates which need never be opened together. Notice also that we need extra electronics and time in the micro-instruction execution cycle to decode the fields.

The control portion of our micro-instruction now takes the form of a number of short encoded fields, each specifying one of a mutually exclusive set of control signals (such as the function to be performed by the arithmetic unit) or one of a mutually exclusive set of processor registers as the source or destination of a transfer. An extension of this is for one field (the *emit* field) to hold a short literal value which can be gated (under control of another field) to any of a number of destination registers.

### *Micro-instruction sequencing*

The sequence bits of a micro-instruction hold the address of the next instruction to be executed, and this field is gated into the SAR of the control store at the beginning of the next micro-instruction cycle. This

Conditional jumps in a microprogram.

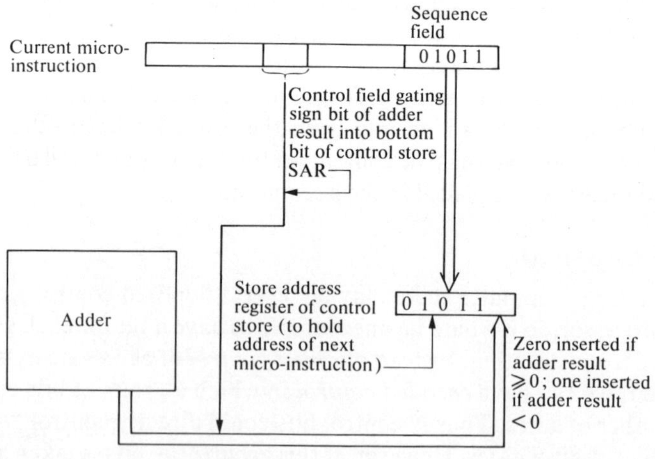


FIG. 3.21

enables us to dispense with a micro-program counter, but at the expense of a next-instruction address in each micro-instruction.

To perform conditional jumps, the computer has to select one from a set of two (or more) next micro-instruction addresses. One method is for the sequence field of the micro-instruction to specify all but the least significant few bits of the next micro-instruction address. These last few bits are then specified by testing various conditions in the processor.

For example, suppose the adder made available as a secondary output the sign of the result of the add operation. Then a field in the micro-instruction could open a gate to insert this output as the least-significant bit of the next micro-instruction address. This is illustrated in Fig-

(a) Horizontal micro-instruction format (on the Data General Eclipse computer)

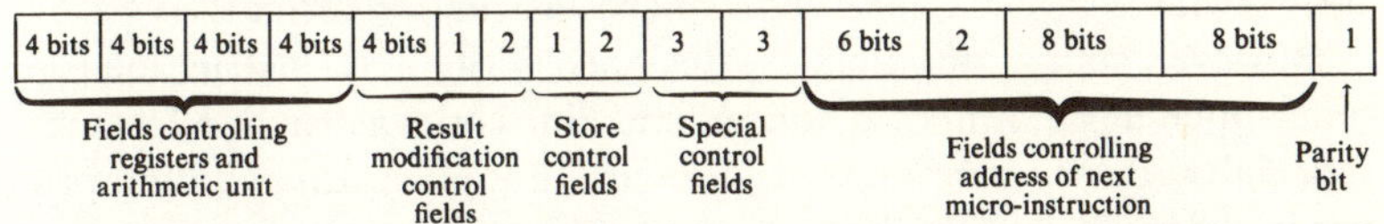


(b) Vertical micro-instruction formats (on the Burroughs B1700 computer)

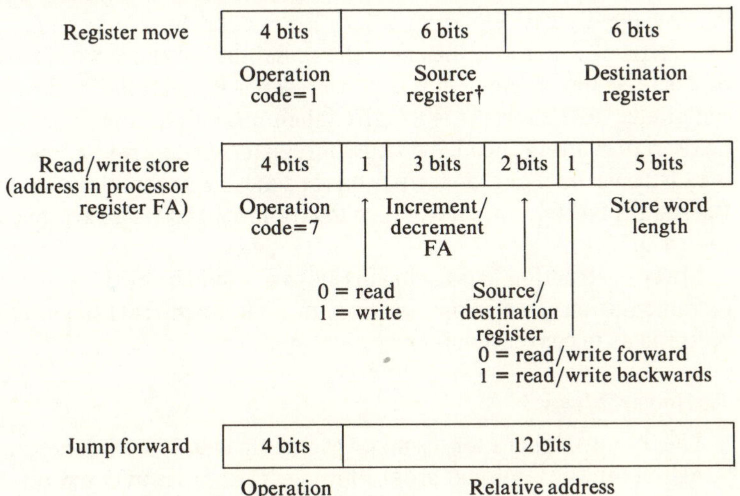


† Possible 'source registers' include various output values from a 24-bit 'function box' (such as binary or decimal sum, logical complement, exclusive or).

FIG. 3.22

ure 3.21: the address of the next micro-instruction is 010110 if the adder result is positive or zero, and 010111 otherwise.

Some computers allow several different test functions to be connected as each of the least significant few bits of the next micro-instruction address, allowing 4-way, 8-way, or even higher order conditional jumps.

### *Horizontal and vertical micro-instruction formats*

The micro-instruction format which we have described is very much oriented towards the hardware of the processor. It is long (perhaps 50 to 100 bits), and is made up of a series of short encoded fields specifying gates to be opened and control signals to be transmitted. An example (of the format of a micro-instruction for the Data General Eclipse computer, taken from Data General 1977) is given in Figure 3.22(a). This layout is called a *horizontal* micro-instruction format.

However, some computers are designed with micro-instruction formats much more similar to normal machine code instruction formats, especially those computers which are designed to be microprogrammed by their users. Here we are trading user convenience against the extra logic levels needed to decode the micro-instruction. We typically have a relatively short micro-instruction format (perhaps 16 bits), part of which specifies how the remainder of the micro-instruction is to be interpreted (that is, it represents an operation code). The remainder of the format is usually taken up with a number of short fields, representing encoded processor registers or control signals. This is called a *vertical* micro-instruction format: some examples (from the Burroughs B1700 computer, taken from Burroughs 1972) are given in Figure 3.22(b).

Micro-instruction sequencing in this case would be by the automatic incrementation of a microprogram counter; jump instructions are then required as in conventional programming.

### *Timing problems*

The timing of operations is much more important in microprogramming than in conventional programming. This arises in two ways.

First, the cycle time of the various parts of the computer are not hidden from the microprogrammer, as they are from the conventional programmer. Thus, a microprogram may have a wait for a store read to be completed, or the result from a test function may not be available for the micro-instruction sequence until several micro-instruction cycles after the function was initiated.

Second, there is the possibility (especially with horizontally micro-programmed computers) of simultaneously performing several operations under control of one micro-instruction if the data paths are available. Thus we may be able to initiate an instruction fetch from store and increment the program counter in one micro-instruction.

### *The advantages of micro-programming*

What are the advantages of implementing the control unit of a processor by microprogramming? Wilkes (1951) introduced the concept as a means by which the design and implementation of a control unit could be carried out in a systematic and logical manner; this advantage is a particularly valuable one today, when uniform electronic layouts are well suited to the technology of LSI.

Microprogramming was first used on a large scale in the IBM System/360 range of computers, where a common architecture and instruction set had to be implemented on a number of different models in the range with widely-varing basic hardware. It has since been used on many small computers as a means of implementing a rich instruction set at a reasonable price. Here then, the advantage is economic; we can design a basic computer hardware to meet certain cost objectives, and then use microprogramming to implement the fetching, decoding, and execution of instructions from a rich set, compatible with the instruction sets of other computers.

As well as the advantages of uniformity (which include ease of maintenance) and cost, microprogramming offers greater flexibility than hardwired logic; it is easier to alter a control store than to rewire a control unit. Thus a computer architecture and instruction set can be frozen at a later stage in the design process, and can be altered as a result of any inadequacies or improvements.

If a computer spends a significant portion of its time in carrying out a particular sequence of steps, then performance could be improved by replacing these steps by a single instruction implemented as a micro-program. Thus in computers oriented to particular tasks, we can tailor the instruction set to the application area; several examples are given in Husson (1970, Chapter 3).

In the operating system area there are many tasks, such as process intercommunication and switching, or transput control, where heavily used sequences of steps could be written in microcode. In the future much of a computer's supervisor may be in microcode: see for example the microprogrammed operating system functions on the experimental VENUS system (Liskov 1972).

A further use of microprogramming is in writing programs to test for and diagnose faults in the computer hardware. Because of the closeness to the hardware, such *microdiagnostics* can drive signals through particular data paths and isolate faults to a much smaller number of units than would be possible with programs written in machine code.

### *Emulation*

One way in which the flexibility of microprogramming can be used is in providing several different computer architectures and instruction sets on one basic hardware. Wilkes and Stringer (1953) suggested the provision of several control stores, one of which could be plugged into the basic hardware to create a particular architecture.

One particular time when we are concerned with several computer architectures is when transferring programs from an old computer to a new one. Instead of converting the programs from one machine code to another, we could envisage writing a program for the new computer to simulate the old computer at the instruction level. In a microprogrammed computer this simulator program could be written in microcode to improve performance; of course, the standard microcode in the new computer is really only a simulator for the new instruction set.

A more common way in which the simulation of the old computer can be improved is to select heavily used portions of the simulator program and replace them with individual specialized instructions (such as for instruction fetching and decoding); these new instructions are then implemented in microcode. Such hardware-enhanced simulation is called *emulation;* it was provided on several models of the IBM 360 range, to emulate second generation computers such as the IBM 1401 and 7090.

### *Writeable control stores*

We have so far assumed that the micro-instructions are held in a read-only control store, although we have considered the possibility of interchangeable plug-in control stores. Instead some computers provide a *writeable control store* (WCS) which can be dynamically loaded with a set of binary patterns as new micro-instructions. Notice that, although we are now able to alter the control store, we need not have the general write-access available with normal main storage; what is required is the ability to reload a portion of the control store at rather infrequent intervals. This might be done by a special (privileged) 'load control store' instruction, which transfers a set of bit patterns in main storage to an area of control store.

It is fairly common to have two areas of control store, one read-only (to hold microprograms for the computer instruction set) and one writeable. Writeable control store is attractive in tailoring a computer for a particular application, but there are major problems, in potential loss of compatibility with the manufacturer's standard software or even between problem programs; this may be compounded by multiprogramming, and errors in microprogramming (particularly as the latter is usually more complicated than conventional programming). WCS is also useful for testing micro-instruction sequences, before placing them in read-only storage for permanent use.

### *The Burroughs B1700 computer*

Computer manufacturers have a continuing problem of protecting their investment in programming and yet persuading their customers to transfer to new computers. One possible solution is the evolutionary approach, by which only minor enhancements are made to a pre-existing architecture so that all programs are upwards compatible to the new computer.

The emulators on third generation computers indicate another possible solution. This is the concept of the *soft machine,* exemplified by the Burroughs B1700 computer. This computer has no machine code instruction set or data formats in the ordinary sense. Instead it provides a writeable control store and a micro-instruction set oriented towards the interpretation of what are referred to as S-languages (for secondary languages).

An S-language could be the machine language of another computer, in which case the B1700 can emulate that computer if an interpreter is written in the microcode. Alternatively it could be an intermediate language into which a high-level language is compiled. Notice that we can have a difference intermediate language (and microcoded interpreter) for each high-level language, designed for the efficient and compact representation of the primitive elements of that language.

The micro-instructions provided for writing interpreters manipulate a number of general-purpose processor registers and function boxes (which produce various functions of two input arguments, such as the binary sum, or the logical disjunction), and access variable-length operands in main store starting at any desired bit address. Thus the B1700 computer can emulate, at the machine code level, any real or hypothetical computer; whether this is the way of the future remains to be seen. Further details of the B1700 computer are given in Burroughs (1972), Wilner (1972a, b), and Tanenbaum (1976, pp. 204–11).

## Problems

**3.1.** A 16-bit computer has two instruction formats:

| 4 bits | 12 bits |
|---|---|
| Operation code | Operand |

| 8 bits | 8 bits |
|---|---|
| Operation code | Subsidiary information |

Two schemes are possible for allocating bit patterns to operations:
(a) One 4-bit pattern (say 1111) in the 4 most-significant bits of an instruction word indicates the second format, while all other 4-bit patterns represent the first format.
(b) The most-significant bit of an instruction word indicates the format.
How many different instructions can be specified under each of the allocation schemes? Why might a computer designer choose the first scheme?

**3.2.** The instruction formats on the Data General Nova computer are shown in Figure 3.2. Ascertain that, despite the variable length operation code, a binary pattern is always uniquely decodable into an instruction.

**3.3.** When a programmer uses an assembler language, he uses mnemonic instruction names and symbolic addresses. Consider a computer with which you are familiar: to what extent must the assembler language programmer be aware of the precise format in the computer of the instructions he writes? For example: does he need to know (and if so, when?) the length of the instruction (if it can vary), the order of fields within the instruction, the value in the operation code field, etc.

**3.4.** Figure 3.5 shows the 'group 1 instruction' on the DEC PDP-8 computer, which uses the two's complement representation for negative numbers. The bits of this instruction can be set so that its execution leaves any one of the following values in the accumulator:

$$0,1,2,3,4,6,64,1024,2047,-1,-2,-3,-1024,-1025,-2048.$$

How can this be achieved?

**3.5.** Suggest a set of sequences of assignment statements, which you would expect to be typical of programs involving arithmetic calculation. Making reasonable assumptions about instruction lengths and speeds (see any recent computer manual), compare the time and store requirements for executing these sequences on computers with zero-, one-, and 1½-address instructions. Estimate how difficult it would be for a compiler to generate efficient code for these three architectures. Perform the same analysis for the Data General Nova computer (see Figures 3.2 and 3.3).

**3.6.** Suppose a computer has an array of accumulators (with the appropriate instructions), and accumulator zero is the computer's program counter. What effect could this have on the design of the computer's jump instructions and addressing modes? Is it a good idea?

**3.7.** For a computer to which you have access, list all the transfer of control instructions. Are symmetric conditions provided: that is, if 'jump on accumulator $\geqslant 0$' is provided, is 'jump on accumulator $<0$' also provided? Is the condition encoded in the operation code or in a subsidiary information field? Are the addressing modes provided the same as for data manipulation instructions?

**3.8.** A simplified version of the 'group 2 operate instruction' on the DEC PDP-8 computer is given as a boolean expression on page 103. How would you describe the significance of bits $x$, $y$, and $z$ in a form suitable for a programming manual?

**3.9.** An 'increment store location and skip if zero' instruction is described on page 105. How could this be used for controlling a repetitive loop?

**3.10.** Suppose that an instruction which specified indexed addressing could also specify whether the index value was to be modified (for example, it could be incremented by one). How would this affect the provision of instructions for performing loops? How useful would it be? How is it related to stack manipulating instructions and to 'auto-indexing' (see § 4.3)?

**3.11.** In § 3.3 and problem 3.10 a number of different groups of instructions were mentioned, which involved modifying the contents of an index register. List the different methods by which this modification value could be specified, and discuss their relative advantages and disadvantages.

**3.12.** Early computers did not have a 'subroutine call' instruction. One technique for getting round this problem was mentioned on page 110, whereby a jump instruction in the subroutine was modified before entry. Another technique (the 'Wheeler linkage') involved constructing a return jump in the accumulator at entry to a subroutine. Program this on a computer with which you are familiar. Extending this idea, we could provide an instruction 'load accumulator with contents of program counter' and this, together with an unconditional jump instruction, would suffice for subroutine entry and return. Discuss this proposed method.

**3.13.** A character string consists of words separated by commas or spaces. Show how the 'translate and test' instruction described on page 117 can be used to search for the first comma.

**3.14.** A <declaration> is defined in BNF as:

<declaration>: := <itemlist>.<br>
<itemlist>: :=<item>|<itemlist><separator><item><br>
<item>: :=<ident>|<ident>[<boundslist>]<br>
<boundslist>: := <boundspair>|<boundslist>,<boundspair><br>
<boundspair>: :=<item>;<item><br>
<separator>: := ,|:|;<br>
<ident>: :=<letter>|<ident><letter><br>
<letter>: := a|b|c|.. x|y|z

Using the 'translate and test' instruction, show how a program could be written to check any character string against this definition, and extract the <ident>s in order to look them up in a dictionary.

**3.15.** Consider a computer with multiple arrays of accumulators and control registers, in which a process's complete context is contained in one array of accumulators and one array of control registers (in particular, the program counter is a control register). What information needs to be changed at a process switch, and therefore how long is the PSW and what does it contain?

**3.16.** (a) What difficulties would you expect to arise in writing a microprogram?

(b) Some microprogrammed computers allow the next micro-instruction to be specified by loading into the control store SAR the contents of some portion of a processor register. Why would this help with the microcode's main task, of decoding and executing machine instructions?

# 4 The addressing space

## 4.1. The requirements of an addressing system

IN THIS chapter we discuss the various ways in which an instruction can specify a store location. We have already introduced the simplest method, called *direct addressing,* on the Von Neumann computer. Here an operand field of **N** bits in each instruction specifies a binary value, and hence a store address, in the range 0 to $2^N-1$. A few character-oriented computers (such as the IBM 1401) have encoded this operand field as a series of decimal digits instead of as a binary value, but this is an inefficient use of the operand field and is not used on modern computers.

In § 1.2 a second addressing method, using index registers, was introduced, and in § 4.2 we discuss variations on this basic method. In the remaining sections of this chapter we go on to discuss other methods of specifying a store address. In this section we consider the inadequacies of direct addressing, and the possible aims of any more sophisticated system for addressing store.

### *The addressing problem*

The first problem with direct addressing is the length of operand field required to address a store of adequate size. This is particularly critical in small computers with a 12- or 16-bit word and an operand field of between 9 and 12 bits, since a maximum of a few thousand words would be directly addressable, while stores of up to 32 000 words are common. On large computers (particularly on byte-oriented computers) store sizes of several million elements are available. Moreover, as we shall see in § 5.2, some computers use the operand field to specify addresses which lie either in main store or on backing storage (such as magnetic disc or drum), so that the range of store addresses must be some tens or hundreds of millions. The use of direct addressing here would require operand fields 20 to 30 bits long; this (in computers with word lengths of 24 to 36 bits) leaves insufficient room for operation codes and other instruction fields.

However, even when the store size can be made small enough or the word length long enough to allow direct addressing of the whole store, there is an economic argument against doing so. Most computer programs or sections of programs exhibit *locality of reference;* that is, the addresses referred to, for instructions and for data, do not range randomly over the whole store, but tend to be clustered in a few areas. Indeed, in a multiprogramming system, each process is allocated a certain area of store, and references to addresses outside the area are illegal. Thus, while each instruction must be potentially able to access a large range of addresses, most of the time its operands will in fact lie in a much more restricted area. It therefore appears that, with direct addressing, several of the more significant bits of the operand field tend to remain constant over some or all of the program. Thus several bits of the instruction word are assigned to provide information which does not change with each instruction. These bits, if not used to specify redundant information, could be used to extend, for example, the operation code field; or the instruction length might be shortened, allowing the computer word length to be shortened.

### *Instruction modification*

The need to modify the operand field of an instruction between executions has been discussed in Chapter 1. This modification may be the simple one of incrementing or decrementing to move from one element of a vector or matrix to the next, or it may involve a more complicated calculation (such as the algorithm for the binary searching of an ordered table) or access to another store location (for example, in a list structure, where each list element contains the address of the next). Since we reject the possibility of direct manipulation of instructions as if they were data, we must have some means (such as index registers) for allowing the store location accessed by an instruction to depend on a previously-calculated data value.

### *The representation of process structure*

Another inadequacy of direct addressing (and of most other addressing systems, including the use of index registers) is its inability to represent process structure. Consider a problem process occupying a certain contiguous block of store. As shown in Figure 4.1(a), the process itself consists typically of a main routine and a set of subroutines, together with a set of data structures. These may vary in complexity from single words of data, through vectors and stacks, to structures interconnected by pointers such as lists. This must all be linearized as

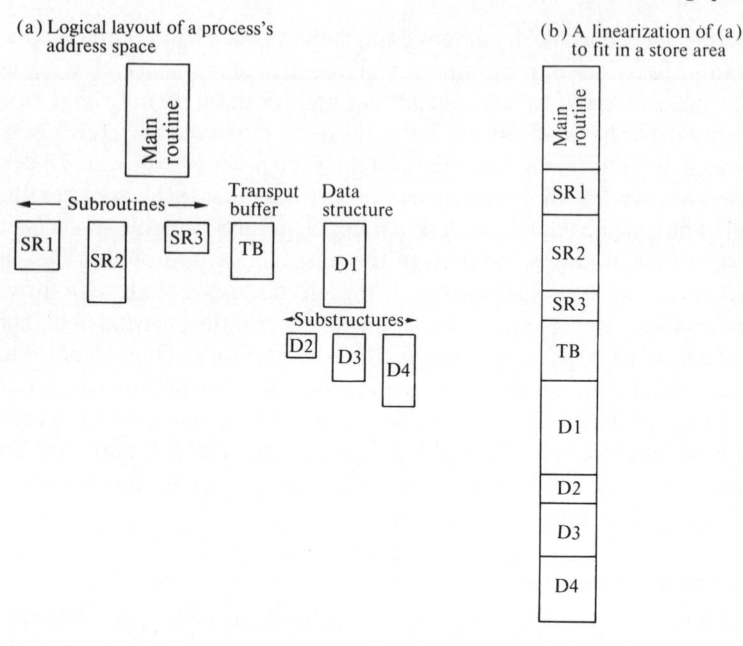


FIG. 4.1

shown in Figure 4.1(b), in order to map it into the single vector of store locations allocated to it.

But in linearizing the process's address space we lose a number of features present in the original, structured layout. First, conceptual understanding of the process is lost when we lose the structure. Second, flexibility is lost by the linearizing, as any modification of a subroutine or data structure changes the addresses of all parts of the process higher up in the store. If alterations to the process of this sort must take place at or before the time at which the process is loaded into the computer, then a suitable linking program can adjust all the relevant addresses, and here some forms of addressing structure reduce the number of such adjustments. However, if alterations to the process are to take place dynamically during execution, the computer must provide suitable addressing facilities, so that the reorganization can be performed economically. Further, the process structure may then be used as a basis for the provision of other facilities by hardware, such as array subscript checking, sharing subroutines or data between processes, and the automatic overlaying of sections of the program or data.

### *The relocation problem*

This leads into the fourth inadequacy of direct addressing, the inability to represent system structure. Typically the store of a computer contains a supervisor and one or more problem processes, the supervisor usually occupying the lower part of store and the problem processes the rest. The problem processes may each occupy a contiguous area of store, or each may occupy a number of areas scattered through the store. Because the various processes have different store requirements, and because we cannot guarantee that the same set of processes will always be run together, we do not wish to fix from run to run the particular area of store which each process is to occupy. If the area occupied by a process is to be fixed each time it is loaded to run, then any necessary adjustment of addresses (or *relocation)* can be performed by the loader program. As before, some addressing structures reduce the amount of work the loader has to do. However, a suitable addressing structure is essential if a process is to be *dynamically relocated:* that is, moved about during its run. Again, the requirement for protection of the problem processes and supervisor from inadvertent or malicious interference by other processes is best provided by a hardware protection system associated with the addressing structure.

It is against the background of these requirements that we look at the various methods of store addressing. It will be seen that most methods aim primarily at reducing the length of the operand field in an instruction, and at providing for instruction modification and relocation. Only the addressing systems of §§ 4.5 and 4.6 attempt to retain the full process structure, although some other systems (such as the multiple base-and-limit system) retain part of the structure.

## 4.2. The use of index registers

Nearly all modern computers provide index registers in some form or another. As described in Chapter 1, each instruction which accesses store specifies whether or not indexing is to take place. If several index registers are provided, then the particular one to be used must also be specified. Then the *effective store address,* that is the address of the location in store to be accessed, is the sum of the contents of the selected index register and the operand field in the instruction.

The number of index registers available in a computer is constrained by the number of bits available to specify an index register, or to specify that no indexing is to take place. A typical situation is three index registers numbered 1, 2, and 3, and a 2-bit addressing mode field encoding the index register to be used, the value zero specifying that no indexing is to take place.

### *Variations on index registers*

The index registers may be special-purpose registers in the processor, used only for indexing. In this case there will be a special group of instructions to manipulate indexing quantities in the registers. However, in most modern computers with an array of accumulators, all, or a subset of, the accumulators are available for use as index registers. The normal arithmetic instruction set can then be used to manipulate indexing quantities. Since an index specification of zero usually indicates no indexing, accumulator zero cannot be used as an index register.

If the index registers are separate from the accumulators, they will be of a length suitable to address the maximum size of store available, although § 3.3 considers cases when the index register has subsidiary fields to hold other data relevant to indexing (such as loop counts). If accumulators are used as index registers, then the indexing quantities are potentially one word long; when the process of indexing results in an effective store address greater than is acceptable, then an error condition may be indicated. Alternatively, some of the more significant bits of the word treated as an indexing quantity may be ignored. For example on the IBM 370 range of computers, where the 32-bit accumulators are used as index registers, the effective address is always truncated to 24 bits: if this effective address refers to a non-existent location, then an interupt is signalled which causes the supervisor to be invoked.

The effective store address resulting from the use of an index register must, of course, be a non-negative integer. However, although in general the two values summed to obtain the effective address are positive, on some computers one of the values may be negative. Thus on the IBM 370 range, the index value and operand field are both treated as positive numbers, the shorter field is extended on the left with zeros, and the fields are added together. On the Data General Nova the shorter field is expanded by propagating its sign bit to the left before addition, so it is treated as a signed number.

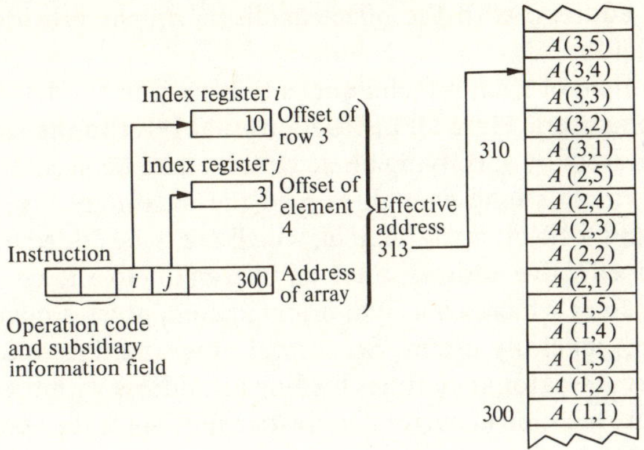


FIG. 4.2

In computers with several index registers, we may allow more than one index register to participate in the generation of an effective store address. Typically, the address mode field of an instruction contains two subfields to specify two index registers, whose contents are to be added to the operand field to provide the effective address. This allows 'two-dimensional' indexing; for example, the operand field in an instruction might hold the address of a matrix, the first index register holds the offset of successive rows of the matrix, and the second index register holds the offset of successive elements within the row.

Figure 4.2 shows an instruction using double indexing to access the element $A$ [3,4] of a two-dimensional array $A$ with three rows and five columns.

### *Base-and-displacement addressing*

It is common, especially in computers whose instructions have an operand field long enough to specify the maximum possible address, to consider direct addressing as the norm, with indexing used to access data structures such as arrays and lists. Thus the operand field is considered to hold the basic address, to be modified as required by an *offset* or *displacement* held in an index register. However, if the store address field is shorter than would be required to hold the maximal address, then the contents of the index register may be considered as the basic address, with the offset or displacement provided by the operand field.

An example of such a technique is that used in the IBM 370 and related computers. Here all instructions that refer to the store designate an address by specifying an accumulator to be used as an index register (which is long enough to hold the maximum possible store address) and a 12-bit operand field, which are to be added together to provide an effective address. Such an operand field allows a range of 4096 addresses which, on a byte-oriented computer, is obviously too small to be generally useful. So normal programming practice is to have an accumulator at all times holding an address within 4096 bytes of each store location of current interest; in fact, since the operand field is assumed to hold a non-negative value, the address held in the accumulator must be within 4096 bytes *and below* the relevant store locations. The only time that indexing can be dispensed with (effectively by specifying accumulator zero) is in addressing store locations zero to 4095, which are allocated to supervisor use and would rarely be used in a problem process.

Because of the way processes tend to access store, only a small number of index registers are normally required to provide addressing of all current store locations. Thus programs can usually be divided into sections, within each of which all addresses are represented by using one of a small number of index values which are held constant throughout the section. The accumulators used in this way are termed *base registers,* the contents of the operand field is referred to as the *displacement,* and the addressing technique is known as the *base-and-displacement* system.

In the simple case of a subroutine whose instructions and data occupy less than 4096 bytes, a suitable value (possible derived from the known entry point address) is loaded into an accumulator at entry to the subroutine, and this is used as a base register for the whole of the subroutine execution. For larger subroutines and programs a base register must be allocated to each block of 4096 bytes of instructions and data, either by the reuse of a single accumulator or by the use of a number of accumulators; and provision must be made in the program to load the base registers with suitable values, either at entry to the subroutine or program, or during execution. The assembler-language programmer is spared the task of detailed address organization, since the assembler calculates suitable base and displacement fields for each instruction, on being informed of the accumulators to be used as base

```
PCI     BALR    15,0      Load acc 15 with address of next instruction
        USING   *,15      Tell the assembler
        L       5,ABC     This would assemble to a displacement from accumu-
        •                 lator 15 (assuming it is within range)
        •
        •
        •
        USING   SCB,10    Tell the assembler that accumulator 10 contains the
        •                 address of SCB (perhaps a data area)†
        •
        •
        •
        •
        L       5,EFILL   This would assemble to a displacement from accumu-
        •                 lator 10 or 15 (whichever is nearer)
        •
        •
        •
        DROP    10        Tell the assembler that accumulator 10 is no longer to
        •                 be used as a base register
        •
        •
        B       NONE      This would assemble to a displacement from accumu-
        •                 lator 15 (assuming it is within range)
        •
        •
        •
NONE    LTR     5,5
        •
        •
        •
        •
```

† The programmer must ensure that the accumulator is in fact loaded with this address.

FIG. 4.3

registers and their contents at run time. Figure 4.3 shows a portion of an assembler-language subroutine using several base registers.

The programmer, of course, often wishes to use indexing in accessing data from structures such as arrays, so some groups of instructions on the IBM 370 range allow an index register to be specified as well as a base register. There is thus no need to alter the contents of the base register to provide indexing. In generating the effective store address, the index and base registers are both added in the same way to the displacement field, so that the effect is equivalent to double indexing.

### *Base registers*

The base-and-displacement addressing technique simplifies the relocation problem on loading a subroutine or program into the store, since the relocatable part of the address referred to by an instruction is usually contained in a base register in current use. Since these are loaded at entry to the subroutine (and for this purpose a main program can be treated as a subroutine of the supervisor), suitably written sets of instructions or data can be moved about in store before being used, but dynamic relocation during use can be done only if great care is taken with address usage.

To ensure that address usage complies with the requirements for dynamic relocation of programs and data, the computer may provide a *base register* which is not accessible to the problem process and which is transparent in use. The contents of such a base register, also known as a *relocation register* or *datum register,* are automatically added to each store address after any indexing or other addressing operation and before access to the store; similarly its contents are added to the contents of the program counter before the next instruction to be executed is extracted from the store.

An example of the use of such a register is shown in Figure 4.4. Here the store of the computer holds a supervisor in locations zero to 8191, and two problem processes in locations 8192 to 28 671 and 28 672 to 61 439. Now the instructions in the processes do not refer explicitly to the store addresses in use by the program; instead they refer to addresses as if each process was loaded from location zero upwards. Thus the first process refers to locations zero to 20 479 instead of 8192 to 28 671, and the second refers to locations zero to 32 767 instead of 28 672 to 61 439.

When the supervisor is about to switch to the first process, it loads the base register with the address of the process's first location, namely 8192. Then, whenever a store access is required (for an instruction or data), the contents of the base register are added to the address designated; thus a reference to *logical* store address 10 by the process causes access to *physical* store address 8192 + 10 or 8202. If the supervisor switches to the second process, the base register is reloaded with the value 28 672. When in supervisor mode the base register is not used, so that the whole of store is accessible to the supervisor. Dynamic relocation is now possible; if the first process terminates, the second can be moved down in the store to occupy store addresses 8192 to 40959, and the only alteration required is that a different value must be loaded in the base register when control is to be switched to the process.

Notice the difference between this use of a base register and the normal indexing technique (including base-and-displacement). In the latter the register is accessible to the programmer and is specified by a

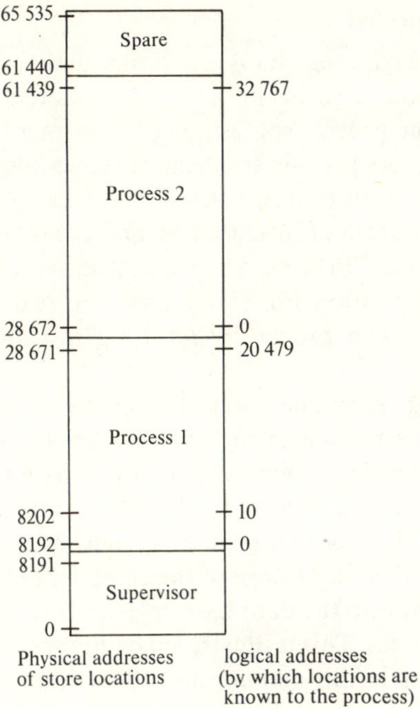


FIG. 4.4

field in the instruction format; the primary use of the technique is instruction modification, though (as we have seen) it may also simplify the relocation problem. The base register, however, is accessible only to the supervisor, and its use is signalled, not by an instruction field, but by the fact of execution in problem mode. The programmer need not be aware of the use of the base register, since the process runs exactly as if the addresses generated (in the range zero upwards) were the physical addresses used. This technique is designed to solve the relocation problem: as we shall see in § 5.1, it can be extended to provide protection of a process's store area from corruption by other processes.

Computers providing such a base register will also have a set of index registers. Thus an effective logical address is generated by adding a specified index register and an instruction operand field: the physical store address is then generated by adding the base register.

***Multiple base registers***

Having just one base register is restrictive, in that each process must occupy a contiguous area in the store, whereas there may be advantages in having the process split among two or more areas of store. A number of computers provide two base or relocation registers, so that the process can be split into two non-contiguous areas. Typically one area holds the program of instructions, and the other holds the data, allowing the hardware to be used to protect the instructions from being inadvertently overwritten For this reason the two registers may be called the *program* or *procedure base register* and the *data base register*.

This addressing technique allows two processes with two separate sets of data to share the same program of instructions. For example if, in a multiprogramming environment, two Fortran subroutines are being compiled, only one copy of the Fortran compiler need be held in the store. When either compiling process is activated the program base register is loaded with the address of the compiler program code, while the address loaded into the data base register is that of the data area unique to that process. This is illustrated by Figure 4.5. Of course, any program to be used in this manner must be written in *pure code;* that

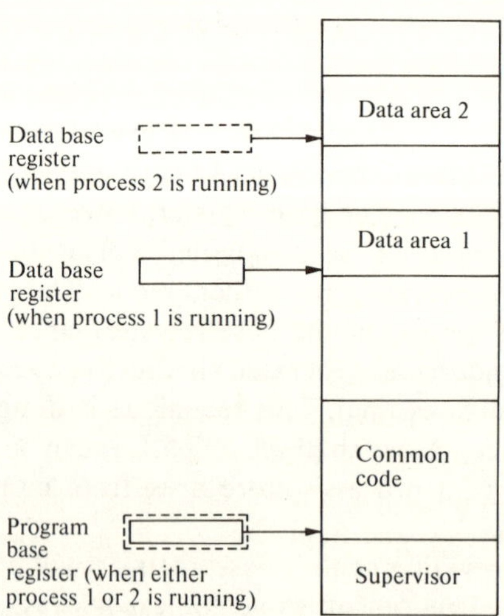


FIG. 4.5

is, the program must store all variables in the data area and must not modify the instruction area in any way.

More than two base registers may be provided; for example, the CTL Modular One computer has three, refered to as the X, Y, and Z registers. The X and Y registers are the normal program base register and data base register respectively. The Z register is a second data base register, which is commonly used for addressing an area of store for communication with peripherals, or between processes in a multiprogramming environment. These base registers are loaded by the supervisor, and the addressing mode field in each instruction indicates (among other things, such as the type of indexing required) which of the three base registers is to participate in calculating the physical store address for the instruction.

Flexibility could be increased further by the provision of more base registers. However, the next step up from two or three base registers is usually to several tens of address mapping registers, and this is described in § 4.5.

## 4.3. Relative, bank, and indirect addressing

### *Relative addressing*

In indexing we have seen that the contents of the operand field are modified by the contents of a register chosen from among a number of accumulators or special-purpose index registers. On some computers, generally the smaller ones with only a small number of index registers, the choice of modifying register may include the program counter. Here the effective address is the sum of the operand field and the contents of the program counter; the latter is the address of either the instruction currently being executed or the next sequential instruction, depending upon the exact point in the instruction cycle at which the program counter is incremented. This technique is often known as *relative addressing*; however, since the term is sometimes used for all forms of addressing involving modification of the operand field, the term *self-relative* addressing is also used.

Relative addressing is a popular addressing mode for jump instructions; usually the operand field contains a signed quantity, to allow jumping both forward and backward in the instruction sequence. It should be noted that relative addressing is very common at the assembler language level in the form of expressions such as * $\pm$ $n$ (where * represents the contents of the program counter); on computers without relative addressing such an expression is translated (at assembly time) into a direct or (perhaps) an indexed address. On a computer with relative addressing, the address remains in this form until the instruction containing the expression is executed.

### *Bank registers*

A variation on relative addressing is the paged store structure found on small computers such as the DEC PDP-8. This use of the term 'paged store' should not be confused with the (more standard) use of the term to describe the 'one-level store' system discussed in §5.2. On small computers like the PDP-8 the operand field can specify only a small range of perhaps 128 or 256 locations. The store is therefore divided into a number of units of this size known as *pages*, and a bit in the addressing mode field of each instruction making reference to the store specifies which of two pages of the store is to be accessed. One of the two possible pages is that starting at store address zero (known as *page zero*); this page contains several special store locations and can be used for intercommunication between programs. The other page is that containing the instruction currently being executed, known as the *current page*, which contains data (and of course instructions) 'local' to the current section of code.

For example on the DEC PDP-8 computer, an instruction at a location in page 27 which specifies an operand field of 15 is referring either to location 15 on page zero (i.e. store address 15) or location 15 on page 27 (i.e. store address 3471, since pages are 128 words long on this computer).

Thus for current page addressing, the top few bits of the program counter are to be considered as a special 'current page' register, to be concatenated on the left of the contents of the operand field to give an effective store address. The bit specifying the page to be used can therefore be seen as specifying whether or not the operand field is to be modified by this current page register.

The use of a current page register can be considered as a special case of the use of *bank registers*. The store of a computer may conceptually be divided into units of a fixed number of locations with contiguous addresses, known as *banks* or *fields*. Historically bank registers were introduced to enable a computer to access stores of larger capacity than the original design; thus a computer designed to access a 16K-word store using direct and indexed addressing might use bank registers to access a 32K or 64K-word store. For this reason, the size of a bank is often the size in which modules of additional store are available for attachment to the processor.

One or more bank registers are provided, each of which can hold a value specifying one bank of store. To obtain an effective address the contents of the bank register are concatenated on the left of the contents of the operand field, so that the bank register supplies the most significant portion and the store address field the least significant portion of the address.

We can see the current page register of the DEC PDP-8 computer as a bank register whose contents are loaded implicitly from the program counter. More usually, the instruction set of a computer using bank registers contains one or more instructions to load the bank registers with suitable values. Similarly, the specification of a bank register to participate in generating an effective address may be implicit or explicit. A simple scheme is to modify all store addresses, whether of instructions or data, by the contents of the (single) bank register. Perhaps the most common technique is for the computer to provide two bank registers, one for instructions and one for data.

As has been mentioned, bank registers were first introduced as a rather *ad hoc* device for extending the addressing range of a computer. In this capacity they are used on some microcomputers to reduce the number of address pins needed by the microprocessor chip (see Aspinall and Dagless 1977, pp. 64–5); the address passed to the store consists of a less significant portion from the microprocessor itself, and a more significant portion from a separate bank register chip, holding a value which can be changed from time to time by the microprocessor.

On larger computers the bank register has tended to fall out of use in its simple form, its place being taken by some form of index and/or base register. It should be noticed however that many computers which provide one or more base registers (as described in the previous section) do not allow an arbitrary physical address to be stored in them. For example the DEC PDP-10 computer (KA10 processor) has two base registers, so that a process can be divided into two portions, a pure code part and a variable data part, but these must be loaded at addresses which are a multiple of 1024. Since an effective logical address on this computer is 18 bits long, the base registers need to be only 8 bits long, and their value is added to the top 8 bits of the effective address to obtain a physical address. On most computers with base registers a certain number of the less significant bits of the base address (six or more) are forced to be zero, so that the base registers have some of the features of bank registers.

***Indirect addressing***

In the addressing techniques we have described, an effective store address is calculated by some means, and this store location either holds an operand, is used to store a result, or is the target of a jump instruction. Instead we may treat the contents of this store location as a store address at which the operand, result or target is to be found. This technique is called *indirect* or *deferred addressing*. Suppose that locations 100 and 200 contain the values 200 and 205 respectively. Then the instruction,

Load accumulator (direct): operand field = 100

loads 200 into the accumulator, while

Load accumulator (indirect): operand field = 100

loads 205 into the accumulator. Direct, indirect, and indexed addressing are the most commonly found repertoire of addressing modes. In a small computer with a paged store (such as the DEC PDP-8) indirect addressing via a location on the current or zero page may be the only means of access to a location not on one of these pages.

In computers which provide only indexed addressing, such as the IBM 370 range, the effect of indirect addressing (required, for example, in moving from one element of a list structure to another by accessing an address field in the first) can be obtained by loading the operand address into an index register. Thus instead of, for example,

Add into accumulator (indirect): operand field = 100

we must write

Load index register 1: operand field = 100
Add into accumulator (indexed by register 1): operand field = 0

One advantage of the indexed addressing version is that an offset can be added to the basic operand address, so that we can write, for example

Load index register 1: operand field = 100
Add into accumulator (indexed by register 1): operand field = 4

whereas, with an indirect addressing system, we would have explicitly to form the address '4 + contents of address 100'. The economics of using the two alternative addressing systems obviously depends on whether such offsets are required, and whether the operand address is used frequently enough to make it worth holding it in an index register for a number of operand accesses.

The above comments assume that the 'cost' of indexed and indirect addressing are the same, which is not in fact the case. The addressing techniques discussed earlier all involve access to a register of some form in the processor, whereas indirect addressing requires access to a general store location. Since the execution time of a store-referencing instruction is dominated by the access time for the instruction and operand, an indirect address adds approximately 50 per cent to the execution time, while an addressing technique which involves only processor registers adds only a few per cent to the execution time.

### *Variations on indirect addressing*

In introducing indirect addressing, we implied that its use is independent of, and orthogonal to, all the addressing systems discussed earlier. That is, an effective store address might be obtained from an instruction by the use of (say) indexing, and an 'indirect' bit in the addressing mode field would then be interpreted by the hardware to

Store locations

| | | | | |
|---|---|---|---|---|
| 100 | Load into accumulator | indirect | index = 4 | 200 |
| 250 | indirect | index = 2 | 302 | |
| 331 | direct | index = 4 | 413 | |
| 463 | | | −999 | |

Index registers

| | |
|---|---|
| 2 | 29 |
| 4 | 50 |

FIG. 4.6

ascertain either that the operand is at this store location or that the contents of the store location are to be treated as an address.

On computers with a short word-length, such as the DEC PDP-8, the whole of this store location is treated as a store address, thus allowing only one level of indirect addressing. However, if the word is longer than that required to hold the maximum store address, as on the Data General Nova, one of the unused bits may be used as an indirect bit at this level, indicating (if set) that the contents of the addressed location are also to be treated as an address. Thus we have a chain of indirect addresses; as long as the indirect bit is set, the contents of the addressed location become a new effective address, while a clear indirect bit indicates that the contents of the addressed location are the final operand.

If it is long enough, the word holding an intermediate address may contain a complete addressing mode field, instead of merely an indirect bit. Thus the intermediate address might, at each stage of an indirect addressing chain, have the contents of a specified index register added to it before accessing the store. For an example consider Figure 4.6, based on the DEC PDP-10 computer. Here an instruction at store address 100 specifies indirect addressing via store address 200 indexed by index register 4. The effective store address is therefore 250, whose contents specify indirect addressing via store address 302 indexed by index register 2. The new effective store address is therefore 331, whose contents specify direct addressing via store address 413, again indexed by index register 4. The final effective store address is therefore 463, which contains the operand.

This example illustrates *pre-indexing,* the most common form of

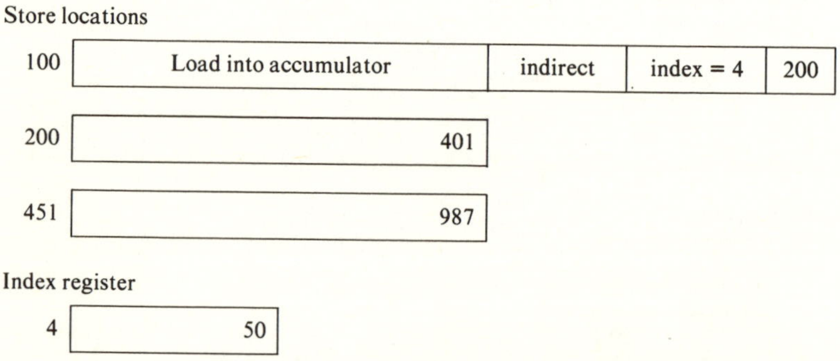

Store locations

100 | Load into accumulator | indirect | index = 4 | 200

200 | 401

451 | 987

Index register

4 | 50

FIG. 4.7

interaction between indirect and indexed addressing, where the index value is added to the address rather than the contents of the location accessed. The less common form of interaction is *post-indexing*, where the index value is added to the contents of the location accessed. A single-level indirect addressing system with post-indexing is illustrated in Figure 4.7, where the result is that the contents of location 451 (i.e. 987) are loaded into the accumulator.

### *Auto-indexing*

One variation on indirect addressing, found on a number of small computers, such as the DEC PDP-8 and Data General Nova, is the use of *auto-indexing registers*. These are a small number (typically 8) of store locations which, if addressed indirectly, are incremented by one before being used to supply an address. Thus in Figure 4.8, store location 10, an auto-indexing register, contains 100. If we load the accumulator from the indirect contents of store address 10, then location 10 is incremented to contain 101, and the contents of store location 101 are loaded into the accumulator. This technique can replace simple uses of an index register, such as processing in sequence the elements of a vector, where each of these elements consists of a single store location; however, it is of course not as flexible as using an index register together with a suitable instruction to modify and test the indexing quantity. Note that if an auto-indexing register is accessed directly as a location holding an operand or to hold a result, then no incrementing takes place; this allows initial values to be set up and final values to be tested.

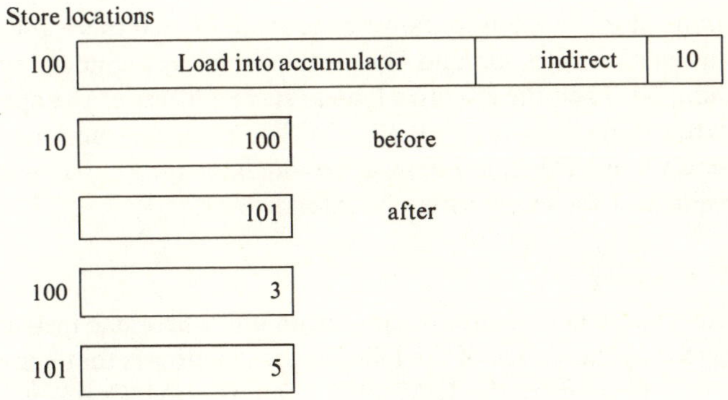

Store locations

100 | Load into accumulator | indirect | 10

10 | 100 | before

| 101 | after

100 | 3

101 | 5

FIG. 4.8

## 4.4. Miscellaneous addressing systems

In this section we first discuss a number of more uncommon addressing systems, and then go on to consider how the addressing mode is specified by an instruction.

On computers with a short word-length we have the problem of allowing any instruction to access any location in store. We have already discussed the DEC PDP-8 solution, using a 'current page' and a 'page zero', together with indirect addressing for locations on other pages. Another solution (used, for example, on the IBM 1800 computer) is to have two formats for most instructions, a short (one-word) format and a long (two-word) format, with each instruction including a one-bit field to specify which format is being used. In the short format only a small address field is provided; this may be used to refer only to a number of store locations with low addresses (i.e. to locations on a 'page zero') or may be supplemented, for example by indexing, as specified in an addressing mode field. In the long format the store address field is the whole of the second word of the instruction, perhaps concatenated with part of the first word; this can be used directly or with address modification, as before.

Another addressing technique allows the operand field of one instruction to be modified by the immediately preceding instruction, without the intervention of an explicit intermediate register (such as an index register). An example of this is the curious instruction 'Supplementary Modifier to Operand of next Instruction' (or SMO) on the ICL 1900 range of computers. Here the value of the operand of this instruction is added to the effective address (after indexing, etc.) of the instruction following. Thus suppose we have an SMO instruction specifying a store location containing the value 24, and this is followed by an instruction with operand field 200 indexed by an index register containing 20. Then the effective logical store address of the operand of the latter instruction is 200 + 20 + 24. The SMO instruction can be seen merely as a (rather *ad hoc*) way in which the range of an instruction's addressable locations may be extended.

### *Address chaining*

A rather more general addressing technique where one instruction modifies the operand field of the following instruction is that known as 'chaining' and used by the IBM 1401 computer (McCracken 1962; Bell and Newell 1971, pp. 225–34). As described in §2.5, this is a two-address computer where each operand consists of a string of characters; an operation is generally performed by processing two characters at a time, one from each operand, until some terminating condition is reached (such as the end of one of the operands).

During execution of an instruction, the store addresses of the characters currently being processed are held in two registers, the A- and B-address registers. Initially these registers hold the addresses of the right-hand characters of the two operands; as the characters are processed from right to left, the registers are suitably decremented. Eventually the instruction terminates when a word mark is reached; at this time, the A- and B-address registers contain the addresses of the first characters to the left of the operands just processed.

If these addresses are the ones required for the second operand or both operands of the next instruction, then the relevant addresses may be omitted from this next instruction and are taken from the address registers. The first store address cannot be omitted from the instruction if the second is present, since this would be indistinguishable from omitting the second and retaining the first store address.

As an example, suppose we have the situation of Figure 4.9: we wish to move operands from two source fields at store address 300–4 and 400–3 to two destination fields at store addresses 200–4 and 205–8 respectively, and there are suitably placed word marks at addresses 300 and 400 in the source fields to terminate the moves. Then the operands could be moved with the instructions:

Move characters to word mark 403 208
Move characters to word mark 304 204

Using chaining, we can obtain the same effect (and save three characters of instruction storage):

Move characters to word mark 403 208
Move characters to word mark 304

The advantages of this chaining technique are that it reduces instruction storage space and increases instruction execution speed, since the time taken to fetch an instruction on a character-oriented computer depends on its length. However such a technique can only be used on a computer with variable-length instruction formats.

On the Honeywell H200/2000 series of computers (Honeywell

(a) Before execution of instructions

| ? | ? | ? |
|---|---|---|

A-address register

| ? | ? | ? |
|---|---|---|

B-address register

| | A | B | C | D | E | F | G | H | I | J | K | L | |
|---|---|---|---|---|---|---|---|---|---|---|---|---|---|
| | 200 | | | | | 205 | | | | | 210 | | |

| | M̲ | N | O | P | Q | R | |
|---|---|---|---|---|---|---|---|
| | 300 | | | | | 305 | |

| | S̲ | T | U | V | W | X | |
|---|---|---|---|---|---|---|---|
| | 400 | | | | | 405 | |

(b) After executing 'Move characters to word mark 403 208'

| 3 | 9 | 9 |
|---|---|---|

A-address register

| 2 | 0 | 4 |
|---|---|---|

B-address register

| | A | B | C | D | E | S | T | U | V | J | K | L | |
|---|---|---|---|---|---|---|---|---|---|---|---|---|---|
| | 200 | | | | | 205 | | | | | 210 | | |

| | M̲ | N | O | P | Q | R | |
|---|---|---|---|---|---|---|---|
| | 300 | | | | | 305 | |

| | S̲ | T | U | V | W | X | |
|---|---|---|---|---|---|---|---|
| | 400 | | | | | 405 | |

(c) After executing 'Move characters to word mark 304'

| 2 | 9 | 9 |
|---|---|---|

A-address register

| 1 | 9 | 9 |
|---|---|---|

B-address register

| | M | N | O | P | Q | S | T | U | V | J | K | L | |
|---|---|---|---|---|---|---|---|---|---|---|---|---|---|
| | 200 | | | | | 205 | | | | | 210 | | |

| | M̲ | N | O | P | Q | R | |
|---|---|---|---|---|---|---|---|
| | 300 | | | | | 305 | |

| | S̲ | T | U | V | W | X | |
|---|---|---|---|---|---|---|---|
| | 400 | | | | | 405 | |

FIG. 4.9

1965; Flores 1969, pp. 194–227), A- and B-address registers are used for holding the operand addresses, and chaining is therefore possible. However, on these computers the technique is extended by allowing the store address specified in an instruction to be two, three, or four characters long. A mode-changing instruction is provided to specify the number of characters per address (if any) in subsequent instructions, since this cannot be deduced from the length of the instruction. When a four-character address is specified in an instruction, it replaces the whole of the contents of the appropriate address register before the operand is assessed, while a two- or three-character address replaces only a low-order portion.

For example the instructions,

Perform operation 1 on operands with addresses 1234–7 and 5678–81
Perform operation 2 on operands with addresses 1345–9 and 5789–93
Perform operation 3 on operands with addresses 1356–7 and 5724–5

could be replaced (using address chaining) by

Perform operation 1 on operands with addresses 1234–7 and 5678–81
Change to 3-character addresses
Perform operation 2 on operands with addresses 345–9 and 789–93
Change to 2-character addresses
Perform operation 3 on operands with addresses 56–7 and 24–5

This is a simplified form of the H200/2000 system, since there the address is in fact held as a binary, rather than a decimal, number. The technique can be seen to be equivalent to a bank register, all or part of which may be concatenated with an operand field, and which is automatically set (in whole or in part) by earlier instructions.

The chaining technique may be characterized by saying that a portion of the store address register (SAR) becomes accessible to the assembler-language programmer. This is taken a step further on many microprocessors, where one particular processor register (which can be loaded and manipulated by the programmer) is assumed to contain the operand address for most store-referencing instructions; for example, on the Intel 8080 most instructions require that the address of the location to be accessed is in the HL register pair. The central processor of the CDC 6600 computer has eight 'operand' registers X0 to X7 and eight 'address' registers A0 to A7 (as well as eight 'increment' or B registers). Whenever a quantity, say Q, is loaded into one of address registers A1 to A5, then the corresponding operand register is loaded from the location with address Q: whenever a quantity Q is loaded into address registers A6 or A7, then the contents of the corresponding operand register is stored at the location with address Q. The address registers therefore act as store address registers, one per operand register.

### *Addressing mode fields*

We have discussed a number of different addressing techniques. In many computers only indexing is available. In this case all that needs to be specified in the addressing mode field of an instruction is the index register to be used, or the fact that indexing is not to take place (usually by specifying an index register number of zero). Of course, the contents of a base register may be implied for all store accesses in a problem process, and this will not require specification in the addressing mode field.

In other computers a selection of addressing techniques are available; a common example is indexing and indirect addressing. For such a computer, the addressing mode field is divided into two subfields; a subfield which holds values zero (for no indexing) or one to $n$ (specifying one of $n$ index registers), and a one-bit subfield to specify whether or not indirect addressing is required. If relative addressing is also available, then usually only $(n-1)$ index registers are provided, so that an index subfield value of $n$ specifies use of the program counter for relative addressing.

An interesting example of the provision of a number of different addressing modes for each instruction is the DEC PDP-11 computer. Each instruction operand is specified by a six-bit addressing mode field; thus a single-operand instruction such as 'clear operand' contains one such field, and a two-operand instruction such as 'add' contains two such fields. The addressing mode field is divided into three subfields; a three-bit field specifies one of the eight accumulators to be used for accessing the operand, a one-bit field specifies whether or not indirect addressing is required, and a two-bit field specifies how the accumulator is to be used for operand accessing.

This latter subfield has four values:

(a) 'Register' mode, in which the specified accumnulator contains the operand.
(b) 'Auto-increment' mode, in which the specified accumulator contains the address of the operand. After the operand has been accessed, the specified accumulator is incremented.
(c) 'Auto-decrement' mode, in which the specified accumulator is decremented, after which it contains the address of the operand.
(d) 'Index' mode, in which the store location following the instruction is treated as an operand field (i.e. the instruction becomes two words long), and the contents of this field are added to the contents of the specified accumulator to give the address of the operand.

The above modes have been described for the case where indirect addressing is not used; if we replace the word 'operand' by the phrase 'address of the operand', we have definitions of the four addressing modes with indirect addressing.

These modes are illustrated in Figure 4.10. In fact this is a simplification of the PDP-11 architecture, since this computer addresses the byte rather than the word; thus the incrementing and decrementing must be by two (rather than one) for word operands in (b), (c), (f), and (g).

Note that the first mode is equivalent to the use of an accumulator in a conventional one-address computer, except that either operand (or both operands) may be held in the accumulator in the PDP-11. The second and third mode may be used for stepping through a vector of store locations to be processed, but are in fact designed for the manipulation of stacks (see §3.3). A further set of addressing modes is obtained by noting that the program counter is in fact one of the accumulators (number 7); direct 'auto-increment' mode specifying the program counter provides an immediate operand in the word following the instruction, while direct 'index' mode specifying the program counter provides a relative address in the word following the instruction.

The discussion of addressing techniques has been expressed mainly in terms of one-address instructions, where an operand field and an addressing mode field provide the effective address of one operand, and any other operands or result locations are implied, or specified in an accumulator field. For a two- or three-address computer a single

Suppose accumulator 3 contains 100
location 99 contains 200
location 100 contains 300
location 600 contains 400
in cases (d) and (h) location 1001 contains 500
location 1000 contains the instruction:

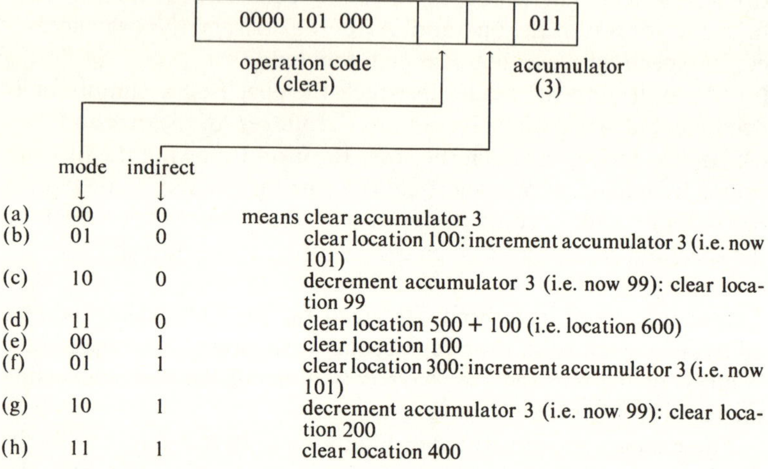


FIG. 4.10

address modification, such as the use of a base or bank register, might be performed on all store address fields in an instruction. More usual, however, is an addressing mode field for each store address field, allowing independent modification of each operand or result address. An example of this is, of course, the PDP-11 computer, where an instruction may have two addressing mode fields and, if required by the mode, two operand fields.

### *Addressing mode specification by the operand field*

In some computers part of the information normally supplied by an addressing mode field is, in fact, encoded in the value of the operand field. A common example of such an encoding occurs in computers which provide a pair of base registers, one for the instructions and one for data. A contiguous range of addresses may be made available to the programmer; addresses below a certain value are considered to be in the instruction space and those above are in the data space.

Thus, in the Univac 1108 computer (Borgerson, Hanson, and Hartley 1978), a problem process runs with three special registers set: a program base register, a data base register, and a 'selection' register. Each effective logical address (after indexing, etc.) is compared with the selection register: if it is lower, the program base register is used to generate a physical store address, otherwise the data base register is used.

In some cases the top few bits of the store address field can in fact be treated as part of the addressing mode field; thus, if our decision as to which base register to use is based on the most-significant bit of the store address field (so that addresses less than some power of two are in instruction space, and the rest in data space), then this most-significant bit should really be considered as a subfield of the addressing mode field.

### *Addressing mode specification by operation code*

We have tended to assume, in discussing addressing techniques, that all instructions which refer to a store address have a similar format, having an operand field and addressing mode field with the same size and significance for all instructions. However, one way of coping with a short instruction length is to use different addressing techniques for different types of instruction; then those instructions which do not need the full generality of addressing available to other instructions can have longer operation code fields or (on computers with variable-length instruction formats) the instructions can be shorter.

One example discussed earlier is the IBM 370 range, where all store addresses are held in base-and-displacement form, but certain groups of instructions allow a second index register, and others (principally the byte string handling ones) do not. A popular grouping of instructions on many computers is a group of data-manipulation instructions, which have fairly general address-modification capabilities, and a group of control instructions (such as the jump instructions), which use more restricted addressing techniques (allowing, for example, a larger number of conditions to be specified in conditional jumps).

The problems with such inconsistencies are the greater likelihood of assembler-language programming errors (for example, specifying an index register in an instruction which cannot accommodate it, by analogy with another instruction), the loss of flexibility in program structure (for example, the inability to code jump tables simply), and the increased difficulty of code generation in a compiler for a computer with an idiosyncratic instruction set.

### *Addressing mode specification by mode register*

A further method of specifying an addressing mode is the use of an addressing mode register, held in the processor and altered from time to time by suitable instructions. We have already met this concept in the Honeywell H200/2000 series of computers, where a special register indicates whether two-, three-, or four-character addresses are currently being used.

The most common case in which an addressing mode is specified for a sequence of instructions in this way is with the use of a base register: store addresses are modified by this register for all instructions in the problem processes, while instructions in the supervisor processes run without it. Thus the use of the base register depends on whether the processor is in supervisor or problem mode, and is specified by the processor mode register (discussed in §3.5).

Another case where an addressing mode register is used is where a computer has been designed for a particular maximum store address, which later becomes inadequate. The addressing system may be altered to accommodate a new maximum store address, but the earlier system will be enshrined in programs for earlier models. To accommodate both old programs and new extended programs on the same computer, a short- and a long-address mode can be provided; the required addressing mode is then selected when the program is loaded, and an addressing mode register set accordingly.

## 4.5. Segmentation

Let us consider again the problem of holding a number of processes in the store of a computer at one time. To ensure flexibility in the positioning of processes within the store, we do not wish to specify absolute store addresses in a process before it is loaded into the computer; indeed, if we wish to be able to move processes about in the store during execution, we must hold all store addresses in a position-independent form, and have hardware to convert from this form to absolute addresses each time a store access is made. One way that this may be done is by providing one or more base registers as described in §4.2.

### *Address mapping registers*

A second method is by the use of a set of *address mapping registers*. Here the store is divided into a number of units of a fixed size, which

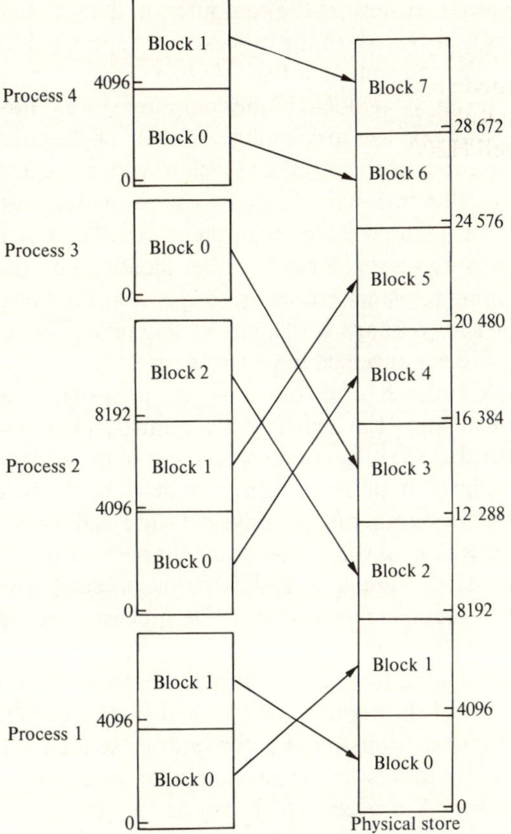


To run process 2, the address mapping registers hold:

| | |
|---|---|
| 7 | — |
| 6 | — |
| 5 | — |
| 4 | — |
| 3 | — |
| 2 | 2 |
| 1 | 5 |
| 0 | 4 |

FIG. 4.11

we will call *blocks;* similarly the addressing range of each process is broken up into a number of blocks of the same size. Each block in the addressing range of the problem process is allocated to a particular block in the physical store of the computer, and a set of address mapping registers is provided (in the processor) to specify the correspondence between the conceptual or logical blocks of the currently running process and the physical blocks of the computer store. Thus there is one address mapping register to each logical block of the current process, holding the number of the physical block to which it corresponds.

Figure 4.11 illustrates this: it shows a computer with eight 4K-blocks of physical store (as, for example, on the Data General Nova) and four processes whose blocks have been loaded into this store. The address mapping registers are set up for process 2 to be run: registers 3 to 7 are marked (perhaps with an extra flag bit) to show that logical blocks 3 to 7 are not accessed in this process.

An effective address (after indexing, etc.) consists of a high-order portion *b*, constituting the logical block number, and a low-order portion *d*, constituting the offset or displacement of the address within the block. The address mapping register number *b* holds the corresponding physical block number $b'$; the physical store address to be accessed is then formed with $b'$ as the most-significant portion and *d* as the least-significant portion. Figure 4.12 shows this process, when a logical address 12345 (octal) is generated while process 2 of Figure 4.11 is running.

The store allocated to a process may therefore consist of a number of blocks scattered throughout the physical store, but to the program the addressing space consists of a consecutive sequence of addresses from zero to some address less than or equal to the maximum store size of the computer. A process which begins to run may therefore be loaded into any set of blocks relinquished by processes which have already terminated, however these blocks are scattered through the

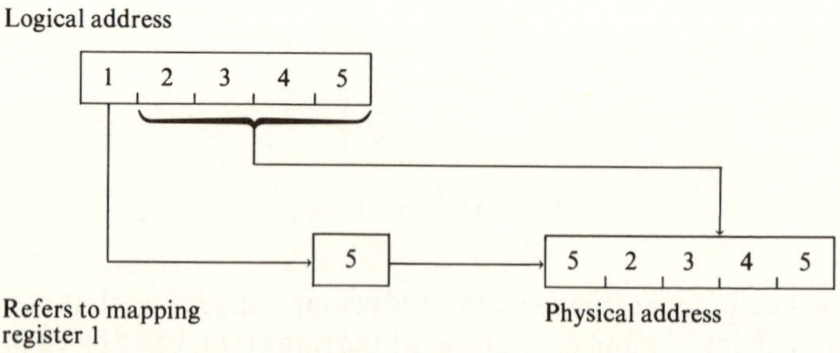


FIG. 4.12

store, as long as there is a sufficient number of them.

On some computers only one set of address mapping registers (or *block index*) is provided, and this must be reloaded on switching from one process to another; on others several sets are provided, and a map selection register indicates which set is in current use.

Notice in this technique how the number of blocks allocated to a process is equal to the number of address mapping registers provided in the processor (and it is of course expensive to provided very many of these). In order to increase the number of blocks per process, the mapping information could be held in a sequence of store locations (and then we need some way of reducing the time penalty of the extra store access); this is the technique of *paging,* which we discuss separately in §5.2. Because of the similarity between these two store management techniques, the term paging is often used for the provision of a small number of address mapping registers in the processor (and a block is then referred to as a *page*), as well as for the more general technique described in §5.2. However we will reserve the term for the latter method, where the aim is to integrate the main store and backing store; we treat address mapping registers in this section as an intermediate form, between two or three base registers on the one hand and segmentation on the other. The address mapping register technique could, in fact, be extended so that integration of main and backing store is possible.

The term *virtual store* is common in discussions of store management techniques, and means any technique in which the set of effective logical addresses generated by a process (the *name space,* or set of *virtual* addresses) is mapped, by a mechanism hidden from the process, onto a set of physical addresses in main (and perhaps backing) store. Thus the use of base registers is an example of a virtual storage technique, although the term tends to be used in a restricted sense to mean segmentation or paging.

### *Segmentation*

Consideration of sets of base registers leads us to view a process as a small number (typically two or three) of independent vectors of contiguous store locations. The technique of *segmentation* is an extension of this to allow large numbers of independent vectors of contiguous store locations.

The basic idea is that the block index described above is held as a table (the *segment table*) in the store of the computer, instead of in a set of special registers in the processor. The virtual address consists, as before, of a more-significant portion, the *segment number* used to access an element of this table, and a less-significant portion, the *dis-*

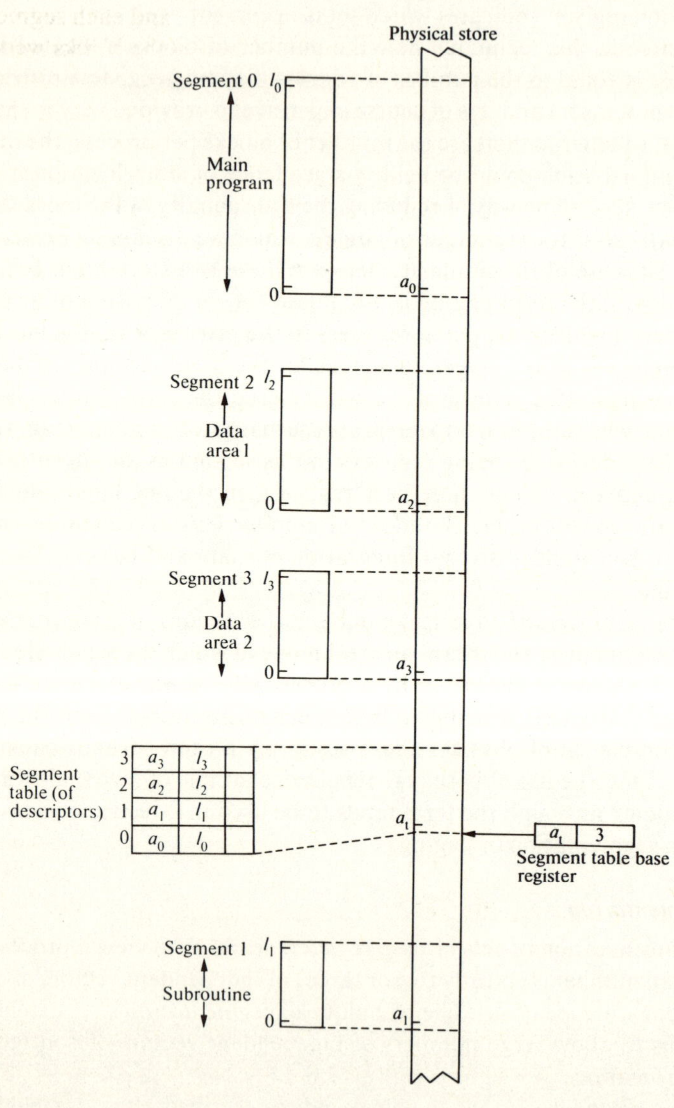


FIG. 4.13

*placement*. Unlike the short displacement fields found with address mapping registers (typically perhaps twelve bits long), here the displacement field is long enough (for example, sixteen to eighteen bits) to address the whole of one logical unit of a program, for example one group of subroutines or one independent data area, and each segment can be of any length up to this maximum (whereas the blocks were a fixed size in the previous technique). A process using segmentation therefore sees a 'two-dimensional' store, of addresses within segments, each of which has some logical significance.

To take a concrete example of segmentation, consider Figure 4.13. In this computer, the effective virtual address generated by indexing, etc., consists of a segment number $s$ (say $m$ bits long) and a displacement, offset or index $d$ (say $n$ bits long); the virtual address is therefore $m+n$ bits long. A segment may be of any length up to $2^n$ words, and each segment is allocated to a vector of contiguous locations in the physical store.

Each segment is refered to by means of a *segment descriptor,* which contains (among other things) the physical store address of the first word of the segment and the number of words in the segment. These segment descriptors are collected together in an area of the store called the *segment table* or (since this table is in fact a segment) the *segment descriptor segment*. The segment descriptors are arranged in the segment table so that the descriptor for segment $s$ is at offset $s$ within the table; the total number of segments in the table must of course not be greater than $2^m$. It would be possible always to start the segment table at a fixed, known location in the store; however, in order to allow each process to have its own segment table, the physical address of the first word of the segment table and the length of the table are usually held in a special hardware register in the processor, the *segment table base register*.

The sequence of steps carried out by the address mapping hardware is therefore as follows:

Split the effective virtual address into the form $[s,d]$

Obtain the descriptor for segment $s$ in the segment table (at offset $s$ from the address in the segment table base register)

Extract the physical segment address $s'$

Access the physical store address $(s'+d)$.

As an example based on Figure 4.13, suppose $m$ is 12 and $n$ is 18. Then the address 0002001234 (octal) is broken down by the hardware to segment number 2 and displacement 1234, and the descriptor for segment 2 is found at $a_t$+2; this gives a physical address of $a_2$+1234 (octal).

In most segmentation systems the low-order portion of a segment address is assumed to be zero (i.e. a segment cannot start at an arbitrary point in store), so the physical store address is obtained by concatenation, rather than addition, of $s'$ and $d$.

Notice that each store access in a segmentation system has the overhead of a further store access to the segment table. To reduce this overhead, we need to keep the commonly accessed segment descriptors in a set of faster registers in the processor, so that for most of the time the virtual-to-physical mapping is via this set rather than the store: we will see how this is done in §5.5.

***Consequences of segmentation***

First, let us consider the process's view of the virtual address space. If there are up to $2^m$ segments, each up to $2^n$ words long, there is potentially a (logically uninterrupted) range of $2^{m+n}$ addresses: this is the view provided, for instance, by a set of address mapping registers. However segmentation is aimed at making the process structure visible to the hardware. So the logical units into which a process's address space can be split (the main program, the subroutines, the several data areas) are allocated one to each segment, which are then treated as independent vectors of store, each numbered from zero up. The size of the logical units into which the process is split (for example, whether to the level of individual arrays, or to the level of a collection of several logically related arrays and scalar variables) will depend upon the implementation and addressing overheads of having a large number of small segments.

There is no suggestion that the last store location in segment $s$ has any particular relationship with the first in segment $s$+1. An attempt to address beyond the end of segment $s$ results in an addressing error interrupt, whereas the attempt to address beyond the end of block $b$ under an address mapping register system results in an access to block $b$+1 (unless $b$ is the last block of the process's address space).

In a multiprogramming environment each process has a number of segments, scattered through the store. The segments for any one process are numbered from zero upwards (with perhaps some unused segment numbers) independently of all other processes in the store, and their segment descriptors are collected together in one segment table for each process. One of the tasks to be performed in switching from one process to another is to load the segment table base register with the address of the segment table for the process being switched to.

When we dynamically relocate a segment (for instance, if it has increased in size and there is insufficient physical space *in situ*), we simply alter its segment descriptor, after which all accesses to store refer to the new area; the problem process is completely unaware of the change.

We have discussed the use of only one field in the segment descriptor, which holds the physical address of the base of the segment in question, but we have mentioned the presence of a segment length field and implied that there are other fields. These fields are used to ensure that the process can access only locations within its own address space, and that only authorized accesses may take place (for instance, a segment may be readable but not writeable by a process). These fields are discussed in §5.1 on storage protection.

***The sharing of segments***

Notice that it is possible for a segment to be shared between two or more processes simply by having a segment descriptor refering to it in each of the segment tables, possibly with different offsets in the table (i.e. different segment numbers); such a shared segment could be common data, or it could be a subroutine (written, of course, as pure code).

An alternative method is for each process to have two segment tables, one (common to several processes) which describes segments to which all processes in the group require access (such as portions of the operating system), and the other (private to the process) which describes those segments belonging to that process.

The University of Manchester MU5 and ICL 2900 range have both these forms of sharing. Segment numbers are in the range 0–16 383. Segment numbers in the range 8192–16 383 (i.e. with the most-significant bit of the segment number set) are used for public segments, accessible to all processes in the system, and descriptors for these segments are held in a single public segment table. Segment numbers in the range 0–8191 are used for segments private to a process, and descriptors for these segments are held in a private segment table for each process. If a small number of processes require shared access to a segment, a descriptor for that segment can be placed in each private segment table; if a large number of processes require access to a common segment, it is made a public segment.

Figure 4.14 illustrates this. There are six public segments, numbers

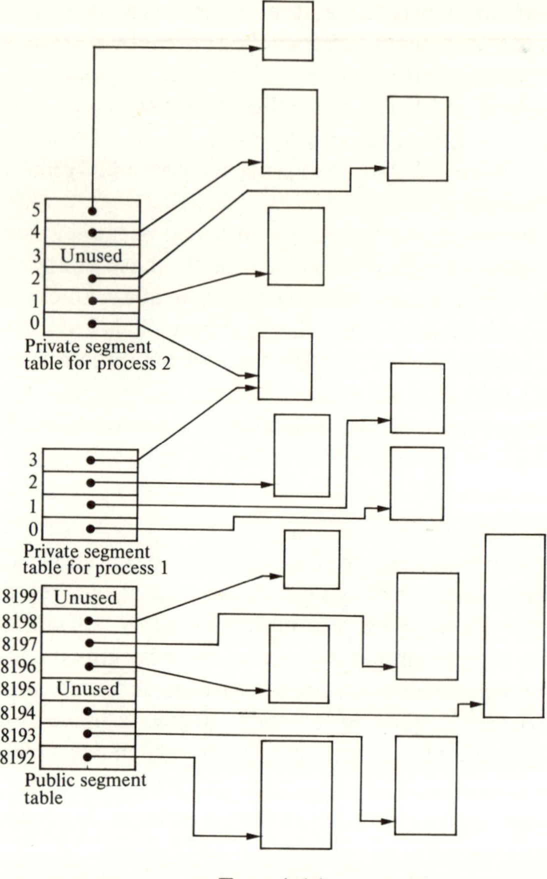


FIG. 4.14

8192–4 and 8196–8, and public segment number 8195 is unused. Process one has four private segments, numbered 0–3, and process two has five private segments, numbered 0 to 2, 4, and 5 (private segment number 3 is unused). Process one's segment 3 is the same as process two's segment 0.

***The generation of virtual addresses***

We have discussed the process of obtaining a physical store address from an effective virtual address in a segmentation system. We now briefly consider how the effective virtual address is arrived at. The operand field of the instruction and a set of index registers are used in the normal way, but two further addressing methods become important: the use of segment registers, and indirect addressing.

(a) A full two-dimensional virtual address $[s,d]$ is rather long, and only a few segments are likely to be referred to over a sequence of store accesses. For this reason a small number of special segment registers in the processor may be provided to hold the numbers of segments being accessed in the current section of the process, and the appropriate register will be specified by a field in each instruction; thus the instruction's operand field and the index registers need provide only the displacement of the address. On the GE (now Honeywell) 645, around which the Multics time-sharing system was originally built, five such segment registers are provided. On the University of Manchester MU5 and the ICL 2900 range a segment register (SN or SSN, the stack segment number) holds the number of the segment in which the process stack is held (and to which many store accesses for data will therefore be directed).

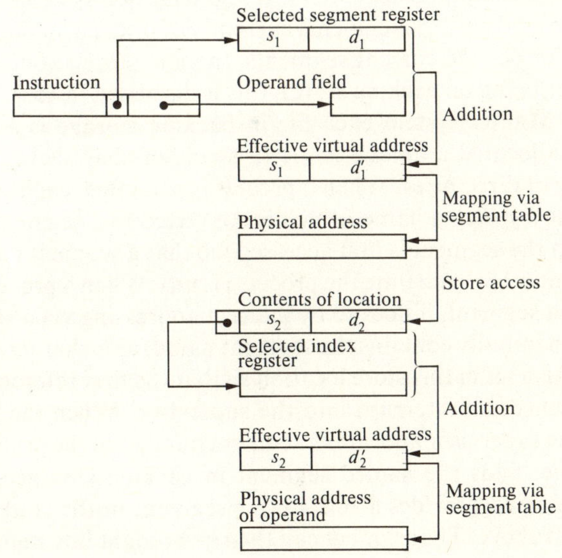


FIG. 4.15

(b) If there are more segments currently being accessed than can be held in segment registers, then the segment numbers could be held in a table in a communication region, and the locations within a segment accessed by indirect addressing via this table. Figure 4.15, based on the GE 645, illustrates this. One of the segment registers (which, on this computer, hold a complete virtual address rather than just a segment number) holds the virtual address of the current communication region in a 'link' segment, and the operand field of the instruction holds an offset into this region, to a location holding the virtual address in the desired segment. This location may specify an index register, whose contents are to be added to this second virtual address before it is converted to a physical address. Notice the overhead that such an addressing technique adds to each store access.

***Segmentation and the backing store***

We have already mentioned that the displacement *d* might be 16 or more bits long, so that a typical segment could be tens of thousands of words long. Furthermore there are usually several segments per process, and several processes in the store at a time. It is therefore unreasonable to require the whole of a process's address space to be held in store simultaneously. In most segmentation systems, provision is made to hold only the segments currently of interest, or only the current portions of the current segments, in main store at one time (the remainder being on backing store); this is discussed in §5.2.

In the Multics system each file in backing storage is a segment, which is allocated a unique name (a string of characters) held in a hierarchy of directories. When a process is compiled, each segment is referred to by such a name, which is converted to a segment number only when the segment is first accessed (so that a segment may have a different number each time the process is run). When a process wishes to access a segment, it does so by indirect addressing via a store location which initially contains the segment name (as a character string). A flag is also set in this store location so that the first reference by the process causes an interrupt into the supervisor. When the interrupt occurs, the supervisor allocates a segment number in the process's segment table, finds the named segment in backing storage using the directories, and provides a link to this segment in the store location referred to above. The segment can then be brought into main store as required by the process, allowing main and backing store to be treated in a unified manner.

Details of the Multics system can be found in Daley and Dennis (1968), Bensoussan, Clingen, and Daley (1972), and Organick (1972). Segmentation in general is discussed in Dennis (1965) and Arden, Galler, O'Brien, and Westervelt (1966).

## 4.6. Descriptor addressing systems

In the last section we used the term *descriptor* to refer to an entity (perhaps one or two words long) which describes an area of store; typically it holds the store address of the first word of the area, the size of the area, and a number of fields describing its contents and what sort of access is allowed to its elements. It can be seen that this is a generalization of the form of descriptors mentioned in §2.5. We introduced the concept of a *block* or *segment* as a unit by which the main store of the computer may be addressed, using the address portion of the descriptor as a base register; the block referred to by a descriptor may also be a unit of storage protection by hardware as described in §5.1, and a unit of allocation of main and backing storage as described in §5.2.

Further the descriptors are collected together as a vector, so that each descriptor is known by its offset within the vector, and there is an inherent order among segment names; this is known as *linear segmentation.* In contrast to this is *symbolic segmentation,* where segment descriptors are referred to by a more general form of name than a linear offset. In the Multics system the programmer is encouraged to think in terms of a symbolically segmented space with addresses of the form[segment name, *d*], although such addresses have to be converted by the system to the basic linearly segmented form of [segment number, *d*]. In this section we will look at a number of other addressing systems with symbolic segmentation.

### *The Basic Language Machine*

In the linear segmentation system described in the previous section there are only two levels of descriptor: those describing the segments available to a process, and the descriptor for the segment table, held in the segment table base register while the process is being executed.

However, the concept of the descriptor is not restricted to two levels. We can conceive of a general tree-structured addressing system where, at all levels except the lowest, there are blocks of descriptors referring to further blocks lower down the tree. Consider Figure 4.16, where we have four levels of descriptor. At the top level the *principal descriptor* is held in a special register in the processor and refers to a block of descriptors, one for each process (in a multiprogramming environment). The process descriptor indicated refers to a block of descriptors, one describing a block of instructions, one a block of data, and the third a further block of two descriptors, each of which describes a block to be used as a transput buffer.

Such a tree-structured addressing system is used in Iliffe's Basic Language Machine (Iliffe 1968), a computer designed as a research project into the use of such addressing structures, and in the Rice University computer (Iliffe and Jodeit 1962; Jodeit 1968; Feustel 1972). On these computers the term *codeword* is used instead of descriptor.

Addressing in these systems is accomplished by applying an index to a descriptor; thus the index 3 applied to the principal descriptor P (written P. 3, so that the term *dot operation* is used for indexing) refers to the descriptor $Q$ for the process shown in detail, and may be said to describe the process. Further P.3.0 refers to the block of instructions in the process, and P.3.2.0.$i$ refers to the $i$th word of the first transput buffer.

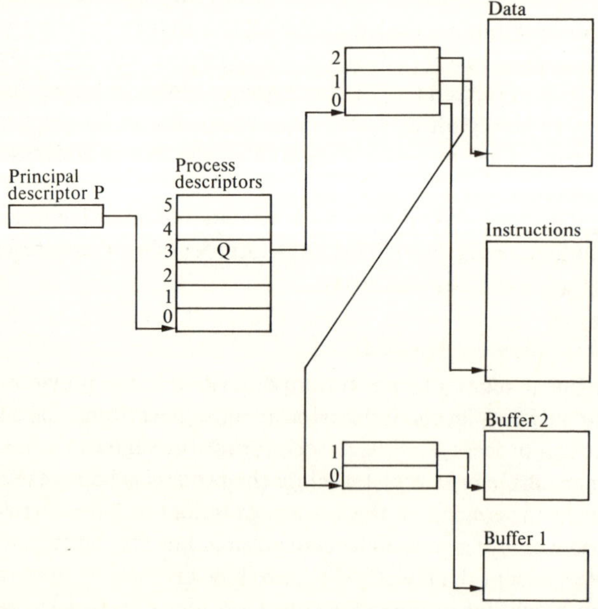


FIG. 4.16

One problem with the use of such chains of descriptors is the conflict between efficiency and flexibility. If all addresses are specified as fully-indexed principal descriptors (in the way that, in the linear segmentation technique, addresses are held in a form equivalent to P.s.d, where P is the segment table base register), then the process of applying indices to successive descriptors for each store access will be very slow for a long chain. But if we short-circuit the process by holding a partially-indexed descriptor in a register and applying only the lower-level indices (for example holding P.3.2.0 in a register and applying the index *i* as it varies), then the system is sensitive to dynamic changes such as relocation of the buffer described as P.3.2.0, since there is no means of recognizing partially-indexed descriptors for alteration.

In the Basic Language Machine each descriptor or codeword has a type field as well as the block address and length fields, and this field indicates the type and size of the elements making up the block; for example, 32-bit binary word, 64-bit numeric value (for example, a floating-point number), 32-bit instructions, or 32-bit codewords. As well as allowing hardware protection, this provides an economic way in which operands can be provided with type fields, as suggested in §2.6. If we execute the function 'add' with two operands addressed by indexed codewords A.*i* and B.*j*, the hardware of the computer can check the compatibility of the type fields of codewords A and B, and select the correct form of addition; if the type fields are incompatible, a function can automatically be invoked to perform a conversion on one of the operands, or an interrupt taken into the supervisor.

Each element of a block now contains, not a full field giving the type of its contents, but a short 'tag' field. This tag indicates either that the element is to be treated as specified by the type field of the codeword for the block containing it, or that it is unusual in some way that has to be treated specially. This special 'escape' action signals the use of a special hardware function, or an interrupt into a user-supplied subroutine or the supervisor. Thus in a block of fixed-point numbers, an element which has not yet been set to a value would be tagged to represent 'undefined', so that if read the element would cause a trap into a subroutine to supply a value or terminate the operation. Similarly, while one of the buffers in Figure 4.16 is being filled or emptied by a transput device, the tag field of its codeword is set so that any attempt to access the buffer causes an interrupt into the supervisor.

### *Capabilities and the Plessey System 250*

We have already mentioned the conflict in tree-structured addressing systems between efficiency and flexibility, since we can specify addresses as fully-indexed principal descriptors or hold a partially-indexed descriptor in a register. The latter alternative is used in the Plessey System 250 computer (Halton 1972; Hamer-Hodges 1972; Leaman, Lloyd, and Repton 1973), where the descriptors or code-words are termed *capabilities* for the blocks they define, to reflect their importance in hardware storage protection.

In this computer 8 capability registers are provided, and each store reference instruction specifies (as part of its addressing mode field) one of these registers as a base register for address modification; a separate set of index registers is also provided. One of the capability registers always contains the capability describing the block of instructions currently being executed, and is therefore a relocation register for the program counter.

A second capability register always describes a block of capabilities available to this process, and these capabilities describe various data blocks, blocks of instructions, and further blocks of capabilities. In order to access one of these blocks, its capability must be loaded into one of the other 6 capability registers. In this way a chain of capabilities may be followed with, at each stage, complete hardware protection of the store contents. The capabilities may be altered only by a subroutine which has write access to a block of capabilities, a situation which obtains only for certain parts of the supervisor.

### *The Burroughs computers*

The technique of symbolic segmentation and the use of descriptors has been a feature of a number of Burroughs computers, beginning with the B5000, and evolving through the B5500, B6500, and B7500 to the B5700, B6700, and B7700. All these computers have a hardware stack to hold operands and subroutine return addresses, as mentioned in §§3.2 and 3.3 respectively, providing a highly-structured operating environment for processes. One of the features of these computers is that they are to be programmed only in a high-level language, and in fact the system architecture is closely related to the block structure of Algol 60.

§3.2 described how a stack is represented in this architecture by a vector of store elements and the A, B, BOS, LOS, and S registers in

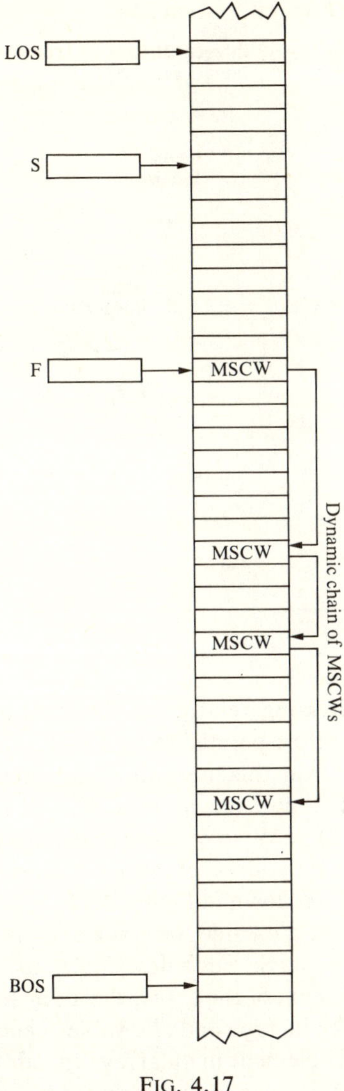


FIG. 4.17

the processor. When a subroutine is entered, a special control word, called the mark stack control word or MSCW, is pushed onto the top of the stack followed by all the parameters and local variables for that subroutine. While this subroutine is being executed, all such variables

| | |
|---|---|
| | **begin** |
| Level = 0, displacement = 1 | **integer** *a*; |
| Level = 0, displacement = 2 | **integer array** *b* [1:10]; |
| | ... |
| | **begin** |
| Level = 1, displacement = 1 | **integer** *c*; |
| | ... |
| | **begin** |
| Level = 2, displacement = 1 | **integer** *d*; |
| | ... |
| | **end;** |
| | ... |
| | **end;** |
| | ... |
| | **end** |

FIG. 4.18

are accessed by addressing relative to the location of this current MSCW, which is therefore pointed to by a special hardware register, the F register. On exit from this subroutine, the stack register S is reset to point just before the most recent MSCW, and F must be reset to point to the previous MSCW; in order to make this possible, a field in each MSCW contains the address of the previous MSCW, the MSCW of the calling routine, as shown in Figure 4.17.

Arrays of data are held outside the stack and are accessed by data descriptor words in the stack. Such descriptors, as usual, contain the address of the first element of the array, the array length, and a number of fields to describe its type and allowable access modes. In order to refer to a particular element in an array, an index must be applied to the descriptor; if valid, the index value replaces the array length field of the descriptor, and a flag in the descriptor is set to indicate that indexing has taken place. When a descriptor is accessed in the stack to load or store an array element, the index and address fields are added to give a physical store address.

So far, the addressing scheme described allows access only to variables or elements of arrays in the current subroutine, that is, variables or arrays with descriptors above the current MSCW in the stack. However, speaking in Algol 60 terms, we wish to be able to refer to data elements in the blocks lexicographically enclosing the current block; in particular we wish to refer to the global variables of the program. Now any variable can be referenced uniquely by an address couple $[l,d]$, where $l$ is the lexicographic level of the block in which the variable is declared (the outermost block being level zero) and $d$ is a displacement to indicate a unique variable (a data element or an array descriptor) at that level, as shown in Figure 4.18.

But $d$ is simply an offset from the address of the MSCW for the relevant block; if therefore we link together the MSCWs, not only by the dynamic calling structure as described above, but also by the static lexicographic structure of Figure 4.18, then we can address non-local variables by tracing the static links back to the relevant MSCW and then applying the displacement. This process is, of course, too slow for frequent use, so that a set of display registers D0 to D31 in the processor holds the addresses of the MSCWs for the current static block structure, and is updated automatically on block entry and exit.

Figure 4.19 adds the static chain of MSCWs and the display registers to figure 4.17, and shows how the variables declared in Figure 4.18 might appear on the stack. Thus, for example, variable $c$ would be addressed with an operand field of 1 and an addressing mode field referring to D1.

We have considered the addressing structure for a single process in the B6700 computer, but in fact the architecture accommodates multiprogramming. This is done by a technique referred to by Hauck and Dent (1968) as the Saguaro stack system, but usually termed the cactus stack system by those unfamiliar with North American flora. Before any processes are run, the operating environment consists of a 'trunk' stack at level zero, containing certain global variables and descriptors for the segments of instructions forming the supervisor.

As each process is initiated, a 'branch' stack at level one is created, containing descriptors for segments of the process's executable code, and a branch stack at level two is set up to hold variables and array descriptors as described above. If two processes are initiated which use the same set of (reentrant) instructions but different sets of data, then they share a stack at level one but have independent stacks at level two. If a process splits into two independent processes, then they share their level-one stack and that part of the level-two stack created up to the

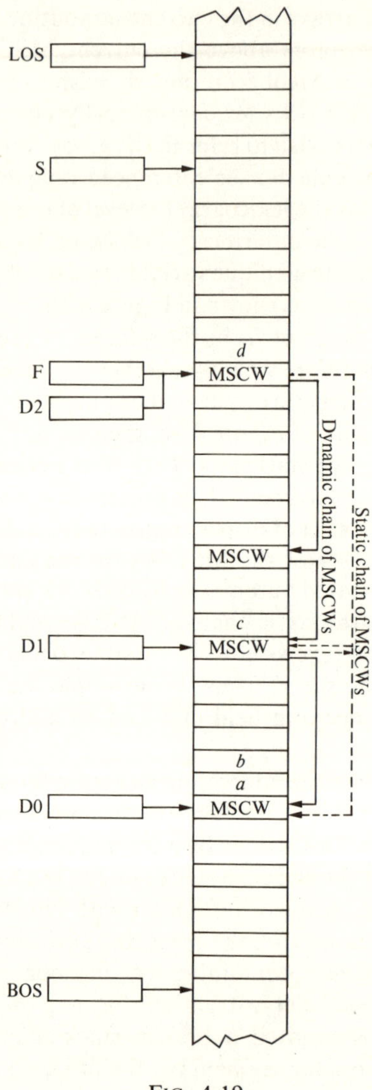


FIG. 4.19

point of splitting, after which they have separate level-two stacks. Figure 4.20 shows a cactus stack for a normal process (process 1), two processes (2 and 3) sharing the same code, and a process which splits into two independent processes (4a and 4b).

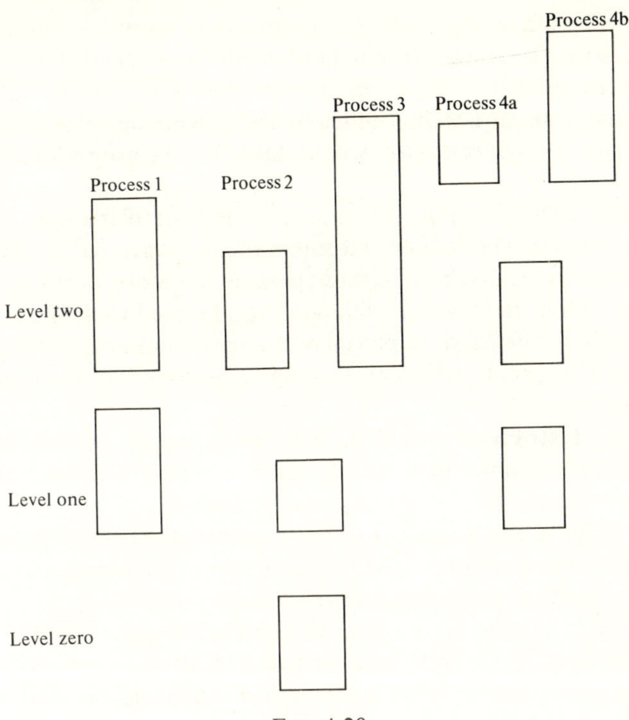


FIG. 4.20

**Problems**

**4.1.** §4.1 discusses four possible aims of an addressing method: the solution of the addressing problem (the need to be able to specify an adequate range of addresses without an excessively long instruction operand field), the provision of instruction modification, the representation of process structure, and the solution of the relocation problem. List the addressing methods described in this chapter, and tabulate the extent to which each method satisfies each of these aims. To what extent can each method help with store protection (see §5.1), the overlaying of store areas, and the sharing of store areas between processes?

**4.2.** (a) Estimate, for a computer with which you are familiar and which has both index registers and indirect addressing, the time overhead (as a percentage of execution time) for use of indirect addressing. How does this compare with the use of index registers?

(b) List the addressing methods described in this chapter, and tabulate their disadvantages (for example, hardware or software complexity, execution time overhead, fragmentation, and wastage of store).

**4.3.** On the IBM 7090 computer, the contents of the index register is subtracted from, rather than added to, the instruction operand field to give an effective address. How would this affect the programmer's use of indexing?

**4.4.** On the IBM 370 range of computers, the assembler allows a set of symbolic names to be defined and automatically converted to displacements from a specified base register, without any store locations being allocated. Show how such a technique can be used to define a 'template' of named fields, to be placed over a particular area of store (for example, a transput buffer) by loading its address into the specified base register.

**4.5.** What restrictions would have to be placed on the assembler-language programmer to make a program or subroutine dynamically relocatable on the IBM 370 range of computers?

**4.6.** Investigate how easy it is to write pure code (that is, programs divided into an invariant instruction area and a variable data area) on a small computer to which you have access.

**4.7.** Consider a computer (such as the DEC PDP-11) which has relative addressing. If a subroutine is written with all addresses relative to the program counter (in what is known as *position-independent code*), how is the relocation problem affected for this subroutine?

**4.8.** Evaluate the ease and flexibility of use of auto-indexing, as compared with normal index registers. How is the instruction execution time likely to be affected by this technique? Why does it shorten the instruction length?

**4.9.** If the jump instruction provides only direct addressing, how could the SMO instruction of page 156 be used to give the effect of indexed addressing for the jump instruction?

**4.10.** Evaluate the ease of address chaining, as discussed in § 4.4, both by an assembler-language programmer and by a compiler for a high-level language.

**4.11.** Investigate the behaviour of the following PDP-11 addressing modes, where the accumulator involved is number 7 (i.e. the program counter):

(a) direct auto-increment;
(b) indirect auto-increment;
(c) direct index;
(d) indirect index.

**4.12.** Consider a computer with segmentation in which two processes A and B share a subroutine C in a common segment. What problem do you see in having the subroutine access its data from the segments of the appropriate process (where corresponding segments in the two processes may have different segment numbers)? How could a communication region in a link segment solve this problem?

**4.13.** Why may the static and dynamic chains of MSCWs on the B6700 be different (as shown in Figure 4.19)? (Hint: what happens if procedure A calls procedure B, where A and B are declared at the same block level?)

**4.14.** The Burroughs B6700 computer provides a set of display registers D0 to D31 to allow access to variables on the stack belonging to the current and surrounding blocks. The University of Manchester MU5 and ICL 2900 range provide only three display registers: NB or LNB (the local name base register) for the current block, SN or SSN (the stack segment number register) for the process's outermost block, and XNB (the extra name base register) which can be set to refer to a point on the stack corresponding to any intermediate block. Investigate the structure of a number of typical Algol 60 programs, and compare these two architectures.

**4.15.** A *floating-point address* (Higman 1966) consists of two portions $[i,e]$, interpreted as the $i$th store unit of length $2^e$ bits. For example,

$[i,0]$ represents the $i$th bit;

$[i,5]$ represents the $i$th 32-bit word;

$[i,15]$ represents the $i$th block of 1024 32-bit words.

Consider a computer whose addresses are expressed in this form (with, say, 10 bits for $i$ and 6 bits for $e$). What effect would this have on the addressibility of store? How could this technique be extended to cover backing and archival storage?

# 5 The structure of the store

## 5.1. Storage protection

FOR ALL but the simplest computer systems the protection of certain areas of the computer store from uncontrolled access is a necessity. In a computer where the store contains a supervisor and a problem process, a store instruction with an invalid address might overwrite and corrupt either an instruction in the problem process (which could cause errors that are difficult to diagnose) or an instruction or piece of data in the supervisor, which would require the (possibly lengthy) process of reloading the computer store. In a multiprogramming environment it is vital that a problem process cannot inadvertently overwrite or jump into the supervisor or the other problem processes; the effect of any errors must be confined to the process in which they appear, otherwise system reliability is impossible to achieve, and great difficulties will be met in attempting to debug supposedly faulty programs.

It is also becoming important, especially in the service bureau environment, where the problem processes being run belong to different and perhaps rival institutions or businesses, to ensure that processes cannot copy information from other processes unless authorized to do so.

In addition to the protection of processes from each other, there are advantages to be gained from protection within a single process. If a process can be divided up into a number of sections, and the types of access to each section controlled, then certain errors can be trapped before data is hopelessly corrupted or, at least, early enough for information still to be available to enable the cause of the error to be easily diagnosed.

### *Software protection*

In some cases protection from programming errors can be provided by software, either by executing all programs interpretively or by adding extra instructions to perform run-time checks. There are two main problems in doing this, apart from the difficulty of ensuring that there are no errors in the interpreter or compiler which would cause errors in the problem process to be overlooked. The problems are:

(a) Speed, since the interpretation or error-checking may slow a program by a factor of up to fifty to one;
(b) Flexibility, since restrictions may have to be made on the types of process executed, in order to reduce the amount of run-time error checking. In particular, programming in assembler language may be disallowed.

Some of the early time-sharing systems, which provided a single language to be obeyed interpretively (for example JOSS (Shaw 1964)), were able to provide sufficient protection by software, but nearly all modern computers make available some form of hardware protection for areas of the main store. Backing storage and other transput devices are still protected by software, since the algorithms for controlling access are usually too complicated and changeable for implementation in hardware. Furthermore, the interpretation of transput requests by the supervisor does not have the speed penalty mentioned above, since any such penalty is absorbed by the speed differential between transput device and processor, and by the low ratio of the number of transput requests to the number of normal instructions. Notice, however, that even here the hardware is normally expected to disallow execution of transput instructions except in supervisor mode (as discussed in §3.5), and to control access to the areas of store holding the supervisor.

***Read-only stores***

One of the most obvious means of ensuring that instructions and constant data are not overwritten is the *read-only store*, often abbreviated to ROS (or ROM as an acronym for read-only memory). In this type of store words are read in the normal way, but the contents of the store cannot be altered by write signals from the processor.

Read-only stores have been built out of many different technologies (see for example, Renwick and Cole 1971, Chapter 10), but functionally they all fall into one of the following three classes:

(a) *Permanent* ROS, where the bit patterns representing the required store contents are imprinted in the store during the manufacturing process.
(b) *Field-Programmable* ROS (often called PROM, for programmable read-only memory, or less commonly *indelible store*), where the store is manufactured so that each bit is capable of holding either a

zero or a one. Then a particular set of binary patterns can later be written into the store, nowadays usually by driving electronic signals through it. After this, the bit patterns are permanent. The writing signals originate in a *PROM programmer*, which may be directly controlled by the computer itself.

(c) *Erasable* ROS (often *EPROM*, for erasable programmable read-only memory), where a method is available (often non-electronic) to erase the contents of the store, after which a new set of binary patterns can be inserted, as under (b). For example, some microprocessors have a ROS which can be erased by exposing it to ultraviolet radiation.

The overriding disadvantage of read-only storage is, of course, its inflexibility. It can only be used for write-protection, and provides protection for the whole store over all time; thus a set of instructions or constants could not be protected for just the life of a process. For this reason, read-only store is used only for information that remains fixed for long periods of time. It is commonly used to hold the microprograms in a microprogrammed computer, perhaps partly in permanent and partly in erasable read-only store, as mentioned in §3.6. Read-only stores have also been used to hold fixed parts of the supervisor (for example, on the University of Manchester Atlas), or to hold the fixed parts of all processes in critical environments such as on airborne and spaceborne computers: in particular most applications of microprocessors use ROS to hold the (permanent) program of instructions for the application.

***Protection bits and keys***

A more flexible method of protecting areas of store is to associate with each store location or block of locations a store protection register, whose contents define the type of access allowed to that location or block. In the simplest case the register is a single bit associated with each location or each fixed range of addresses (for example, each block of 256 words) which, if set, allows only read access to that location or within that range; if not set, full read and write access is allowed. For example, Figure 5.1 shows part of a store, with a store protection register associated with each block of 256 words; addresses 4096–351, 4352–607, and 4864–5119 can be read but not written, while addresses 4608–863 can be both read and written. The protection bits are set by a privileged instruction, so that a problem process cannot inadver-

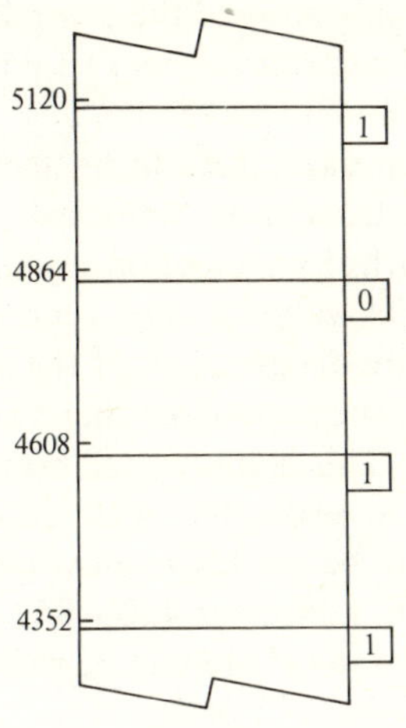


FIG. 5.1

tently or maliciously clear the protection bits of protected areas.

Consider a computer using this technique. While a problem process is running, all the store except the data areas of the problem process can be write-protected by setting the protection bits. However, to switch from one process to another in a multiprogramming environment, a number of protection bits will have to be set or cleared. For this reason the technique is used only on smaller computers where the expected environment is one problem process together with the supervisor. For a multiprogramming environment, a more sophisticated system, that of *protection locks* and *keys*, can be used.

In this protection system the store is again divided into a number of fixed blocks of contiguous addresses, and a small register (the *protection lock*) is associated with each block; a privileged instruction is provided to place values in these locks. Then each problem process is supplied (again by supervisor action) with a unique *protection key* value, which is held in a protection key register in the processor while that process has control of the computer. Whenever a store access is made for writing, the value in the protection key register is automatically compared with the value in the protection lock of the block containing the location being accessed. Only if the two values match is the access completed; otherwise an interrupt is taken into the supervisor.

Thus a different protection value is associated with each process currently residing in the main store of the computer (up to the maximum which can be held in the protection lock), and switching between processes requires only that the protection key register be reloaded. In order to allow common data areas to be accessed, a protection lock value of zero may be treated as 'unlocked', so that write-access is allowed to processes with any protection key value. Conversely if a process has a protection key value of zero, then this may be treated as a 'skeleton' key with write-access to all of the store, irrespective of the protection lock values; the supervisor therefore normally runs with a protection key of zero. This is illustrated by Figure 5.2, where a protection lock register is associated with each block of 256 words; addresses 4096–607 can be written to only by a process with a protection key value of 3 or 0, addresses 4608–863 can be accessed by any process, and addresses 4864–5119 can be written to only by a process with a protection key value of 7 or 0.

As we have described it, the protection lock and key system covers only write accesses; however, the protection lock could have a second one-bit field specifying, for each block, whether read accesses are also to be controlled. The former system is used on the IBM 360, the latter on the IBM 370: in both cases the maximum lock value is 15.

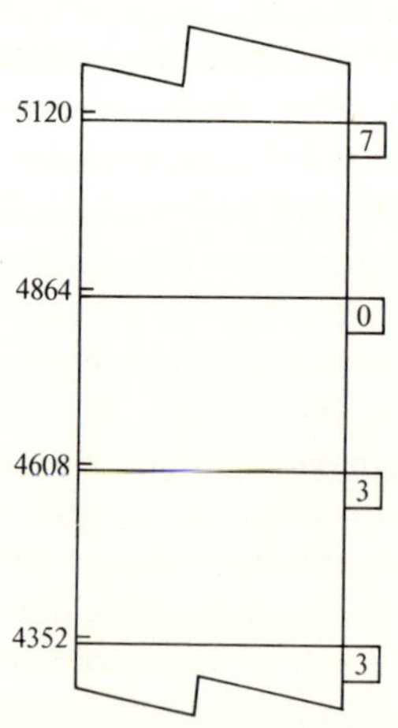


FIG. 5.2

### *Protection based on address mapping*

The above store protection systems are independent of any addressing structure on the computer, but often an addressing system which allows access to certain parts of the store can be employed to give protection of the rest of the store.

In §4.2 the concept of a base register was introduced: this base register, inaccessible to the problem process, holds the address of the lowest location occupied by the process and is used for relocation of that process. Computers using this system also have a *limit register* (or boundary or barricade register), containing the address of the highest location occupied by the process. Thus in Figure 4.4 the limit register would hold 28 671 when process one is running, and 61 439 when process two is running. The hardware adds the contents of the base register to each store address generated by the problem process, and also checks that the resultant address still lies between the values held in the base and limit registers before accessing the store. If the address lies outside this range, then an attempt (malicious or otherwise) has been made to access unauthorized areas of the store, and an interrupt is taken into the supervisor.

Notice that only two levels of protection are supplied; none for addresses within the acceptable range, total for addresses outside that range. If two base registers are provided, each is paired with a limit register to disallow access outside the two ranges of addresses specified; the values held in the base and limit registers can be changed only in supervisor mode, of course. Normally the two ranges of addresses have different allowable types of access: thus there is total protection for addresses outside the two ranges, read-only access to the range of addresses defined by the program base and limit registers (for constants and pure code instruction sequences), and full read and write access to the range of addresses defined by the data base and limit registers. There will be similar features in computers with three or more base registers.

We have considered the process of obtaining a physical store address, using base and limit registers, to be the addition of the base register contents followed by a check against the base and limit registers. The address added to the base register is usually assumed to be non-negative, so that the physical address need be checked only against the limit register. A common variation is for the limit register to contain the maximum address which may be specified by the problem process (20 479 or 32 767 in Figure 4.4), so that the check against the limit register may proceed in parallel with the addition of the base register contents.

### *Protection in segmentation systems*

In segmentation systems, the segment descriptor contains a segment length field as well as the segment base address field. The displacement (considered as a non-negative value) is checked against the contents of this length field before, or in parallel with, addition of the segment base address; an out-of-range displacement causes an interrupt into the supervisor. Further, the segment table base register is associated with a register holding the number of the highest segment in the table, and any generated segment number is compared with this before access to the table.

With segmentation it is not possible to allocate a fixed set of allowable access modes to each segment, as it was with two pairs of base and limit registers. So a further field in the segment descriptor specifies the access modes allowed if the displacement is in range; such a field is set up by supervisor action, when the length and base address fields of the descriptor are loaded.

In some computers, such as the Basic Language Machine, the allowable access modes are implied by the type field (for example, instructions must be read-only), but in a normal segmentation system the access mode field could allow or disallow each of three access modes:

Reading of instructions for execution;
Reading of data;
Writing of data.

In our earlier discussions of store protection the reading of instructions has been subsumed with the reading of data under read access, but there are advantages in separating them. On the one hand we can ensure that attempts are not made inadvertently to execute constant (read-only) data; and conversely we can ensure that the code of a subroutine is executable but not readable, for example a subroutine performing a security operation such as cryptographic decoding, or a subroutine in a service bureau where usage is charged. Also in earlier discussions write access to data implied read access, but we might wish to allow write access while disallowing read access to a segment, especially if the hardware does not distinguish between read access for data and read access for instructions. A fully general access mode field would allow any combination of these three modes, but often only a subset of these combinations is provided, such as read and write access together with read access alone.

A capability system (such as in the Plessey System 250 computer) is organized in a similar way: a capability consists of a base address, a length field, and a field defining the access rights to the block of locations described by the capability. Apart from the access modes discussed above, we now require a 'read capability' mode which allows a word from the block to be loaded into a capability register, giving addressability to a new block of locations. Further access modes are required to allow protected entry to subroutines. For further discussion of capabilities see Dennis and Van Horn (1966), Needham (1972), Fabry (1974), and Lister (1975, pp. 118–23).

### *Ring protection systems*

Consider the following situation. An instructor wishes to run a process consisting of a program which runs and assesses a student's program and then updates a mark list. Under a segmentation system the mark list occupies its own segment, but we wish to allow write access from the assessment program, but not from the student's program.

Here we have a common situation, where a process consists of two or more portions with differing levels of access rights. Similarly a process which normally runs at a user level of access rights will occasionally invoke portions of the operating system, and this requires access to various system tables, etc. What we appear to need is a generalization of the two-level problem/supervisor mode system described in §3.5. This is the *ring protection* system (Graham 1968), introduced on the Multics system (Organick 1972, Chapter 4; Schroeder and Saltzer 1972) and used on the ICL 2900 range. It is an extension to the basic segmentation system already described.

In this system we assume a range of levels of privilege (zero to 8 on Multics, zero to 15 on the ICL 2900 range). Whenever a process runs, it is at some one of these levels. The level a process runs at may change over the lifetime of the process, and its current level is specified in a processor register while the process occupies the processor. The lower the number of the level, the higher the level of privilege. A diagram of the levels of privilege can therefore be drawn as shown in Figure 5.3, where the closer a ring is to the centre the higher its privilege.

Each segment in the addressing space of a process is now allocated a fixed level number, as well as its usual access mode field. If a process

Rings of privilege.

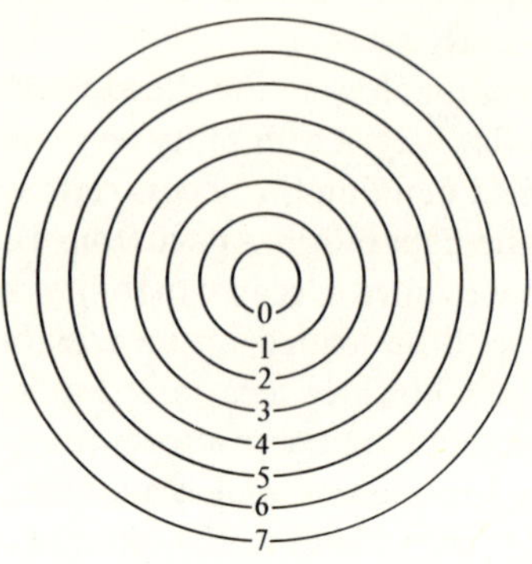


FIG. 5.3

attempts to access a segment, the usual access checks are made (the displacement must be less than the segment length, and the type of access must be authorized by the access mode field), but also the segment's level number is checked against the process's current level number. Only if the process's current level is less than or equal to the segment's level, is access allowed.

A process running at a particular level can therefore access only segments at the same or a higher-numbered (less privileged) level, and cannot access segments at a lower level. Thus a process's address space is divided into a number of levels of decreasing privilege. In fact the innermost (lowest-numbered, most-privileged) few levels are allocated to the operating system, with the most highly privileged part occupying level zero. This is the level at which the privileged instructions of §3.5 are executed, and the amount of code at this level is quite small. Thus it is possible to eliminate most of the sacrosanct nature of the supervisor, which becomes a collection of segments of code and data, with certain access rights, residing in the address space of each problem process. The highest-numbered (lowest-privileged) few levels are available for use by problem processes. Thus the instructor would run his assessment program at one of these levels, with the student's program at a higher-numbered level.

We have as yet said nothing as to how the process's current level is changed. This level is in fact the level number of the segment currently being executed. To change to a higher-numbered level (or of course the same level) the process simply jumps to an appropriate segment of code: it is assumed that the segment knows what it is doing. If an attempt is made to jump to a segment of code with a lower level number, then the jump must be directed to one of only a few locations in the segment. These are 'gates' or entry points to the segment, where as many checks as required can be programmed.

## 5.2. One-level store systems

The concept of the one-level store may be approached from two directions. First, there are many situations where a program and its data require more store than is physically available. Traditionally this problem is overcome by organizing some of the data into files held in backing storage, and explicitly programming read and write operations to transfer sections of the data into the main store as required by the program logic; and by dividing the program code into sections, and using overlaying techniques (probably with some help from operating system software). A problem with this reorganization is that the programmer may find it difficult to do efficiently, since the best organization depends on how much physical space is available and the exact sequence of operations the process carries out, and these will vary from run to run of the process.

Secondly, in a multiprogramming system, we wish to hold a number of processes in main store, so that the processor can be shared among them. But unless the store capacity of the computer is large (or we restrict the size of the processes' address spaces), the total store requirement of the processes may be greater than the computer's store capacity. Thus the switching from one process to another may involve dumping all or part of the store areas associated with the first process from the main store to magnetic disc or drum, in order to make room for the second process. Swapping the whole of each process is costly in backing storage transfers, while swapping only part of a process involves the trapping of accesses to those parts of the process's address space not currently in the main store.

The techniques we consider in this section involve dividing a process's address space into units which can be transferred between main and backing storage without intervention from the problem process. Since the transfer unit is commonly called a *page*, the term *paging* is normally used for this technique. The term *one-level store* is also used, since the unified virtual store that the problem process sees is physically partly in main and partly in backing storage, as organized by the hardware and supervisor. Such a one-level store system was first introduced on the University of Manchester Atlas computer (Fotheringham 1961; Kilburn, Edwards, Lanigan, and Sumner 1962), allowing the programmer to disregard the physical capacity of the main store when designing a program. Paging is discussed in Randell and Kuehner (1968), Denning (1970), and Parmelee, Peterson, Tillman, and Hatfield (1972).

### *Paging hardware*

In a typical paging system the main store is divided up into a number of fixed-size blocks of contiguous locations known as *page frames,* and the virtual store seen by the problem process (which may be much larger than the physical store of the computer) is divided into a number of blocks of contiguous addresses, the same size as the page frame, known as *pages*.

The effective virtual address generated by the problem process is split into two fixed-length fields in the form $[p, d]$, where $p$ is the page number and $d$ is the displacement within the page, which must be long enough to address any location in the page. The page and page frame size is always a power of two, to simplify the division of a virtual address into page number and displacement. The choice of page size depends on a number of factors. The larger it is, the smaller the amount of hardware and software involved in manipulating the paging system, and the more efficient the transput of pages from backing storage (in the sense that one transput operation brings in a large block of data). But conversely the larger the page, the more likely it is to hold unused locations, and the higher the cost of rounding up a process's address space to an integral number of pages (Denning 1970, pp. 169–71; Chu and Opderbeck 1974). A typical page size is 1K (1024) words.

At any point in time a particular page of the process is either in a page frame in the main store, or it is held in backing storage (magnetic disc or drum). There are two main methods of getting from the page number to the appropriate page frame. On the Atlas computer each page frame has associated with it a *page address register* which holds the number of the page currently occupying that page frame. The conversion from virtual to physical addresses performed by the hardware of the Atlas computer is then as follows:

Split the effective virtual address into the form $[p, d]$.
Compare $p$ with all page address registers (simultaneously).
If there is no match, then we have a *page fault* (see below).
Replace $p$ in $[p, d]$ by $p'$, the number of the matched page address register.
Access physical store address $[p', d]$.

This is illustrated in Figure 5.4. Notice its similarity to the technique of address mapping registers in §4.5.

In this method of performing the virtual-to-physical address mapping, we require one page address register per page frame, against all of which each generated page number is compared. Instead we can provide the address mapping information in an area of main store, the *page table*, similar to the segment table described in §4.5. This is by far the most common method of performing the mapping. However, notice that it introduces an extra main store cycle for each store access;

Examples of address mapping: virtual address (2,147) gives physical address (1,147); virtual address (1,147) gives a page fault.

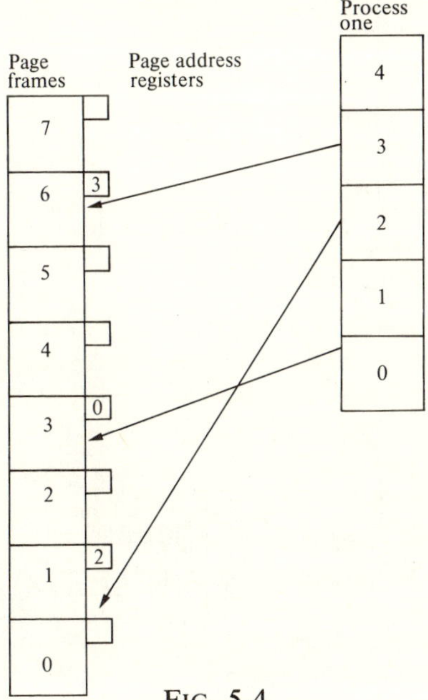


FIG. 5.4

in §5.5 we describe how this overhead is reduced.

In this second method there is one *page descriptor* in the page table for each page of the process, the descriptor for the *p*th page being at offset *p* in the table. The descriptor indicates whether the page is in main or backing storage, and its location (either its page frame number in main storage, or its block address in backing storage). Then the address translation performed by hardware is as follows:

Split the effective virtual address into the form $[p,d]$.
Obtain the descriptor at offset *p* in the page table.
If the page is currently in backing storage, generate a page fault.
Extract the physical page base address $p'$.
Access physical store address $[p',d]$.

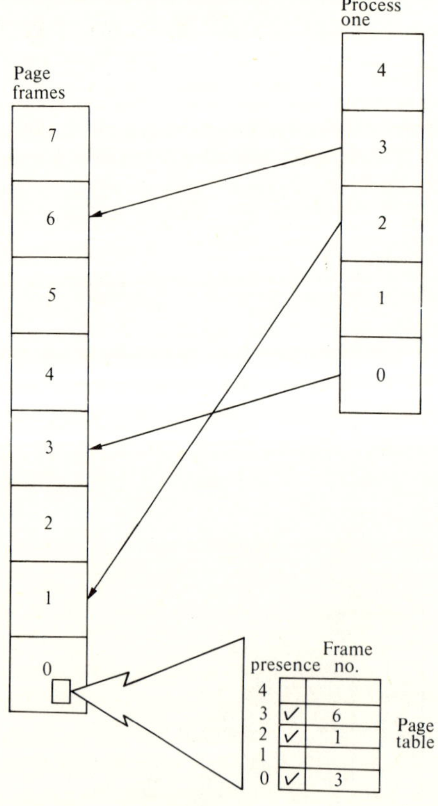


FIG. 5.5

This is illustrated in Figure 5.5. Notice how we have shown the page table as occupying a certain area in the main store: this is a further overhead of the method.

A paged computer is usually run with multiprogramming, so there must be some way of distinguishing pages which belong to different processes but have the same page number. If a page table system is used, then a separate page table is provided for each process; the switching between processes involves reloading a *page table base register* so that it refers to the page table of the new process. On a system with page address registers, two schemes are possible. One is to allocate a unique process number to each currently active process, and to extend the page address register with a field holding the process number to which the page belongs; the comparison operation in the address translation now compares the current process number and the page number with the two fields of the page address register. The other scheme, used on the Atlas computer, adds a 'lockout' bit to each page address register; on switching to a new process, all page frames are locked out (so that page comparison fails) except for those frames containing pages of the current process.

### *Page faults*

If the page to be accessed is not currently in a page frame in the main store, we have a *page fault* which causes an interrupt into the supervisor. The supervisor must move the required page into main store, so it initiates a read operation to transfer the page from a backing storage address specified in a supervisor table (perhaps the page table itself) to a suitable empty page frame in the main store. We have glossed over the problem, to which we will return later, of ensuring that there is an empty page frame when it is needed.

When the page transfer is complete (and the processor time may be used by another process in a multiprogramming system), the page address register or page descriptor is brought up to date, and the required store access can then be completed. Notice that a page fault causes the current instruction to be abandoned, but we must be able to return and complete it later, when the page fault has been dealt with. Usually the whole instruction is re-executed after the page fault has been serviced. There must therefore be restrictions on the order in which the sub-operations of instructions are performed, so as to ensure that all store accesses which could potentially cause page faults are initiated before any non-repeatable sub-operations.

***Paging and segmentation***

There are obvious similarities between paging and the system of linear segmentation described in §4.5, and in fact the terms are sometimes confused. The system of paging is aimed at making available a large, contiguously-addressed, one-level store, and (at least in theory) the programmer or compiler should be unaware of page boundaries and the fact that the addressing space is at any time partly in main and partly in backing storage. Segmentation is a system of reorganizing a linear store into a number of independent, contiguously-addressed areas or segments, and the programmer or compiler is aware of the separateness of segments and the allocation of segment names or numbers.

It is common for segmentation and paging to appear together in a computer (for example, on Multics, the IBM 370 range, and the MU5 and ICL 2900 range), so that segments can be very large and only a small portion of each active segment is in page frames in main store at any time. Typically an effective virtual address is made up of three fields; a segment number *s*, a page number *p*, and a displacement *d*, in the form [*s*,*p*,*d*]. The segment descriptor now refers to the page table of a segment rather than to the segment itself. The address translation performed by hardware is now:

Split the effective virtual address into the form [*s*,*p*,*d*].
Check *s* against the segment table length register.
Obtain the segment descriptor at offset *s* in the segment table (whose address is in the segment table base register).
If the segment's page table is not in main store, generate a *segment fault*.
Check *p* against the segment length.
Check the type of access against the segment's access rights (and perform any testing for the ring protection system, if present).
Extract the base address *x* of the segment page table.
Obtain the page descriptor at offset *p* from *x*.
If the page is not in main store, generate a page fault.
Extract the physical page address *y*.
Access physical store address [*y*,*d*].

This is illustrated in Figure 5.6. We have incorporated the protection checking discussed in the previous section, and a *segment presence bit* so that a non-active segment (and its page table) can be removed from

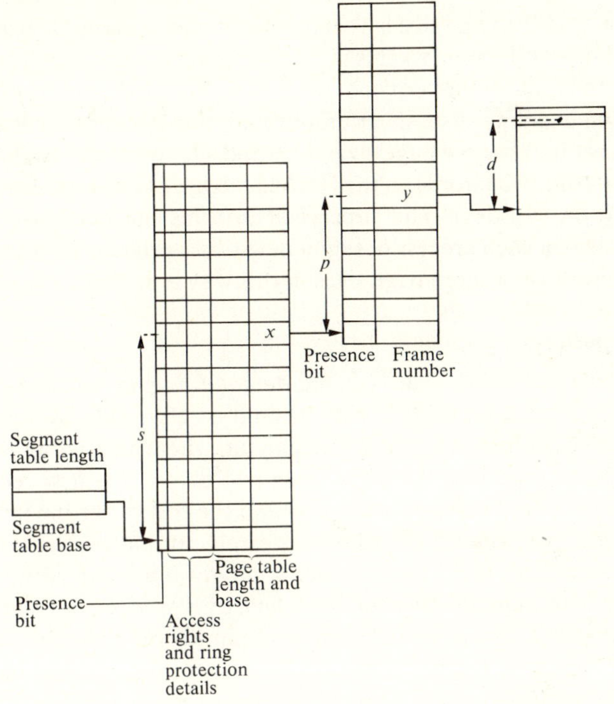


FIG. 5.6

main store. If the segment table is very large, it may also be paged into main store as required. Note the number of extra store cycles required for each store access, and the complexity of the hardware translation process: it is matched by the complexity of the software required to support it (as for example on the Multics system, described in Organick 1972). Note also the amounts of store taken up by page and segment tables, and by rounding each segment up to an integral number of pages.

On the Burroughs computers discussed in §4.6, a rather different scheme is employed. Instead of paging a segment into main store, the whole of each segment is either in main or in backing storage. As above, each segment descriptor contains a presence bit, to indicate whether or not the segment is in main store; an access to a segment not in main store causes supervisor action to transfer the segment from backing storage. Thus on these computers the page is the same as the segment, and the page size is variable from one to many thousands of words. For small segments this is, of course, very economical, since an allocation of main store does not need to be rounded up to the nearest page. Some paging systems attempt to provide part of this flexibility by having two possible page sizes (2K and 4K bytes on the IBM 370 range, 64 and 1024 words on the GE 645, although the former size was not used on Multics). The supervisor informs the hardware of the chosen size for each process or segment within a process. How valuable it is to have two or more page sizes in this way is unclear.

***Paging policies***

We have described what is called *demand paging,* where a page is transferred to the main store only when it is referred to by a process. This is to be compared to *predictive* paging, where an attempt is made to transfer a page into the main store just before it is first required. Because of the difficulty of prediction and the cost of getting it wrong, such predictive paging by hardware is rarely attempted. Some operating systems have facilities by which a programmer can request that pages be held in main store for the whole of a process, or can inform the supervisor that a page will soon be required or is no longer needed, but such features are not common. The operating systems on most paged computers provide demand paging as the policy for bringing pages into main store.

When a page has to be brought into main store from backing storage, an empty page frame must be available to hold it. We can ensure that at all times there are a number of empty page frames available, or we can free a page frame only when required. In either case, the supervisor must, from time to time, choose a page frame to free, copy the page it contains to backing storage, and update the relevant page descriptor or page address register. If the page to be returned to backing storage has not been altered since it was last transferred into main store, the recopying can be omitted and the page frame simply marked empty. For this reason an *update* or *change* or *write bit* is usually associated with each page frame. This is set to zero when a page is copied into a frame, and is forced by hardware to one whenever a write access is made to any word in the frame. When a page frame is to be freed, the page contained in it need be recopied to backing storage only if the update bit is set to one.

A number of strategies have been considered for choosing the page to be relegated to secondary storage; these may take account of update bit settings to cut down on transput traffic where possible. The strategy chosen is built into part of the supervisor known as the *page turning algorithm;* although it is part of the software, the strategy chosen will require certain hardware support, so two popular strategies are mentioned below. Any strategy can, of course, be defeated by a suitably pathological process or set of processes, resulting in the phenomenon of *thrashing,* when pages are swapped wildly in and out of the main store.

What we wish to do is relegate the page that will not be accessed for longest, and it is usually assumed that a good estimate of this is the page which has not been referenced for longest. This is the basis of the *least recently used* or *LRU* algorithm. This algorithm could be implemented as a list of all page frames in order of recency of reference, to be reordered by hardware after each store access. However, because of the length of the page list which would have to be reordered, paging systems tend to rely on the technique of *use* or *reference* bits. A use bit is associated with each page frame, is set to zero when a page is copied into the frame, and is forced by hardware to one whenever an access (for read or write) is made to a word in the frame. If the use bits are periodically reset to zero by the supervisor, then at any time those page frames with zero bits have not been accessed in the current interval; at a page fault one of these pages is relegated to secondary storage, as an approximation to the least recently used page.

A more recent algorithm is that of the *working set,* introduced by Denning (1968a). This technique, which marks for relegation any pages of a process not referred to over an interval of recent process time, can be implemented with use bits. However more sophisticated hardware, such as on the Maniac II computer (Morris 1972) at the University of California, preserves the recent reference history of each page and automatically sets the relegation marker. For a more detailed discussion of paging policies see Belady (1966), Denning (1968b), and Madnick and Donovan (1974, pp. 148–65).

### 5.3. Special uses of store locations

In the classic Von Neumann computer a rigid distinction is made between the collection of named store devices or registers in the processor, each of which is allocated its own small set of functions, and the (much larger) collection of store elements making up the main store, which are used interchangeably and are distinguishable only by their addresses.

However, on many computers, certain store addresses refer to locations which are distinguishable in some way from the generality of store locations. This can occur in three ways:

(a) A store location may have additional electronics associated with it, so that it can carry out some special function.
(b) a register forming part of the processor may be allocated a store address, so that it can be referred to by that address as well as (or instead of) by an explicit register name.
(c) a hardware function (for example, the transput system), which requires to access store may have fixed store address 'wired into it', rather than using any specified location. This location is distinguishable then, not because it performs some special action, but because it is the source or destination of some data associated with the hardware function.

Examples in each of these classes can be found in this section (see problem 5.8).

There are several possible reasons for distinguishing store locations in this way. Chief of these is cost, since it is cheaper to provide a location as one of a set of store elements than as a special register, although this must be set against the loss in speed in accessing the register where necessary. Second, it may be more convenient in programming to treat certain registers in the same way as store elements. Third, when an instruction addresses one of these special store locations, the operand field can be considered as an extension of the operation field or accumulator specification field, thus effectively extending the length of the instruction word.

### *Index registers and accumulators*

One candidate for implementation as store elements instead of as special processor registers is the set of (one or more) index registers. We have already seen an example of this in the auto-indexing registers of the DEC PDP-8 computer described in §4.3. Instead of providing a set of index registers in the processor and an extension of the addressing mode field to specify them, reasons of cost required that index registers be implemented as store elements, and the auto-indexing mode of addressing provided a convenient way of overcoming the need to extend the addressing mode field.

In small computers which provide conventional indexing, it is fairly common for some or all of the index registers to be implemented as store elements. For example, store addresses 1–3 might represent index registers 1–3, although there is no need for the index register number to be matched by the address of the store element implementing it.

We have already mentioned the provision of accumulators in a computer in the form of a small array. The accumulators can be allocated specification or index numbers within the array independently of the store addresses (as on the IBM 370 range), or they may replace the first few locations in the addressing range (as on the DEC PDP-10 computer). Thus we might have a computer in which store addresses zero to 15 specify the accumulators zero to 15.

Notice that inter-accumulator operations can now be expressed in a single-address instruction by specifying one accumulator in the operand field; thus 'add accumulator 4 to accumulator 5' is represented by the instruction 'add store address 4 to accumulator 5'. This technique may be used to reduce the number of different operations in the instruction set. However in a computer with a variable-length instruction format there are advantages in extending the operation codes so as to provide inter-accumulator operations with a shorter instruction length.

On a small computer the accumulators might in fact be implemented as store elements; however, on larger computers we will wish to take advantage of faster (and more expensive) technologies. Thus we simply interpret a store address in the range zero to, say, 15 as a reference to one of the fast store elements or accumulators, and addresses above 15 as references to a normal store element. There are then no normal store elements with addresses below 15.

However this raises a problem when the main store is shared between a supervisor and one or more problem processes, since each process is allocated one or more contiguous address ranges which include virtual addresses representing the accumulators, and the physical addresses representing the accumulators will be in the protected area of the supervisor.

Consider for definiteness a computer, with a single pair of base and limit registers, in which store addresses zero to 15 represent the accumulators; suppose a single problem process is running which requires a virtual address range of zero to 20 479, as shown in Figure 5.7. The virtual addresses 16–20 479 might be allocated to physical addresses 8208–28 671. Then the address translation hardware is simply

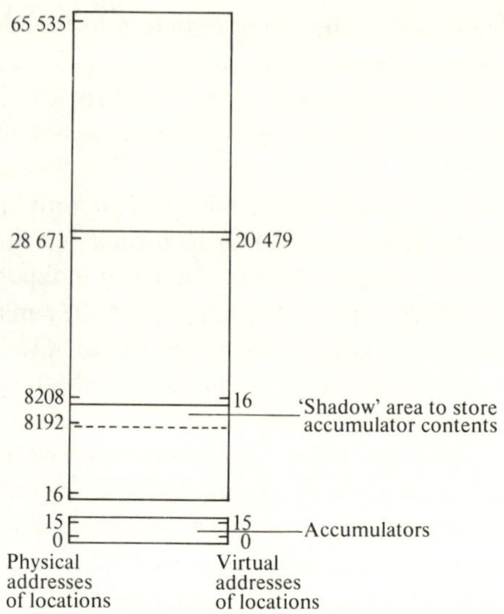


FIG. 5.7

bypassed for virtual addresses zero to 15, so that the physical accumulators are referred to.

On entry to the supervisor, or switching to another problem process, the current accumulator contents must of course be saved. A common technique is to allocate virtual addresses zero to 20 479 for the problem process instead of 16–20 479, so that the virtual addresses zero to 15 can be used as an area in which to save the contents of the accumulators at a process switch.

If the accumulators can be addressed as store locations, we may be able to move instructions into the accumulators and execute them there; this can be done on the DEC PDP-10 computer, for instance, and is used for fast execution of an iterative loop.

### *The V-store or image store*

Together with the accumulators and index registers, the program counter is the other important program-accessible processor register. The program counter has never (to the author's knowledge) been implemented as a store element, although on a few computers it is addressable as one of an array of accumulators.

Transput operations are a fertile source of dedicated store locations, and some examples will be mentioned in §§ 6.2 and 6.3. One technique (discussed on page 249) is worth anticipating, since it can be generalized for non-transput use: this is the allocation of a store address to each of the transput control registers, so that the transput system is controlled by normal data manipulation instructions rather than by special transput instructions.

Consider now the different control registers we might expect to find in the processor. There will be a process mode register, a number of registers for the store mapping and protection system, sets of flags indicating hardware conditions (such as faults), etc. One way of organizing this heterogeneous mass of registers was suggested in § 3.5, as an array of control registers to be manipulated by a rather general group of instructions. A second method is to allocate a store address to each register, so that normal data manipulation instructions can be used to read or alter register values as if in store locations (but only in supervisor mode). We may extend this technique by assigning store addresses to all processor registers. Such a range of addresses referring to the processor registers, and accessible only from supervisor mode, is called a *V-store* (a term introduced on the University of Manchester Atlas: Sumner, Haley, and Chen 1962), or an *image store;* it is used, for example, on the ICL 2900 range.

### Clocks and interval timers

A requirement for any computer used for real-time or time-sharing work is a means for measuring the passage of time. Even in a simple batch-processing system, it is desirable to be able to put the time of day on the printed output. This requirement is met by the optional or standard provision of a clock. The clock may be a special transput device or a special register in the processor, but it is commonly implemented as a dedicated location in main store, and we will discuss it in that context.

There are several possible forms of clock. On the IBM 370 range a 'time-of-day' clock is provided. This is a binary counter which is incremented by hardware at a fixed rate (once per microsecond). Conventionally it is initialized so that a zero count would represent 0000 hours GMT on the first of January 1900, so that the current date and time can be deduced from an inspection of the clock value (the cycle length of the counter is well over a century). A second register, the clock comparator, can be loaded with a value which the hardware continuously compares with the clock value, causing an interrupt as soon as the clock value is greater. This allows the supervisor to take control from a (possibly overrunning) problem process at a certain time or after a certain period of time.

On many computers an *interval timer* is provided rather than a clock. This is a dedicated store location whose contents are automatically decremented by one at a fixed rate. On the IBM 370 range two timers are provided, one running at 300 cycles/second and one at one million cycles/second. When the contents of the interval timer reaches zero, an interrupt is generated into the supervisor.

The contents of the interval timer can be loaded with a suitable value to generate an interrupt after a certain period of time, or the contents can be read to measure time intervals. By keeping track of the number of times the interval timer has reached zero, the supervisor can provide the time of day, assuming suitable operator initialization at the beginning of the day.

We have assumed that the clock or interval timer is updated at a fixed rate as long as power is available; on some computers the updating is done only when the processor is executing instructions, or only when the processor is in problem mode (why is this useful?).

### *Miscellaneous constants and functions*

Occasionally a number of registers or store locations are dedicated to holding fixed values required by the process and are therefore protected from being overwritten. A common case is where accumulator or index register zero always holds the value zero, as for example processor register B0 on the CDC 6600 computer. This is to be distinguished from an addressing mode field of zero meaning 'no indexing', rather than 'index with register zero'. Some of the earlier computers provided several useful constants; for example the Ferranti Pegasus computer had dedicated, write-protected store locations holding zero, minus one, one-half, $2^{-10}$, and $2^{-13}$. A further example of store locations containing fixed values is one form of bootstrap loader, discussed in § 8.3.

Finally mention should be made in this section of the allocation of data manipulation operations to particular store elements. This is not a common technique. It was used on the National Physics Laboratory's Pilot ACE computer (Wilkinson 1953). In this early computer, transferring a number from store address *n* to store address 16 (written *n*-16) simply performed a copy, overwriting the previous contents of location 16. However, transferring a number to store address 17 or 18 caused it (respectively) to be added to or subtracted from the contents of store address 16. Thus address 16 had some of the functions of an accumulator, and destination addresses 17 and 18 could be seen as the input to the adder/subtractor unit. The instruction '15–17' was therefore equivalent to the single-address instruction 'add to accumulator the contents of store address 15'. Other functions could be obtained by quoting a suitable source or destination address in a transfer instruction of the form '*n–m*'.

Such techniques have occasionally been used to extend the instruction set of a small computer. Thus, on the Apollo Guidance Computer (Alonso, Blair-Smith, and Hopkins 1963; Savage and Drake 1967), shifts are performed by sending values to one of four special store locations; for example, if an instruction is performed which stores a value in location 17, the value is in fact stored arithmetically shifted right one bit. The shifted value can then be reloaded from location 17 for further processing.

## 5.4. Improving store access time

The maximum rate at which accesses can be made to the main store is governed by the *cycle time* of the store; that is, by the time which must elapse for the store to recover after a read or write access, before a further access may be made. In some computers there is a close connection between the timing of the processor and the cycle time of the main store; the rate at which the processor accesses the store for instructions and data is synchronized with the cycle time of the store.

However there is a great disparity between the speed attainable by the electronics of the processor and the cycle times attainable by main store techniques, especially store techniques which can economically provide large capacities. In order not to slow down the processor unnecessarily, the store can be uncoupled from the processor, so that both operate independently and asynchronously, except when intercommunication is required.

The processor from time to time sets up a store address to be accessed and (for a write access) a data word to be written, and then requests the store to perform a read or write. For a write, the store signals when the operation is complete. For a read, the store signals when the requested data is available from the store, and (if necessary) when the operation is complete and a further operation can be requested.

The processor may then continue with other tasks or await the signal from the store as required. This uncoupling of store from processor is necessary if there are several processors accessing a common main store, and makes it easier to attach transput devices which directly access the store. Further, if the store access time is variable (as discussed below), the processor operates as fast as it can access data rather than being tied to the length of the 'worst case' access time; this is particularly important in computers with functional parallelism, as discussed in § 8.2. Decoupling the processor and store is considered in more detail in problem 5.10.

***Multiple store modules***

If the store is uncoupled from the processor, then we can attach several *modules* or *banks* of store to one processor, each module operating independently and asynchronously. We hope that, by making successive accesses to different modules of store, the effective access time of the store as a whole will be less than the cycle time of the individual store modules.

For example, suppose we have two modules of store as shown in Figure 5.8. A store access (to, say, module zero) for an instruction is normally followed by an access to store for data. If this piece of data were held in module one, the access could be commenced before the first module was ready for a further access.

If, as in this example, a main store is implemented as a number of store modules each holding a contiguous range of addresses, we have what is known as *high-order interleaving* of store modules, since the particular module is chosen by inspection of the high order bits of the store address. The supervisor might attempt to hold the instructions and data of a process in different store modules.

Another more common means of allocating addresses among a number of store modules is by *low-order interleaving,* where the store module is specified by the low-order bits of the address. If there are $m$ modules, then a particular module holds every $m$th store address; thus with two modules, one module holds all even addresses and one all odd addresses. The rationale behind this technique is that store accesses for instructions, and often for data, tend to be consecutive store addresses. Consecutive addresses should therefore be allocated to different modules in the hope of improving access time.

Some computers, (such as the DEC PDP-10) allow interleaving on both high and low order bits. Thus with four modules we would have

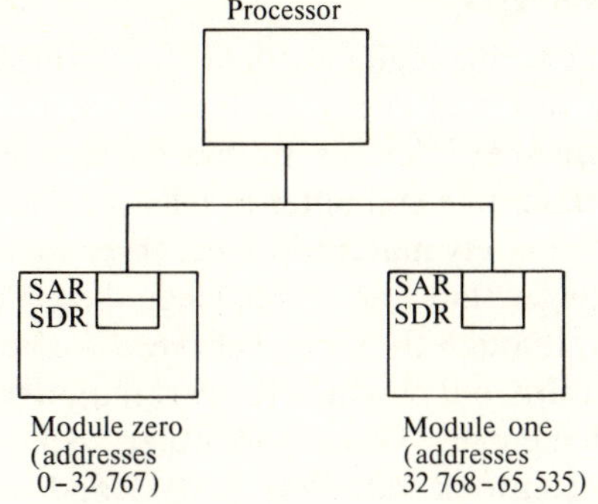


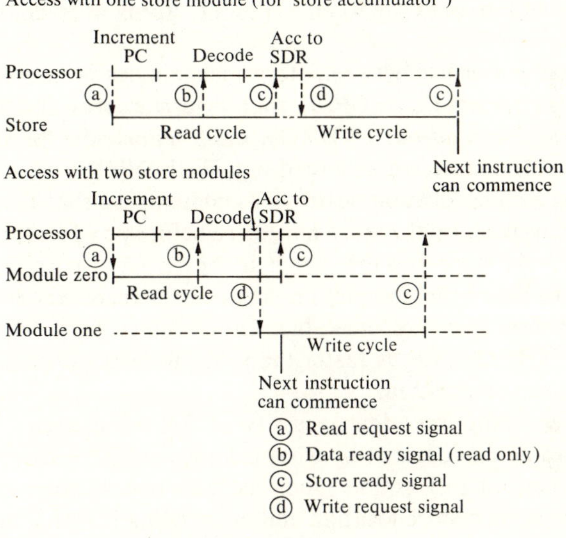


FIG. 5.8

even and odd addresses in the first half of the range in modules zero and one respectively, and even and odd addresses in the second half of the range in modules two and three, respectively. We are thus endeavouring to separate both consecutive addresses and concurrently used blocks of addresses (such as instructions and data), in order to reduce the effective access time below the cycle time. Interleaving is discussed in Lorin (1972, pp. 66–8) and Burnett and Coffman (1970, 1975).

### *A variety of store technologies*

When we consider the technologies available for main store, we see a spectrum from very fast and costly devices, through a range of medium-priced, medium-speed devices, to slow storage media which are cheap enough to attach to a computer in massive quantities. The three ranges are approximately matched by the three main technologies: semiconductor stores; thin film stores (including plated wire); and ferrite core stores, although the second of these is much less common than the first and third, out of which the vast majority of modern main stores are implemented. These and other technologies are described in detail in Renwick and Cole (1971) and Middelhoek, George, and Dekker (1976). Here we are concerned only with the functional differences between types of store, as seen from the processor.

One major division between store technologies is between stores with *destructive read-out* (DRO), such as ferrite cores, and those with *non-destructive read-out* (NDRO); most semiconductor stores are operated with non-destructive read-out. With DRO stores, the action of reading a store location destroys its contents, so that the contents must be rewritten by the store hardware before any further accesses are made to the store. It is this which, in the earlier discussion, we have assumed to delay the completion signal for a read access after the requested data becomes available. Other things being equal, read access to NDRO stores is faster than that to DRO stores, since the rewrite process is omitted.

However, sometimes the necessity of following each read by a rewrite can be made use of by what is known as the *split-cycle* technique. When an instruction (such as 'add one to store contents') involves reading a store location and overwriting it with a new value, the overwriting can take the place of the rewrite which must follow the (destructive) read.

Another division is between *passive* stores (such as ferrite cores) which retain the data stored in them when power is cut off, and *active* stores (such as semiconductor store), which require power to retain data. The latter are therefore *volatile,* losing stored information if power is cut off. A computer which must restart itself and continue operating as soon as power returns after a power failure must have at least some non-volatile storage.

Some stores lose information if it is not regenerated from time to time. These stores must initiate a periodic regeneration pass over all elements, to read and rewrite the information being held. An early example of a store technology requiring regeneration is the electrostatic storage tube: some forms of semiconductor store also require regeneration. The processor is not normally aware of this regeneration, since it is performed by the store hardware when it is not satisfying read or write requests.

Apart from store technologies, the effective access time of the processor to main store is affected by the size of the unit of store accessed, or *width* of the store. An example of this is the range of main stores on the IBM 360 (see Bell and Newell 1971, p.563). Here a large range of store access times was required for different models in the series, based on only a small range of store cycle times. This range was attained partly by interleaving store modules, but also by having the store width range from 1 byte on the slower models to 16 bytes on the faster models.

In some computers the main store can be made up of several modules, implemented in a number of different store technologies, but functionally indistinguishable to the processor. For example DEC supply a ferrite core module and two different forms of semiconductor store for the PDP-11 computer, and a main store may be built up from a selection of several of these. Thus we have a range of addresses designating store elements, some of which have a shorter access time than others. Typically the faster store elements are allocated the lower addresses, but it is up to the supervisor to be aware of these boundaries and to allocate store areas to processes appropriately.

### *A hierarchy of stores*

In many computers several different types of main store are distinguishable. If we add backing and archival storage media, we obtain a storage hierarchy diagram as shown in Figure 5.9, where capacity increases and speed decreases in a downwards direction. It is unlikely that all these levels would be present on any particular computer.

Level a represents the accumulators and other registers in the processor; as we have seen, these may in some cases be assigned main store addresses or (less commonly) be implemented as main store locations. Level d is the standard main store, and levels f to k are transput devices; level f may be integrated with main store in a 'one-level store' system.

Let us first consider e, the *mass store*. This consists of large quantities (several million words) of random access storage, typically fer-

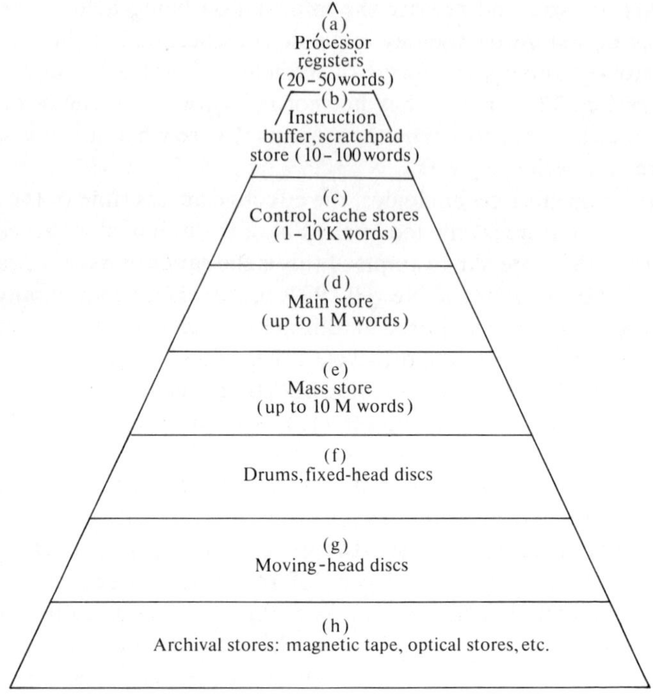


FIG. 5.9

rite cores. The transfer time for a block of words may be similar to that for the faster devices in level f (such as magnetic drums), but the advantage of the mass store is its access time, since devices at level f have to rotate to the correct position before the transfer can begin. Mass storage is used to hold seldom-accessed blocks of instructions and data, or provides a buffer between levels d and f in a 'one-level store' system. In some computers the mass store is distinguishable from the main store only by the range of addresses allocated to it and by its speed: this is the case with LCS (large capacity store) on the IBM 360 and 370. In such cases instructions and data are stored and accessed similarly in either store, although for efficiency commonly used instructions and data will be held in main store. In other computers, the main and mass stores are functionally distinct and have independent addressing ranges, as on the ECS (extended core store) of the CDC 6600 computer. Here instructions and data cannot be individually accessed in mass store, and instructions are provided to transfer blocks of words between the mass and main stores. It is probable that as mass store becomes cheaper and new technologies become available at this level, it will take over some of the storage functions currently carried out by level f.

As shown in Figure 5.9, there are a number of possible forms of small fast store at levels b and c. These stores are usually accessible directly only by the hardware and are transparent to all software. The accumulators and other special processor registers may be implemented as elements of a very small array of fast storage, instead of as a miscellaneous collection of registers; this store is usually termed *local* or *scratchpad* store. The *control* store is the store (often read-only) containing micro-instructions to implement the instruction set on a microprogrammed computer.

### *Cache stores*

The 'one-level store' system of the Atlas and other paged computers attempts to simulate a large main store by means of a small main store together with a large backing store, by taking advantage of the observed patterns of store access. The same technique can be used to simulate a large, fast main store by means of a small, fast store together with a large, slower main store. This technique of the *slave* or *look-aside* store was proposed by Wilkes (1965). It is used on the IBM 360 model 85 computer and several models of the IBM 370 range, where it is known as the *buffer* or *cache* store. The latter term seems to be the one in most common use for this technique.

At any point in time, the cache store contains copies of the contents of several locations in the main store, each tagged by the store address to which it corresponds. When a store location is to be read by the processor, its address is searched for in the cache store. If found, the contents are passed to the processor immediately. If the address is not found in the cache store, the required word must be read from the main store to the processor, and a copy of it (together with its address) is placed in the cache store to speed up subsequent accesses.

Rather than copying just the word required, the hardware may copy several words (including the required word) into the cache store, in the hope of taking advantage of *locality of reference* (that is, the tendency for a sequence of store accesses to be clustered close together), to obviate later main store accesses.

The cache store technique attempts to simulate a large and fast store with a large, slow store together with a small, fast store. The effective speed of the cache store depends on its *hit rate:* that is, how often a required store access can be satisfied from the cache store rather than from the main store. This in turn depends on how well clustered store accesses are. If each effective store address is equally likely to be anywhere within the process's address space, then the cache store would have to be a large fraction of the main store size before it would have any significant effect on performance. In fact processes exhibit to a greater or lesser degree (depending on the kind of tasks they are performing) the phenomenon of locality of reference, both in space and time: after a store location has been accessed, it is likely to be accessed again, and other nearby store locations are likely to be accessed. Figures of more than 90 per cent success in finding a required store word in the cache have been reported with quite small cache stores (Liptay 1968; Murphey and Wade 1970). Figure 5.10 (taken from Madnick and Donovan 1974, p.196) shows the effective size, cost per byte, and access time of the IBM 370 model 158, assuming a 90 per cent hit rate.

When the cache store becomes full, there is the problem (as with paging systems) of deciding which words are to be relegated to the main store, exacerbated here by the fact that for speed the decision must be made by hardware. On the IBM 360 and 370 only read access causes words to migrate to the cache store. A write access alters the relevant location both in the main store and (if present) in the cache store. Thus no recopying from cache to main store is required at relegation, and the selected part of the cache is simply overwritten. The technique of use bits, described in § 5.2, could be used, but since there is only a small number of entries in the cache store, they are reordered by recency of access after each read access; the least recently used entry is then the one to be relegated.

| | Cache store | Main store | Effective store |
|---|---|---|---|
| Size (bytes) | 8K | 1M | 1M |
| Cost (per byte) | $4.00 | 50¢ | 53¢ |
| Access time (average) | 230ns | 1μs | 307ns |

FIG. 5.10

We will meet cache stores again in the next section, when we discuss the technology out of which they are constructed. Cache stores are discussed in Katzan (1971b), Kaplan and Winder (1973), and Bell, Casasent, and Bell (1974).

### *Instruction buffers*

Cache stores derive their effectiveness from the statistical properties of processes such that accesses exhibit locality of reference, and read accesses are much more common than write accesses. *Instruction buffers* are based on the rationale that access to store for instructions is effectively read-only and exhibits strongly non-random behaviour.

An instruction buffer enables one or more instructions expected to be required in the future to be automatically read from main store into the buffer while the current instruction is being executed. Then these instructions can be executed from the buffer more quickly than they could be executed from main store.

A very simple example occurs in computers which store two instructions to a word. The fetching of the first instruction of a pair causes the second also to be read, and saved in an instruction buffer, until the first instruction has been executed. Thus, if we ignore jumps, about half the instructions executed would not need a store access to fetch them.

More generally an instruction buffer is likely to hold some tens of instructions, so that a short loop of instructions can be executed directly from the buffer, with no main store accesses for instructions. Since such buffers are common on the functionally parallel computers of § 8.2, we discuss them further there.

## 5.5. Associative stores

The main stores that we have considered in this book are all *coordinate-addressed.* That is, the store is a vector of elements, any one of which may be accessed by specifying its coordinate or index within the vector. With several store modules, the effective address is still a coordinate or index, within a vector implemented as a number of separate shorter vectors. The addressing schemes described in Chapter 4 are all attempts to interpose some form of structure between the instructions and this linear store.

Suppose now that we wish to search for a particular item in a block of main store. This involves inspecting all or a selection of the items in the block until the required item is found, or until it becomes clear that

that item is not in the block. As described in §3.4, search instructions are provided on some computers. This drastically reduces the number of store accesses for instructions during the search, but at best the number of store accesses for data is of the order of the logarithm to base two of the number of items in the block.

We would like to be able to compare the required item simultaneously with all the items in the block, and obtain a result in only a few store cycles. Since we are attempting to access a store location by its contents which are associated in some way with the required item, this would be a *content-addressed* or *associative* store. We use these terms as synonyms, although some writers (for example, Bell and Newell 1971, p. 76) would use only the term *content-addressed* for the stores discussed in this section, reserving the term *associative* for a storage system with a more general ability to relate one piece of data to another.

An associative store, as shown in Figure 5.11, consists of a number of store elements each equipped with some electronic logic to perform matching. An item to be searched for is placed in the *interrogation*

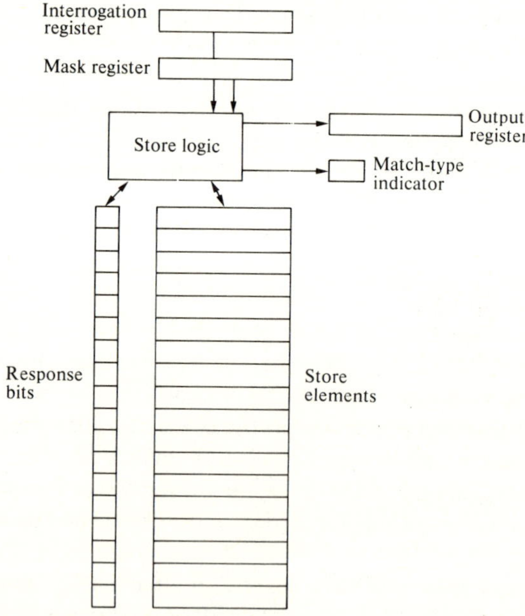


FIG. 5.11

*register* (or *argument, search, comparand register*). and the store is placed in *search mode*. The logic attached to each element then compares the contents of the element with the contents of the interrogation register. A single *response* or *match bit* is attached to each store element; this is set to one if the element matches, and to zero otherwise. Since all comparisons are performed simultaneously, one operation cycle after search mode has been entered the response bits which are set to one indicate which store elements match the contents of the interrogation register.

In some applications of associative stores the interrogation register is always compared against the same fixed subfield of the store elements. However, a general-purpose associative store would have an interrogation register of the same length as the store elements, and a *mask register* to select those parts of the interrogation register which are to be compared. Only those parts of the interrogation register corresponding to bit positions set to one in the mask register are compared to the store elements. A zero bit in the mask register indicates a 'don't care' bit position in the interrogation register, which always matches 'true' whatever the contents of the corresponding bit in the store element.

Thus the response bit is set for each store element which matches the contents of the interrogation register in those positions corresponding to one bits in the mask register, irrespective of the contents of other parts of the store element. An example is given in Figure 5.12 of the result of a search. In some associative store technologies it is possible to set a value of 'don't care' (as well as zero and one) into the bit positions of the store element itself, and this can be used for more complex forms of matching.

Over the years many research papers and articles have been written suggesting technologies for, and applications of, associative stores (Slade and McMahon 1956; Kaplan 1963; McAteer, Capobianco, and Koppel 1964; McKeever 1965; Hellerman and Hoernes 1968). However, computer main stores are still coordinate addressed, because associative stores (with their requirement for a certain amount of search logic attached to each element) cannot compete economically at module sizes of several tens of thousands of words. Thus, apart from research projects into their construction and use, practical associative stores are found in two forms:

(a) Small associative stores (several tens of words, up to a few hun-

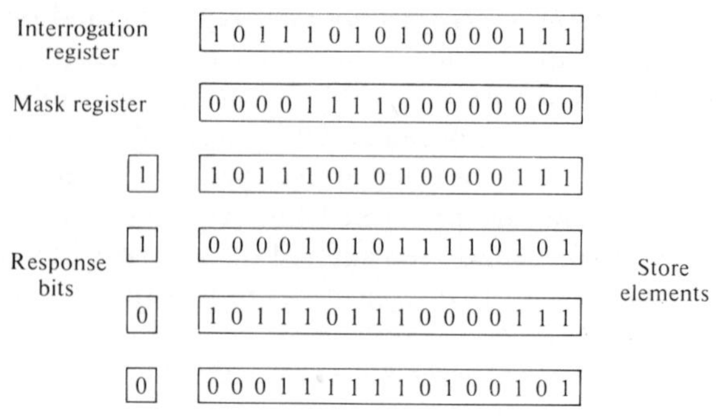


FIG. 5.12

dred) added to computers with conventional main stores, in order to manage this main store better.

(b) Large associative stores (thousands of words) on computers whose architecture has been designed to exploit such a store. These unconventional computers are used only in application areas where their cost is outweighed by the inability of a conventional computer to cope.

In the remainder of this section we first consider the architecture of a rather general-purpose associative store, supposing it to be feasible, and discuss various ways in which it might function. We then consider the application of associative stores in conventional computers (as in (a) above), where they would be specialized for a particular restricted function. We deal briefly in §7.2 with the application of more general-purpose associative stores in unconventional computers (as in (b) above).

### *Variations on search mode*

We have assumed the existence of only an 'exact match under mask' search, but this could be used for implementing more sophisticated forms of matching. For example, by testing in turn each bit of the interrogation register against the corresponding bit position in the store elements, we could construct a 'less than or equal' search operation. For this reason general-purpose associative stores may work in a *word-parallel, bit-serial* fashion: that is, all words are (of course) searched simultaneously, but the search is for equality at a single selected bit position. Other forms of search (word equality, greater than, etc.) can then be microprogrammed out of a sequence of basic searches (Falkoff 1962). Note that we need to be able to manipulate response bits: for example, to save their values (in a specified bit of the corresponding element), and to search only elements with their response bits set.

Note further that we could similarly construct a sequence of operations to perform *ordered retrieval* (Seeber and Lindquist 1962) from an associative store: that is, to select the numerically lowest value, then the next lowest, and so on. Thus the associative store could be used for sorting as well as searching.

### *Read-out mode*

After a search is complete we have zero, one, or many response bits set in the associative store. A match-type indicator may indicate which of these conditions is the case, and in certain circumstances this would be all that we need to know.

However, we usually now enter *read-out mode* to retrieve the contents of the matched element, assuming for the moment that there is exactly one. The contents of the matched element, or some fixed part of it, or that part corresponding to one bits in the mask register, is read to an output register, where it can be accessed by the processor.

Alternatively, if the store is both content- and coordinate-addressable, the address of the matched element is placed in the output register. The store can now be accessed by the processor in the normal way using this address.

In associative stores designed for the special-purpose applications discussed later in this section, a successful search automatically causes read-out of the contents of the matched element to the output register. An unsuccessful search simply provides a match-failure signal.

Let us now consider the problem of read-out if there are two or more successful matches. In some applications of associative stores we can be sure that such a situation never occurs, or we may have to re-enter search mode with a refined match condition until only one successful match remains. Alternatively, we may be satisfied with any one of the successfully matched elements, perhaps that with the lowest physical address in the store; additionally the match-type indicator could show that multiple matches have occurred, or provide a count of the number of successful matches. If all successful matches must be retrieved automatically, then the associative store will have to make these available successively in the output register.

### *Write mode*

We have considered search mode and read-out mode for an associative store; the third mode of use is *write mode,* to insert information into the store. In the spirit of content-addressing, write mode may imply writing data to all store elements whose response bits have been set to one by the last search (called *multi-write).* Possibly only those parts of each element corresponding to one bits in the mask register will be affected. Alternatively, if the store is both content- and coordinate-addressable, all write accesses could be coordinate-addressed.

If additional data is added to the store from time to time, the store logic could keep track of unused elements and provide a 'write into empty word' facility. In the applications of associative stores discussed later in this section, this may be the only form of write-access to the store: provision must be made for ensuring an empty word is available when required, of course.

### *Associative stores in paging systems*

The main use of associative stores in commercially available computers is to improve the efficiency of segmentation and paging systems, by reducing the number of main store accesses in the address mapping process.

The set of page address registers on the Atlas computer (see §5.2) forms an associative store, all the elements of which are compared in parallel with the page number of the virtual address in order to find a page frame number.

In the more normal paging and segmentation systems, using page or segment tables in main store, associative stores have no such logically necessary place. However, each access to store involves a second store access to obtain a page or segment address. Indeed if we have a system involving both paging and segmentation, we could have up to three such accesses.

If we consider first a paging system without segmentation, we insert an associative store in parallel with the address mapping hardware. Whenever the processor accesses the main store, it inserts the page number and page frame number in the associative store. Now whenever the page table must be accessed for a page address, the address mapping hardware also searches the associative store for the page number, in the hope of obtaining the page frame number more quickly. If the search of the associative store is successful, the page table access can be terminated. If not, the page table access will eventually be completed, the store is accessed, and the page and page frame numbers are inserted in the associative store to speed subsequent accesses to that page.

On a computer using segmentation and paging, the pair (segment number, page number) is the search field for the associative store, in the hope of obtaining the page frame number. If it is not present, the full address mapping process continues, involving access to the page table for the segment table (if it is paged), to the segment table itself, and to the page table for the relevant segment. On the GE 645 computer used in the Multics system (Organick 1972, Chapter 1), a more complex algorithm is used to bypass some of these three store accesses, even if they cannot all be eliminated.

As mentioned above, these associative stores are small in comparison with main store sizes; for example 32 entries on the DEC PDP-10 (KI10 processor), up to 64 entries on models in the ICL 2900 range, and 128 entries on the larger models in the IBM 370 range. They can therefore hold only the last few page or segment addresses. However because of locality of reference, these will tend to be the majority of the addresses required. When a new page or segment address is obtained which is not in the associative store it must be inserted. The new entry in the associative store usually replaces the least recently used entry, the LRU algorithm being implemented either by dynamically reordering the entries or by means of use bits. At a process switch all entries in the associative store are set to 'empty', to prevent an invalid match with a page number from an earlier process. With such a system a success rate of 90 per cent or more is claimed, for finding the required information in the associative store rather than the page or segment table; Schroeder (1971) suggests that on the Multics system, with an associative store of 16 elements, less than 4 per cent of main store accesses are caused by the address translation process.

### *Associative stores as cache stores*

The cache stores of the previous section are obviously implemented as special-purpose associative stores. The search argument is a main store address, which is compared with all the entries in the cache store. A successful match (and, of course, not more than one such match can occur) results in the appropriate store contents being sent to the processor. A failure causes main store to be accessed, and the cache store updated.

Such a cache store, where a main store location may be brought to any empty cache store element, and where the search is performed over all cache store elements, is called *fully associative* or has *unconstrained mapping*. On the IBM 360 model 85 and IBM 370 computers, where the caches contain from 8K to 32K bytes, this would require rather a lot of logic to implement, even though on these computers a cache store element holds a group of 64 or 32 bytes (respectively) rather than a single byte. These computers therefore use a cache store in which a particular store location can be brought only to one of a limited set of cache store elements, and the search for an element in the cache store can be similarly limited. Such a cache is called *set associative,* or uses *congruence mapping.*

The IBM 370 cache store (Katzan 1971a, pp. 193–7, 214–20; Madnick and Donovan 1974, pp. 189–98) is illustrated in Figure 5.13. For the purposes of implementing the cache store system, the main store is considered to be a two-dimensional array of 32-byte groups or *blocks.* 128 of these blocks (64 on some models) make up a *row*; the number of blocks to a *column* (the number of rows) depends on the size

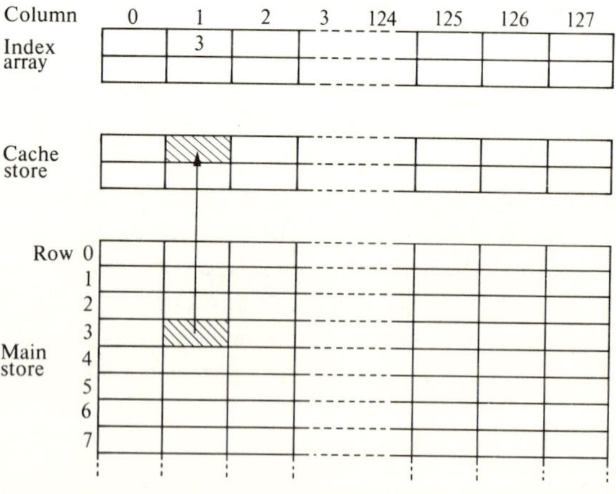


FIG. 5.13

of the main store. Thus a 24-bit address consists of a 12-bit (or less) row number, a 7-bit column number, and 5-bit byte-within-block number.

The cache store is made up of 128 columns (one corresponding to each main store column) and two or four rows, depending on the size of cache store: we show two rows. At a particular row and column of the cache store is a cache element proper, capable of holding one block of 32 bytes, and an index array element, holding the row address of the block occupying the corresponding cache store element. Now a particular main store block is brought, not to any element in the cache store, but to an element in the cache store column corresponding to the main store column containing the block.

Thus each cache store column acts as an independent cache store for the column of main store to which it corresponds, with its own LRU relegation algorithm. The column number of an address specifies which column of the index array to search for the row number. Thus a decimal address 12 346 would give a row number of 3, a column number of 1, and a byte-within-block number of 26. So column 1 of the index array would be searched for a row number 3; from Figure 5.13 this would be successful, and the 26th byte would be accessed from the corresponding cache element.

The IBM 360 model 85 works in a rather different way, with the same intention of reducing the size of the associative store required: it is described in Liptay (1968).

### *Associative stores in the MU5 computer*

The MU5 computer built by the University of Manchester contains three associative stores to increase the rate of instruction execution: a fourth associative store is used by the paging and segmentation hardware in the usual way. Since this computer has a pipeline processor of the type discussed in §8.2, a continuous flow of instructions into the processor is required, despite jump instructions. An associative store is therefore provided into which are loaded the address of each recent instruction which has caused a jump, and the address jumped to. If a jump instruction is soon to be executed, a search for its address is performed in the associative store. If the instruction address is found, the address previously jumped to is a prediction of the new jump address, and is used to access further instructions. Simulation studies suggest a prediction success rate of 75 per cent when the technique is applicable (Ibbett 1972).

The other two associative stores, referred to as *name stores,* are a refinement of the cache store technique. Here only certain types of data migrate from the main store. Essentially, index values and descriptors for arrays enter what is known as the B/D name store, and other values enter the A name store.

Each name store can be seen as a set of accumulators, which tend to hold the most active data variables of the appropriate type. The rationale behind the normal accumulator sets of §3.2 is that the programmer or compiler can ensure that they hold the most active variables, in order to take advantage of their speed of access. By making the migration of variables to the name store automatic, we relieve the programmer or compiler of a difficult job, which could not always be performed well (except at run time) because of data-dependencies in the frequency of use of variables. The performance of the MU5 name stores is discussed in Ibbett and Husband (1977).

## 5.6. Cyclic stores

Access to all current conventional main stores is organized around three basic principles: that the processor gains access to a store element by quoting its name; that the name of an element is its coordinate or index within a vector of store elements; and that the access times to all elements are (at least approximately) the same. Since any store has its elements laid out in a linear manner, the second principle is almost a consequence of the first. The previous section showed an alternative to the first principle, in the form of associative stores.

Another alternative is the type of store where, after a store element has been accessed, the subsequent access is to the 'next' element in the store in some sense. Examples of this are magnetic tapes and shift registers; a schematic example of the latter is given in Figure 5.14. Conventional coordinate-addressed stores can be accessed in this way (for example to access successive elements of a vector) by performing arithmetic operations on addresses. However, here we are concerned with stores whose only means of access is in this way, and which are designed for particular applications where such access is adequate. Two application areas where shift stores have been used are some of the stacks discussed in §3.2 and the transput buffer stores mentioned in §6.1; note also that the cyclic stores discussed in this section are essentially a form of shift register (why?). A generalization of this type of store would provide a list-structured main store, as suggested by

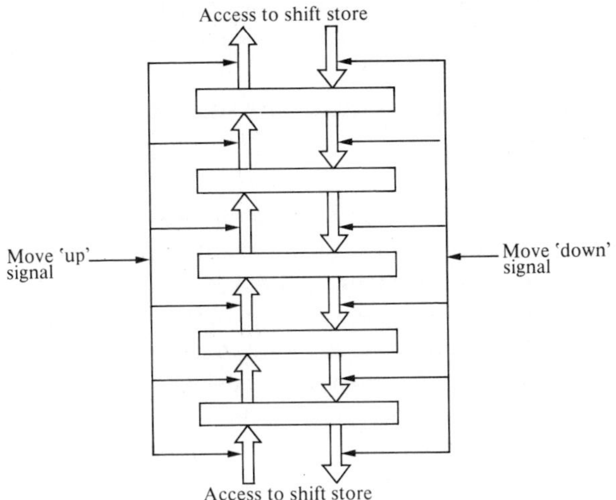


Each rectangle represents one bit (for a shift register) or a larger unit (e.g. a word, for a shift store).

FIG. 5.14

Shaw, Newell, Simon, and Ellis (1958) for a computer to execute the IPL-6 language directly. No conventional computer has been provided with a main store of this form, although it could be implemented on a microprogrammed computer.

The third principle is broken by cyclic stores, which are the subject of this section. A problem associated with all early computers was the provision of sufficient quantities of random-access main store in the days before ferrite cores became available at an economic price. A common solution was to provide a very small quantity of random-access main store combined with a larger quantity of storage of a cyclic nature; that is, any particular store element could be accessed only at one particular time in a cycle which was long when compared with the internal operations of the processor.

The two common implementations of such a cyclic store were the magnetic drum, where each element was accessible only as the portion of the drum containing it rotated past the read/write heads, and the delay line, where the pulses specifying the value of an element continually circulated through a device such as a mercury tank, and could be accessed only when they were being reflected and amplified at one end of the delay line. These are discussed in Renwick and Cole (1971,

Chapters 2 and 4) and Middelhoek, George, and Dekker (1976, Chapters 2 and 5). Thus the feature of such cyclic stores which concerns us is that the access time for an element depends on where in the store it, and the element previously accessed, are situated.

### *The IBM 650*

The IBM 650 (Hamilton and Kubie 1954) was a typical example of a computer with a cyclic main store, in this case a magnetic drum which could hold one or two thousand words. The only random-access store elements were three processor registers: an upper and a lower accumulator, which could be used as one double-length accumulator, and a subsidiary register known as the distributor. The basic data-manipulation instructions of the computer used the one-address system, each instruction specifying the operation code and a store address for one operand; one of the processor registers would contain the second operand and the result.

If instructions were placed in successive store elements on the drum, then a complete drum revolution would have to take place between successive instruction accesses. Suppose however that the multiply instruction took a time equal to one-tenth of a drum revolution; then when a multiplication had been completed the drum would have rotated to a position one-tenth of the way from the position from which the operand was accessed, and we could have saved part of a drum revolution if the next instruction was on the drum soon after this point.

For this reason the IBM 650 instruction held a second store address, that of the next instruction to be executed. This is called a *one-plus-one address* format, and in general an *n*-address computer which also specifies an explicit next instruction address is called an *n-plus-one address* computer. Note that, for conditional jump instructions, both addresses refer to instructions; one to be jumped to when the condition is satisfied, and one for when it fails.

With the provision of instruction timing information, programs could now be organized in such a way that the next instruction on the drum would be positioned under the read/write heads soon after the current instruction was completed. This technique of program organization is known as *optimum coding* or *minimum-access coding*.

### *The Ferranti Pegasus*

In the model of the IBM 650 computer described above no random-access storage was available apart from the three processor registers.

Later models had index registers and small ferrite core stores to buffer data flow to and from transput devices.

If a small random-access store is added between the processor registers and the cyclic store, we have what is known as a *'two-level store'* system. In theory any computer with random-access main store and backing storage devices such as magnetic drums or discs answers to this description. Here, however, we are concerned with early computers where the random-access store (variously called the 'computing' or 'working' store) is considerably smaller than the typical program size, so that the housekeeping operations of transferring instructions and data between the two stores become frequent, and the operation of the cyclic store is closely integrated with the processor rather than being treated as one of several transput devices.

The two-level store system is exemplified by the Ferranti Pegasus computer, where 55 words of main (random access) store and a magnetic drum of 5120 words were provided. The primary store was made up of 7 accumulators and 6 blocks, each of 8 store elements, to hold instructions and data. Single words could be transferred to and from the drum via accumulator one, but the drum store was in fact divided into blocks of 8 elements, and instructions were provided to perform a transfer of data between a block on drum and one of the 6 blocks of main store.

Thus the data-manipulation instructions of a program would be interspersed with the housekeeping operations of transferring instructions and data between drum and main store. We can see the similarity of these block transfer instructions to instructions on more recent computers for block transfer between main and mass stores.

### *Current uses of cyclic stores*

Cyclic stores were extensively used for the main store of early computers. The ferrite core and newer storage technologies soon ousted them from main to backing storage, where they are treated as transput devices. These are invariably magnetic discs or drums nowadays, delay lines no longer being used; however, there are a number of new technologies (such as magnetic bubbles and charge-coupled devices: Stone 1975, Chapter 5; Middelhoek, George, and Dekker 1976, Chapter 3), which may be expected to replace rotating magnetic devices in the future.

Cyclic stores are sometimes still used as the main store on specialized computers where speed in a random-access mode of operation is not required; for example, on the display processors and programmable calculators of Chapter 7.

## Problems

**5.1.** To be fully secure, a computer system needs
(a) A store protection system;
(b) A supervisor mode and privileged instructions;
(c) Some means of controlled entry to supervisor mode.
Explain why all three are necessary. Are these three sufficient? (Hint: consider the problem of a run-away process.)

**5.2.** Consider a computer being run in a multiprogramming environment, so that the main store is occupied by several processes and by part of the operating system. What are the comparative advantages and disadvantages of the following protection systems?
(a) Protection bits;
(b) Protection locks and keys;
(c) A single base and limit register pair;
(d) Segmentation.

**5.3.** In the protection lock and key system, access is allowed if 'protection key value equals protection lock value'. Investigate the consequences if 'equals' were replaced by 'less than or equal'.

**5.4.** In §5.1 we describe a protection system using segmentation together with a ring structure. In what ways might such a system be inadequate? Hint:
(a) How does the system establish the identity of an authorized user?
(b) Have you perfect confidence in the operating system under which your programs run? More generally, could you have two pieces of coding which are mutually suspicious?

**5.5.** Discuss the similarities and differences between the store management techniques of address mapping registers, segmentation (§ 4.5) and paging (§ 5.2). Can the first technique be clearly distinguished from the other two? Look at the virtual storage system available on the DEC PDP-11 computer (DEC 1972b): which of the three techniques is this?

**5.6.** On page 199 we assume that a page fault causes the instruction being executed to be abandoned. After the page has been brought in by the operating system, the instruction is re-executed. What consequences does this have on a paged computer which has instructions to perform character-by-character operations on long character strings?

(For example, consider 'and byte string A with byte string B, leaving the result at byte string A' on the IBM 370 range, where the strings may be 256 bytes long.) What would be the consequences of wishing to resume an instruction partway through its execution, at the point where the page fault occurred?

**5.7.** In § 5.2 we mention two page replacement strategies, LRU and working set. Another possible strategy, which would be simple to implement, is first-in-first-out (FIFO): when a page fault occurs, the page relegated is that loaded longest ago. What is wrong with this strategy?

**5.8.** On page 204 three classes of distinguishable store locations are described. Place each of the examples of § 5.3 into its appropriate class. Do the same for the examples of distinguishable store locations mentioned in §§ 6.2 and 6.3.

**5.9.** Assume that a computer of your choice has a hardware clock or interval timer. Design a program to enable any user process to ascertain the date and time, or to request an interrupt after a specified interval of time.

**5.10.** Consider a computer where the processor and store are synchronized. The processor alternately executes a fetch and an execute cycle, both the same length as the store cycle. Each of these *major cycles* is divided by a pulse generator into a fixed number of *minor cycles,* and all register transfers and control signals are initiated at the beginning of one of these. At the start of the fetch cycle the program counter is sent to the SAR and a read is initiated. At a fixed point later in the cycle the instruction is available in the SDR; by the end of the cycle the store will have been regenerated and the instruction decoded. For an add instruction the execute cycle will cause a read, to get the store word contents into the SDR; again the store is regenerated while the add is being performed. For a store instruction the execute cycle will cause a write. In either case, at the end of the execute cycle we are ready for the fetch of the next instruction. Some extensions to this simple system are necessary:

(a) An unconditional jump (for example) requires only a fetch cycle.
(b) An instruction with indirect addressing requires one or more extra 'defer' cycles between the fetch and execute cycles.
(c) For direct store access by a transput device (see § 6.1) each store cycle could be offered to the transput system before being used by the processor.

Investigate what inefficiencies arise in such a system because of the following problems:
(a) Some instructions have an execution phase which does not match a fixed multiple of the store cycle time; for example, accumulator-to-accumulator instructions, which do not require a store access but cannot be done during the fetch cycle, or multiply and divide instructions, which may require a lengthy processing phase after the store access.
(b) The store cycle time may not be fixed, either because a range of stores with different speeds can be attached to the processor, or some parts of the store are faster than others (this covers the case of interleaved store modules and cache stores).

Suppose now we uncouple the processor from the store. We assume that the processor still has a fixed-length minor cycle (i.e. it is synchronous), but now a store access is achieved by sending a request to the store (or store module) which, if not busy, immediately starts a store cycle, and signals the processor when it is done. How does this affect the problems discussed above? How does it affect access to the store by transput devices or by a second processor, or by the functionally parallel computers of § 8.2?

**5.11.** Choose several typical pieces of program code (e.g. those used in problem 3.5). Suppose that any read access to store causes the accessed value to migrate to the least recently used element of a cache store of, say, 8 or 16 elements. What is the hit rate for your chosen pieces of code (assuming one-address code with a single accumulator)? Consider now a name store of the MU5 form, rather than a cache; i.e. only data values, and not instructions, migrate from the main store. What is the hit rate? How does this compare with your answers to problem 3.4?

**5.12.** Write a program for a conventional computer which searches a table for a specified entry. Estimate how many store cycles are required on average per search, and compare this with the associative stores of § 5.5.

**5.13.** Consider a word-parallel, bit-serial, associative store with the following operations:
Set all response bits.
Search all words whose response bits are set, clearing the response bits of those which do not match the interrogation register at the *i*th bit.
Write the *i*th bit of the interrogation register to the corresponding bit position of all words whose response bits are set.
Test if any response bits are set.

Assuming the usual instructions to manipulate registers and transfer control, write subroutines to do the following:
(a) Set the response bits of all words equal to the interrogation register.
(b) Set the response bits of all words (numerically) less than or equal to the interrogation register.
(c) Set the response bits of the words containing the (numerically) lowest value in the store.
(d) If each store word contains two fields A and B, add field A to field B.

You may assume there are some free bit positions in each word which can be used as marker bits.

**5.14.** Choose a program to carry out some typical operation, such as inverting a matrix. What proportion of the instructions executed are conditional jumps? How often does the MU5 type of prediction work?

**5.15.** Investigate the difficulty in programming (in assembler language) on a computer with a cyclic store. How could the situation be improved with additional software?

# 6 Transput and autonomous processors

In the first chapter of this book a basic computer was divided into three parts, and Chapters 2–4 discussed two of these, the processor and the store. Here we deal with the third part, the peripheral, input/output or transput system, which provides communication between the computer and the outside world.

In the first two sections of this chapter we discuss in general architectural terms the control of transput devices, and some of the consequences of having both device and processor operating at the same time.

In § 3.5 we introduced the term *process* for an independent sequence of operations. In a similar manner we can redefine the term *processor* to mean anything which can carry out a sequence of operations; in this book it would always be a piece of electronic logic. Now the processor defined in Chapter 1 is obviously still a processor by the new defininition, but so is any transput device which operates independently and autonomously when it has been set going. So we can use the term *processor* for any piece of hardware capable of independent execution of a sequence of operations. A computer system may therefore contain several processors, including one or more processors which execute the sets of operations described in earlier chapters (i.e. processors by the old definition). We refer to these (especially when there is only one of them) as *central processors,* but we often use the term processor when no confusion can arise.

The third section discusses the receipt of interrupt signals, from transput devices and elsewhere, and their handling by the central processor. The fourth section deals with the provision of autonomous special-purpose processors, or channel controllers, to allow the transput system to perform more complex operations without placing a burden on the central processor. The last two sections introduce systems containing two or more interconnected general-purpose processors, either in the form of a multiprocessor system or as a network of computers.

It should be mentioned that there is much more variation in the areas discussed in this chapter, even among mainstream computers, than in areas discussed in earlier chapters. Moreover, no completely standard terminology has emerged, and the same term (such as channel) may be used by different manufacturers to refer to equipment with very different functional capabilities. On the whole we will follow the terminology used by IBM for the System/360 and /370 series of computers, as it is something of a *de facto* standard in this area.

### 6.1. The attachment of transput devices

Early computers had only a small fixed complement of transput devices, such as printing equipment and a reader and punch for paper tape or punched cards. Nowadays there is a vast range of transput devices which could be attached to a computer, including communication lines to terminals and other computers, and such exotic devices as audio-response units and Olympic scoreboards. The transput hardware of a computer must therefore be designed to provide general facilities to control any of the wide variety of devices that we might wish to attach to the computer, even a device introduced long after the computer has been designed and built.

The common feature of all transput devices is that they do not operate at the electronic speeds of the processor and store; typically they will be electromechanical in nature, with speeds several orders of magnitude slower than the processor. Thus a computer capable of executing a million instructions per second might be communicating with a user at a terminal at 10 characters per second, with a line printer operating at 1000 lines per minute, with a moving-head disc with an average access time of 10–80 ms and a transfer rate up to half a million characters a second, and a drum with an average access time of 4 ms and a transfer rate of a million characters a second. Between successive moments at which the processor has to supervise these devices (and in the last three cases a complete line of 100–50 characters or block of, say, 4000 characters would have been transferred) it could execute 100 000, 60 000, 18 000 or more, and 8000 instructions respectively.

Thus we expect a transput instruction to invoke a particular transput device and, over some (perhaps lengthy) period of time, cause a set of bits of data to be transferred between the computer and the outside world. Further there is a requirement for certain types of control over the device which do not invoke any transfer of data (such as selecting a mode in which the device is to operate), and for interrogating the current state of the device (such as to ascertain the details of an error condition). This involves transferring data to and from the *control registers* of the device, which govern the device's operation. In the remainder of this section we therefore consider the provision only of such general facilities, leaving their interpretation for individual devices to the reader.

In § 5.4 we described a hierarchy of computer storage devices, ranging from accumulators to archival storage (see Figure 5.9). Storage media below a certain level in the hierarchy are electromechanical in nature (magnetic drums, discs, and tapes on current computers). They are therefore too slow to hold the instructions currently being executed and their operands, as can the storage media above this level (for example, the main and perhaps the mass storage). Instead they are treated as transput devices, to be controlled by the type of facility described in this and the next sections.

### *The effect of the operating system*

Much of the complexity of the transput hardware is nowadays hidden behind an operating system (Madnick and Donovan 1974, Chapter 5; Lister 1975, Chapter 6). Even in a low-level language, transput operations will be invoked by an extracode or supervisor call instruction with suitable parameters, and it will be the task of the supervisor to issue the detailed transput instructions and deal, for example, with transput errors. Thus programs can be written which are independent of particular transput devices or even particular types of device.

An extreme example of this is in the Multics system, where the technique of segmentation allows much of the magnetic disc backing storage to be seen by the applications programmer as part of the main store. A more common example is that of *spooling* or *pseudo-offlining,* whereby programs communicate with slow devices (such as card readers and line printers) indirectly via storage areas on disc rather than directly.

### *Character-oriented transput*

Within the computer the basic unit of data is usually the word, while in the outside world it is usually the character (of 6 to 8 bits). The most basic form of transput operation therefore transfers one character or word between computer and device. As discussed in Chapter 1, on early computers the processor was halted until the transfer was complete, when the computer would fetch and execute the next and subsequent instructions. The destination of data on input, or source on output, could be a fixed processor register (typically the accumulator) or a store location (at an address either fixed for the device, or specified in the transput instruction).

Because of the difference in speed between processor and transput device, all computers now allow the two to operate concurrently, so that the transput instruction simply initiates the input or output of a character or word, allowing the processor immediately to proceed to the next instruction. In order to take advantage of this concurrency, the transput operation must not require further use of any of the facilities to be used by the processing instructions. For example, if a transput operation retained control of the (single) accumulator until it was complete, then very few instructions could be executable concurrently with this transfer. Some early computers used a subsidiary processor register (such as the MQ register) as source or destination of the data transferred by a transput operation, so a rather larger class of instructions could be executed during the transfer. If we make a (fixed or specifiable) store location the source or destination, then we can use all the normal instructions during the transput operation (as long as we refrain from accessing this particular store location).

An alternative common solution (see, for example, many devices on the DEC PDP-8 computer) is to provide a one-character or one-word buffer in the device, which holds the data during transfer. Thus an input instruction initiates a transfer of data to the buffer (at electromechanical speeds); when the operation is complete, a further transput instruction loads the buffer contents into (say) the accumulator at electronic speeds. Similarly, an output instruction transfers the output data from accumulator to buffer, again at electronic speeds; the processor then continues with the fetching and execution of subsequent instructions, while the data is output from the buffer at electromechanical speeds.

The programmer wishes to establish when the transput operation is complete, so that a further transput operation can be initiated, or so that the input data can be processed. In early computers the programmer would have to take into account the detailed timing of processor and transput devices in writing programs, in order to access the devices at the correct rate. Greater flexibility is provided by a *done flag* for each transput device; that is, a one-bit register indicating whether or not the device has completed an operation. Such a flag is automatically cleared when a transput operation is initiated, and set to one when it is complete. A further transput instruction is then necessary for testing this flag to ascertain when the operation is complete.

Such an instruction could be executed from time to time after a transput operation has commenced, but nowadays the setting of any done flag will cause an interrupt. We might then have to use this flag-testing instruction to establish which device caused the interrupt; however, there are other possible ways of doing this, to be discussed in § 6.3.

### *Block-oriented transput*

We have assumed above that the data transferred to and from the transput device is an undifferentiated stream of characters or words. This is often not the case. Instead many transput devices manipulate data in a basic unit, or *block,* of a number of characters or words. Thus for a card reader the block is a group of 80 characters on a punched card, while on a magnetic tape the block might be from a few tens to several thousands of characters, as determined by the format in which the tape was written.

The *block,* defined by physical means on a particular transput device, is to be distinguished from the *record,* which is a grouping of a number of characters or words to form a logical unit. Thus the personal data of each employee in a payroll file would constitute a single record. In the simplest case the record and the block are coterminous, but in general there will be several (logical) records to a (physical) block, or (more rarely) a record may spread over several blocks.

In early computers with only a few types of transput device, it was possible to specify a fixed block length for each transput device, and to build these various block lengths into the processor's hardware. Thus an instruction to read a punched card would imply the block length of 80 characters.

On a modern computer, with no standard set of transput devices, it is not possible to build such fixed block lengths into the processor. Instead each transput instruction must specify the length of the block to be read or written, most commonly as a count of characters or words to be transferred. Alternatively, since we have to specify the address of the store location allocated to the first element of the block, the length of the block could be indicated by also specifying the address of the store location allocated to the last element of the block. A third possibility is for a particular character or word value to mark the end of the block, and for the processor to terminate the transput operation when it has been recognized; this method is nowadays rarely used, since it limits the generality of the data which can be transmitted.

### *Early methods of block transput*

There are a number of methods found on early computers for transferring complete blocks of data between computer and transput device. Perhaps the most obvious is to utilize a sequence of transput operations of the type described earlier, each of which transfers a single character or word. Thus a transput control instruction would be issued to commence the transfer of a block; for example, with a magnetic tape unit, the tape must be set in motion. Then a succession of single-element transput instructions would transfer successive elements of the block, accompanied by appropriate updating of block count and store address. Eventually the end of the block would be reached, signalled either by the transput device or by the block count reaching zero. A further transput control instruction would then need to be issued to terminate this block transfer; with a magnetic tape unit, for example, the tape would be brought to a halt.

Instead of dealing in detail with individual words or characters, we can organize the computer in such a way that a transput instruction causes the transfer of a complete block, with the detailed transfer of individual elements carried out by the hardware. The problem here is what is to be done about processor access to the store while data is being transferred between transput device and store.

One solution is to halt the processor while a block transfer is taking place. Thus a transput instruction causes the transfer of a block of data to or from an area of store, after the completion of which the processor proceeds with the next instruction.

A second and very common solution on first-generation computers was to provide a *buffer store,* capable of holding a complete (usually fixed-length) block, an obvious extension of the single-element buffer discussed above. A transput instruction then initiates a block transfer between device and buffer store, and the processor immediately proceeds to the next instruction. When the transfer is complete, a further transput instruction empties the buffer (at electronic speeds) into main store (for input) or refills the buffer from main store (for further output). Such a system was often extended to the provision of several buffer stores, each of which could be simultaneously in communication with a different transput device, while the processor and store continue to perform non-transput operations.

There are disadvantages in the use of all these methods, as means of decoupling the transput devices from the processor. The first method requires processor intervention for every element of the block, which limits the extent to which it can carry out other tasks. Also, for a fast device, the extraction of instructions and data for the transfer of each element may overload the store. The second method eliminates any processor and store overload, but only by eliminating all processor overlap. The third method allows the processor and transput device to operate in parallel, but at the expense of extra data movement from buffer to main store, and of inflexibility in such things as block size.

### *Direct store access*

A fourth method for block transput is *direct store access,* which allows processor and transput device to operate independently with the minimum of interference. Other names for this method are *direct memory access* (and hence the acronym *DMA*), *cycle-stealing,* and *data break*. Nearly all modern computers provide some form of direct store access, either for all transput devices or for only the faster devices, the slow devices being processed (under interrupt control) by transferring individual characters or words.

For direct store access, the main store and processor are decoupled, as described in § 5.4. The store control registers (the SAR and SDR) are now accessible to both the processor and the transput devices.

To initiate a transput operation, the processor executes a transput instruction which passes to the appropriate device the address and size of a buffer area in main store. This information, together with other details passed by the transput instruction (such as direction and mode of transfer), is stored in *control registers* in the device. We will suppose that the buffer address (or rather, the address of the next word in the buffer to be processed) is placed in register BA, and the buffer size (given as a word count) is placed in register BC.

The transput operation then commences, with data words being passed directly between transput device and store without involving the processor, which is independently fetching and executing instructions. The only interference is when device and processor or two devices are simultaneously attempting to access the store, when the conflict is generally resolved by giving priority to the transput device (or the faster of two), since its timing is usually more critical.

Consider first the input of a block of data, for each word of which the device hardware carries out a cycle such as the following:

Read next word of data from input medium.
If none left (or error recognized), terminate transfer.

| | |
|---|---|
| Send this word to SDR of store.<br>Send contents of BA to SAR of store.<br>Initiate store write cycle. | The processor and other transput devices are locked out of the store during these three steps. |

Increment contents of BA register.
Decrement contents of BC register.
If contents of BC are zero, terminate transfer.

For output the cycle becomes:

| | |
|---|---|
| Send contents of BA to SAR of store.<br>Initiate store read cycle.<br>Receive into device the word read from store (via SDR). | With the processor and other transput devices locked out. |

Write this word to output medium.
Increment contents of BA register.
Decrement contents of BC register.
If error recognized by device, or contents of BC are zero, terminate transfer.

The termination of the transfer involves the end-of-block action appropriate to the device, and the setting of a flag to indicate this termination to the processor. The setting of this flag usually causes an interrupt to be signalled to the processor.

It is common for the BC register to hold minus the count of words in the buffer, so that only incrementing hardware need be supplied for both BA and BC. Alternatively, an end-of-buffer address might be used instead of a word count.

Not that we have assumed the transput device to work in units which the store can handle directly (i.e. in words); the cycle of operations would be the same for a byte-oriented device on a byte-oriented computer. For a character-oriented device on a word-oriented computer, the cycle must perform several device reads to build up a word to be written to store, or several device writes to deal with the individual characters of a word from store.

### *Hardware for direct store access*

Figure 6.1 illustrates the layout of a typical computer with the features we have discussed. In this diagram we have a processor, containing such storage registers as program counter and accumulators, directly connected to a number of slow transput devices. Each of these

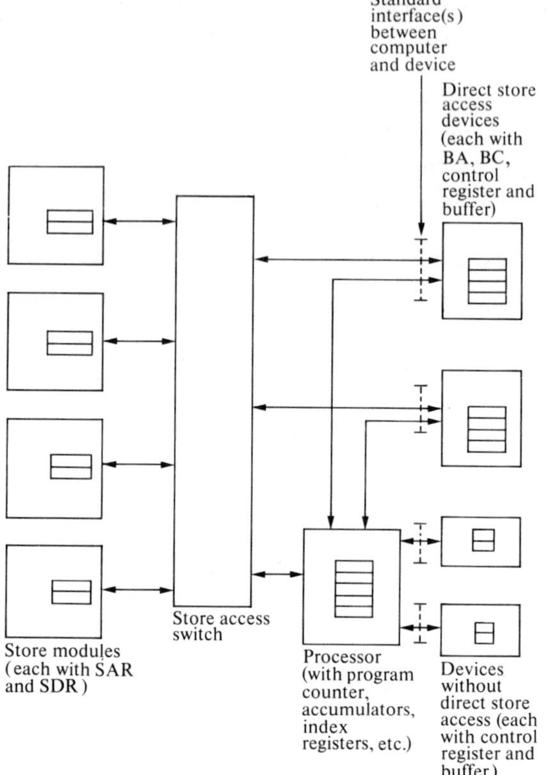


FIG. 6.1

contains a control register and a buffer for one character or word, and is controlled (one character or word at a time) by the processor.

Then there are a number of transput devices which operate under direct store access, and contain buffer address and buffer size registers as well as control registers. Each device is connected to the processor, both to receive control information and to cause an interrupt (signalling termination of a transput operation). After initiation of such an operation, each of these devices operates independently of the processor and all other devices, transferring data between store and transput medium until the operation is complete.

On the left of the diagram the main store has been divided up into a number of independent store modules, each with its own SAR and

SDR. Now there is no interference between device and processor, or between device and device, in simultaneously making access to the store, as long as each access is to a different module. Only if two accesses are made simultaneously to the same module does one have to await completion of the other.

The active elements (processor and devices) are connected to the store modules via a *store access switch* or *exchange*, whose task is to route each access to the appropriate module, and to resolve any conflict or contention for the same module. Any contention is dealt with by allocating each active element a fixed priority, with the faster devices having the higher priority and the processor the lowest. Then, if several active elements all access the same store module simul-

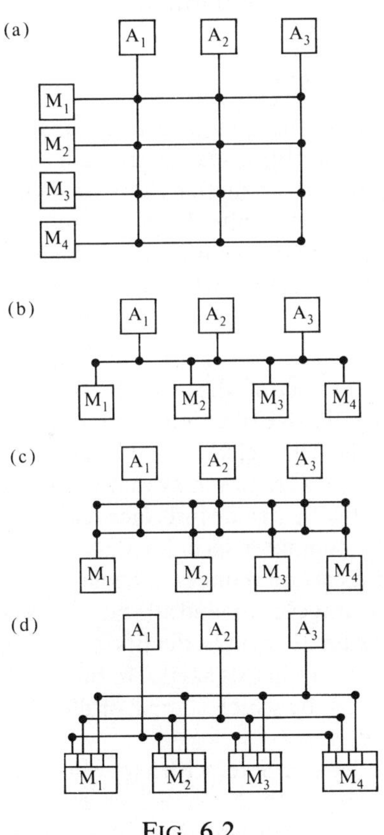


FIG. 6.2

taneously, that with the highest priority is given access and the remainder are delayed for one store cycle.

Such a store access switch may be implemented in various ways (Enslow 1974, Chapter 2):

(a) As a *cross-bar* switch illustrated in Figure 6.2(a), where each active element ($A_1$, $A_2$, $A_3$) has its own route to each store module ($M_1$, $M_2$, $M_3$, $M_4$);
(b) as one or more common *bus*, illustrated in Figure 6.2 (b) and (c) respectively, providing a small number of routes to be time-shared among the active elements; or
(c) As a *multiport* system, illustrated in Figure 6.2 (d), where each store module has several access ports, each with its own SAR and SDR, and conflicts are resolved within the store module.

## 6.2. Transput instructions

Having discussed the features of various transput methods, we now consider possible forms of transput instruction. In modern computers the whole of this group of instructions is privileged; that is, the instructions can be executed only while the processor is in supervisor mode. This ensures that all transput request by problem processes are intercepted and checked by the operating system.

### *Transput ports*

In early computers a set of idiosyncratic transput instructions was provided, each to invoke one function on one of the devices attached to the computer. Similarly the electronic connections from computer to device would be just those required by that particular device. We start by generalizing at this electronic interface level.

The designer of a computer specifies a *standard interface* for transput, consisting of a certain number of signal wires, with binary zero and one at certain voltage levels, and allocated to pre-determined functions (such as data signals, signals identifying how the data signals are to be interpreted, and timing signals). He further designs a *protocol*, or sequence of actions, by which control or data bits are to be passed across the interface.

He then provides his computer with a (perhaps expandable) number of transput *ports*, each with this standard set of wires, and arranges that the computer interprets signals on these wires according to the fixed protocol. Then any peripheral device which is designed to adhere to the standard interface can be attached to any of the transput ports.

As a slight complication we might have several standard interfaces rather than one; thus we might have several ports into the computer for direct store access, adhering to one standard, and several non-DSA ports adhering to a second. This is illustrated in Figure 6.1, where we see the transput ports as (in some sense) marking the boundary of the computer proper. Notice that for the DSA ports some signals are routed to the store via the store access switch, and some are routed to the processor.

We have shown a separate link from processor to each transput port, as this is an architectural view. We might implement the connections in this way, or we might connect a single set of wires from the processor to all the ports in series. It is then for the device on a port to select which signals from the processor are to be obeyed and which ignored (as they are directed to another device), and to identify itself when sending signals to the processor.

***Device numbers***

Suppose now that we number all the transput ports on the computer and build these numbers into the hardware. If now a port number is specified in each transput instruction executed, then the standard signals are directed to the device attached to that port and no other.

Since devices are attached to ports rather permanently (to be changed only by maintenance engineers, or by the type of reconfiguring discussed in § 8.1), we can use these port numbers to refer to devices, as *device numbers*. Notice that any device numbers or names available to problem processes (*symbolic* device numbers, *stream* numbers, or *data set* names) are likely to be distinct from the (physical) device numbers discussed here, and are mapped onto them by the action of the operating system.

Thus we can envisage a group of general transput instructions, each of which sends an appropriate set of signals to whichever device is specified by number in the instruction. It is only when the signals reach the device side of the standard interface that they are interpreted in accordance with the particular type of device involved.

***Types of transput instruction***

Let us now consider the types of transput instruction provided. One system would be to have a facility for sending any valid combination of control signals through a specified transput port, and leave it to the programmer and device to associate a meaning with each combination.

A simple example of this is the DEC PDP-8 computer, which has a 12-bit word divided up (for the transput instruction) as shown in Figure 6.3. Thus a transput instruction on this computer causes a combination of up to three control signals to be sent to a particular device. It is for the programmer and device to know that a particular combination sent to a particular type of device means, say;

> Load contents of accumulator into punch buffer, clear done flag, and start punching contents of buffer on paper tape, setting done flag on completion

It is, however, fair to say that on this computer some attempt has been made to provide consistent interpretations of particular combinations of control signals over a range of device types.

A second example of such a system is the Data General Nova computer, which provides six transput instructions:

> Transfer content of accumulator to register A (or B, or C) in device *n*
>
> Transfer contents of register A (or B, or C) in device *n* to accumulator

The function of particular fields of these three device registers (and even their existence) depends on the type of device *n*. This computer also provides facilities to test and manipulate a 'busy' and a 'done' flag associated with each device.

The above are examples of transput instructions which do not have a standard functional interpretation. Instead we could establish a

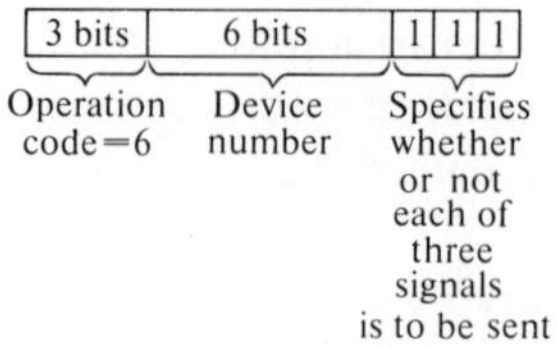

| 3 bits | 6 bits | 1 | 1 | 1 |
|---|---|---|---|---|
| Operation code=6 | Device number | Specifies whether or not each of three signals is to be sent | | |

FIG. 6.3

primitive set of functions required by transput devices, and then provide a set of instructions to implement these functions.

If we consider first block transput, we can distinguish four basic functions, leading to a set of four transput instructions to be used for all devices, as follows:

(a) *Read* (or Data In); transfers a block of $c$ data words from device number $n$ to the store at address $a$, where $n$, $c$, and $a$ are specified by fields in the instruction. This instruction is rejected by a device which can perform only output.
(b) *Write* (or Data Out); transfers a block of $c$ data words from the store area at address $a$ to device number $n$, where $n$, $c$, and $a$ are as before. This instruction is rejected by a device which can perform only input.
(c) *Control* (or Control Out); transfers a block of $c$ control words from the store area at address $a$ to device number $n$. How these control words are interpreted by the device to change control modes, load control registers, initiate actions not involving data transfer (such as to rewind a magnetic tape), etc. depends on the particular type of device.
(d) *Sense* (or Control In); transfers a block of $c$ status words from device number $n$ to the store area at address $a$. How these status words are to be interpreted by the supervisor as done flags, details of error conditions, details of the current position of the device, etc. depends on the particular type of device.

This set of four instructions is an idealized version of those provided on the IBM 370 range, and in any real computer (including the IBM 370) things are in practice rather more complicated. We describe later a number of secondary facilities which may be provided for block transput (such as scatter read-gather write), so a field of flags would be provided in the read and write instructions to specify the options required. Some devices required extra information for a transput operation, such as mode of operation, or disc address of the block to be transferred. We can either provide further fields in the read and write instructions to hold this information for devices that require it (other devices ignoring these fields), or we can pass this information across in a preceding control instruction.

An equivalent set of instructions for non-block (character or word) transput would probably not have the elegance of the above set, but might be as follows:

(a) *Read;* transfer into the accumulator the contents of the buffer in device number *n*.
(b) *Write;* transfer to the buffer of device number *n* the contents of the accumulator, and initiate output of this character or word, signalling on completion.
(c) *Control;* set up the control registers of device *n* in a manner specified in a sub-operation code field, possibly transferring the contents of the accumulator. One important control sub-operation is to initiate input of a character or word into the device buffer, signalling on completion; the input would then be completed by a read instruction.
(d) *Sense;* receive status information from device *n* into the accumulator, which part of the status is required being specified in a sub-operation code field.

### *Variations on transput instructions*

We have suggested that the sense instruction transfers some or all of a device's status information to an accumulator or store area. A popular variation is a conditional jump instruction, testing a specified status bit. A typical example is

Skip next instruction if done flag set in device *n*, where *n* is specified in an instruction field.

Some sense instructions incorporate control functions, in that they clear a status bit in the device after reading it. Conversely, read, write, and control instructions may subsume sense functions, in that they skip the next instruction (or set a condition code register) if the device rejects the transput instruction as invalid in some way (for example, the device is already busy); alternatively, an immediate error interrupt may be signalled. It is then the supervisor's task to issue sense instructions to obtain more details.

If the amount of information to be passed in a transput instruction is too large to fit in an instruction word, then the instruction may specify the address of a control block of store locations containing some or all of this information. Alternatively the information may be placed in a fixed store location before the transput instruction is executed, and the device copies the information into its own control registers before allowing the processor to proceed to the next instruction. For example, when a transput operation begins on the IBM 370 range, some of the information is specified in the transput instruction, but some is extracted by the transput system from store location 72 (the channel address word or CAW).

A fairly common way of saving on the cost of storage registers in transput devices using direct store access is to utilize two fixed main store locations per device to hold the BA and BC registers described earlier. This is slower than having these registers within the device, since three store cycles (instead of one) are required to transfer each word of data; one to extract, use and increment the BA register, one to extract, use, and decrement the BC register, and one to transfer the data word between device and store.

One interesting alternative to the provision of transput instructions is to allocate store addresses to the control registers of each device. The control of transput operations by placing information in control registers, and the sensing of transput conditions by reading control registers, is then by normal data-manipulation instructions operating on the appropriate store addresses. Thus, on the DEC PDP-11 computer the top 4K of addresses refer to device control registers and buffers, rather than store locations. One advantage of such a system is that it may be possible to extend the store protection system to cover the device control registers, allowing a finer degree of control over device use by problem processes than is possible with the all-or-nothing system of privileged transput instructions.

### *Device control units*

So far we have treated the transput or peripheral device as a single entity; it is now time to look at it more closely. It can usually be divided up into the transput device proper, which is predominantly electromechanical in nature and performs the basic functions of reading, writing, and storing data, and the transput *control unit* or *device controller*. This contains the electronics to send the appropriate sequence of detailed control signals to the device, in accordance with the generalized signals received from the computer through a transput port. This is illustrated in Figure 6.4.

Where there is a single device connected to a control unit, there is no architectural reason for distinguishing the two. However, the distinction may be useful at an implementation level, since a manufac-

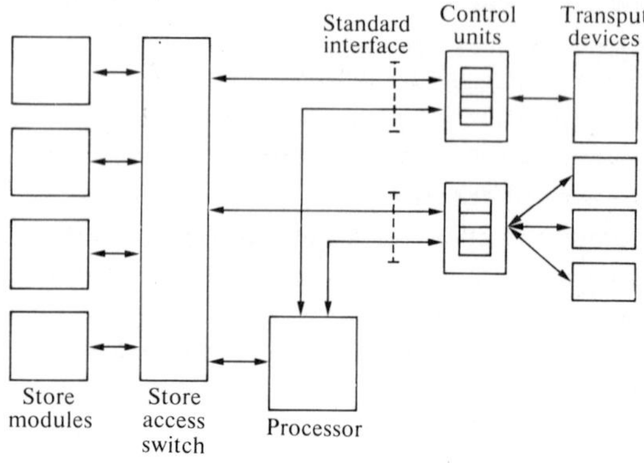


FIG. 6.4

turer might design a single transput device and several control units for the device, each adhering to the standard interface conventions of a different computer. The device can then be attached to any of these computers by a suitable selection of control unit.

Sometimes we wish to distinguish between control unit and device even at an architectural level, since several devices of similar type can be attached to one control unit, as shown in Figure 6.4. Instead of the transput port and control unit responding to a single device number, they now respond to a range of numbers, and the control unit routes signals to the appropriate device.

While a transput operation is being carried out which involves the transfer of data (that is, a read or write), the control unit and specified device operate as a single unit. However, it may be possible for a device to carry out some non-data transput operations (such as rewinding a magnetic tape) without the supervision of the control unit.

At any time, then, several devices in the group may be operating. No more than one is performing an operation involving the control unit, while the rest may be performing simple operations on their own. Note that the signal indicating that one of these simple operations is complete must pass through the control unit to the computer, and must therefore await the completion of the transput operation which it is currently supervising.

The advantage of such shared control units are a reduction in electronic hardware in the system, at the expense of delaying access to a device until the control unit is free, and reducing simultaneity of operating among a group of devices.

A typical control unit has a number of storage registers, to hold the store address, word count, and other details of the current transput operation. Furthermore there will be a data buffer register, to hold data on its passage between device and store. In the simplest case, where the main store and transput devices use the same basic unit of data (whether character, byte or word), this buffer register is of a size to hold one such basic unit, and is used to match the speeds of the store and device. In cases where there is a mismatch between data units, the buffer register is also used for data assembly and disassembly. Thus, for input from a character-oriented device to a word-oriented store, a number of characters are collected together in the buffer before transmission to the store as a word.

### Further transput functions

There are a number of possible further transput functions, over and above the basic transfer of a single block of data between device and store, such as the following:

(a) Many transput devices have some form of error-detection. For example, most backing store devices have parity-checking, the more common character sets used on punched cards provide some degree of redundancy, and some output devices are able to reread and check each character as it is written. If an error is detected, the transput operation is terminated immediately and the processor informed. This is usually by an interrupt, causing entry to a process which issues a sense instruction to establish exactly what error has occurred, and then takes suitable corrective action. On some recent backing store devices parity bits have been replaced by full error-detecting and error-correcting codes, so that certain types of error can be automatically corrected.

(b) Instead of transferring a block of transput data to or from a single contiguous store area, we may wish to read a block of data and transfer various portions of it to different store areas, or create and write a single block of data from a number of separate store areas. This is callled *scatter read–gather write*. Instead of a single store address and count, the transput instruction indicates a chain of elements, each of which consists of an address and count. In transferring a block, the control unit uses the address and count of the first element until the count is exhausted, when it moves on to the next element. This continues until either the count of the last element in the chain has been exhausted, or the device indicates the end of the block (or, of course, an error is detected).

(c) While using scatter-read to decompose a block into a number of portions on input, it may be that some portions are of no interest. We would like to use the count field of a chain element to define the size of this portion to be read but ignored, so that the store is not updated from it. Each chain element would therefore contain, along with the store address and count, a flag to indicate that data is to be read but not passed to the store; the address field would, of course, not to be used in this case. Facilities (b) and (c) are provided in the IBM 370 range : they are illustrated in Figure 6.5.

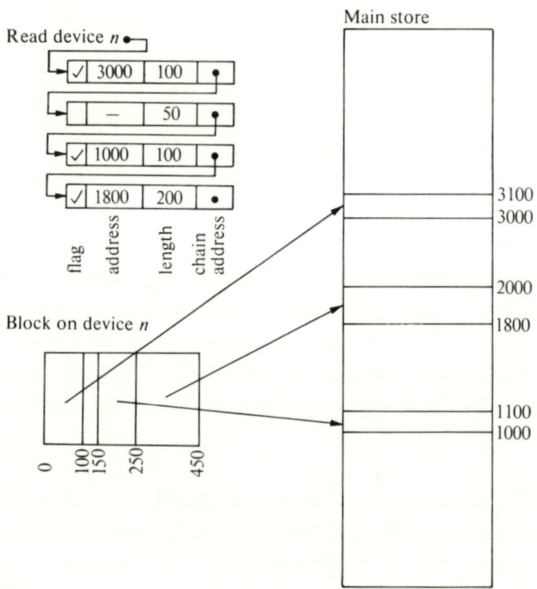


FIG. 6.5

(d) Some control units may translate data from one character code to another during transput, according to a table stored within the unit. This translation table may be wired-in for a particular device, or transferred from the computer by a control instruction when required.

(e) There are also a number of more device-specific functions. An example is reading backwards on magnetic tape, where the input data is transferred to main store commencing at a high address and working towards a low.

### *The transput system and the store*

In Chapters 4 and 5 we saw how the processor's view of the store was mediated by store protection and store mapping systems, and perhaps by a cache store. The transput device's view of the store is likely to be rather more basic. In the simplest and most common case the device sees a linear, Von Neumann store. All mapping of virtual store addresses in transput requests to physical store addresses, and all checking that those addresses may be read from or written to, is done by the supervisor before issuing the transput instruction.

In computers where each word or block of words has an associated store protection register to limit access by the processor, we can make store accesses by transput devices be subject to the same tests. For example, in a system of store protection locks and keys such as on the IBM 370 range, one of the items of information passed to the device by the transput instruction is the protection key value to use. At each store access by the device, this key is matched to the lock value for the area of store accessed, and any mismatch terminates the operation.

Notice that such techniques check only that the transput operation is authorized to use that area of store. Checking the issuing of transput instructions is done by making them privileged instructions, and checking that the device is properly used (for example, that only authorized areas of backing storage are accessed) remains the task of the supervisor.

A few computers provide for a base and limit pair to be passed to the transput device, to allow a certain degree of store mapping and protection. However, a full store segmentation system for transput devices would introduce excessive overheads for a little gain.

How a cache store is integrated with a transput system depends on whether the cache store is part of the processor or the store. If it is part of the store (that is, it has the form of Figure 6.6(a)), then all store

(a)

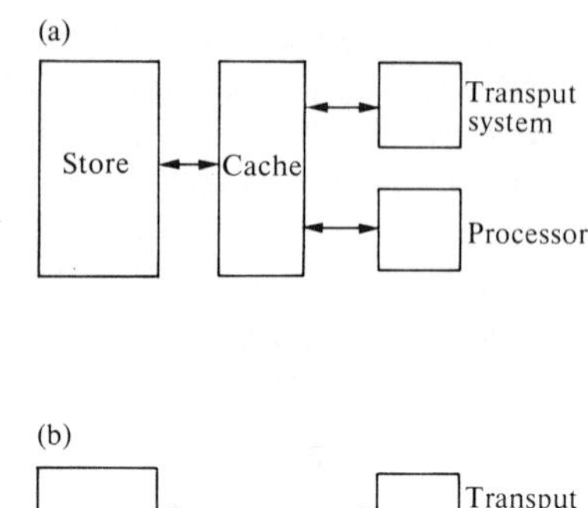


(b)

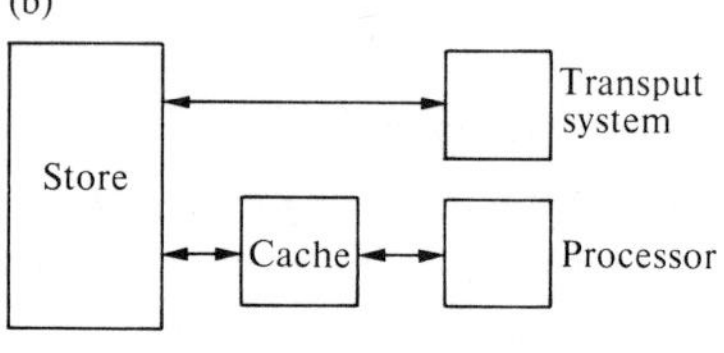


FIG. 6.6

accesses, whether from processor or transput system, are automatically routed via the cache store, so that it is always up to date. However we have to guard against the cache store containing mainly entries called for by the transput system rather than by the processor. If the cache store is between the processor and the store access switch (as in Figure 6.6(b)), then it is bypassed by store accesses from the transput system. This is the manner in which the IBM 370 cache store is attached. When the transput system writes to a store location of which a copy is held in the cache store, care must be taken either to update the copy with its new value, or simply to delete the copy (so that the next read access to that location by the processor calls up the new value into the cache store).

***Pseudo-transput devices***

We have considered transput devices as including both means for communicating with the outside world (including other computers at a distance) and backing store devices. To these we may add other devices which receive a block of data and process it in a time long in comparison with a typical processor instruction. These devices are then attached to the transput system in the normal way. One fairly common device of this type is a block transfer unit, which autonomously transfers a block of data from one area of main store to another.

On a number of computers, particularly the smaller ones, transput instructions directed to device number zero are interpreted as control instructions for a wide range of miscellaneous functions, such as the console switches, the store mapping system, and particularly the interrupt control system.

## 6.3. Interrupts and interrupt handling

In this section we discuss the hardware action taken by a processor on receipt of an interrupt signal.

### *Causes of interrupts*

The interrupt signal indicates the occurrence of any one of a number of events, such as the following;

(a) Certain conditions in a transput device cause an interrupt signal to be sent to the processor; this signal is sent by the device's control unit, or by the channel controlling it (as discussed in the next section). Such a signal indicates that action is required from the processor to further the transput operation. Thus, for a device using direct store access, a block of data has been successfully transferred, a non-data operation has been completed (such as a rewind on a magnetic tape), or an error (such as a parity failure) has occurred. On a non-direct store access device, the signal might indicate that the device buffer is ready to be refilled or emptied by the processor.

(b) Most transput interrupts are 'solicited'; that is, they are the result of the execution of a transput instruction by the processor some time in the past. However, certain transput devices may be able to send an unsolicited or 'attention' interrupt signal, to indicate the occurrence of some event not connected with any of the device's preceding transput operations. Thus such a signal might be given by an operator's pressing a start button on a card reader, after a deck of cards has been placed in the input hopper.

(c) A further set of attention interrupt signals may be received from non-transput sources. One such source is often an interrupt button on the operator's console, to initiate communication between operator and computer. Another example is the signal line from another processor in a multiple computer system.

(d) In 5.3 we discussed the provision of clocks and interval timers in a computer, and mentioned that certain events (such as an interval timer reaching zero) cause an interrupt to be signalled to the processor.

(e) There are several classes of interrupts generated by events during store access, such as a processor's attempting to access a store address not available on the computer, or its attempting to access a store location in a mode for which it is not authorized. Another important example of a store access interrupt is the 'page fault', signalled in a paged computer when the required page is not in main store, to invoke the page-turning algorithm.

(f) Various data conditions can signal an interrupt, causing entry to the supervisor to take the appropriate corrective action, perhaps terminating the process in error, or entering a user-supplied routine to modify the data at fault. Conditions causing such an interrupt include operands in invalid formats, and overflow in fixed- or floating-point arithmetic.

(g) In §8.1 we discuss the possibility of using one process to monitor the progress of another, perhaps one which is incompletely debugged. To this end another set of interrupt signals may be provided, to cause entry into the monitoring process after each instruction or when a certain set of conditions obtains.

(h) particular instructions will cause an interrupt into the supervisor; these will include extracodes and supervisor call instructions, unallocated operation codes, and privileged instructions when in problem mode.

(i) Some computers provide an instruction whose execution causes the processor to act as if an interrupt has been signalled, a field in the instruction specifying which interrupt is to be simulated. This is useful for testing interrupt-servicing routines.

(j) Finally the processor and store will cause interrupts when a hardware fault is detected, allowing the supervisor to enter a diagnostic program or bring the computer to an orderly halt.

Some writers make a distinction between *traps*, generated within the processor or store synchronously with the interrupted process, and *interrupts*, generated asynchronously and usually from some other part of the computer system (in particular, the transput devices). In this book (unless we indicate to the contrary) we use the generic term interrupt for convenience to cover both interrupts and traps.

We assume that interrupts can take effect only after the execution of one instruction is complete and before the execution of the next has begun. Thus any interrupt (in the specific sense) received while an instruction is being executed is held until it has finished. The signalling of a trap usually marks the termination of the instruction execution, either prematurely (for example, an invalid data format) or normally (for example, a supervisor call). Traps in which the supervisor action is expected to be followed by normal completion of the interrupted instruction (such as page faults) usually arrange for all such traps to be signalled before any irrevocable action is taken by the instruction: then the supervisor can process the traps and simply call for the execution of the instruction to be reinitiated.

### *A simple interrupt system*

In the simplest interrupt handling system there are two interrupt modes in which the processor can run: with interrupts *enabled*, so that if an interrupt request reaches the processor it is accepted immediately the execution of the current instruction is complete, and with interrupts *disabled*, so that no interrupt requests are accepted by the processor.

The processor is normally running a problem process with interrupts enabled. When an interrupt request occurs, the processor automatically switches to interrupt disabled mode and enters an interrupt service routine. This routine is entered by having its first instruction at some fixed standard location in the store, typically in one of the first few locations.

In order that the processor will be able to return to the interrupted process, the contents of the program counter at interruption (that is, the address of the next instruction to be executed in the interrupted process) is automatically stored at another fixed standard location in the store. Thus a typical hardware sequence on receipt of an interrupt request is

Complete execution of current instruction.
Switch to interrupt disabled mode.
Store contents of PC in (say) location zero.
Load into PC the address (say) one.
} if interrupts are enabled.
Fetch and execute instruction referred to by PC.

It is the task of the service routine (which starts in this example at location one) to save any critical register or store contents likely to be overwritten by the routine (such as the contents of the accumulator), establish what condition has caused the interrupt, service that condition, and return to the interrupted process.

The latter is effected by some form of 'interrupt return' instruction, which simultaneously switches to interrupt enabled mode and jumps to the address saved by the interrupt hardware (here in location zero). Immediately after execution of this instruction, the processor is once more in interrupt enabled mode and executing the interrupted process, until the next interrupt request occurs.

It is of course possible for an interrupt to be requested while a previous interrupt is being serviced. This interrupt is not accepted, since the processor is in interrupt disabled mode; this is necessary in order not to lose the return address and register contents of the interrupted process. Normally the interrupt request remains outstanding until the 'interrupt return' instruction has been executed, after which the interrupt is immediately accepted. No further instructions will have been executed from the interrupted process, but the contents of the program counter and other processor registers will have been correctly restored, and can be resaved at the new entry to the service routine.

### *Establishing the cause of the interrupt*

On entry to the interrupt service routine the condition causing the interrupt must be established. The most obvious way in which this can be done is for there to be a flag associated with each possible interrupt condition, and an instruction (or set of instructions) with which the current value of each of these flags can be tested: for transput conditions these will be what we have termed sense instructions. When an interrupting condition occurs, the appropriate flag is set by hardware. The interrupt service routine then contains a chain of instructions, testing in turn each flag associated with a condition which might have caused an interrupt, until a flag is encountered which has been set. This system is used, for example, on the DEC PDP-8 computer.

If there are a large number of possible interrupting conditions, then the establishing by this means of the condition to be serviced is a lengthy process. There are several ways in which it is speeded up. One method is to have the flags collected together as an interrupt register, so that one particular bit of this register is associated with each possible interrupt condition. An interrupt request causes the appropriate bit to be set. The establishing of which condition has occurred is now reduced to scanning the interrupt register for a bit set to one.

If there are more conditions than can be accommodated in a single register, then the interrupt conditions are divided into groups, each with its own interrupt register. The interrupt group is then established by an over-all interrupt register with one bit per group. This technique could, of course, be extended to more than two levels.

A second method is for a code number to be allocated to each possible interrupt condition, and for the interrupt hardware to make available the number of the condition causing the interrupt. This number could be returned as a result of the execution of a special 'establish interrupting condition' instruction (as on the Data General Nova), or it could be placed in a known store location on entry to the interrupt service routine.

A third method is for the code number of the interrupting condition to modify the address of the initial entry point to the interrupt service routine. Thus, instead of storing the current PC contents at, say, location zero and fetching an instruction from location one,the hardware might store the current PC contents at location $2n$ and fetch an instruction (presumably a jump) from location $2n+1$, where $n$ is the number of the interrupting condition. Now, the fact that we find ourselves in a particular part of the interrupt service routine means that a particular condition has occurred. This method is sometimes referred to as a *vectored* interrupt system, since it makes use of a vector or table of interrupt entry points. It is the most common method of establishing the interrupting condition.

We could of course combine several of the above methods in a single system. For example, the IBM 1800 computer has one entry point for each group of interrupt conditions, and a register of flags to differentiate between conditions within each group.

### *The need for multiple interrupt levels*

In the simple interrupt system we have described, there are just two interrupt modes or levels, interruptable and non-interruptable. The processor will not accept any interrupt signals which it receives while in non-interruptable mode; instead any signals that occur are held pending in a queue by the hardware, until the processor returns to interruptable mode. However, if the interrupt condition is transient, the interrupt signal may be lost if it is not accepted within a certain length of time. In this situation we have a condition with a *crisis time,* within which a response must be made to the interrupt.

If the processor is in interruptable mode when the condition occurs, the response time depends upon the maximum instruction execution time (during which the interrupt cannot be accepted). This can be kept short, if the hardware prohibits such things as lengthy indirect addressing chains. More rarely, lengthy instructions could have points within their execution at which interrupts can be accepted.

However, in the worst case, the response time includes the maximum execution time for any of the interrupt service routines. Many computer systems therefore need a facility such that the interrupt service routine for a less critical condition can be interrupted by an interrupt signal from a more critical condition.

This is achieved by having the processor, on entry to the interrupt service routine, decide (by hardware or software means) to enable or disable individual interrupt conditions or groups of conditions. If an interrupt condition is disabled, any signal by that condition is held pending until the condition is enabled. Notice that such disabling of a condition is to be distinguished from switching a condition (such as overflow) so that its occurrence does not cause an interrupt to be signalled at all.

Such a system for the selective enabling and disabling of interrupts allows us to build an interrupt priority structure, within which higher priority conditions can interrupt the servicing of lower priority conditions (and, of course, the problem process). Thus we have a hierarchy of conditions, from high priority alarms (such as power failure) through to low priority conditions where response time is not critical. This is illustrated in Figure 6.7, which shows high priority interrupts having precedence over low priority interrupts. The systems to be described vary in the degree to which the priority of a particular condition can be changed.

### *Interrupt-on and interrupt-off instructions*

The most straightforward hardware extension we can make to the simple interrupt system, in order to allow several priority levels, is to

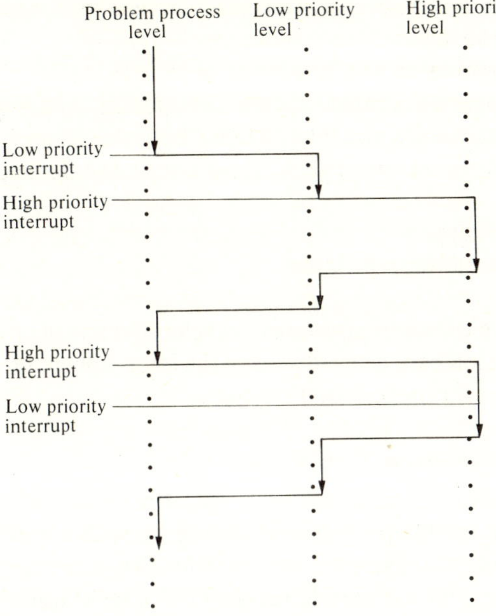


FIG. 6.7

provide an instruction which switches the processor between the interruptable and non-interruptable modes, as for example on the DEC PDP-8 computer.

In such a system the acceptance of an interrupt puts the processor in non-interruptable mode as before. But now the interrupt service routine can establish what condition has caused the interrupt, and hence at what priority level it should be running. It can then issue the instruction to return the processor to interruptable mode, having first saved any information that would be overwritten by a subsequent interrupt. Later in the interrupt service routine, when any interrupt would be difficult to cope with (when restoring saved information and preparing to return to the interrupted process), the processor can be switched back to non-interruptable mode.

Since the instruction to switch modes affects all interrupts equally, the interrupt service routine must be able to cope with the fact that any interrupt may occur on returning to interruptable mode (a lower priority interrupt, or even an interrupt for the condition currently being serviced). So the interrupt software may be complex because of the naivety of the hardware.

We have postulated two instructions to manipulate the interrupt system; this over-all enable/disable instruction, and the 'interrupt return' instruction. On the DEC PDP-8 only the former is provided. To return from an interrupt service routine we use the sequence:

Enable interrupts
Jump via saved return address

The enabling of the interrupts must not take effect until after the jump, for obvious reasons: so the hardware of the interrupt enable instruction delays its effect for one instruction cycle.

***The multilevel interrupt system***

Instead of implementing an interrupt priority system in software, we can build it into the processor hardware. In such a multilevel interrupt system (used, for example, on the IBM 1800 computer), each possible interrupt condition is assigned to one of a set of interrupt priority levels, and this assignment is built into the processor. Instead of being in a simple interruptable or non-interruptable mode, the processor is in one of a set of modes, one for each interrupt level, together with one (with the lowest priority) for the problem process.

If an interrupt signal is at a priority level lower than, or the same as, that in which the processor is running, it remains pending. If it is at a higher level, then the hardware accepts it as soon as the current instruction is complete. When the interrupt servicing is finished at a certain level (and higher priority interrupts may have been serviced at intervals during the processing), an 'interrupt return' instruction is executed. This causes the processor to revert to the next highest interrupt priority level which has an interrupt pending, eventually returning to the problem process at the lowest priority level.

If, for example, the processor is dealing with an interrupt at priority level 4 when an interrupt at priority level 7 occurs (where a higher number means a higher priority), then the processor would switch to level 7 and deal with that interrupt; when an 'interrupt return' is executed at this level, and assuming that no higher level interrupts have occurred, then the processor reverts to level 4.

Thus the hardware for this type of interrupt system implements a stack, allowing interrupt service routines to be interrupted only by higher priority interrupts, and ensuring an orderly return through the interrupt levels. In order that interrupt levels do not overwrite information saved for lower levels, it is usual for a vectored interrupt system to be provided, with a separate entry point and location for saved program counter contents for each level.

One problem with the multilevel interrupt system described above is that the connection between interrupt condition and priority level is wired into the hardware. A more flexible approach is provided by the DEC PDP-10 computer, where a set of interrupt priority levels is provided, and the processor accepts an interrupt signal only if it is of higher priority than the currently running process. However, instead of interrupt conditions being permanently assigned to particular levels, a set of instructions is provided which can tell the hardware which priority level an interrupt condition is to be attached to. For example, transput instructions can attach a device's various possible interrupt conditions to appropriate levels. The interrupt priority structure can therefore be dynamically reconfigured to take account of changing requirements.

***The masking interrupt system***

The multilevel interrupt system is built round the idea that the service routines for the various priority levels are self-contained entities, which are invoked by a particular interrupt condition, perform their function, and terminate, reverting to the interrupted process. However, a more complicated relationship between processes may be required, in which termination of a process at one interrupt level requires entry to a process at a different level than the interrupted one. While it is possible to implement such a structure using a multilevel interrupt system, more flexibility is provided by a masking interrupt system.

In this system a bit-pattern in an interrupt mask register in the processor specifies which interrupts are to be accepted. Each bit-position in the interrupt mask register corresponds to a particular interrupt condition or group of conditions, and only those conditions corresponding to a bit-position set to 'one' are enabled, so that an interrupt signal will be accepted. All other conditions (corresponding to zeros in the mask register) are disabled until the mask register is changed.

On receipt of an interrupt signal from an enabled condition, the contents of the PC are saved and the interrupt service routine is entered in the usual way. Furthermore, all interrupts must be disabled until sufficient is known about the interrupting condition for the mask register to be reset. This can be done by having an over-all interruptable/non-interruptable mode, and this is set to non-interruptable automatically on interrupt acceptance. Thus an interrupt signal is accepted only if the over-all mode is interruptable, and then only for conditions corresponding to a 'one' in the mask register. A typical interrupt processing sequence for an acceptable interrupt is then

Complete execution of current instruction.
Switch to non-interrruptable mode.
Store contents of PC.
Load into PC the address of the interrupt service routine.
} carried out by hardware

Save accumulator contents, etc.
Ascertain interrupting condition.
Reset interrupt mask register.
Switch to interruptable mode.
Service interrupting condition.
Switch to non-interruptable mode (why?).
Restore (or modify) interrupt mask register.
Restore accumulator contents, etc.
Switch to interruptable mode.
Return to interrupted (or other) process.

Notice that the over-all enabling of interrupts must again be delayed by hardware until the return has taken place. This technique is used on the Data General Nova computer.

***The PSW revisited***

The over-all interruptable/non-interruptable switch has been reintroduced as a means by which the contents of the program counter and interrupt mask register are changed in effect 'at the same time' on entry to and exit from an interrupt service routine.

A more general solution to this problem is the process state word or PSW introduced in §3.5. In this method each process runs under the control of a PSW which contains a number of processor registers, the only two of importance at present being the program counter and interrupt mask register.

Each interrupt condition, or group of conditions, is allocated two store locations, as under the vectored interrupt system, but these locations are now large enough to hold a pair of process state words, the 'old' PSW and the 'new' PSW. When an interrupt signal is accepted, the current contents of the processor registers are collected together and stored as the old PSW, to be replaced by the fields of the new PSW. The processor is now running in the appropriate interrupt service routine with the appropriate mask bits set. On completion of the processing of an interrupt, the routine executes a 'load PSW' instruction directed to the old PSW location. The processor is then back in the interrupted process, with the interrupt mask register reset to its original value.

This system is used on the IBM 370 range, where there are six groups of interrupt conditions, and hence six pairs of store locations to hold their PSWs. To establish the interrupting condition, the hardware stores an interrupt code number in the old PSW when the interrupt is accepted.

### *Saving the process context*

The process state word generally holds all the registers in the processor except for the accumulators, index registers, and (if they are present) the control registers. Thus the PSW-switching technique automatically saves the contents of all the miscellaneous registers (the condition code, the overflow flags, etc.) when an interrupt occurs, and re-initializes them for the interrupt service routine; they are then all restored by the 'load PSW' instruction. The processor mode register is one of these miscellaneous registers, and normally this field is set in the new PSW to cause entry to supervisor mode; however, note that it is now possible to route an interrupt directly to problem mode where it is appropriate.

We still need to save and restore the accumulators, index registers, and control registers. There are three general methods of solution:

(a) any registers required by the interrupt service routine have their contents saved and restored by the software. Special intructions may be provided to speed this task, as on the IBM 370 range.
(b) Several sets of registers are provided (as on the DEC PDP-10), and the PSW contains a field specifying which set of registers is currently in use. Then, as long as the sets of registers used by interrupting and interrupted processes are different, no register saving is required. If

two register sets are provided, one for the problem process and one for the interrupt service routines, then the register sets must be saved only when we decide to switch from one problem process to another. (c) The hardware automatically saves the contents of the registers in a suitable store area, replacing them with a set of values loaded from another store area. Essentially we are extending the PSW to a process state 'package' containing all the processor registers. This method is much less common than (a) or (b).

### *Interrupt stacking*

If each interrupt service routine is independent, returning control on completion to the next interrupt level, then the interrupt handling is done in a last-in-first-out fashion. Because of this, some computers which incorporate a stack as part of the processor hardware (for example the DEC PDP-11 computer and the Burroughs B6700 computer) make use of this stack in the handling of interrupts.

When an interrupt is accepted, a new PSW is taken from a fixed store location assigned to that interrupting condition. However, instead of storing the old PSW in another fixed location, it is pushed onto the stack used for subroutine linkage. When the interrupt has been serviced, an instruction pops the old PSW from the stack and returns to the interrupted process.

It will be seen that processor traps can be treated as 'involuntary' subroutine entries, making use of the stack in the same way as conventional subroutines entered in a 'voluntary' way by subroutine call instructions.

## 6.4. Transput channels

The tasks to be carried out by a device control unit may be complex. Generalized transput instructions have to be interpreted for a specific device, data words assembled and disassembled, the current store address and block count held and updated, status information and interrupts routed back to the processor, and there may be further facilities such as scatter read–gather write to be provided. Some of these tasks are device-dependent, but those involved with the transfer of data into and out of the store are common to all devices.

It may be more economic for several devices to share a single piece of equipment which provides a device-independent path to the store. Such a piece of equipment, called a *channel controller* (or simply *channel)*, is illustrated in Figure 6.8. In this diagram we show just one channel, but most computers provide two or more such independent channels to transfer data between transput device and store. Note that the channel is a processor by the definition given in §6.1. Some manufacturers therefore refer to this piece of equipment as an *input/output processor*: we prefer to reserve this word for use only when the transput system has a rather general data manipulating ability.

Now the co-operation of a channel and a device (and its control unit) is needed to transfer a block of transput data to or from the store, so that for the duration of a data operation the two operate as one unit. When the operation is complete, the channel is free to co-operate with another (or the same) device for a further operation. For the duration of the transput operation the channel is exclusively concerned with one device, so that no other device can gain access to the store through that channel.

The exact allocation among device, control unit, and channel (and store access switch) of the various tasks to be performed for a transput operation varies from computer to computer. The device-independent ones (such as maintenance of the store address and block count) tend to be in the channel, and the rest in the control unit. Also (especially in the smaller computers) the channel and the processor may share a certain amount of electronic logic, rather than be completely independent. We have assumed a single type of channel for all types of transput device; for economy a range of logically-equivalent channels may

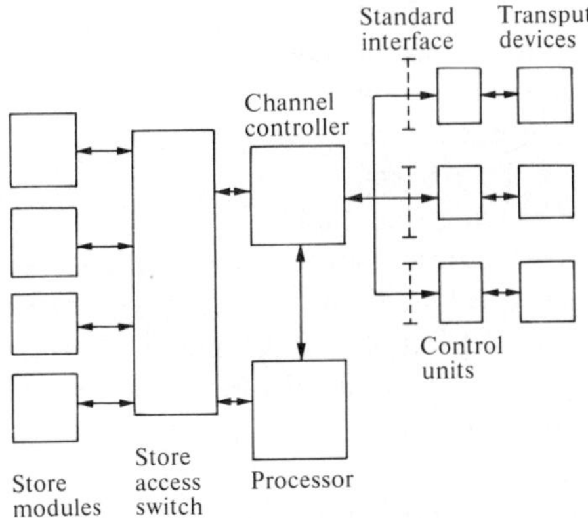


FIG. 6.8

be provided, tuned to the speed ranges and data widths of different sets of device types.

### *A simple channel*

As an example of a typical transput operation, consider a block read. The read instruction has to specify both a channel and a device. If either of these is non-existent or busy, an immediate error condition is signalled (perhaps by an interrupt). Otherwise a path is opened between channel and device for the operation, and the information is extracted from the instruction and passed to the relevant unit; the block address and length to the channel, the operation code to the device control unit, and so on.

The operation is then carried out independently of the processor, the data being passed from the device via the channel to the store. When the block is completely tranferred, the channel brings the device to a halt and sends an interrupt signal to the processor. All the channels may of course be in simultaneous use, any conflicts being resolved by the store access switch in the usual way.

Notice that at the hardware level the possible sources of transput interrupts are not now the set of devices but the (smaller) set of channels. In general, by the introduction of channels, we reduce the amount of equipment in processor and device, at the expense of reducing the potential transput parallelism.

### *Sequences of transput operations*

Having reduced the amount of equipment in each device by the introduction of channels, we can consider increasing the sophistication of these channels. We can allow each channel to control a sequence of transput operations, rather than a single operation, without requiring the intervention of the processor.

To do this we provide the channel with an instruction set, and a register to act as a program counter.The instruction set consists of at least read, write, control, and sense (or their equivalents). Some computer manufacturers (notably IBM) make a distinction between instructions, which are interpreted by the central processor, and commands, which are interpreted by the channel: we will use this convention.

Before starting a channel, the supervisory program builds up a sequence or program of channel commands to carry out the desired operations, and places them in an appropriate area of store. It then executes a 'start channel' instruction specifying the channel number and the address of the first command in the sequence. If this channel does not exist or is busy, there is an immediate interrupt.

Otherwise the channel copies the program address into its own program counter, extracts and interprets the first command, and initiates and controls the consequent operation. When this is complete the channel updates its program counter, and initiates and controls the next operation. This continues with the channel carrying out the program of transput operations, independent of both the processor and other channels. From time to time the channel accesses the store, either to extract a command, or to extract or insert a word from the current block of transput data, and any confllict here is dealt with by the store access switch.

Eventually the end of the program of commands is reached, indicated by an explicit 'stop' command or by a flag in the last command. The channel brings the device and itself to a halt, sending an interrupt signal to the processor.

We have as yet said nothing about the specification of which device is involved in any particular operation. Each command might specify the device involved, so that the association is formed between channel and device just for the one operation; or there might be a 'start device' command, so that the association lasts until the next such command or until the end of the channel program. The most common method (used, for example, in the IBM 370 range) is for the 'start channel' instruction executed by the processor to specify a device with which the channel is associated for the duration of the channel program.

### *Further channel functions*

There are a number of extra features that a channel might have;

(a) For a transput operation involving data transfer, the channel remains associated with the device for its duration. After initiation of a non-data operation (such as a tape rewind), the channel need not be involved, but normally remains associated with the device to deal with the next command. If there are no further commands in the program, the channel may initiate the operation, and immediately send an interrupt signal to the processor indicating that it can now be allocated a new channel program. The interrupt signal from the device, indicating that the operation has been completed, will have to wait for the channel to be free again, in order to route it to the processor.

(b) On the IBM 370 range scatter read–gather write is provided by allowing a subsequence of commands in a channel program to specify (by means of flags), not a sequence of transput operations, but a single read or write operation and a sequence of store areas.

(c) Only one processor transput instruction has been mentioned, 'start channel'. Other possible transput instructions are 'test channel', to establish its current status, and 'stop channel', to force termination of a current channel program.

(d) To the basic transput commands executed by the channel we may add an unconditional jump to allow greater flexibility in placing channel programs in store.

(e) We have assumed that all channel programs run to completion. There is of course the possibility that an error will arise in a transput operation. This causes the channel and device to halt immediately, sending an interrupt signal to the processor. The supervisory program may then use the 'test channel' instruction mentioned above to establish the cause of error.

(f) Finally some conditional jumping flexibility could be built into the channel command set. A simple scheme is for some commands to incorporate a skip on a data condition. For example, a disc search command compares the next disc block against some specified condition and skips if the test is successful. Then a channel program to search for and read a particular block would be

Search for condition, and skip if found.
Jump to previous command.
Read block.

Katzan (1971a, Chapter 9) discusses such a conditional skip on the IBM 370 range.

If we follow this path, of adding more power to the command set of the channel, we arrive at the concept of one or more general-purpose processors for transput in a multiprocessor system, to be discussed in the next section.

### *Multiplexor channels*

We have shown the channel as associated with one transput device for the duration of a sequence of (one or more) operations. This leads to problems with slow devices (such as card readers and line printers), since they are likely to be in near-continuous use, although the actual channel hardware is invoked only rarely because of the device's speed of operation.

In order to obviate the need for a large amount of hardware to be tied to slow devices and spend most of its time waiting for infrequent transput events to occur, we introduce what is usually called a multiplexor channel. We arrange for each slow device to be connected to what appears to be its own channel. However, we implement all these channels by sharing or multiplexing a single piece of channel logic. We refer to each of the logical units to which a device can be connected as a *subchannel*, and refer to the set of subchannels as a *multiplexor* channel. A multiplexor channel thus consists of a single piece of hardware to update store addresses and block counts and transfer data between device and store. This piece of hardware is then shared between a number of subchannels, to which the slow devices are connected, and which have all the logical functions of a conventional channel. The fact that the channel hardware spends only a small proportion of its time dealing with each device is hidden by the slow speed of operation of the device.

A normal channel holds its current context (store address, block count, etc.) in registers to ensure a fast response speed. In a channel dealing with many slow devices a large array of registers would be needed; instead a small store is provided within the channel, or an area of main store is allocated to hold the subchannel contexts.

Some computers provide one or more multiplexor channels, together with one or more channels which control one device at a time (sometimes called *selector* channels). In other computers any channel can be used in either mode.

### *Interconnection of devices to channels*

Finally let us consider the possible forms of interconnection between channels and devices. Figure 6.9(a) shows a scheme in which a group of devices is allocated to each channel. Each of the devices 1 to 3 can be controlled by channel A, so that only one of these devices can carry out a data operation at a time (although others of the group may be carrying out non-data operations). The merit of this scheme is the

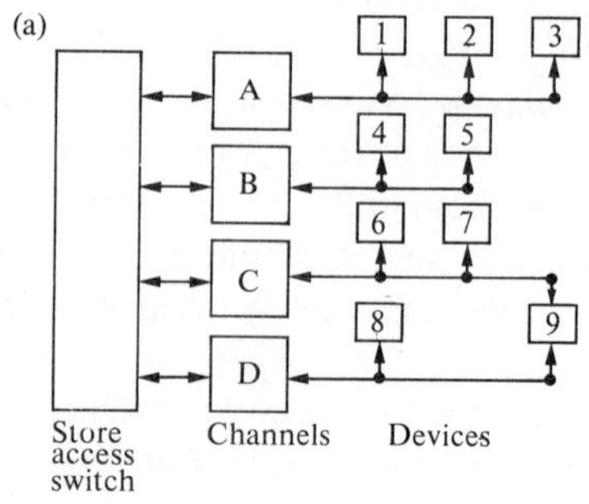


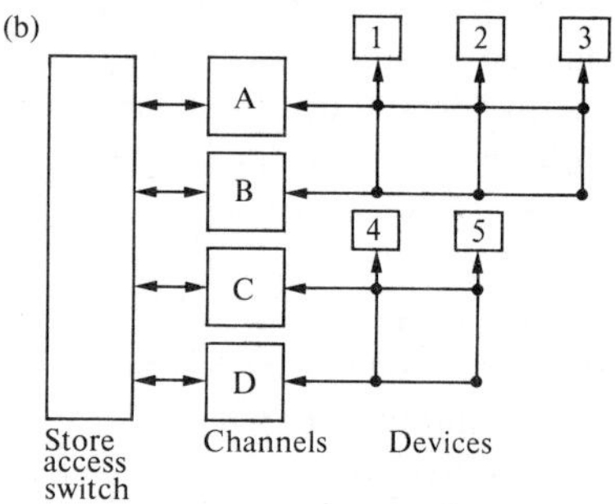


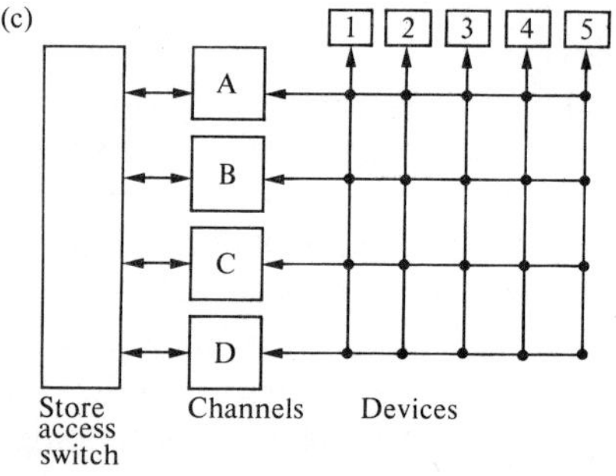


FIG. 6.9

small number of interconnections required, at the expense of pre-planning the allocation of devices to channels when the computer system is initially set up. Note also that the device identification number can be short, since it may be concatenated with its channel number for uniqueness. This scheme is that of the IBM 370 range. Note in Figure

6.9(a) that each device shown in fact consists of a control unit and one or more transput devices.

Device 9 could be a critical one (such as a disc unit) which has been connected to two channels, in order to provide duplicate paths to the device in the event of congestion or hardware faults in one channel. Alternatively device 9 could be an adaptor to connect together two channels back-to-back; this allows blocks of store to be rearranged without tying up the processor.

Figure 6.9(b) illustrates an interconnection scheme where each group of devices is connected to all of a group of channels; thus each of devices 1 to 3 could be controlled by either of channels A or B, and two of the devices could carry out data operations simultaneously. Figure 6.9(c) shows a cross-bar interconnection scheme, where each device can be controlled by any channel.

In this section we have discussed transput channels mainly in terms of the facilities on the IBM 360 and 370 ranges. Here the design approach has been to provide a rather small number of channels (up to eight on the IBM 360, up to twelve on most of the IBM 370 models) with sophisticated facilities. On other computers a different approach has been taken, of providing a larger number of simpler channels. For example, the Burroughs B6700 computer has up to three 'input/output processors', each attached to a group of devices. Each of these processors contains twelve 'channels', which can control a single operation (rather than a sequence) on any device attached to the processor. Thus a B6700 with a single input/output processor would have the interconnection scheme shown in Figure 6.9(c); the addition of a second input/output processor would produce an interconnection scheme of the form shown in Figure 6.9(b).

### 6.5. Systems with several processors

In this section we discuss multiple computer systems; that is, systems in which two or more general-purpose processors are electrically connected. The fact that we require the processors to be general-purpose, to have a program counter and a reasonably comprehensive instruction set, means that a system with one central processor and a number of channel controllers, as described in the previous section (even if the channels are termed input/output processors), is not admissible as a multiple computer system by this definition.

Note further that we require direct electrical connection between the processors. We thus exclude systems of computers communicating by transferring punched cards or magnetic tape from computer to computer, and also systems which consist of several processing and other units which can be configured in various ways into two or more disjoint computers.

### *Reasons for interconnecting computers*

The first multiple computer system is believed to have been formed by the setting up in 1954 of a direct computer-to-computer link between SEAC and DYSEAC, two computers owned by the U.S. National Bureau of Standards (Nisenoff 1966). Since then many multiple computer systems have been built, ranging from closely connected multiprocessors to geographically dispersed computer networks.

There are four basic reasons for the setting up of such systems (apart, of course, from the wish to do research into the problems presented by computer intercommunication):

(a) To increase the computer power available. It is sometimes more economic or convenient to enhance a computer system by adding one or more extra processors than by replacing a single processor by a larger model, which perhaps does not exist or has the wrong performance/cost ratio. It must, of course, be possible for the increased power to be usable in multiple computer form; that is, the tasks to be performed must be capable of being carried out at least partially in parallel to take advantage of such a system.

A particular case of this method for increasing computer power is 'load-sharing'. If we have several (usually geographically remote) computers, then we may find that their peaks of activity do not coincide. If we interconnect them, then an overburdened computer can pass some of its work-load to a more lightly loaded computer.

(b) A further enhancement to computer power is provided by functional specialization. Suppose we have several tasks to be carried out, and we assign each of them, on a more or less permanent basis, to a particular computer or processor. This eliminates the overheads of switching a single processor between a number of tasks, and the supervisory software (and perhaps the hardware) is simplified by this reduction in task switching.

If we assign markedly different tasks to different parts of the system on a permanent basis, each computer or processor can be designed for the tasks it is to perform. For example, if we assign all transput tasks to one processor and all data-processing tasks to another, the former can be small and have a limited range of data-types, while the latter can be optimized for performing processing without having to control transput.

In a network of computers we may assign particular classes of job to particular computers and design their configurations accordingly. For example, jobs with large store requirements might normally be run on one computer, jobs with large line-printer output requirements or using specialized transput devices on another, and jobs using a certain application program on another, at a location where expertise has been built up.

(c) If we have a system with multiple computers or processors, we may have increased resilience to hardware faults, since there could still be sufficient processing power to continue with at least the system's more important tasks. Such resilience is not, of course, available if all processors are involved in the processing of each task.

(d) Finally, we can connect geographically distant places by computer-controlled links, either as the best means of providing a communications network for purposes not directly connected with computers (for example, a computer-controlled telephone exchange), for access to computer power or specialized computers (for example, remote job entry systems), or for access to banks of data stored elsewhere.

***The user's view of a multiple computer system***

We will shortly look at the physical means by which multiple computer systems are constructed. But we will first look at the user's view of such systems.

In the computer-controlled telephone system mentioned above, the user is, of course, unaware of the presence of computers. In a system in which the user is aware of the presence of computers, he is likely to see one of three basic systems: a network; a symmetric system; or an asymmetric system.

In the first case he sees a number of geographically remote computers or computer systems interconnected by links. He may not know (or care) whether these are permanent or switched links, or what subsidiary computers are involved along with the main-frames at the ends of each link.

In the case of a multiple computer system at one location, the user sees either a set of approximately equivalent processors or computers on any of which each job could be run, or a small processor/computer dealing with transput and a larger main-frame performing data processing. He may not know whether the active units are processors or independent computers, and whether they are interconnected by a common main store, a common backing store, a communications link, or even a non-electrical link such as by transferring reels of magnetic tape.

### *Forms of computer intercommunication*

If we turn from the external view, we can distinguish two dimensions of direct electrical link between processors, as shown in Figure 6.10. On one dimension we distinguish between sending a message as a stream of signals (what we might term 'dynamic' communication) and placing a message where it can be read ('static' communication). This is analogous to the difference between speaking to someone and leaving a written message.

On the other dimension we distinguish between direct processor-to-processor communication using the processor's non-transput instruction sets, and communication using the transput systems, so that each processor sees the other as a transput device. These methods may be

| Control | | Communication: Dynamic | Communication: Static |
|---|---|---|---|
| | Direct | A | B |
| | Transput | D | C |

FIG. 6.10

further distinguished by the distances involved, since the former of necessity involves close proximity, while the latter may allow links over any distance from a few feet to world-wide (or even over interplanetary distances).

As the diagram shows, this gives us four intercommunication classes, A to D. These are not mutually exclusive, of course, as two processors might be connected in several ways for different types of message. Class A includes a number of miscellaneous interconnection methods, which tend to appear in computer systems in conjunction with other methods from classes B to D. Class B involves processors sharing a common main store; we speak of the system as a (single) *multiprocessor* computer. Classes C and D involve intercommunication through transput systems, via either a link or a shared backing storage device. We consider the system to consist of *several* computers, and speak of a *multi-computer* system. Class D includes all the numerous examples of geographically dispersed computer networks.

### *Class A links*

As we have already mentioned, class A includes a group of miscellaneous direct processor-to-processor links, such as the following:

(a) We could provide instructions on one processor to start, stop and interrogate the current status of another processor. We have already seen one example of this, the channel control instructions discussed in the previous section, although there a special rather than a general-purpose processor is being controlled. Another example is the 'exchange jump' instruction on the CDC 6600 computer, which we discuss later. Note that a system with such instructions is potentially asymmetric, with one processor the master and the other the slave.

(b) A number of unconventional computers have been built which provide a group of processing units which operate in closely-coupled parallelism to complete a task, where the parallelism is between what would be successive instructions (or groups of instructions) from a single task in a conventional computer, rather than between separate tasks.

An example is the early NBS Pilot computer (Leiner, Notz, Smith, and Weinberger 1958, 1959) where one processor performed the normal data-processing, while another performed the housekeeping functions for this processing (address modification, iteration counting, etc.); a third processor dealt with transput.

Such computers have instructions to couple together the processors so that they co-operate on the current task, but the instructions required depend on the particular architecture. Where such parallelism is provided, it is nowadays disguised (for ease of programming) as a conventional single-instruction-stream computer, so that the intercommunication is invisible at the instruction level.

(c) A third possibility is to make some of the registers in one processor accessible to another processor. This could be seen as an example on the border of class B, but it is included here as it is more asymmetric and idiosyncratic than the method described there.

An example of this technique is the accessibility of the central processor's program counter to the PCPs of the CDC 6600 computer. Another is the accessibility of various registers and counters in the central processor to a diagnostic computer, as discussed in §8.1.

(d) The most common class A method of communication is for one processor to be able to send a signal causing an interrupt in a second processor. This could be seen as on the border of class D, but again we find it convenient to treat it as part of the 'miscellaneous' class A.

There are two main possibilities here. One is for the circuitry of a processor or computer, on detection of a hardware fault, automatically to send a signal to interrupt a stand-by processor or computer, causing it to set in motion procedures to take over the first's workload. The second is for there to be an instruction (for example 'signal processor' on the IBM 370 range) which causes the interrupt signal to be sent to a specified computer, and the signal then has a significance dependent on the process issuing the instruction. It might, for example, be a signal to draw the attention of the second processor to a message left in common main store in a class B system.

### *Class B links—multiprocessors*

Class B consists of the various multiprocessor systems (Enslow 1974). Here a system (considered to be a single computer) contains a number of general-purpose processors sharing a common main store, as illustrated in Figure 6.11. We show three processors, each with a full set of registers (program counter, accumulators, overflow flag, etc.) and each able to access any of the whole range of store locations, here

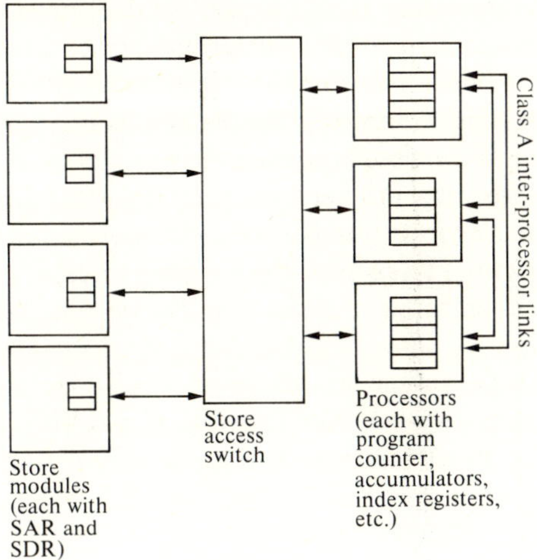


FIG. 6.11

divided up among four store modules. Any of the possible implementations of the store access switch shown in Figure 6.2 could be used.

Each processor autonomously fetches and executes instructions, and its store accesses are routed to the relevant store module by the store access switch. The only interference by one processor with another is when both attempt to access the same module at the same time, when the switch invokes a priority-ordering among the processors to complete one store access before commencing the other. If two processors are executing the same piece of code or accessing the same table of constants, then only one copy is required and the processors can independently access the same store area, mediated if necessary by the store access switch.

The implication in Figure 6.11 is that all the processors in the system are similar, with the same architecture and instruction set: this is therefore a *symmetric* multiprocessor system. Any process once initiated can run unchanged on any processor; indeed, a process may run on several different processors in the course of its lifetime. Even if all the processors are identical, it may be necessary for a process to be able to ascertain on which processor it is running (for example, a process logging processor hardware faults), so an instruction may be provided which delivers the identification number of the processor on which it is executed. Examples are 'store cpu address' on the IBM 370 range, and 'read processor identification' on the Burroughs B6700.

An alternative configuration is an *asymmetric* multiprocessor system, with two or more non-identical processors sharing a common main store. The most common example of this is a system of one or more small general-purpose processors to deal with transput, and one or more larger processors to perform the data-processing: the former could be seen as having evolved from the channel controllers of the last section. Less commonly each of the larger processors could be specialized for a limited range of tasks from the system's workload.

In Figure 6.11 we show a further means of interprocessor communication, as well as the common store. This is to suggest that such a multiprocessor system may also provide class A links, usually in the form of a facility for each processor to send an interrupt signal to any other.

### *The store of a multiprocessor*

So far we have assumed that the whole main store is common to all processors. It is possible for each processor to have access to its own private range of store locations as well as to a range of common store locations. Note that the distinguishing feature of a strict multiprocessor computer is that the shared main store can hold instructions for direct execution and data for direct manipulation by the normal instruction set.

If a symmetric multiprocessor holds all its main store in common then there is a problem with the wired-in addresses of store locations dedicated to a fixed processor use. Thus each processor may expect to find, starting at the same fixed address $x$, a vector of addresses for interrupt service routines, and we may wish each processor to have its own vector rather than there be a system-wide one.

One way of dealing with this is for each processor to have a *relativisor* or *prefix,* wired in when the system is set up, and this is added to all addresses generated for an area at the bottom of the store containing the dedicated locations. Suppose, for example, that all the processor's dedicated locations are in the first 2048 locations of the store. Then in a two-processor system we might have relativisors of zero and 2048, so that a physical address $x$ in the range zero to 2047 (generated either automatically by the processor hardware or by an instruction for a process) would cause access to either location $(x+0)$ or $(x+2048)$, depending on the processor involved. This is illustrated in Figure 6.12.

A further problem in a multiprocessor system is the placing of a

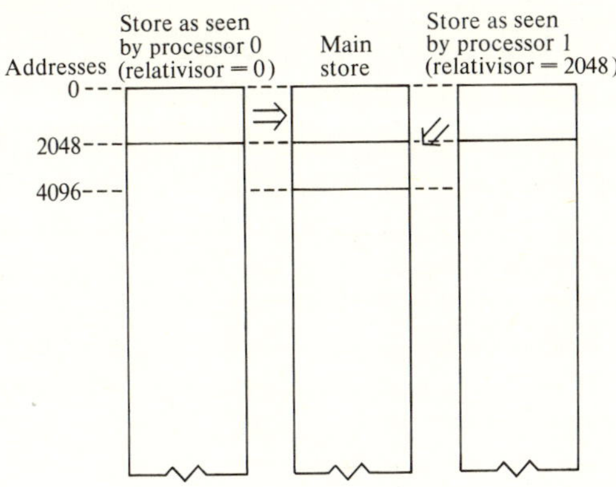


FIG. 6.12

cache store, whether a single one across the access paths to store of all processors, or an individual cache store for each processor. In the former case we may exacerbate the store access interference between processors, while in the latter we have the problem of one processor updating a store location of which another processor is accessing a cache store copy. The latter method is used on the multiprocessing models in the IBM 370 range.

### *The transput system of a multiprocessor*

Figure 6.11 does not show any transput system. There are a number of possibilities here. One is for each processor to have its own transput system, as shown in Figure 6.13(a). Here each group of transput devices and channel controllers is accessible from just one processor, and the channel controllers are connected to their own devices, their controlling processor and the common store. At the other extreme we have Figure 6.13(b) where there is a single system-wide transput system, here consisting of two channel controllers, accessible to all processors via a cross-bar switch. The first system is used on multiprocessing models in the IBM 370 range, while the second is used on multiprocessing Burroughs B6700 computers.

In Figure 6.13(a) it is fairly obvious which processor is to receive any interrupt or trap. Each processor receives its own traps, interrupts from its own transput system, and interrupts directed to it from the other processor. However, in Figure 6.13(b) things are not so clear-

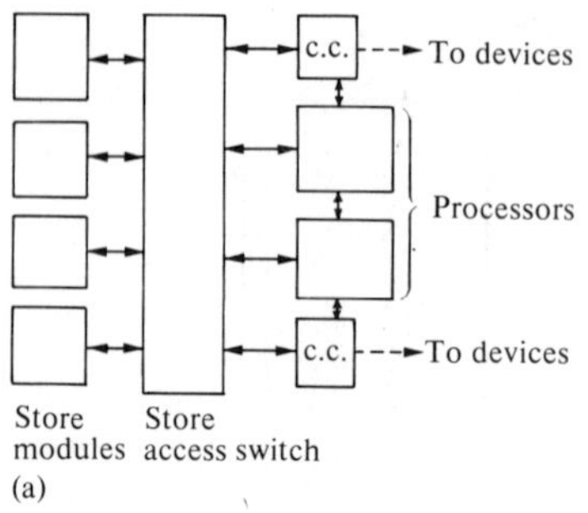


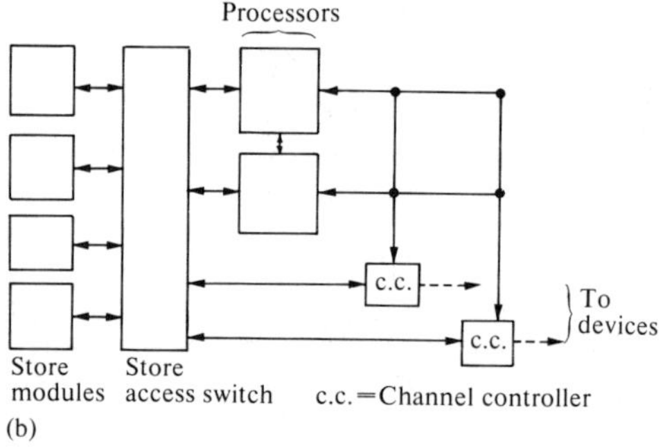


FIG. 6.13

cut. Traps from a processor (overflow, invalid operation code, processor hardware faults) are directed to that processor. Interrupts from the transput system could be routed to any of the processors, so the transput hardware routes the interrupt to the 'most-interruptable' processor; that is, whichever processor has indicated its willingness to accept such interrupts. In such a system a single copy of the supervisory programs may be supplied, and this is run on whichever processor is available when a supervisory function is required.

### *The CDC 6600 computer*

The CDC 6600 is an example of a computer on the border between classes B and C, since the common storage is seen as the main store by one processor but not by the others. This computer was designed for performing scientific calculation at great speed, and for a long time it held the title of 'the largest computer in the world' (Bell and Newell 1971, p.476). Its architecture is illustrated in Figure 6.14.

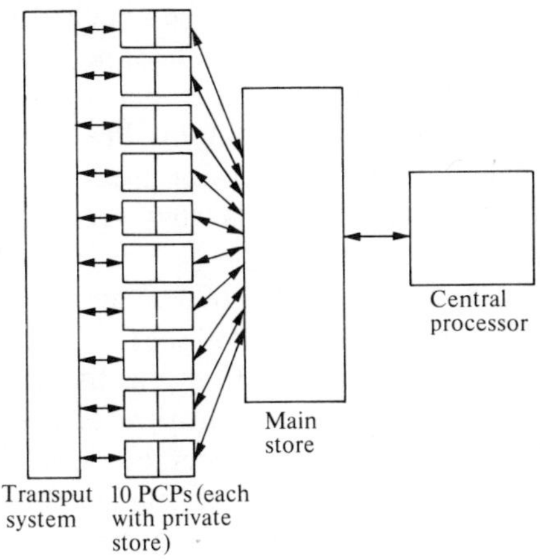


FIG. 6.14

It consists of a single central processor, oriented towards providing great processing power and speed for scientific calculation, and obtaining its instructions and data from a 60-bit word main store: and 10 smaller peripheral control processors or PCPs (all identical), each with a private 12-bit word store holding its own instructions and immediate data. Each PCP has instructions with which it can read or write the central processor's store, allowing it to send messages to the other PCPs or to the central processor.

The PCPs control all transput devices attached to the computer. Since there is no interrupt system in this computer, the PCPs monitor the devices by *polling,* that is , by explicitly checking the device status at a suitable frequency. As the PCPs are small 12-bit computers, they can be used for more general processing than simply controlling transput devices. Under the SCOPE operating system, one of the PCPs holds a set of supervisory programs to control management of the central processor and allocation of the remaining nine PCPs to transput operations.

In order to allow the PCPs to monitor and control the central processor, they have six special instructions: four to read and write the central processor's store, one to read the central processor's program counter, and the 'exchange jump' instruction. When the latter is executed on a PCP, the central processor stores its current process context in a specified area of main store, loads a new context, and continues. This allows the central processor to be switched very quickly from process to process, under the control of the supervisory PCP.

In the later CDC 7600 computer, a similar pattern of central processor and group of PCPs (now 15) obtains, but there are several conditions which can cause central processor interrupts, unlike the CDC 6600 in which there are no interrupts whatever, and all synchronization is by polling.

Architecturally we see the CDC 6600 computer as a system of 11 independent processors. In § 8.2 we will see that one of these, the central processor, is implemented as 10 physically separate processing units, interconnected in such a way as to operate as a single logical processor. Conversely the PCPs are implemented as a single piece of physical hardware, time-multiplexed to appear as the 10 independent PCPs. The conceptual layout is shown in Figure 6.15 (taken from CDC 1966).

Each PCP requires 51 bits of current processor context (accumulator, program counter, etc.), and the 10 processor contexts can be imagined as laid out as a 'barrel'. The physical hardware's major cycle of 1000 ns is divided into 10 minor cycles of 100 ns, and each PCP has the use of the logic of the instruction control for one such minor cycle, to execute one step of an instruction (which might in some cases be the whole instruction). The physical hardware simply moves the next processor context into the instruction control and executes one step for

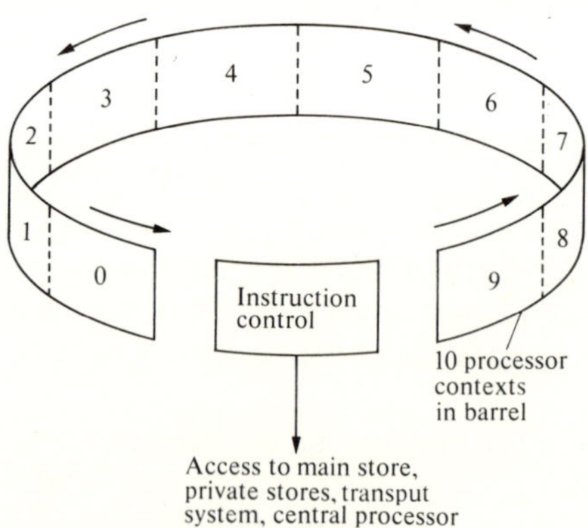


FIG. 6.15

that PCP. The PCP private stores are independent of one another, and have a read/write cycle of 1000 ns; if a PCP requires an access to private store, it is arranged to be complete when the PCP next reaches the instruction control.

This is an example of a common technique whereby we implement a set of independent processors as a single piece of time-multiplexed hardware. We saw one example of this, the multiplexor channel, in the last section. Another example is the second-generation Honeywell H800 computer (Lourie, Schrimpf, Reach, and Kahn 1959). This used a similar 'barrel' principle on a single piece of hardware to implement 8 logically autonomous processors, each of which executed a separate process. In the CDC 6600 all PCPs are allocated a minor cycle in each major cycle, even if they are idling. In the H800 however, the physical processor executed instructions only for the active processes, which meant that they ran faster if there were only a few of them.

Both the CDC 6600 and the H800 were designed to allow the processing load to be seen at the architectural level as a set of independent processes, without requiring large amounts of multiprocessing hardware and without the large process-switching overheads of multiprogramming. The technique of multiplexing has also been used to achieve compatibility across a range of computers, for instance the IBM 360 and 370 ranges. Here the larger and faster models have (both architecturally and physically) a processor and a set of independent channel controllers. On the smaller and slower models the architectural independence between units is preserved, but is implemented by microprogramming a single physical processor.

### *Class C links—shared storage devices*

Class C includes systems where several separate computers can each access a shared backing storage device. Currently there are two main configurations in this class:

(a) 'Front-ending' systems communicating by means of a disc. Several second-generation computer systems had a small satellite or *front-end* computer which controlled all slow devices, in order to relieve the main-frame computer of the task. Work for the main computer would be written by the front-end computer to a reel of magnetic tape, which would then be physically transferred by an operator to a tape deck attached to the main computer. An improvement on physical transference of the tape reel is to make a single magnetic tape deck electronically connectable to either computer by means of a manually-operated switch. If we replace the tape deck by a magnetic disc unit, we have a typical example of a class C system. Work for the main com-

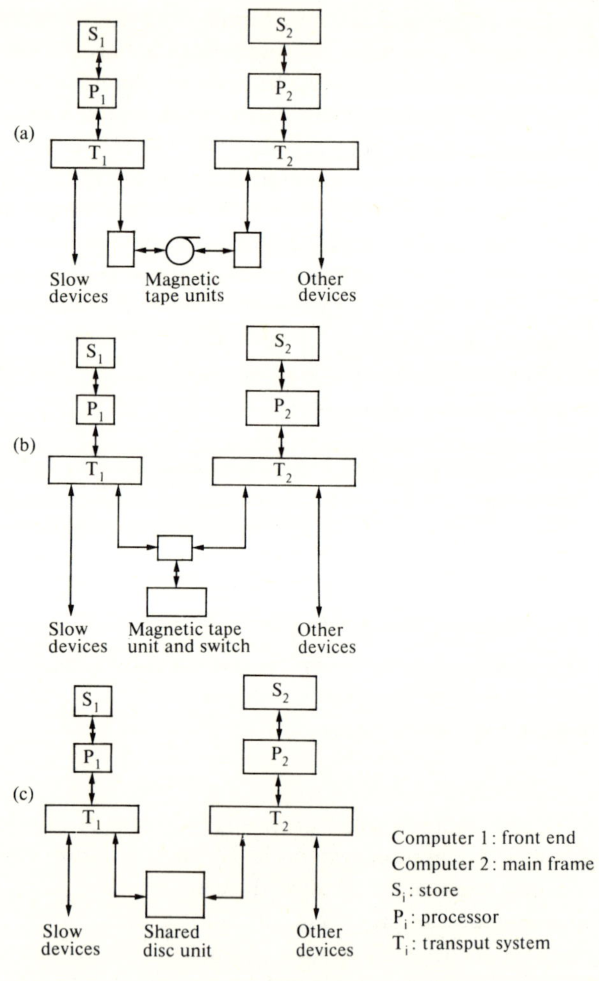


FIG. 6.16

puter is written by the front-end computer to a suitable area of the disc in a mutually-understood format, from which it is processed by the main computer and the results returned to the disc for output by the front-end computer. These three systems are illustrated in Figure 6.16.

(b) Sharing of backing storage resources between computers. In the simplest case this involves being able to make use of a backing storage device such as a magnetic disc (or, of course, other transput devices) from any of several computers, care being taken to avoid conflicting accesses to the device. Such a system may ensure reliability by the duplication of hardware. We provide two separate computers (processor and store) which share all (or most of) their transput devices. Normally one computer is processing the input data. If the computer breaks down, it sends a (class A) signal to the other computer, which immediately takes over the transput devices and continues with the processing.

***Class D links***

In class D, intercomputer communication involves transfer of characters, words, or blocks of data over a link under control of the transput systems of the two computers. Thus transfer of a block of data from computer A to computer B involves the execution of a 'write block' instruction by the transput system of computer A in conjunction with a 'read block' by computer B, and each computer sees the other as a sophisticated transput device. If the two computers are close together

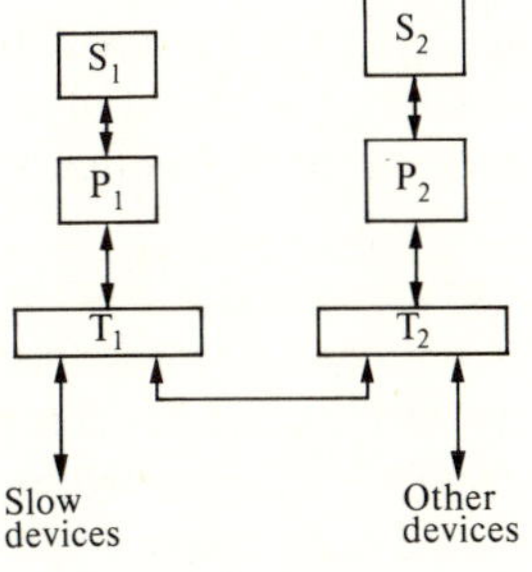


FIG. 6.17

(some tens of feet) we may simply (at least in architectural terms) connect their transput systems back-to-back, with some provision of logic to resolve conflicting control signals received from the two sides.

This is a common method of attaching a front-end computer to a main-frame. It is illustrated in Figure 6.17, using the same symbolism as Figure 6.16. Examples of this are the ASP or attached support processor system, where the two computers are models in the IBM 360 series (for example, a model 40 and a model 65), and the University of Manchester Regional Computer Centre where the front-end is an ICL 1906A and the main-frame a CDC 7600. We have shown the front-end computer as dedicated to the control of slow devices (card readers, line printers, and the like). Alternatively the front-end might be used to control only remote devices (for example, a number of interactive terminals), or we might attach several front-end computers to a single main-frame, each to control a range of devices.

### *The replacement of hard-wired logic*

So far in this chapter we have seen the transput devices and their control units as pieces of hard-wired logic. However, if the transput operations to be carried out are sophisticated, it may be more economic to implement the control unit of the transput device as a small computer. The central processor need not be aware of this. It simply sends details of required transput operations in a suitable format through the transput system (i.e. a class D link), irrespective of whether the control unit is hard-wired or computer-based. Two main classes of device have until recently been candidates for this technique, backing storage and remote devices.

If we replace the hard-wired control unit for a backing storage device (such as a magnetic disc) by a small computer, it is easier to implement (for example) queuing systems for transput requests to take advantage of the rotational ordering of blocks on the device, and more complex search commands to reduce the load on the central processor.

If we have a number of remote devices (in particular terminals), then characters have to be received from a number of lines and multiplexed onto a single line into the central computer for input, and the converse for output. Such a task (line controlling and message concentrating) is usually performed most conveniently by a small computer, which is able to buffer data and use the complete message (rather than the individual character) as the unit of transfer to and from the central computer. It may also be delegated some of the simpler processing tasks to be carried out for the terminal user (such as reaction to the pressing of control keys). Such a computer may be seen from the central processor either as equivalent to a hard-wired control unit and multiplexor for the network of remote terminals, or as a subsidiary computer relegated the task of front-ending the system to this network.

With the introduction of microprocessors, it is becoming increasingly common to use them as controllers for a wide range of devices (such as line printers and individual visual display units). Thus instead of having all the processing power concentrated in the main-frame, it is tending to be spread throughout a computer system; this is called *dispersed* or *distributed intelligence.*

### *Computer networks*

Only if the distance involved is short can we set up a class D link between two computers by directly connecting their transput systems. If the distance is more than some tens of feet, and more especially if the computers are geographically dispersed, then the data to be transmitted must be converted to a form more suitable for long-distance communication. Thus the simplest link between two remote computers is a cable interfaced to the two transput systems by equipment providing this two-way conversion.

Rather than provide a fixed path between each pair of potentially communicating computers, we generally make use of a private or public switched communications network, which may have been designed for use by computers or may be basically for other purposes (such as the public telephone network). Such switched networks are of two kinds, circuit-switched and packet-switched. If two computers are to communicate over a *circuit-switched* network, a direct circuit or path is opened between the two computers for the period of the dialogue (or 'call'), and messages are then sent over this path. In a *packet-switched* network, no such permanent path is opened. Instead the dialogue is broken up into addressed blocks or *packets* of data, which are fed into the network and relayed from point to point towards the destination over any currently-available path, so that subsequent packets may follow different paths through the network. The network itself may incorporate computers, to control the paths in the circuit-switched case, or to receive and retransmit the packets in the packet-switched case.

The software to communicate across such a network is more complex than over short-distance links, since it needs to adhere to a convention or *protocol*, which specifies the format of each packet (including address of sender and receiver, priority level, etc.), how a dialogue is initiated, and how errors are detected and corrected; on the larger networks such a protocol has to be suitable for use by a wide range of computers, perhaps produced by different manufacturers. This is a very brief introduction to the large and rapidly evolving field of computer communications and networks; for further reading see Abramson and Kuo (1973), Bacon and Bull (1973), and Davies and Barber (1973).

A common form of computer network is the *star*, shown in Figure 6.18 (a), where remote sites are connected to a single central facility providing computer power. Typically we have a number of remote job entry (RJE) stations, each consisting of a card reader and a line printer together with a hard-wired or computer-based controller, transmitting

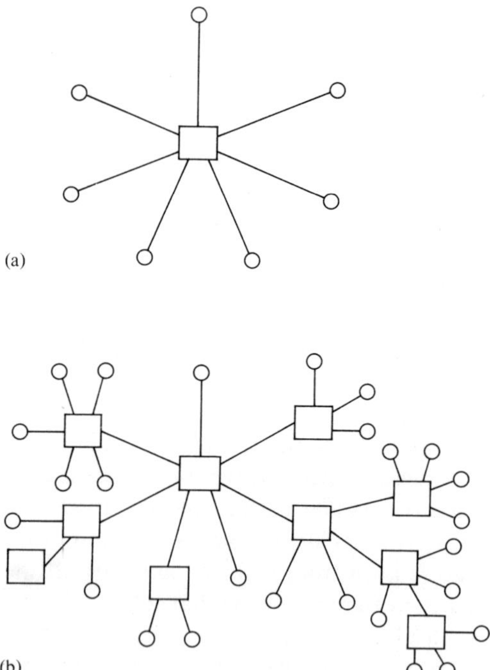


FIG. 6.18

jobs to a large remote central computer and subsequently receiving the output for local distribution. A more complex system might have a hierarchy of several levels of computer power between remote sites and central computer, as shown in Figure 6.18 (b). The central facility might more generally be any shared resource, such as common data base (see, for example, Marill and Stern 1975).

A more general scheme of intercommunication gives us the *distributed* network shown in Figure 6.19, where each computer may be connected to several others. An example of this is a distributed processing system for a firm, where each department or section has its own small computer dedicated to performing local tasks, and the computers are interconnected to transfer common data from one section to another. There may also be common computing resources accessible from all sectional computers.

Another example is the Advanced Research Projects Agency network ARPANET (Roberts and Wessler 1970) linking computers (or local computer networks) at various universities and research laboratories in the USA and Europe. Figure 6.19 is in fact a diagram of the logical layout of ARPANET, abstracted from Kirstein (1975). Since the computers at each node are diverse and independently managed, they are not connected directly into the network. Instead each 'host' computer is connected to a dedicated Interface Message Processor or IMP (originally the Honeywell DDP-516 (Heart, Kahn, Ornstein,

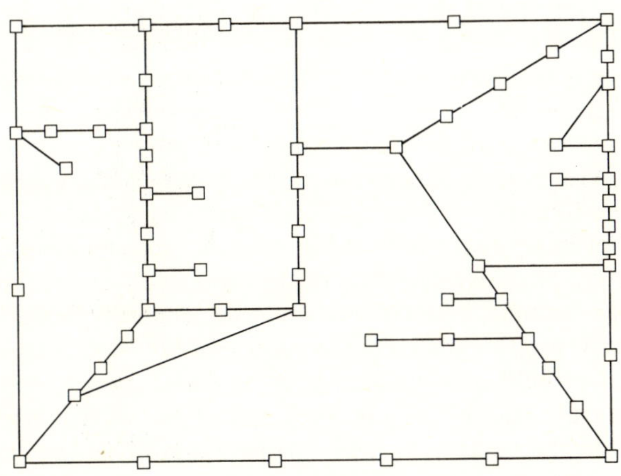

FIG. 6.19

Crowther, and Walden 1970), now being replaced by the Lockheed SUE computer (Heart, Ornstein, Crowther, and Barker 1973)), and these form the nodes of the network. Access to ARPANET is from any host computer or from a terminal attached directly to one of the IMPs.

## 6.6. Semaphores

Consider two or more processes which interact, in order either to co-operate on a task or to share a common resource. The processes may need to send synchronization signals to each other, or they may need to ensure that only one process at a time is operating in a critical area. The simplest mechanism for policing such interaction is to have a counter accessible to all processes, and these can alter the counter value or test it for a critical value.

This mechanism was formalized as the semaphore by Dijkstra (1968) in the paper 'Co-operating sequential processes'. A *semaphore* is a counter which, after being initialized to a suitable value, can be accessed only by two primitive synchronizing operations, called P or *wait* and V or *signal*. The wait primitive tests the value of the semaphore and, when it is greater than zero, decrements it by one and allows the process to continue. The signal primitive increments the semaphore value by one and allows the process to continue.

The process 'hangs' at the wait primitive as long as the semaphore value is negative or zero. It either executes a 'busy wait' continually retesting the value of the semaphore, or (more usually) the process relinquishes use of the processor until it becomes unblocked. The unblocking is eventually caused by another process executing the signal primitive on that semaphore. If several processes are waiting on a semaphore when a signal is performed, only one process will find the semaphore to have a positive value so that it can continue; the others will remain blocked.

These primitives are *indivisible*; that is, no semaphore can be accessed by a primitive while it is being operated on by another primitive. If, for example, a semaphore could be accessed after a wait had found it to be positive and before its value had been decremented, then timing flaws would arise in the interaction under certain conditions.

By declaring and initializing a semaphore for each synchronizing event and each critical area, and implementing wait and signal as subroutines to operate on any specified semaphore, we can build a system of processes with demonstrably safe interaction. Figure 6.20 (a) shows

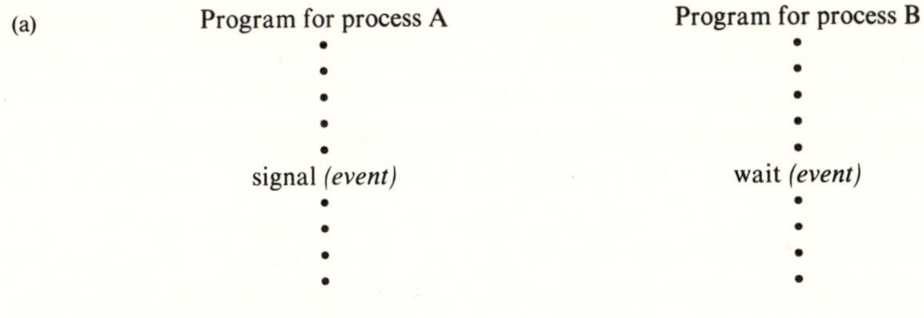


*event* is a semaphore initialized to 0.

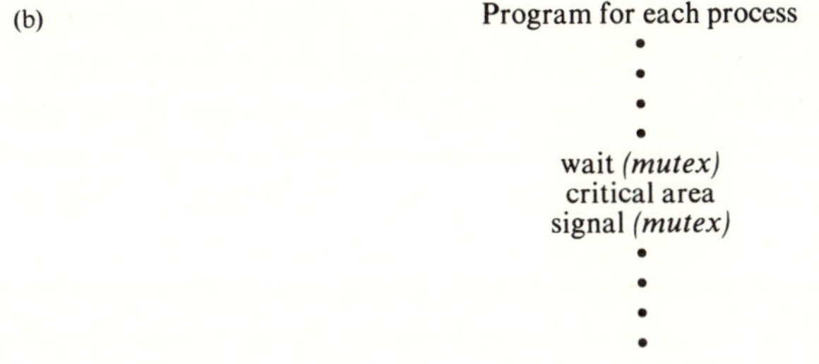


*mutex* is a semaphore initialized to 1.

FIG. 6.20

a semaphore being used to ensure that process B does not proceed until process A has reached a certain point. Figure 6.20 (b) shows a semaphore ensuring not more than one process can enter a critical area at a time. For further discussion of the use of semaphores see Dijkstra (1971) and Lister (1975, Chapter 3).

***The implementation of semaphores***

In order to allow flexibility in the declaration of semaphores we implement them as ordinary store locations. How then are we to implement the indivisible primitives, wait and signal? We might implement them as normal subroutines using load and store instructions, relying on speed differentials between processes to make simultaneous access to the semaphore unlikely, but such an assumption of relative speed is dangerous.

If the processes are run under a multiprogramming system on a single processor, then we can implement the primitives as subroutines which run in non-interruptable mode, so that no other process can take control until the primitive has finished. This means that they are in fact implemented as subroutines in the supervisor, called by extracode or supervisor call instruction. In fact the two primitives, and the associated process switching, could be implemented directly in hardware or by microprogramming (Wirth 1969; Liskov 1972).

Consider now a multiprocessor system, with the interacting processes running on separate processors and with semaphores implemented as locations in common store. The synchronizing primitives consist of sequences of load and store instructions accessing this common store. Now the store access switch ensures that the individual store accesses do not interact, so that (for example) a read access to a store location used as a semaphore is not accepted until a preceding write access from another processor is complete. However, there is nothing to stop a sequence of accesses from one processor being interleaved with a sequence of accesses from another. So, if two (or more) processors start executing the code of one of the synchronizing primitives at the same time, we have the possibility of timing faults.

There are two practical ways of getting round this, both of which are variations on the theme of having a central arbitrating mechanism. We can organize an asymmetric multiprocessing system, designating one processor the master and the rest slaves. Then the master processor acts as the arbiter, to which all requests for access to critical areas are routed for granting or refusal.

The second method retains the symmetric multiprocessor system. The common code of the synchronizing primitives is treated as a critical area, to be protected by a 'metasemaphore' or 'lock', as described in Lister (1975, Chapter 4). The difference between this lock and an ordinary semaphore lies in the action taken while waiting. An ordinary semaphore causes the process to relinquish control of the processor, while the lock causes a 'busy wait' until the code of the primitive is free. The lock is again some designated location in common store, taking values of (say) zero for closed and one for open. Now signal takes the form.

Load accumulator with one
Store accumulator at lock location

This is indivisible as far as the lock location is concerned. However, the wait requires the indivisible operation;

Test (designated) location for one and, if so, set to zero.

We must therefore provide such an operation, using the store access switch as arbiter.

Most multiprocessors have an instruction which implements this indivisible operation. A common one is the 'test and set' instruction (as on the IBM 370 range). This accesses a specified store location and changes its value to some constant (say zero), while at the same time informing the processor of the previous value by performing a conditional jump, setting a condition code, or loading the accumulator. The store access switch allows no other accesses to the store location (or more likely to the store module in which it lies) until both the read and write accesses are complete.

A variation on this is an 'exchange' instruction, which (indivisibly) interchanges the values of one location (the semaphore) and either the accumulator or another location (private to the process causing execution of the execution).

Indeed we can use any of a selection of instructions described in earlier chapters, such as

> Add contents of accumulator and store location, leaving the result in accumulator and location

or

> Increment contents of store location and jump if result is zero

as long as the read and write store accesses cannot be separated by accesses for another instruction.

### *Some final comments*

There are three comments to be made about the use of semaphores, and their implementation in this way. First, problems may arise with instructions like 'test and set' on computers which have cache stores or instruction overlap. For example, when a 'test and set' instruction is executed any cache action must be overridden (why?).

Second, the use of semaphores assumes co-operating processes, which are aware of what interactions are possible and the protocol for dealing with them.

Third, because these primitives are so basic, it is difficult for their use to be checked for correctness. We may therefore use semaphores to build higher-level primitives for process interaction, so that the use of these new primitives can be checked at compile-time (see Hansen 1973, Chapter 3).

## Problems

**6.1.** Investigate the transput devices attached to a computer to which you have access.
(a) For each device, what is the time taken to complete an operation? How many instructions could the central processor execute in that time?
(b) For a program you have written in a high-level language, how easy is it to change the device from which it reads input or to which it writes output? In other words, how independent of particular devices is your program?
**6.2.** Investigate the transput instructions on a computer to which you have access.
(a) How well do they match the types of transput instruction described in § 6.2?
(b) How are the requirements of particular devices to receive control information and to send status information accommodated within these transput instructions?
**6.3.** When reading a block of data from an input device, the block count as specified by the transput instruction may not match the actual length of the block. On the IBM 370 range it is possible to suppress the error indication usually caused by the mismatch, and to pass to the processor the residual count at the end of the operation (i.e. block length as specified by the instruction minus actual block length). How is this useful in reading blocks which vary in size in an unpredictable way?
**6.4.** Write a program to copy paper tapes on a small computer to which you have access. The program should use the computer's interrupt system and the technique of double-buffering, with buffers of 100 (decimal) characters. Reading should terminate when a particular character (say an asterisk) is read; punching should continue until this character has been output, and then terminate. Write documentation for this program so that it can be used as a general tape-copying facility.
**6.5.** On page 258 a simple method is described for establishing the cause of an interrupt, by executing a series of sense instructions. How does the order of these instructions affect the time taken to respond to

the interrupt from a particular device? For each of the other methods described for establishing the cause of interrupt, what mechanism determines the order in which devices at the same interrupt priority level receive attention?

**6.6.** Consider a simple interrupt system with only two modes, interruptable and non-interruptable. Suppose a second interrupt occurs while an interrupt is being serviced. List the exact sequence of events which occur as the servicing of the first interrupt is completed. How many instructions are executed in the interrupted process before the second interrupt is accepted?

**6.7.** Instead of jumping to a fixed address on receipt of an interrupt request signal, some computers (such as the DEC PDP-10) simply execute the instruction at a fixed address and then clear the interrupt request signal. What is the effect of this if the executed instruction is a subroutine call? What if it is some other instruction?

**6.8.** Sketch the software required to implement an interrupt system with multiple interrupt levels, using each of the following types of interrupt hardware:

(a) Interrupt-on and interrupt-off instructions,
(b) Multilevel,
(c) Masking.

What are the relative advantages and disadvantages of the three types of hardware? Are they suited to particular application areas?

**6.9.** Pages 264-5 describe how a process state word system works under a masking interrupt system. Explain how a PSW system would work under a multilevel interrupt system.

**6.10.** Ought we to see interrupts as a form of process switch, rather than as entries to servicing routines? Should interrupts be implemented as signal operations on semaphores within the transput control system (For examples see Wirth 1969; Liskov 1972; Lister 1975, Chapter 6)?

**6.11.** On a medium or large computer about which you have access to information, investigate the provision of facilities equivalent to the channel controllers described in § 6.4. To what extent are the differences merely matters of nomenclature, and to what extent are they more fundamental?

**6.12.** On page 280 we describe the use of a relativisor or prefix to map a processor's access to certain store addresses onto different sets of physical store locations. In Figure 6.12, is there a problem with the store areas accessible to processor 1? On the IBM 370 range the method of prefixing is slightly different from the description in the text. If the prefix is $x$, then addresses in the range zero to 4095 are routed to physical locations $x$ to $(x+4095)$, and addresses in the range $x$ to $(x+4095)$ are routed to physical locations zero to 4095. Redraw Figure 6.12 to illustrate this method.

**6.13.** On a multiple computer system about which you have access to information investigate the links provided between processors. Allocate the links to the classes A, B, C and D described in § 6.5.

**6.14.** (a) The concept of multiplexing occurs frequently in operating systems and hardware design. Write an essay on the subject of 'multiplexing'.

(b) The concept of distributed intelligence has occurred several times in this chapter. Write an essay on the subject of 'distributed intelligence'.

**6.15.** The subroutine call instruction on the DEC PDP-8 computer is illustrated in Figure 3.14. Devise a 'lock' or 'metasemaphore' using this instruction (Hint: if the instruction uses indirect addressing, it both reads and changes the store). In order that your mechanism should work, what assumptions must you make about the 'indivisibility' of the subroutine call instruction?

# 7 Computers for specialized tasks

IN THIS chapter we briefly consider a number of computer-types lying outside the main-stream of development, being designed to carry out specialized functions.

In Chapter 1 we mentioned that a rudimentary instruction set entitled a computer to be considered (at least in theory) as general-purpose. On the other hand all computers are oriented to particular applications areas; thus a computer designed for commercial data-processing may not economically perform scientific calculations or process control. So any attempt at an exact definition of 'specialized' computer is doomed to failure.

We will not discuss special-purpose computers which are capable of performing a single closely-specialized task, such as sorting a vector of data items (Barsamian 1970) or performing calculations for Fourier transforms. Instead we will look at three areas to which general-purpose computers have been oriented, and at the non-standard architectures that have evolved to deal with them. These three areas are; computers for transput control, computers with unusual forms of parallelism, and computers oriented towards executing a language different from the conventional assembler language.

Since this book is a survey of typical computer architectures, and since each different non-standard approach is likely to result in a radically different architecture, we will consider only a small number of representative examples for description in each section.

## 7.1. Computers for transput control

Functional specialization for transput control has taken two forms which we discussed in Chapter 6. One form is the channel controller, where the detailed control of each transput operation is by a special-purpose processor, with an instruction set of read, write, control, sense, and (perhaps) jump. The other is the provision of a small computer as a (programmed) control unit for a transput device, instead of a hard-wired controller. Because of the economies of scale, such a computer has a conventional architecture and instruction set; nowadays a microprocessor would be used. The only architectural way in which it differs from a data-processing computer is in possibly having a read-only store to hold the control program.

In a network of computers we are likely to see a degree of specialization of particular computers for particular transput tasks, especially with the decreasing cost of processing power. Thus small computers are dedicated to the control of communications lines; in a message-switching system the nodes could be medium or large computers. The implication is that such computers are general-purpose, the specialization being provided by the control programs residing within them, although there may be architectural specialization towards high reliability operation, short word lengths, lack of floating-point arithmetic, and well-developed interrupt systems. Some computers, especially those marketed as communications controllers, have instructions to help with the generation of error-detecting or error-correcting codes.

### *The control of graphics displays*

The problems of controlling one particular transput device, the graphics display (see Davis 1969; Newman and Sproull 1973), have resulted in the appearance of special-purpose processors to support it.

The picture on the screen of a display has to be regenerated 30 to 60 times per second to prevent flicker, so that the data required to specify the picture to be drawn (known as the *display file)* has to be accessed repeatedly for the period of time the picture is to be displayed.

In the simplest displays, the data consists of the coordinates of the set of points to be illuminated. However, on displays with vector and character generators, the display file consists of a series of references to the various generators with the required parameters. For example Figure 7.1(a) shows a display file for drawing Figure 7.1(b) on a hypothetical display. The display program consists of an interpretive loop, which reads the display file and issues the appropriate display commands. The display file can therefore be considered as a program of instructions in a high-level display language.

Continuing this line of development, we can implement the interpretive loop in hardware as a special-purpose processor; this is illustrated in Figure 7.2. Here we see a computer consisting of a general-purpose processor A, to provide conventional processing power, and a special-purpose processor B, to refresh the display, both accessing the common store; this contains both the display file or program for processor B and the conventional program for processor A. We also show a communication line to a medium or large computer C, which provides further

(a)

Draw a line (not illuminated) to (100, 100)
Draw a line to (360,100)
Draw an arc, centre (400,100), to (440,100)
Draw a line to (700,100)
Draw a line (not illuminated) to (440,100)
Draw a line to (440,180)
Draw a line (not illuminated) to (360,100)
Draw a line to (360,180)
Draw a line (not illuminated) to (200,100)
Draw an arc, centre (400,100), to (600,100)
Draw a line (not illuminated) to (340,200)
Draw a line to (280,240)
Draw a line (not illuminated) to (460,200)
Draw a line to (520,240)
Draw a line (not illuminated) to (260,20)
Change to character mode (size 2)
WOT NO BYTES?
Change to command mode
Repeat

(b)

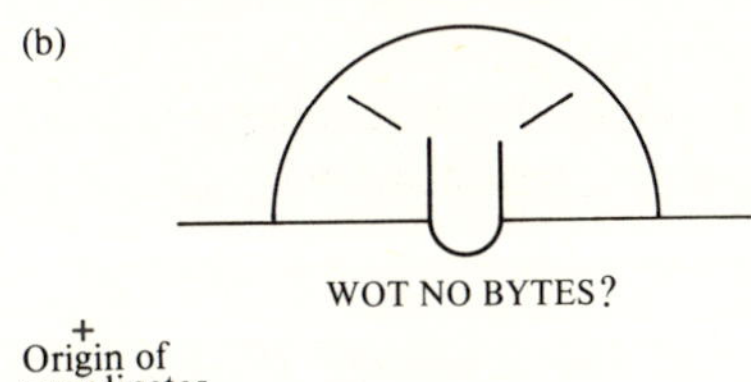


FIG. 7.1

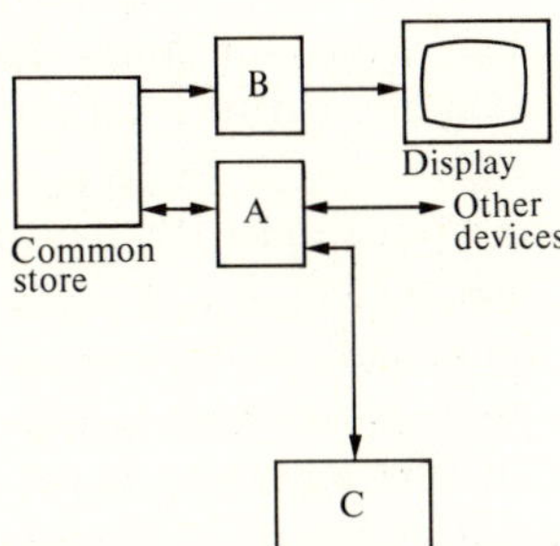


FIG. 7.2

processing power and contains programs (written in a high-level language) and data structures for the particular application for which the display is currently being used.

Thus the applications programs in C initially generate a display file, which they send via A to the store it shares with B, and B continuously displays it as a picture. The user interacts with processor A to modify the display file (and hence the picture). If extensive or application-oriented processing is required, C is invoked again. We thus cut down the overheads in A and (more importantly) in C of supporting a display, and reduce the data flow across the communication line.

The display processor B (Watson, Myer, Sutherland, and Vosbury 1969; Bell and Newell 1971, pp. 305–14) is now a special-purpose processor with instructions such as:

Display a point at a given location on the screen
Draw a line or vector in a number of possible modes; short or long, continuous or dashed, illuminated or not (the latter for positioning the beam which draws the picture)
Draw an arc of a circle
Draw a character, in one of various sizes or styles
Set display parameters: for example beam intensity, colour, character size

Having provided this instruction set, there are a number of possibilities for its extension. Pictures typically contain a number of instances of each of a set of sub-pictures; consider for example a graphical computer-aided design process, such as for an electronic circuit. So there is a requirement for a subroutining facility, whereby a single series of display instructions which generates a sub-picture can be invoked several times, at different locations on the screen. In a sophisticated system, each invocation might specify a rotation and scale transformation to be applied to the basic sub-picture as it is displayed.

We have shown user interaction with the display (by light-pen, push-buttons, or other means) as through processor A in Figure 7.2. Alternatively, if we dispense with this processor, the display processor itself may be equipped with instructions to sample the input devices and conditionally jump to different points in the display file.

We could extend the instruction set in this way until we have a general-purpose processor specialized for display control (Myer and Sutherland 1968).

### *Hybrid computers*

Throughout this book, the computers discussed are *digital*; that is, the electronic signals passing through the computer have two significant voltages, representing the binary values of zero and one. The other main family of computers is *analog*; here the voltages can assume any value within the range for which the computer has been designed.

An analog computer consists of a collection of electronic units, each capable of performing a certain function on one or more input analog signals, for example summation, integration, multiplication, function generation, etc. These units are connected together by means of patching wires on a patchboard, and potentiometers are set to represent various constant values required by the problem to be solved. In this way an electrical circuit is set up to represent a differential equation, which in turn represents some physical system which it is desired to study. For example, Figure 7.3(a) shows an analog circuit set up to solve the differential equation given in Figure 7.3(b).

When the electrical circuit is complete, the analog computer is placed in *compute* mode. The voltages in the different parts of the circuit are allowed to fluctuate with time in a similar way to the dependent variables of the physical system being studied. The voltages are measured as they vary, or the computer is placed in a frozen state or *hold* mode, while measurements are taken.

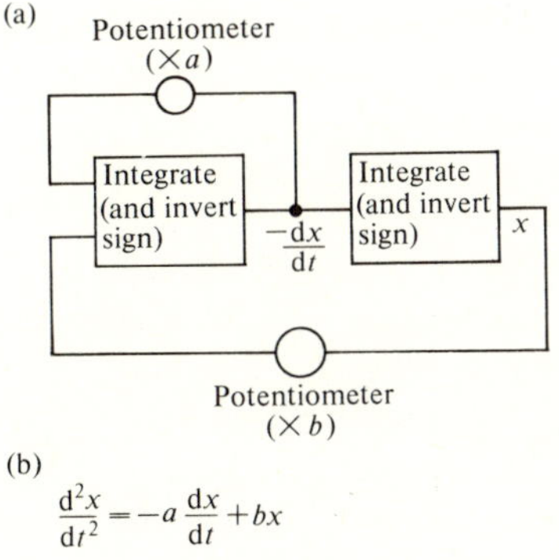


$$\frac{d^2x}{dt^2} = -a\frac{dx}{dt} + bx$$

FIG. 7.3

In order to increase the flexibility of the analog computer, it is nowadays usually provided with a number of digital electronic units as well as analog ones; these include store units, comparators, and switches. A second (digital) patchboard is provided to enable logical decisions to be made from analog results in order to modify subsequent analog computations. An analog computer with such digital units can thus perform iterative calculations.

As the complexity of the digital and analog networks increases, it becomes more difficult to design, set up, and check an analog computation, and the digital computer must be brought in to help. Programming languages such as APACHE and APSE have been implemented in which an analog computation is described, and which then generate patchboard connection maps, tables of potentiometer settings, and expected check results.

Instead of using such off-line assistance, we can directly attach a digital computer to the analog computer through an interface unit, resulting in a *hybrid computer* as shown in Figure 7.4. Here control signals are passed from the digital to the analog computer to set the potentiometers and mode of operation and, perhaps, to perform some of the patching. Initial values are sent to the analog computer via a digital-to-analog converter, and results are read by the digital computer via an analog-to-digital converter. These results can be stored, further processed, and made available in a form suitable for human scrutiny. In addition it may be possible for the digital computer to perform some or all of the tasks which would have been carried out by the patched digital units described earlier.

Note that we have introduced the hybrid computer from the analog point of view, with the digital computer as a sophisticated and flexible

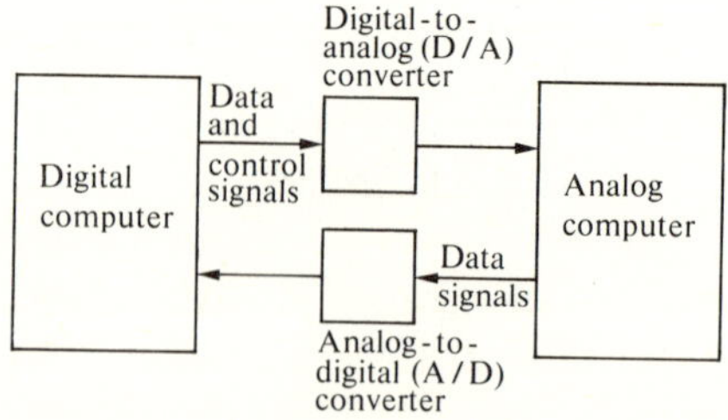


FIG. 7.4

set of control and digital processing units. If we look at it from the digital point of view, we see a collection of transput devices capable of solving certain classes of differential equations.

For further reading on analog and hybrid computing see Bekey and Karplus (1968) and Hyndman (1970); for a brief introduction to hybrid computation see Girling (1967).

## 7.2. Unconventional forms of parallelism

We have seen how designers of computers soon saw the advantages in making transput devices autonomous, so that transput could proceed in parallel with the processing of data. But this idea could be extended to the internal operations of the processor. Obvious candidates were multiplication and division, since these took significantly longer than the other arithmetic and logical operations.

Thus some early computers (such as the Ace (Wilkinson 1953) and Deuce (Haley 1956)) allowed multiplication and division to be carried out in parallel with other instructions. Once a multiplication (for instance) had been initiated, the processor could be made to fetch and execute subsequent instructions. The programmer had to be aware of how many normal instructions he could cause to be executed before the product was available, and he had to take care that none of them interfered with any of the registers involved in the multiplication.

We could extend this concept further, by building a processor with several autonomous units, each capable of executing a subset of the instruction set. A well-known example of this was the second-generation Bull Gamma-60 computer (Dreyfus 1958a, b), which had four processing units (for decimal arithmetic, logical operations and binary arithmetic, comparisons, and character code translation) and several transput devices, all of which could operate autonomously.

A problem with such systems is the difficulty of conceptualizing and writing a program to take advantage of the parallelism available, unless it can be structured into a set of loosely-coupled but otherwise independent processes, or into a single stream of instructions operating simultaneously on several similar sets of data.

The former encompasses the transput autonomy and multiprocessor systems described in Chapter 6, while the latter covers the associative and array processors treated later in this section. Most modern computers which provide several autonomous instruction-executing units disguise them so that they appear to be conventional single-instruction-stream computers; this is discussed in §8.2.

Parallelism in general is discussed in Hobbs, Theis, Trimble, Titus, and Highburg (1970) and Thurber and Wald (1975).

### *Degrees of multiprocessing*

Until recently the multiprocessor systems described in Chapter 6 would contain no more than 3 or 4 processors. However, with the advent of cheap microprocessors, we can consider interconnecting a large number of them, either through a common store or by some other means, in order to carry out a designated task. The task is thus executed not by multiprogramming a set of processes on a small number of processors, but by allocating each process to a dedicated processor. The fact that each processor is dedicated to a single process simplifies the coding of the task to be performed and the supporting software, while the cost of several microprocessors being idle for much of the time is tolerable.

Given a computer consisting of a store and one or more general-purpose processors, we can add special-purpose processors to which the central processor delegates some of its tasks. A common example is, of course, the channel. Several minicomputer manufacturers now offer processors capable of executing a sequence of floating-point instructions from common store, once initialized by the central processor; such a floating-point processor is available on the DEC PDP-8 for example.

Much theoretical work has been done on *cellular automata* and *tessellated* computers. Consider an infinite configuration of cells laid out in a regular one-, two-, or three-dimensional pattern. Each cell is occupied by an automaton or computer capable of being in one of a set of states, and of changing to a new state which is a function of its current state and those of its near neighbours. The transition rules from state to state are the same for all cells.

It has been shown, for example by Von Neumann (1966) and Codd (1968), that even with small numbers of possible states and simple transition rules (very much simpler than even the smallest conventional computer), configurations can be constructed which are in some sense universal. They can simulate a universal Turing machine and reproduce themselves.

There have been various suggestions for such tessellated computers (see for example Holland 1959, 1960) which would have a simple replicated structure (well suited to LSI technology) and would be able to sustain a number of parallel processes. It remains to be seen whether such architectures lead to designs capable of being programmed to solve real problems. For further discussion and references in this field see Foster (1976a, Chapter 12).

### *Associative processors*

We now turn to computers in which the execution of each instruction causes an operation to be carried out, not on a single set of data, but simultaneously on a number of sets of data. We refer to such computers generically as SIMD (single instruction stream/multiple data stream) (Flynn 1966). A conventional computer is SISD (single instruction stream/single data stream) using this terminology, and multiprocessors are MIMD (multiple instruction stream/multiple data stream); there are no very convincing examples of MISD computers.

In §5.5 we discussed the use of associative stores, which are accessed by presenting, not an address, but a search argument which is compared simultaneously with all the elements in the store. We gave examples of the use of such associative stores in conventional computers. Instead we could design a processor with a main store which is exclusively associative or content-addressed; this is an *associative processor* (Foster 1976b; You and Fung 1977).

Such a computer would have facilities for searching, reading from, and writing into the associative store, for establishing how many responses have occurred, and for moving data from a store location to any of its near neighbours. Such a computer is used for processing tasks involving simple operations on large arrays of data. An example is picture-processing, where a picture (a rectangular array of numbers representing intensity levels) is to be treated to remove noise and sharpen contours.

### *Array processors*

Much scientific computing revolves around performing the same operation (typically a floating-point arithmetic operation) on all elements of a vector or matrix. Conventionally this is implemented by means of a loop, on each iteration of which one element of the vector or matrix is operated on. Obviously any decrease in the amount of processing to be performed on each iteration step improves the over-all processing time.

One means of achieving this is to design a special-purpose processor capable of performing a variety of arithmetic operations on vectors of data. This would be attached to a conventional computer in the same way as a transput device, or as one processor in a multiprocessor system. An example is the IBM 2938 array processor (Ruggiero and Coryell 1969). Alternatively we could provide a general-purpose processor with a subset of array-oriented instructions, such as vector multiplication and addition.

A speed improvement is achieved here because the instruction fetch and decoding is performed only once per operation instead of several times per iteration of the operation. Further we may be able to overlap the processing of one group of operands with the accessing of the next.

To improve the speed of array processing still further, we must introduce parallelism in the processor so that an operation is performed on several data elements simultaneously. Such an idea was put forward in the proposed Solomon computer (Slotnick, Borck, and McReynolds 1962). The best-known implementation is the Illiac IV computer, built by the University of Illinois and Burroughs Corporation (Barnes, Brown, Kato, Kuck, Slotnick, and Stokes 1968; Slotnick 1971).

This computer was designed to have 256 processing elements (PEs), each capable of performing various floating-point operations on 64-bit words, 32-bit half-words, etc. Since the same operation is to be performed on a number of data elements simultaneously, these PEs are not independent (as, for example, are the processors in a multiprocessor system). Instead there is a control unit (CU) which fetches instructions from a single instruction stream, decodes them, and broadcasts each of them to all the PEs for execution on their own data streams.

Illiac IV was designed as four quadrants, each of 64 PEs with their own control unit, and the quadrants could operate together or independently. However, only one quadrant has been built, and this is illustrated in Figure 7.5. Each PE has its own 2048 words of store, and the control unit is able to access all the store associated with its own quadrant. To allow data communication between PEs, a quadrant is considered to be an 8 by 8 array, and every PE is connected to its 4 orthogonal neighbours. 'Housekeeping' operations such as array configuring and program loading are performed by an attached Burroughs B6500 computer.

The Illiac IV was designed to tackle problems where parallel processing could be applied to large numbers of pieces of data simultaneously, such as linear programming and the solution of large sets

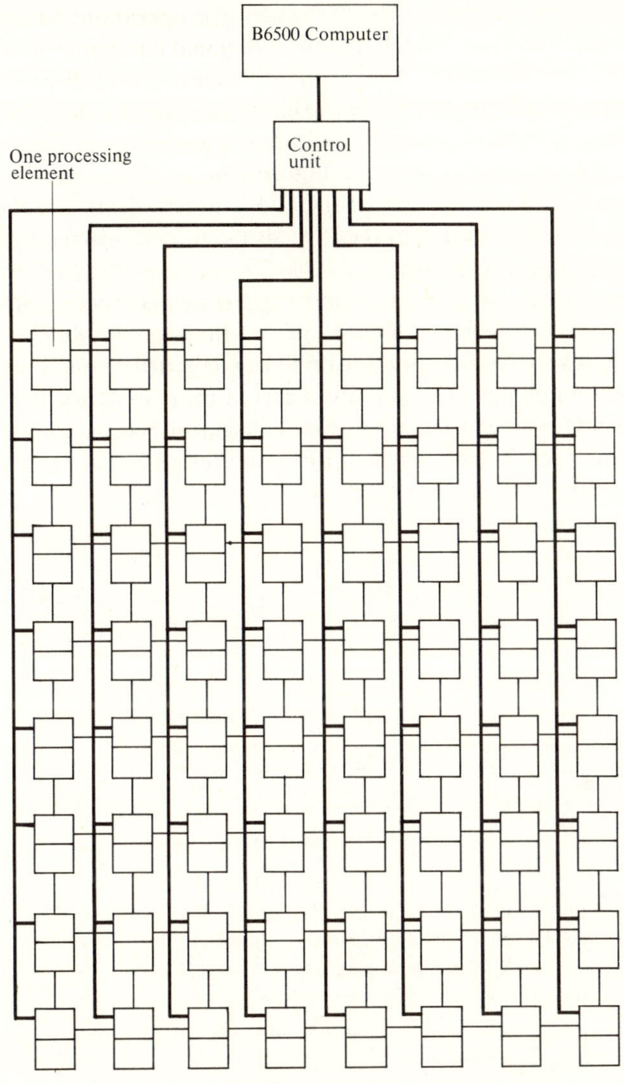


FIG. 7.5

of partial differential equations (for example, hydrodynamic flow and weather forecasting).

Sometimes the processing of a particular data stream is dependent on an earlier test. Each PE therefore contains a register of flags which can be set and cleared by the execution of condition-testing instructions in the PE, or by the CU broadcasting one bit of a 64-bit word to each PE. The execution of subsequent instructions by the PE can be made conditional on the value in this register. Thus the conditional statement '***if*** B ***then*** $S_1$ ***else*** $S_2$' would be executed in parallel on several processing elements as shown in Figure 7.6.

As we have said, the task of the CU is to broadcast a sequence of operations to be executed by the PEs, although some instructions (such as jumps) are executed directly by the CU. Data is extracted by the PE from its store (using a private index register), or is broadcast from the CU (for common data). There are several ways in which the CU becomes aware of what is going on in the PEs; error conditions (such as overflow) in any PE cause an interrupt to be signalled to the CU, and the CU has an instruction which causes it to receive a 64-bit word made up of one bit sent by each PE. Other examples of array processors are discussed in Enslow (1974).

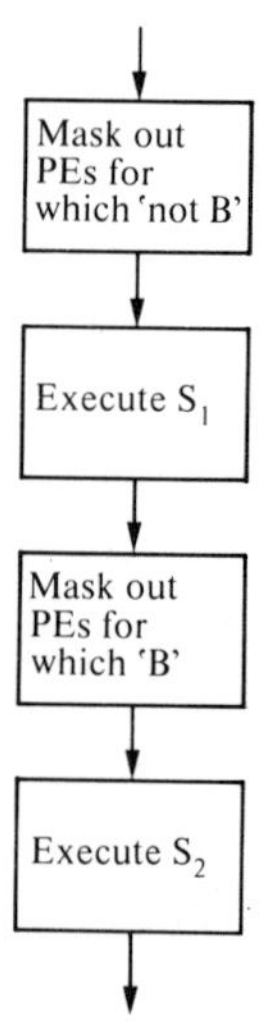


FIG. 7.6

## 7.3. Language-oriented computers

The basic aim of a computer's system software is to give the user a better interface than the computer's raw hardware (as exemplified by its assembler language); that is, to provide a 'virtual' computer which is more convenient to use than the 'real' one. Such a virtual computer will have facilities to improve the efficiency with which it is used, for example by multiprogramming or by collecting statistics of usage, but that is of interest to the user only indirectly as it reduces the cost of processing power. The system software may provide other facilities to simplify the user's access to the computer; a one-level store using paging, more flexible and powerful transput facilities, or extensions to the instruction set by means of extracodes. But the most obvious difference between the virtual computer and the real computer upon which it is based is the use of high-level languages for describing algorithms.

### *Architectures for high-level languages*

Conventionally high-level languages are implemented by means of a compiler performing a once-for-all translation into a machine code program, which is then executed. Because most programs are generated by compilers rather than assembler-language programmers, a computer's instruction set should nowadays be designed to simplify the compiler's code-generation phase (Capon 1974). For a discussion of the problems raised for the compiler-writer by current architectures see Wirth (1968, 1972). What is required is a pattern within which all instructions fall, without individual quirks or exceptional cases which have to be treated separately. For example, the University of Manchester MU5 (Kilburn, Morris, Rohl, and Sumner 1968) was designed to facilitate generation of programs by compilers, with a simple and rational instruction set.

The Burroughs range of medium to large computers (from the B5000, through the B5500, B6500, and B7500, to the B5700, B6700, and B7700) provides an important example of a computer architecture related more closely than usual to the requirements of a high-level language. The architecture and form of the instruction set are similar to the (interpreted) intermediate language produced by the Whetstone Algol 60 compiler, described in Randell and Russell (1964). Thus, for example, the architecture provides a stack to allow direct evaluation of expressions in reverse Polish notation, and a block structure with local and global variables. In fact, these computers are designed to be programmed only in high-level languages, including an extended version of Algol 60 in which the supervisory programs are written.

### *Direct execution of high-level languages*

An alternative way of implementing a high-level language is to build hardware upon which it can be executed directly. Various proposals, such as Bashkow, Sasson, and Kronfeld (1967) for a 'Fortran machine', have been put forward, but progress required computers with a microprogrammed architecture (principally the IBM 360), since this allows the construction of processors for high-level languages without the cost of building a new computer from scratch.

Various languages have been experimentally microprogrammed on the IBM 360 range. Weber (1967) describes the implementation of the Algol-like language Euler on an IBM 360 model 30. The language interpreted by the microprogram (i.e. the language replacing the IBM 360 instruction set) is, in fact, an intermediate language into which the Euler statements are translated by a microprogrammed compiler. In Hassitt, Lageschulte, and Lyon (1973) the language APL is microprogrammed on an IBM 360 model 25. Here again the microprogram interprets an intermediate language, into which the APL statements are translated. However the compiler is not microprogrammed but is written in APL (and is therefore executed in the intermediate language). For further examples see Melbourne and Pugmire (1965) and Rice and Smith (1971).

In §3.6 the Burroughs B1700 computer was described. This is a 'soft' machine, provided with a flexible micro-instruction set by which the computer can be made to take on any appropriate architecture and instruction set. We can therefore design an intermediate language for each high-level language, into which it can be compiled simply and efficiently. We then write an emulator, a microprogrammed interpreter, for each of these languages.

Thus the B1700 can be made to have an architecture matched to whatever high-level language the current program is written in, at the expense, of course, of a rather general micro-instruction set, not tuned to any particular architecture. Since we may wish to run programs written in several different high-level languages at the same time, we may have to have several emulators simultaneously resident in the control store, and process switching will include switching emulators.

Further intermediate languages could be provided. There is one supporting the PL/l-like language in which the supervisory programs for the B1700 are written, and the instruction sets of other computers could be emulated. We could also emulate the instruction sets of unconventional computer architectures.

***Programmable calculators***

The simplest forms of electronic calculator differ only in implementation and speed from the mechanical calculators which preceded them. Three registers are provided; a data entry register, an accumulator, and a register to hold multipliers and similar subsidiary values.

The depression of one of the keys on the keyboard causes either a numeric digit to be entered into a register or an operation to take place between values held in the registers (such as a transfer, addition, subtraction, multiplication, division, or square root). The result of the operation is returned to one of the registers, which is continuously displayed for the checking of input values and the reading of results.

A small number of extra registers may be provided, together with extra keys to transfer values to or from the registers. This allows constants and intermediate values to be retained in the calculator during a calculation.

Such calculators are not computers, of course, since they are externally programmed, the program being the sequence of key-depressions made by the user. However over the last 10 years a number of calculators have been marketed in which such a sequence of key-depressions may be stored within the calculator and subsequently executed. Such *programmable calculators* (Bell and Newell 1971, pp. 235–56; Valéry 1974) can thus be classified as computers.

A programmable calculator has a set of keys to enter numeric data and perform the usual operations, and it can be used as a normal calculator where each operation is invoked by a key-depression. There are a number of registers (perhaps a few tens) which can hold numeric values, but some or all of them are capable of holding symbols which represent key-depressions.

The calculator can be placed in a special mode in which a sequence of key-depressions is stored as a sequence of symbols, rather than executed. When such a sequence has been entered, the calculator can be started under program control. Successive symbols are interpreted as key-depressions and executed, the control passing sequentially from symbol to symbol, until a conditional or unconditional jump symbol is reached, which transfers control to the symbol in a specified location or to a specified label symbol.

These calculators are designed for statistical and engineering calculations, where data can be requested, iterative calculations performed, and results displayed. There is some similarity to on-line interactive languages such as APL.

As with ordinary electronic calculators, all programmable calculators have a keyboard for data and program entry and a display for results. They may also have provision for the permanent storage of the steps of a program, often in the form of magnetic cards. In a special mode of operation, the calculator writes a sequence of program steps to a card, and these can later be read back into the calculator for execution. Thus a program library of useful calculations can be built up; for large calculations, a sequence of cards may be required. Those programmable calculators which reside on the top of a desk may have a range of peripherals which they control; a printer, a paper-tape reader, perhaps even a communication line to a main-frame computer. On programmable calculators to be held in the hand (such as the Hewlett-Packard HP-65 and HP-25, and the Sinclair Cambridge Programmable) only a keyboard, a display, and perhaps a magnetic card unit are feasible. On wristwatch calculators (which may be programmable by the time this book appears) there is a problem with fitting even a usable keyboard and display in the space available.

Notice that the number of basic data-manipulating operations on a programmable calculator is usually greater than on a conventional computer. Apart from register transfers, the four basic arithmetic operations, reciprocal, square root, and absolute value, many calculators also provide such operations as logarithms to base ten and exponential e and their inverses, the circular and hyperbolic functions and their inverses, and conversion between polar and rectangular co-ordinates.

We have already mentioned that the 'language' of key-depressions bears a resemblance to an interactive computer language. Because of this, some programmable calculators (such as the Wang 2200) have taken the further step of having one key to each of the symbols in the vocabulary of the BASIC language, which thus becomes the language in which the calculator is programmed.

## Problems

**7.1.** For a programmable graphics display to which you have access, write a software system to display text in an alphabet other than the Roman alphabet (for example the Greek, Russian, or Arabic alphabet).

**7.2.** The game of 'Life' (Gardner 1970, 1971), invented by the Cambridge mathematician J. H. Conway, uses an infinite two-dimensional board divided into squares, each of which is either occupied or empty. At each move or 'generation' a new configuration of occupied squares is constructed from the previous configuration, by the application of the rules:

(a) An occupied square remains occupied if exactly 2 or 3 of its 8 immediate neighbours are occupied.

(b) An occupied square becomes empty if 0, 1, or 4 or more of its neighbours are occupied.

(c) An empty square becomes occupied if exactly 3 of its 8 immediate neighbours are occupied.

(d) An empty square remains empty if 2 or less, or 4 or more of its neighbours are occupied.

Figure 7.7 shows one move of a particular configuration called a 'glider'; investigate its behaviour. Write a program which, given an initial configuration of occupied squares, will generate and display successive configurations until a stable state is reached (if ever). How could such a cellular automaton simulate a Turing machine? (Hint: use streams of gliders to represent signals.)

**7.3.** Suppose that, when the first computers were built, the store technologies had resulted in content-addressed rather than coordinate-addressed main stores. Would the development of programming have

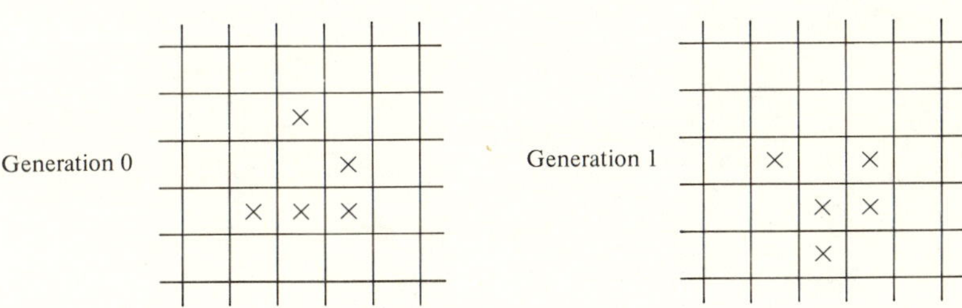


FIG. 7.7

been different, or does the programmer naturally think in coordinate-addressed terms?

**7.4.** Consider a word-parallel, bit-parallel associative processor and an array processor. Is there a clear distinction to be made between these two concepts, or are they the two ends of a continuous spectrum?

**7.5.** Suppose a problem requires manipulation of an $N \times N$ matrix $A_{ij}$ on an array processor with $N$ processing elements $PE_1$ to $PE_N$. We could store array element $A_{ij}$ at the location with address $i$ in the private store of processing element $j$, as shown in Figure 7.8(a). Then a complete row can be manipulated at a time, one array element by each processing element. Is the same true for manipulating a column at a time? Consider the *skewed storage* format shown in Figure 7.8(b). If each processing element has its own private index register, how could one row or one column be manipulated at a time?

**7.6.** Figure 1.1 gives a diagrammatic view of a 'typical' computer. To what extent is this matched by

(a) the 'system' consisting of a non-programmable calculator and its user, and

(b) a programmable calculator?

Do you consider the introduction of calculators which are programmed in BASIC to be an advance or a retrograde step, as bringing calculators closer to the world of computers and programming?

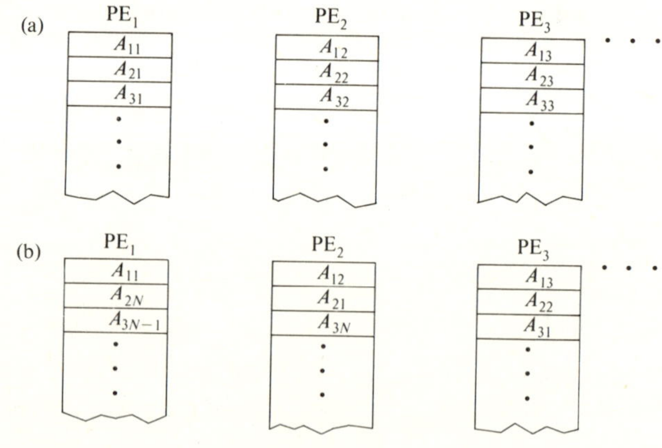


FIG. 7.8

# 8 Miscellaneous features

## 8.1. Faults, errors, and monitoring

A MAJOR worry with the first computers was whether such unwieldly collections of electronic equipment could be made to work for long enough to enable useful calculations to be performed. Reliable operation of computer hardware is still a major design aim; it is measured by the *mean time between failures (MTBF)* of components, and the subsequent *mean time to repair (MTTR).*

We can divide the techniques for dealing with hardware failures into three classes;

(a) Hardware provision for extending the MTBF, and for detecting and indicating to the computer operator that a fault has occured.
(b) Hardware provision for easing the task of the maintenance engineer in detecting, isolating and correcting faults, and thus reducing the MTTR.
(c) Provision for making some of the failure signals and maintenance facilities of (a) and (b) available to the computer's supervisory software, thus allowing it to take recovery action when a hardware fault occurs.

While (c) is within the field of computer architecture, (a) and (b) are more properly part of the implementation level. We will briefly discuss each of these areas in turn. We will then go on to look at the provision of facilities in the hardware to catch programming errors (and other unusual conditions) in running processes. For further reading and references on hardware faults see Friedman and Menon (1971), Bennetts and Lewin (1971), and Breuer and Friedman (1976).

### *Low-level redundancy*

At the most basic level, electronic components (and the techniques by which they are manufactured and their quality is controlled) are chosen to give an appropriate level of reliability, taking into account other factors such as cost and speed. The operational reliability of components in electronic computers is improvéd by the facts that, first, preventive maintenance is carried out on the equipment from time to time and, second, that components are used as two-state devices, so that the definition of successful operation is less stringent than in other fields of electronics, such as analog computing.

At the next higher level we can design functional units using redundancy techniques to mask the effect of any one (or, more generally, any $n$, for fixed $n$) component failures in the unit. There are two problems here. First, we are increasing the number of components in the system, which makes the likelihood of component failure greater. Second, the masking of the effects of faults makes the isolation and correction of those faults more difficult, thus potentially increasing the MTTR. For this reason such techniques are most commonly used in situations where continuous fault-free operation is required over a relatively short period of time, and component repair or replacement is not possible, for example on computers for space vehicles or satellites.

A redundancy technique, known as *N-modular redundancy* or *NMR* (Mathur and Avizienis 1970) is illustrated in Figure 8.1. Here a unit has (reliably) to compute the function $f$. We have a number $N$ of irredundant circuits $F_1$, $F_2$, . . . $F_N$ each computing the function $f$, and a decision circuit or vote-taking unit D to choose an output value for the unit, based on the set of output values supplied by the $F_i$. Here $N$ is 5. A common value of $N$ is three, when the technique is termed *triple modular redundancy* or *TMR:* it was used in the Saturn V

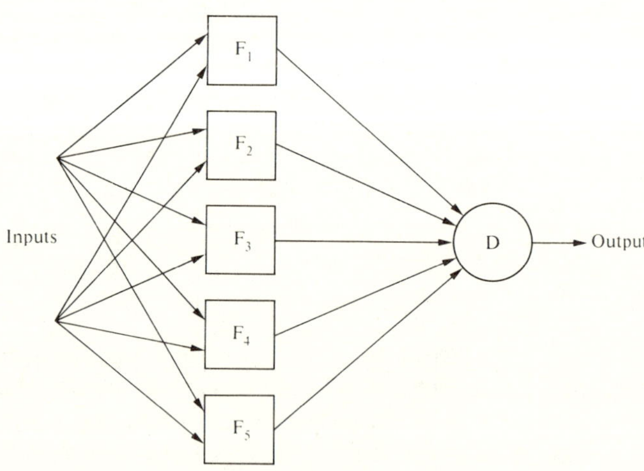


FIG. 8.1

launch vehicle computer to provide high reliability for a 250-hour mission (Dickinson, Jackson, and Randa 1964).

The usual decision rule for $N=3$ is to output the value taken by at least two of the circuits $F_i$. If all three circuits produce different output values, then we have a catastrophic circuit failure. If only two of the $F_i$ agree, we have a result with a certain level of assurance that the third computing circuit is at fault.

This technique can be used at several levels, for example at the basic electronic component level, when the term *massive redundancy* is sometimes used, or at the level of the major sub-units of the processor. The latter is illustrated by the Univac I (Eckert, Weiner, Welsh, and Mitchell 1951), one of the first commercially-available computers, which had extensive facilities for fault-detection. The adder and various other pieces of equipment within the processor were duplicated, allowing two independent results to be produced by each duplicated element. The two results would then be compared by the hardware; a match allowed processing to continue, while a mismatch caused the computer to halt.

### *Data encoding for reliability*

Another type of redundancy technique is derived from coding theory (Peterson 1961; Berlekamp 1968). Here a set of *check bits* is associated with each group of data bits, and circuits at various points within the computer generate logical functions of the data and check bits, to establish whether the group has been corrupted and, possibly, what the correct group should be.

The simplest and most common technique in this class is the addition of a single (*parity*) check bit to each group of data bits. The value of the parity bit is chosen so that the number of bit positions (parity and data) set to one is either always odd or always even. This detects all single bit faults. Most computers have a parity bit attached to each word of the main store, which is set on writing to store and checked on reading.

For further fault protection some computers provide several check bits per word, each a parity bit for a different portion of the word: this is particularly convenient when these part-words are independently used as instructions or data. Alternatively, and becoming increasingly common, a set of check bits is used for a degree of fault detection and correction over the whole word. Using the popular Hamming code, a set of eight check bits can be used to correct all single bit faults and detect all two bit and many multiple bit faults in a word with 64 data bits. Each check bit is an even parity bit for a certain selection of the bits of the word, as discussed in problem 8.2. This technique is used, for example, in the main store of the IBM 370 range.

Instead of treating some bits in a word as data bits and others as check bits, we can treat all bits as data bits and agree that only a selection of the possible binary patterns are to be used to encode data. The unused patterns then provide some degree of fault detection or correction. This technique has been more common on decimal computers (where there is some redundancy in the way decimal digits are represented by binary patterns) than on binary computers. For example the two-out-of-five coding of decimal digits shown in Figure 2.18 detects any single bit fault (how well do the other codings in Figure 2.18 detect faults?).

### *Instruction retry*

Some of the hardware faults that occur in a computer system are likely to be transient rather than permanent. This is the rationale behind such software techniques as attempting to reread a magnetic tape a number of times when a fault arises, in the hope that the fault will disappear.

This technique can also be used at the implementation level. If, while an instruction is being executed, an unexpected condition occurs or one of the above fault-detection systems indicates a fault, then (provided that none of the operands required by the instruction have been destroyed) the hardware can make another attempt to execute the instruction. This continues until either the execution is successful, or until some maximum number of attempts has occurred. This technique of *instruction retry* is used, for example, on the IBM 370 range.

### *The problem of hardware fault diagnosis*

The presence of a fault is indicated by a signal from the fault-detection hardware, or it becomes apparent through the process of testing during preventive maintenance, or through erratic behaviour during normal use of the computer.

Using this information as a starting point, the maintenance engineer must firmly establish the presence of a fault in the hardware, and isolate it to a particular electronic module which can be replaced or repaired. This is done by driving sequences of test signals through each suspect area and observing the output signals.

The implementation of a computer therefore involves providing adequate access to all units, the ability to isolate each subsystem for testing, and the provision in each subsystem of suitable points at which test signals can be inserted and output signals observed. Further, the circuits in each subsystem can be designed to reduce the number and complexity of the test sequences which need to be generated in order to detect and locate all faults. Notice here that the wish to improve the MTTR may affect other aspects of the design, such as cost, speed, or the MTBF.

### *Hardware fault interrupts*

In first- and second-generation computers the detection of a hardware fault in the processor or store would bring the computer to a halt, leaving it to the operator and maintenance engineer to take appropriate action. However, on most modern computers a fault in the processor or store causes a 'hardware fault' interrupt to take place, allowing the supervisor to decide what action should be taken (unless the fault is so severe as to incapacitate the computer).

Such an interrupt is allocated one of the highest priority interrupt levels available on the computer (why?). It may make available to the supervisor a certain amount of information as to the type of fault, the area in which it occurred, and the contents of internal registers which are not normally accessible.

There are several possible courses of action that the supervisor can take. In the simplest case it records as much data as possible as to the circumstances of the fault (for the use of the maintenance engineer), and then brings the computer to a halt. Alternatively, after recording the fault, the supervisor may attempt to continue to run the computer, terminating or restarting any processes corrupted by the fault.

If a fault occurs but is corrected at the hardware level by some form of redundancy, the supervisor may still wish to be informed, in order to estimate the reliability of the results computed, as well as for maintenance purposes. Thus as well as the 'hard' fault interrupt described above, caused by the detection of a permanent hardware fault, there may be a 'soft' fault interrupt, indicating that a transient or correctable hardware fault has occurred; for example, an instruction has successfully been retried, or a single-bit fault has been corrected in a store word. The supervisor simply records the circumstances of the fault and then resumes normal processing.

### *Diagnostic programs*

In order to drive the hardware of a computer through a sequence of tests, the maintenance engineer generally makes use of diagnostic programs, as well as the externally applied signals mentioned above. Such diagnostic programs are written to exercise the various data paths and functional units of the computer, and must therefore be designed taking into account the implementation details of the computer and their likely classes of fault.

They will be run by the engineer for assurance that the computer is operating correctly, and in order to isolate a fault to a particular unit. In the latter case the diagnostic program may apply a series of increasingly refined tests, or simply place the computer in a regular cycle of operations which can be further investigated by external means (such as an oscilloscope).

Alternatively the occurrence of a fault interrupt may cause the supervisor directly to invoke diagnostic programs to locate the fault or show it to be transient. In systems requiring a high degree of reliability, the supervisor periodically runs a diagnostic program, to ensure that all parts of the system are operating satisfactorily.

A problem with diagnostic programs is that some minimal part of the hardware (called the *hard-core*) must be working without faults for the programs to be run. For engineer-run diagnostic programs, he will presumably have checked the hard-core by other means. For supervisor-run diagnostic programs, the programs must be able to perform some degree of self-checking (see, for example, Leaman, Lloyd, and Repton 1973). As more of the computer hardware is checked out, it is added to the hard-core to simplify subsequent tests.

Notice that a diagnostic program written in microcode is able to exercise the computer hardware more exhaustively than one written in machine code. Many microprogrammed computers can therefore enter a mode in which the computer is controlled by a sequence of *microdiagnostic* programs, in order to locate faults in more detail (see, for example, Barstow and McGuire 1970).

### *Diagnostic computers*

Instead of providing the test and observation points required by the maintenance engineer on the electronic subsystems themselves, some of these points and diagnostic controls may be collected together at a single diagnostic console, either at the computer site or connected to it remotely via a communications line.

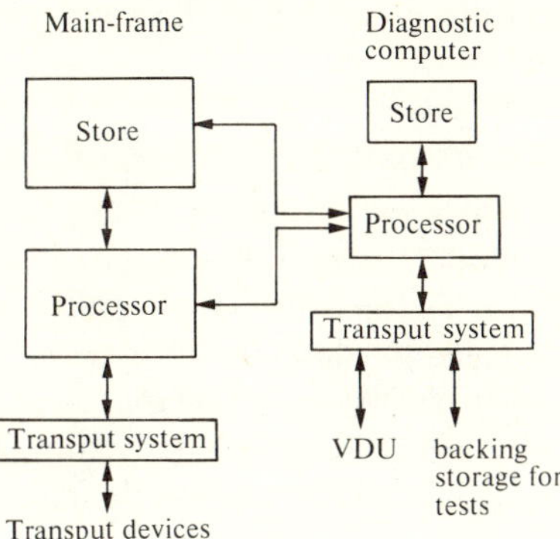


FIG. 8.2

Once these diagnostic features are controllable from a single point, a small computer may be provided to perform the routine parts of the maintenance procedure; this is becoming increasingly popular with the availability of microprocessors. A schematic example of such a system is shown in Figure 8.2. This diagnostic computer reads a sequence of tests from a backing storage device, applies test signals and observes the results. The sequence of tests would first check for the presence of faults in the various subsystems of the computer, and then locate the faults in detail by an appropriate sequence of tests selected from the backing storage.

Here we have assumed that the diagnostic computer is in use only during periods of maintenance, but it could also be used continuously to monitor the running of the rest of the system. In this case all computer faults detected by the hardware of the central processor and store are routed to the diagnostic computer, instead of causing an interrupt in the central processor. The diagnostic computer would then decide on appropriate action.

### *High-level redundancy*

Many computer systems derive their performance from the duplication of a number of units; that is, the system is made up of several processors, several store modules, several transput channels. As well as providing computer power, such duplication may improve reliability by what is known as *high-level redundancy*. Thus a failed processor would be removed from a system, which could then continue to run, albeit at a degraded level.

In order to allow a system to be *reconfigured* in this way, the interfaces of each unit are brought to a reconfiguration console, rather than being permanently connected to other units. By means of switches, the operator or engineer partitions the various units into one or more independent systems, removes units for testing, and specifies the numbering scheme by which one unit accesses another. For example, consider a system with one processor and four store modules, providing four-way interleaving on the bottom two bits of the store address as shown in Figure 8.3(a). If one store module failed, the system might be reconfigured so that it runs with each fault-free store module holding a consecutive sequence of addresses, since low-order interleaving would be difficult: this is shown in Figure 8.3(b).

Instead of providing manual reconfiguration, we might provide some degree of automatic reconfiguring. Thus a reconfiguration computer (usually the diagnostic computer discussed earlier) would real-

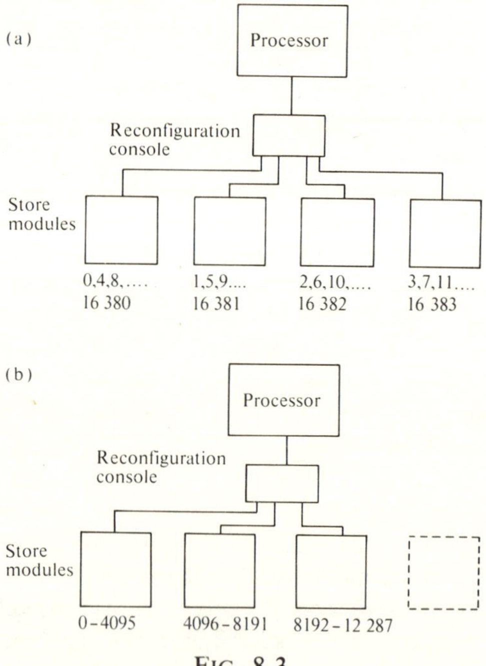


FIG. 8.3

locate data paths and access numbering schemes between units, on the basis of fault reports received. It would then make available to each enquiring processor details of the new configuration.

In a multiprocessor system, each processor may be able to remove itself from the system if it appears to be faulty, or reconfigure the system in the light of fault reports from other processors. On such a system there is also the possibility of having several processors compute the same function and 'vote' on the result, or for each processor to have a diagnostic interface by which it can be put through a series of tests by another processor.

We may also be able to reconfigure the system at a more detailed level than the processor or store module. Thus a processor in the IBM 370 range can disable its cache store if it appears to be at fault, and continue to run at a slower speed. Similarly, in a computer with a paging system, any page frames containing faulty words could simply not be used.

The technique of high-level redundancy can be used to design computers for environments where operation is required without human intervention for long periods of time. An example is the STAR (for Self-Testing And Repairing) computer, designed by the Jet Propulsion Laboratory to control an unmanned interplanetary spacecraft (Avizienis 1968).

This computer is divided into a number of subsystems, of each of which several identical copies are provided. All copies of each subsystem are permanently connected into the computer, but only one copy of each subsystem is supplied with power (and therefore active) at any time. The unpowered copies have no effect on the rest of the computer. Each subsystem has extensive fault-detecting hardware. If a non-transient fault is detected in a subsystem, it is powered down and made inactive, and power is supplied to one of the spare copies of the subsystem.

This replacement of subsystems on receipt of fault signals is performed by the Test-And-Repair Processor or TARP, which also restarts processes which may have been corrupted by the fault. Since we have to guard against faults in the TARP, several copies of this subsystem are provided, and all TARP processing is checked by voting between a number of active copies. Any TARP disagreeing with a majority decision is made inactive, and a standby copy is powered up. Even in this computer certain switches and buses cannot be replicated, and must be designed for reliability and 'fail-safe' operation.

### *Faults outside the processor and store*

In the above discussion we have concentrated on faults occurring in the hardware of the processor and store. Many of the techniques discussed can be applied to the hardware of the transput system. For example, most forms of backing storage provide at least parity checking, and many nowadays have fault detection and correction systems.

The detection of a fault by the hardware of a transput device results in a distinctive transput fault interrupt. The supervisor then issues a sense instruction to obtain more details of the type of fault. Following this it can retry the transput operation, enter a diagnostic program to locate the fault, log details of the fault, and (if necessary) reconfigure the system to exclude the faulty unit.

For transput faults we do not have to consider the possibility of faults in the processor and store hard-core which is performing the tests. However there may be a problem of obtaining test programs from backing storage, or of communicating fault information to the outside world.

A further type of fault which may have to be dealt with (especially in real-time systems) is a failure in the environment supporting the computer, in particular a power failure. If power begins to fail, a special very high priority interrupt causes entry to a supervisor routine, which has sufficient time to save in non-volatile storage such volatile data as the processor registers. Instead of restarting manually (as discussed in §8.3), the computer will receive a restart interrupt when steady power has returned, enabling supervisor action to be taken to restart processes corrupted by the power failure.

In some cases provision is made for power to be maintained for a sufficient time after a power failure for further corrective action to be taken, perhaps including switching to stand by power generators.

### *Process errors*

Moving on from the consideration of hardware faults, we consider the provision of interrupts on detection of a process error, such as an illegal operation code or an unauthorized store access. There should be a clear distinction between interrupts from detected hardware faults and interrupts from process errors, although in some circumstances the latter may of course be indicative of hardware failure.

The interrupt causes entry to the supervisor, which may terminate or attempt to restart the offending process. Alternatively supervisor services may be provided as a consequence of certain interrupts, for example the segment and page fault interrupts discussed earlier. A third possibility is to return control to a section of the offending process nominated to deal with that error condition; thus a process may be able to take appropriate action on the occurrence of such conditions as overflow or invalid data.

We have already met the concept of an interval timer in §5.3. This can be used to provide another type of error check, sometimes called a *watchdog timer.* Before transferring control to a problem process, the timer is set to count down a suitable interval. If the timer reaches zero and causes an interrupt before a return is made from the problem process, then the supervisor assumes the process is caught in a 'dead' state.

***Process monitoring***

In testing a newly-written program, we wish to run it under the control of some form of monitor, which will periodically bring the program under test to a halt, take copies of critical pieces of information for analysis, and restart the program (perhaps in a modified form) from the point reached or from some other point.

In early computers such a facility was provided in one of two ways. One way was for the monitor to be the programmer himself, manipulating a number of specially provided controls, of the form described in §8.3. The disadvantages of this are the rudimentary nature of the facilities provided and the need for dedicated use of the computer. Such techniques are now used on only the most primitive computers, or for the testing of only the most basic supervisory programs. A second way is for the monitor to be a trace program which interprets the program under test, instruction by instruction; the disadvantage here is the slow running speed.

On more recent computers a solution to the problem is provided by hardware facilities which allow control to be transferred at appropriate times from a process under test to a monitoring process. Between monitoring points the process under test runs at full hardware speed, but at the monitoring points the full facilities of the instruction set are available for implementing a test strategy. The monitoring process may, of course, be in contact with a programmer at an on-line terminal. Other processes (production or under test) may be running on the processor while this monitoring is going on.

The simplest facility of this type is the provision of a mode of running in which an interrupt is generated after each instruction of a problem process is executed. The supervisor reroutes this interrupt to a monitor process for appropriate action. Thus the process under test runs within its own environment, with no possibilty of inadvertent entry into the monitor.

Alternatively the monitor interrupt may be generated only by the execution of certain types of instruction in the problem process. On the IBM 370 range the monitor interrupt is generated by the execution of a 'monitor call' instruction. This instruction has a subsidiary information field which holds a value in the range zero to 15. A field in a processor register specifies, while the process is running, which of these values causes the instruction to generate an interrupt, and which cause it to be treated as a null instruction. Thus the monitoring process can inform the hardware which classes of monitor call are to be enabled and which disabled.

On the IBM 370 range a system called 'program-event recording' or PER is provided for more extensive monitoring of a process. When the system is enabled (by loading appropriate values into the PSW and some of the control registers), the hardware generates an interrupt if any of a number of events occurs while the process is running. The events which can be selected are: the execution of a (successful) jump instruction: the alteration of the contents of an accumulator: the execution of an instruction from a specified store area: or the alteration of any of the contents of a specified store area.

## 8.2. Instruction overlap

At each stage in the evolution of computers there is a requirement for faster operating speeds than the available circuit technology can support with a conventional computer architecture.

At several points in this book techniques have been discussed to improve processing speeds. Thus an instruction set will be provided which allows common sequences of operations to be carried out with a small number of instructions; microprogramming may be used further to tailor an instruction set to a particular task. Autonomous channel controllers relieve the central processor of transput tasks, and the remaining tasks may be shared between several processors in a multiprocessing system. Since access to the main store is a perennial bottleneck, much attention has been given to improvements in this area, leading to the use of such techniques as arrays of accumulators, the interleaving of store modules, and cache stores.

However, at some point we reach the limit set by the maximum speed at which the central processor can execute instructions, even with all operands available as soon as they are required. This limit is set by the currently available technology, but beyond this there is an ultimate limit set by the speed at which electronic signals are propagated, of one nanosecond per foot.

The answer to this problem lies in the concept of *parallelism* or *concurrency;* that is, in having several parts of the processor in operation simultaneously rather than in sequence. Thus we mentioned in Chapter 1 the speed improvement achieved by moving from serial to parallel processing of the bits of a computer word, and in Chapter 6 we discussed the concurrency of transput operations with processing. In §7.2 one possible method of organizing a parallel computer architecture was introduced, in which each instruction caused the same operation to be carried out on a number of operands at the same time.

In this section we discuss a different method of providing parallelism, by what we term *instruction overlap.* Here we retain the conventional (SISD) computer architecture, of a processor executing in sequence a single stream of instructions and operating on a single stream of data. However, before the execution of one instruction is complete, the hardware may begin to execute one or more of the succeeding instructions. In this way the rate at which instructions are executed is related to how quickly successive instructions can be initiated, rather than to the time to complete the average instruction.

We have introduced the term instruction overlap for this concept, but it is also commonly referred to as *instruction lookahead, pipelining,* or *functional parallelism.* The first term describes an instruction buffer pre-fetching instructions from main store; instruction overlap is generally accompanied by instruction lookahead, but it is possible to have the latter without the former. The second term we use later in this section to refer to a specific (common) type of instruction overlap. The third term, functional parallelism, describes the division of the processor into a number of independent units, each able to carry out its function in parallel with the other units; this is obviously a necessary part of instruction overlap.

As we shall see, the implementation of instruction overlap has to cope with interdependencies between instructions. For this reason, instruction overlap may have visible effects at the architectural level. Even where this is not the case, a knowledge of how overlap is organized may enable more efficient programs to be written. Instruction overlap is discussed further in Flynn (1966), Lorin (1972), and Stone (1975, Chapter 9).

### *Processor design for instruction overlap*

Let us ignore for the moment the problem of interdependencies between instructions. Figure 8.4 illustrates some possible layouts for functional parallelism within a processor, to allow instruction overlap. Layout (a) represents a conventional processor, where instructions are

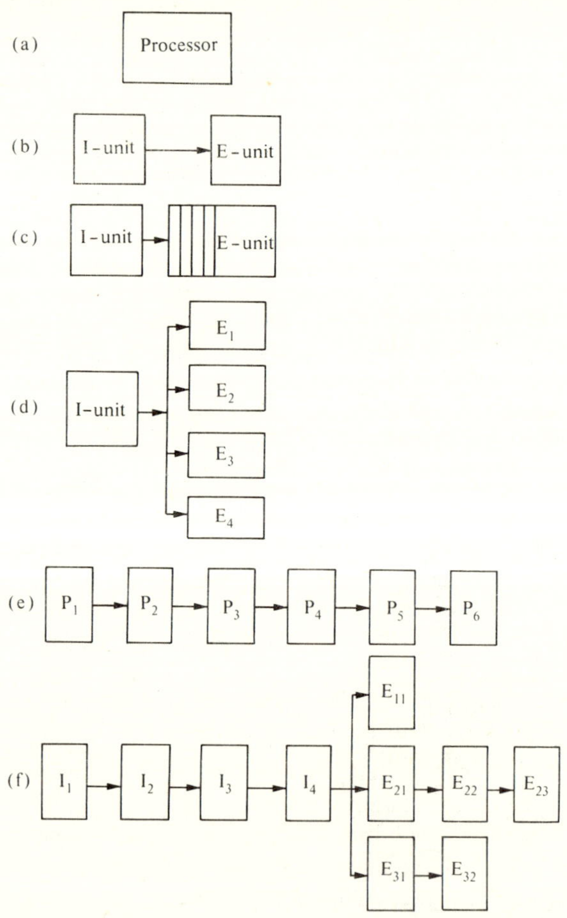


FIG. 8.4

executed sequentially, each being completed before the next is fetched.

In layout (b) the processor is split into two parts, the I-unit and the E-unit, which can be in operation simultaneously. The I- (or Instruction-) unit fetches the next instruction (possibly from the main store, but often from some form of instruction buffer), partially decodes the operation code field, performs any required modification of the operand address (for example, adding the contents of an index register), initiates a store read for the operand if this is necessary, and passes details of the instruction to the E- (or Execute-) unit, which executes the instruction. Meanwhile the I-unit proceeds to the next instruction. Some classes of instruction, such as index manipulation and unconditional jumps, are executed by the I-unit, leaving only the more complex operations to the E-unit. Since most computers with instruction overlap have been oriented towards scientific applications, the E-unit is typically concerned mainly with floating-point arithmetic operations.

Layout (c) introduces a buffer between the I- and E-units capable of holding a number of instructions which have been dealt with by the I-unit and are awaiting execution. Such a layout is used in the IBM 7030 (Bloch 1959; Buchholz 1962), one of the first computers to attempt to provide instruction overlap within a conventional architecture. The design of this computer (termed Project Stretch) aimed at a hundredfold performance increase on large scientific calculations over the current state-of-the-art, as represented by the IBM 704 computer. Since the available technology would support only a tenfold speed increase, this necessitated the overlapping of several instructions.

In this computer, therefore, the I-unit fetches the next instruction, performs address calculations, initiates any required read accesses to main store, and (unless the instruction is executed directly by the I-unit) places the partially-processed instruction in one element of a four-element buffer, called the lookahead unit. When the operand (if any) arrives from the store it is placed in the appropriate element of the buffer. A mechanism called *forwarding* ensures that, if several instructions in the buffer all require the same operand, only one store access takes place, and when the operand arrives from the store it is passed to all buffer elements awaiting it.

Independently of the I-unit (but of course with suitable interlocks) the E-unit extracts instructions from the buffer and executes them. The results of many operations affect only the accumulator within the

E-unit. However, from time to time a store instruction requires a result to be returned to the main store. The E-unit then returns the result to a location in the buffer, which initiates the store access and, eventually, frees the buffer element for further use. Again the forwarding mechanism may come into play to pass this result directly to an instruction in the buffer which is waiting to access it from main store.

Thus the IBM 7030 attempts to ensure that, while one instruction is being executed, it is looking at instructions far enough ahead to initiate all store accesses in time to keep the arithmetic unit operating at full speed. A number of more recent computers, such as the IBM 370 model 165 (Katzan 1971a) and the ICL 2960, provide instruction overlap by a layout of the form (b) or (c).

One way in which we might extend the parallelism of layout (b) is to provide several E-units, each capable of executing one instruction at a time from a subset of the instruction set. This is illustrated in layout (d) and is exemplified by the CDC 6600 central processor. This processor has ten independent E-units: two perform multiplication; two perform incrementation; and there is one unit each for fixed-point addition, floating-point addition, division, shifting, logical operations, and jumping.

The common portion of the processor (corresponding to our I-unit) includes the various accumulators and index registers from which the E-units obtain operands and to which they return results, the mechanism for accessing the main store, and a control unit called the 'scoreboard' or 'reservation control'. This unit keeps a record of the current usage of all E-units and processor registers, and assigns successive instructions to the appropriate E-unit if it is free and the operands and result register are available; if not, the scoreboard records the delaying condition, and allocates the instruction when the condition has been satisfied. Thus the scoreboard attempts to keep as many as possible of the 10 E-units in continuous operation, with appropriate interlocks between instructions. It is reported (Bell and Newell 1971, p. 471) that the CDC 6600 is 2½ times faster than the CDC 6400, which has exactly the same architecture, but does not have instruction overlap.

In the above discussion we have split the processing of an instruction into two steps, one performed by the I-unit, and one by an appropriate E-unit. Instead we can consider breaking down the processing of each instruction into a sequence of rather smaller steps. We then provide a set of autonomous functional units, each of which performs one of these steps on an instruction and passes it on to the next unit, as shown in layout (e). Thus successive stages might fetch the instruction, decode it, calculate the effective address, access an operand from main store (or a cache store) if required, perform the appropriate processing, and return a result to store if required.

We can thus imagine the processor as a pipeline or assembly line along which instructions pass. At any point in time several instructions will be at different stages of partial completion in the pipeline, and instructions will enter and leave the pipeline at a rate determined by the time taken to complete a stage rather than the time taken to complete the processing of an instruction.

Typically different classes of instruction proceed through different stages after the first four described above (which are common to most instructions). Thus a more realistic layout is (f), where we have a pipelined I-unit and a number of more or less pipelined E-units to deal with different classes of instruction. Examples of such a system are the IBM 360 models 91 (Anderson, Sparacio, and Tomasulo 1967) and 195 (McLaughlin 1969; Murphey and Wade 1970), the central processor of the CDC 7600 (which has 9 pipelined E-units), and the University of Manchester MU5 (Ibbett 1972).

Any particular scheme for parallelism must take into account the speed lost by the extra logic introduced, and the fact that the maximum possible overlap is never sustained in practice, because of instruction interdependencies.

### *The fetching of instructions*

In order to take advantage of instruction overlap we need to be able to fetch instructions at a suitable rate. Most high-performance computers therefore interpose an instruction buffer between the main store and processor, capable of holding a small number of instruction words. The instruction buffer on the CDC 6600 holds 8 words (up to 32 instructions), that on the IBM 360 models 91 and 195 holds 64 bytes (again up to 32 instructions).

While the processor is fetching and decoding an instruction from some point within the buffer, store accesses are made to fill the buffer with words from the instruction stream ahead of this instruction; that is, the computer is 'looking ahead' down the instruction stream. Thus the instruction buffer attempts to eliminate waiting for the store access for the next instruction, and also protects the processor from variations in store access speed (due for example to conflict with operand accesses by the processor, and with transput accesses to store).

The occurrence of a conditional jump instruction of course invalidates this simple lookahead technique, since the processor has to await the setting of the test condition before choosing which path to follow. Unfortunately about 20 per cent of instructions executed will be jumps (see for example Sumner 1969), so this is a major problem for overlapped computers.

There are three possible ways of dealing with conditional jumps:

(a) Wait for the condition to be set before proceeding further;
(b) Continue processing down both paths; or
(c) Guess which path is likely to be followed, and continue down that path.

In (b) and (c) the processor must be able to eliminate the effect of following a path that turns out to be incorrect.

Method (a) is used in the CDC 6600 computer. If a conditional jump instruction is decoded by the central processor, no attempt is made to execute later instructions until the jump condition has been established and the new instruction path chosen.

In method (b) instructions are prefetched down both instruction paths into two separate instruction buffers. Suitably marked instructions are then processed from both buffers up to a point just before an unrecoverable action takes place, when the instruction awaits the establishing of the jump condition. Instructions from the invalid path are then eliminated, while instructions from the valid path complete their processing. This method is not used in practice, because of the complexity of the interlocks that would be required.

Method (c) is the most common technique. Typically a static choice is made of the most likely path to be followed for each class of conditional jump instruction, and this is built into the lookahead control logic. When a conditional jump instruction is decoded, the appropriate path is selected and the processing of instructions from that path continues. Instructions from beyond the jump are marked and are held up when they reach the point where they are to be executed by an E-unit, until the jump condition is established. If the correct choice has been made, the processor continues down this path. If not, the instructions from beyond the jump are eliminated, and the processor restarts from the beginning of the other path.

To speed the recovery action after an incorrect choice of path, some processors fetch into a separate buffer the first word or two down the unchosen path, while following and partially processing the chosen path in the main instruction buffer. This jump or *branch buffer* is used to refill part of the instruction buffer if the jump choice turns out to be wrong. Thus we obtain some of the effects of method (b) without its extra complications.

A simple method of choosing a path, used on the IBM 7030 computer, is to assume that all conditional jumps will fail; that is, control is expected to proceed to the instruction in the location following that containing the jump. A slightly more sophisticated system (used, for example, on the IBM 370 model 165) is to assume that conditional jumps fail, except for those based on tests upon index values, which are assumed to succeed. We have described in § 5.5 the way the MU5 computer selects the path to follow.

The instruction buffer not only holds instructions awaiting execution but can also act as a repository for the last few instructions executed. If a successful jump is made backwards in the instruction stream to one of these instructions, the processor automatically enters a special 'loop mode', in which the instruction buffer is not refilled from main store, and the sequence of instructions is executed repeatedly from the buffer for the remaining iterations of the loop.

***Instruction interdependencies***

In the computers of this section we wish to preserve the fiction of conventional sequential execution of instructions, by interlocks to preserve dependencies between instructions. These can be divided into three types; operational, procedural, and data dependencies (Tjaden and Flynn 1970).

An *operational dependency* is one where two instructions both require the same processing resource. Thus if instruction A is using the fixed-point E-unit, instruction B cannot use it at the same time. If the cost warrants, we could of course provide several fixed-point E-units, or split the single E-unit into several (pipelined) stages, so that instruction B can enter the first stage of the E-unit as soon as instruction A enters the second stage.

A *procedural dependency* is one caused by the sequential nature of the instruction stream. It is exemplified by an instruction whose execution depends on the path chosen by a preceding conditional jump instruction. Methods for dealing with this type of dependency have already been discussed.

A *data dependency* is illustrated by the following piece of code,

Load into accumulator 1 the contents of $x$
Add to accumulator 1 the contents of $y$
Multiply accumulator 1 by the contents of $z$

In the second and third instruction the source of one operand is the result (or 'sink') of the preceding one. Similarly an address modification may require an index register whose contents are evaluated in the preceding instruction. The processor logic has to recognize such dependencies, and attempt to bypass (by extensions to the forwarding technique described earlier) the delays inherent in sending the result of an operation first to an accumulator and then to the unit which requires it as a source operand.

Overlapped computers operate at their full speed only in portions of a process which are relatively free from procedural and data dependencies and this imposes a burden on the programmer or compiler. Interdependencies between simultaneously-executed instructions could be reduced by interlacing instructions from several independent instruction streams (Aschenbrenner, Flynn, and Robinson 1967), and this is illustrated in Figure 8.5. At the architectural level we see several independent processors each operating on its own instruction stream. However these processors are implemented as a number of independent I-units sharing a set of E-units.

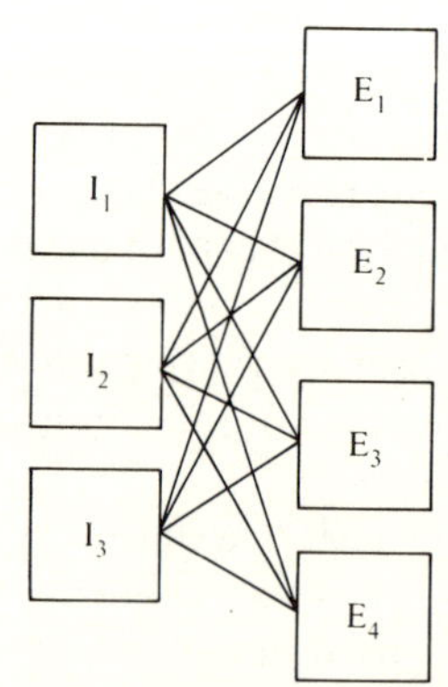


FIG. 8.5

### *Vector processors*

Instead of having a functionally parallel processor which operates only on conventional data-types, we may provide data-types which take advantage of the processor's overlapped operation. On these *vector processors* (for example the CDC Star-100, the Texas Instruments ASC, and the Cray-1) instructions specify operations, not on single operands, but on vectors of (fixed-point, floating-point, or logical) operands. Then the processing of one operand from a vector is overlapped with the accessing and processing of subsequent operands from the vector. Some writers (for example, Enslow 1974, pp. 41–4; Foster 1976a, p. 253) reserve the term pipelined computer for this type of vector processor, where there is provision for explicit specification of vectors whose elements are to be processed by a pipeline of functional units. Vector processors are discussed in Ramamoorthy and Li (1977).

### *Other consequences of instruction overlap*

We have already discussed possible interactions between instructions in the instruction stream; for example an index quantity required by one instruction might be computed by an instruction closely preceding it. In the worst case we have the possibility of an instruction modifying a location containing an instruction which is about to be executed (although such bad programming practice should nowadays be rare). Some computers with lookahead (such as models in the IBM 370 range) provide interlocks to detect and recover from these situations. However many others (including the CDC 6600) do not provide interlocks, and programmers are simply warned against modifying instruction words within a certain distance of the instruction being executed.

Further problems in overlapped computers are caused by the occurrence of interrupts. First, the occurrence of an interrupt forces the emptying of the instruction pipeline and the restarting of the processor on a new instruction sequence, causing a loss of overlapping efficiency. Thus we should attempt to minimize the number of interrupts which arise, for example, by removing most transput activity to satellite processors (see, for example, the architecture of the CDC 6600).

Second, interrupts may not arise in an overlapped computer in the same sequence as they would in a non-overlapped computer, since instructions are being executed out of order. We are in effect introducing unforeseen instruction interdependencies because of such *imprecise* interrupts (Anderson, Sparacio, and Tomasulo 1967).

Overlapped computers may not be able to guarantee recovery to a state equivalent to the operation of a non-overlapped computer in these circumstances.

Because there are times at which the programmer wishes to have control over the exact sequence in which operations are carried out, some instructions may force *serialization* (IBM 1970, pp. 20–1); that is, all preceding instructions are completed before the instruction is initiated, and no subsequent instructions are initiated until it has been completed. A semaphore operation is obviously a candidate for such serializing action.

Apart from the special cases discussed above, programs can be written ignoring the means by which overlapping is achieved, and the required processing will be carried out correctly but at possibly a less than maximal rate. However, compilers ought to be able to produce machine code which takes advantage of the overlapping provided by the processor. Thus, when generating code for arithmetic expressions, the compiler should attempt to minimize the data dependencies between successive instructions. This is discussed for example in Lorin (1972, Chapter 10) and Baer (1973).

## 8.3. Operator–computer dialogue

In early computers an intimate relationship was assumed between the computer and the programmer. Programs were written in machine code, and were tested by being run on the computer while the programmer observed their behaviour through the interpretation of binary patterns of lights at the computer console.

Since then, of course, computers have become too complicated and expensive to allow such techniques. The vast majority of computers are in the hands, not of programmers, but of professional computer operators, whose scope for intervention is controlled by an operating system. The possibility of on-line interaction with one's program (for debugging or man-machine problem-solving) has reappeared with multi-access computer systems, but here the required facilities are provided by software, aided by the process-monitoring hardware discussed in § 8.1.

We begin this section, then, by discussing hardware facilities to allow direct debugging of programs at the computer console, with the proviso that these are in regular use only on the smaller modern computers. On medium and large modern computers such facilities are commonly still provided, but only for use by the maintenance engineer in running diagnostic programs or in debugging the most basic supervisory software. On microprocessors there are no facilities at all for direct access to the processor; in the software testing phase extra hardware called a 'development system' (Aspinall and Dagless 1977, Chapter 9) is attached to the microprocessor system to run and debug programs.

### *Direct debugging of programs*

Our first debugging requirement is for some form of breakpoint facility, by which a running program can be brought to a halt from time to time for inspection, without interspersing the program with halt instructions. The types of facility which are provided parallel the monitoring facilities discussed in § 8.1. Corresponding to the interrupt after each instruction is the provision on most computers of a *single-instruction* mode, in which the computer stops after each instruction is executed, to await manual inspection and restart.

An alternative method is to provide a 'selective halt' instruction which specifies one of a group of switches at the computer control panel. If the specified switch is set, the computer comes to a halt; otherwise the instruction is treated as a null instruction. Such a feature was common on first- and second-generation computers, but is not often provided nowadays.

Corresponding to the monitoring of program events, we have the fairly common provision of a means for halting the computer if access is made to a store address specified at the computer console; such a facility is provided on the IBM 370 range, for example.

After the occurrence of a breakpoint, the programmer wishes to examine the current values of process variables. The contents of the processor registers, such as accumulators, the program counter and the condition code register, are usually displayed continuously on the console, either as a row of binary lights or as sets of octal or hexadecimal digits. A set of toggle or rotating switches is also provided at which a store address may be set up; a console switch then causes the display of the contents of the selected location, or of successive locations starting at the selected address.

A further requirement is to alter the contents of selected store locations. Switches are provided to establish a bit pattern one word long; a console switch then causes this value to be deposited at a store location whose address has previously been set up, or at the next store location of a series starting at such an address.

### *Operator controls*

In order to control the computer system, the operator needs the following;

(a) A power on/off switch for the whole computer system. Since the use of this switch to turn the power off causes a lengthy sequence of actions to be followed, so that units are powered down without damage to equipment, an emergency power off control may also be provided to remove power from the whole system instantaneously.

(b) A switch to reset all electronic equipment (especially all processor and transput flags) to some initial condition. The power-on sequence may also include this resetting action. Some computers provide a switch to clear the whole of main store to zero.

(c) A switch to start and stop the processor executing instructions. The start is at the instruction referred to by the current contents of the program counter, set by the processor before it was brought to a halt (for a restart) or by means of a set of switches (for initial startup). Each piece of transput equipment normally has similar power, reset, and start switches; the start switch simply places the device in a state ready to respond to processor signals.

(d) The operator must be given some indication that the computer is running correctly. Thus a small number of signal lights are provided to indicate, for example, whether the processor is receiving power and whether it is executing instructions. This may be extended to calibrated dials measuring activity in the various units, or to a meter for total computer hours used.

(e) Saltzer (1974) draws attention to the fact that the operator's console (particularly if it includes the examination and patching facilities discussed earlier) provides a possible route for bypassing system security controls. Thus a console lock may be provided to disable some or all of the features we have discussed, forcing operator intervention only under the control of the operating system.

All these controls could of course be collected together with the direct debugging and maintenance facilities on a single control panel, resulting in a large and impressive array of flashing lights. Nowadays it is more common to have two control panels. One, the operator's console, contains only the controls (a) to (e), together with the interrupt and initial load buttons (which are discussed later); the other, maintenance console contains all the remaining direct controls.

All other operator intervention is via an operator's terminal (an on-line typewriter or visual display unit), and this is treated by the operating system and hardware as just another peripheral device, and controlled by the usual transput instructions. Indeed on the larger computer systems there may be several operator terminals in different parts of the computer room, limited by software control to accepting certain sets of operator directives.

### *Communication with processes*

Normally-running processes (that is, processes not involved in fault tracing from the maintenance console) generally converse with the computer operator, if at all, through the operator's terminal. However, there are three other means by which a process might interact directly with the operator; that is, not via the standard transput instructions. These are as follows:

(a) Many modern computers provide an interrupt button, pressure on which causes a special interrupt (that is, an interrupt not associated with a transput device) to be signalled to the processor. This interrupt is normally used to indicate (probably at a high priority level) the operator's wish to enter into a dialogue with the operating system via his terminal.

(b) In the past, computers have often had a number of console 'sense' switches, which could be individually set by the operator, and whose setting could be tested or read into the accumulator by a non-transput instruction (see, for example, the 'or with switch register' instruction on the DEC PDP-8 computer).

On second-generation computers this instruction was often a conditional jump,

Jump to address $x$ if sense switch $i$ is set

Similarly a number of console signal or 'sense' lights could be set and tested by non-transput instructions. By means of these sense switches and lights a rudimentary form of communication could be set up between operator and computer. The technique became incorporated into early versions of Fortran in 'IF (SENSE SWITCH i)' and 'SENSE LIGHT j' statements. When multiprogramming was introduced such facilities became the prerogative of the operating system, and they are nowadays likely to be found on only the smaller computers.

(c) We have already mentioned the need for the operator to have some clear indication that the computer is running. To this end some computers provide a loudspeaker through which a continuous note is produced while instructions are being executed. An alternative use of such a loudspeaker is to give an alarm signal; thus a 'hoot' might be generated when a halt or a special 'alarm' instruction is executed.

A third possibility is for the loudspeaker to be stimulated each time a certain condition obtains within the processor, so that the note produced by the loudspeaker depends upon the frequency with which the condition arises. The condition is often the execution of a certain type of jump instruction, or the occurrence of an overflow from the accumulator. The note produced by the loudspeaker is supposed to indicate gross process behaviour during debugging, but this hardware was often used on early computers for playing tunes on open days (see, for example, the description in Bowden 1953, pp.75–6 of the Manchester Mark I computer).

### *Bootstrapping*

Before we can press the start button, we must have some means of placing a suitable program in the initially empty store of the computer. This is done by a process known as *bootstrapping,* whereby a sequence of increasingly sophisticated loaders is prepared, and each is used to load (and perhaps transfer control to) the next loader in the sequence.

Thus, when we have introduced a minimal loader into the computer, it is used to load a larger and faster loader with error-checking and other facilities, and this is used to load the required application program. A common early technique (on computers with punched card input) was to precede each program deck with a single card containing a loader for the program; the minimal loader would then be required simply to load this card at a standard location and transfer control to it. Nowadays the bootstrap technique loads an operating system, which incorporates its own loader and controls the loading of all other programs.

It remains to discuss how the minimal loader is to be placed in the main store of the computer. One possibility is to have a small read-only area in main store, into which a loader program is placed during manufacture of the store. Such a program operates in a normal fashion, except that it cannot be overwritten. This technique raises a problem if we wish to alter the input device from which the next loader is to be read. A slightly more flexible scheme is to provide a main store area for which all write accesses can be disabled by a console switch: a loader in such an area is unlikely to be corrupted unintentionally, but allows the possibility, under operator control, of modifying the loader.

Earlier in this section we discussed the provision of sets of console switches by which the operator can enter words into the main store, and this facility can be used to insert a loader program. Such a loader must be designed for shortness, to minimize the amount of switch manipulation needed to insert it. For example the DEC PDP-8 computer, which uses this method, has a minimal (RIM, or Read-In Mode) loader sixteen words long.

A more sophisticated solution (common on modern computers, such as the IBM 370 range) has an *initial load* sequence built into the processor. When the operator presses an initial load button on the console, this reads a block of words from an input device into main store starting at a fixed location, and control is then transferred to this location (which is the beginning of some form of loader to bring in the operating system). The operator usually has a switch with which he can select the input device from which reading is to take place. The address of the block to be read is usually fixed; on paper tape or magnetic tape typically the next available block is read, while on a magnetic disc block zero of cylinder zero of the selected disc drive might be assumed.

In this section we have talked in terms of a single-processor system. If the system contains several processors, one processor may be able to set up an initial program and start each of the other processors executing it. For example, the initial load sequence on the CDC 6600 computer loads the contents of a panel of manually-set switches into the private store of PCP number 0. starts PCP0, and sets the remaining PCPs ready to accept data from PCP0; subsequently one of the PCPs will start the central processor.

**Problems**

**8.1.** On page 317 it is suggested that techniques for dealing with hardware failure can be divided into three classes. To what extent do the techniques described in § 8.1 fit neatly into these classes? Which of the techniques do you consider to be at the level of architecture, which at the level of implementation, and which a mixture of the two?

**8.2.** Consider a group of *n* bits $[b_i]$, some of which are data bits and the rest of which are check bits. Suppose we place one or more even parity constraints on the binary patterns which can be held by the group: for a single even parity bit, the constraint is

$$\sum_{i=1}^{n} b_i = 0$$

(where addition is modulo two). A set of constraints can be represented by a $c \times n$ *parity-check matrix* $[m_{ij}]$, where $c$ is the number of constraints, each of the form

$$\sum_{j=1}^{n} m_{ij} b_j = 0,$$

Thus, for a word of two 8-bit data bytes each with its own parity bit, the parity-check matrix is

$$\begin{bmatrix} 111111110000000010 \\ 000000001111111101 \end{bmatrix}$$

Suppose we wish to detect and correct all single bit faults. What restrictions does this impose on the values taken by the columns of the matrix? Hence design a code for 64 data bits and 7 check bits, which will detect and correct all single bit faults (if we assume not more than one fault occurs at a time). By adding an over-all parity bit, design a code for 64 data bits and 8 check bits, which will detect all two bit faults and correct all single bit faults. (Hint: see any reference on Hamming codes, such as Berlekamp 1968, Chapter 1).

**8.3.** The *residue* of a number *modulo k* is the remainder on dividing the number by *k*. How is the residue of the sum, difference, and product of two numbers related to the residues of the original numbers?

The residue of a number modulo 9 is easily generated from its decimal representation by summing the digits (why?). How might this be used for checking arithmetic operations? Are there better moduli than 9 for binary computers?

**8.4.** What facilities would you like to see in a program to aid in the debugging of assembly language programs? How could such a program make use of the process monitoring hardware discussed in § 8.1, and how would its use be an improvement over the use of the direct debugging facilities discussed in §8.3? How would your debugging program need modification to deal with a high-level language?

**8.5** In § 8.2 we discuss how a computer may attempt to predict the result of each conditional jump, and provide a special 'loop mode'. How could a programmer make use of his knowledge of the effect of this part of the hardware, in order to write more efficient programs? Are the same techniques available to a compiler?

**8.6.** Consider two computers to which you have access, one a small computer and the other a medium or large one. What direct controls are provided on each computer's console? How easy is it to obtain this information from the manuals on the computer? Which of the controls are provided for the operator, which for the maintenance engineer, and which for the programmer? To what extent is one set of switches or lights made to serve several functions?

# Bibliography

ABRAMSON, N. AND KUO, F. F. (1973). *Computer-communication networks.* Prentice-Hall, Englewood Cliffs, New Jersey.

AIKEN, H. H. AND HOPPER, G. M. (1946). The automatic sequence controlled calculator. *Elect. Enging,* **65,** 384–91, 449–54, 522–8. [Reprinted in Randell (1975), pp. 199–218.]

ALONSO, R. L., BLAIR-SMITH, H., AND HOPKINS, A. L. (1963). Some aspects of the logical design of a control computer: a case study. *IEEE Trans. electron. Comput.,* **EC-12** (6), 687–97. [Reprinted in Bell and Newell (1971), pp. 146–56.]

AMDAHL, G. M., BLAAUW, G. A., AND BROOKS, F. P. (1964). Architecture of the IBM System /360. *IBM J. Res. Dev.,* **8** (2), 87–101.

ANDERSON, D. W., SPARACIO, F. J., AND TOMASULO, R. M. (1967). The IBM System /360 Model 91: machine philosophy and instruction handling. *IBM J. Res. Dev.,* **11** (1), 8–24.

ARDEN, B. W., GALLER, B. A., O'BRIEN, T. C., AND WESTERVELT, F. H. (1966). Program and addressing structure in a time-sharing environment. *J. Ass. Comput. Mach.,* **13** (1), 1–16.

ASCHENBRENNER, R. A., FLYNN, M. J., AND ROBINSON, G. A. (1967). Intrinsic multiprocessing. *AFIPS Conference Proceedings,* **30,** 81–6. [Spring Joint Computer Conference 1967.]

ASPINALL, D. AND DAGLESS, E. L. (eds) (1977). *Introduction to microprocessors.* Pitman and Academic Press, London and New York.

AVIZIENIS, A. (1968). An experimental self-repairing computer. In *Information processing 68: Proceedings of IFIP Congress 1968* (ed. A. J. H. Morrell), Vol. 2, pp. 872–7. North-Holland, Amsterdam.

BACON, M. D. AND BULL, G. M. (1973). *Data transmission.* MacDonald and American Elsevier, London and New York.

BAER, J. L. (1973). A survey of some theoretical aspects of multiprocessing. *Comput. Surv.,* **5** (1), 31–80.

BARNES, G. H., BROWN, R. M., KATO, M., KUCK, D. J., SLOTNICK, D. L., AND STOKES, R. A. (1968). The ILLIAC IV computer. *IEEE Trans. Comput.,* **C-17** (8), 746–57. [Reprinted in Bell and Newell (1971), pp. 320–33.]

BARSAMIAN, H. (1970), Firmware sort processor with LSI components. *AFIPS Conference Proceedings,* **36,** 183–90. [Spring Joint Computer Conference 1970.]

BARTOW, N. AND MCGUIRE, R. (1970). System /360 model 85 microdiagnostics. *AFIPS Conference Proceedings,* **36,** 191–7a. [Spring Joint Computer Conference 1970.]

BASHKOW, T. R., SASSON, A., AND KRONFELD, A. (1967). System design of a FORTRAN machine. *IEEE Trans. electron. Comput.*, **EC-16** (4), 85–99. [Reprinted in Bell and Newell (1971), pp. 363–81.]

BEKEY, G. A. AND KARPLUS, W. J. (1968). *Hybrid computation.* Wiley, New York.

BELADY, L. A. (1966). Study of replacement algorithms for a virtual-storage computer. *IBM Systems J.*, **5** (2), 78–101.

BELL, C. G., KOTOK, A., HASTINGS, T. N., AND HILL, R. (1978). The evolution of the DECsystem 10. *Commun. Ass. Comput. Mach.*, **21** (1), 44–63.

BELL, C. G. AND NEWELL, A. (1971). *Computer structures: readings and examples.* McGraw-Hill, New York.

BELL, G., CADY, R., MCFARLAND, H., DELAGI, B., O'LAUGHLIN, J., NOONAN, R., AND WULF, W. (1970). A new architecture for minicomputers—the DEC PDP-11. *AFIPS Conference Proceedings,* **36,** 657–75. [Spring Joint Computer Conference 1970.]

BELL, J., CASASENT, D., AND BELL, C. G. (1974). An investigation of alternative cache organizations. *IEEE Trans. Comput.*, **C-23** (4), 346–51.

BENNETTS, R. G. AND LEWIN, D. W. (1971). Fault diagnosis of digital systems—a review. *Comput. J.*, **14** (2), 199–206.

BENSOUSSAN, A., CLINGEN, C. T., AND DALEY, R. C. (1972). The Multics virtual memory: concepts and design. *Commun.Ass.Comput.Mach.*, **15** (5), 308–18.

BERLEKAMP, R. (1968). *Algebraic coding theory.* McGraw-Hill, New York.

BLAAUW, G. A. AND BROOKS, F. P. (1964). The structure of system /360: part I—outline of the logical structure. *IBM Systems J.*, **3** (2) and (3), 119–35.

BLOCH, E. (1959). The engineering design of the stretch computer. *Proc. Eastern Joint Computer Conference 1959,* pp. 48–59. [Reprinted in Bell and Newell (1971), pp. 421–39.]

BORGERSON, B. R., HANSON, M. L., AND HARTLEY, P. A. (1978). The evolution of the Sperry Univac 1100 series: a history, analysis, and projection. *Commun. Ass. Comput. Mach.*, **21** (1), 25–43.

BOWDEN, B. V. (ed.) (1953). *Faster than thought.* Pitman, London.

BREUER, M. A. AND FRIEDMAN, A. D. (1976). *Diagnosis and reliable design of digital systems.* Pitman, London.

BUCHHOLZ, W. (1962). *Planning a computer system: Project Stretch.* McGraw-Hill, New York.

BUCKLE, J. K. (1978). *The ICL 2900 series.* MacMillan, London.

BURKS, A. W., GOLDSTINE, H. H., AND VON NEUMANN, J. (1946). Preliminary discussion of the logical design of an electronic computing instrument, Part I, Vol. I. Report prepared for U.S. Army Ordnance Department. [Reprinted in Von Neumann (1963), pp. 34–79; Bell and Newell (1971), pp. 92–119.]

Burnett, G. J. and Coffman, E. G. (1970). A Study of interleaved memory systems. *AFIPS Conference Proceedings,* **36,** 467–74. [Spring Joint Computer Conference 1970.]

——, —— (1975). Analysis of interleaved memory systems using blockage buffers. *Commun. Ass. Comput. Mach.,* **18** (2), 91–5.

Burroughs (1972). *B1700 systems reference manual.* Reference number 1057155. Burroughs Corp., Detroit, Michigan.

Capon, P. C. (1974). Order codes that suit programming languages. In *Infotech state of the art report 17: computer design* (ed. C. Boon), pp. 457–67. Infotech Information Ltd, Maidenhead, Berkshire.

Case, R. P. and Padegs, A. (1978). Architecture of the IBM System /370. *Commun. Ass. Comput. Mach.,* **21** (1), 73–96.

CDC (1966). *Control Data 6000 series computer systems reference manual,* Publication Number 60100000, Control Data Corp.

—— (1971). *Control Data Star-100 computer system hardware reference manual,* Publication Number 60256000, Control Data Corp.

Chu, W. W. and Opderbeck, H. (1974). Performance of replacement algorithms with different page sizes. *Computer* **7,** 14–21.

Codd, E. F. (1968). *Cellular automata.* Academic Press, New York.

Conway, M. E. (1958). Proposal for an UNCOL. *Commun. Ass. Comput. Mach.,* **1** (10), 5–8.

Creech, B. A. (1970). Architecture of the B6500. In *Software engineering (COINS III)* (ed. J. T. Tou), Vol. 1, pp. 29–43. Academic Press, New York.

Daley, R. C. and Dennis, J. B. (1968). Virtual memory, processes and sharing in Multics. *Commun. Ass. Comput. Mach.,* **11** (5), 306–12.

Data General (1971). *How to use the Nova computers,* Reference Number DG NM-5. Data General Corp., Southboro, Massachusetts.

—— (1977). *User's manual: programmer's reference: S/130 micro programming WCS feature,* Reference Number 015–000069–00. Data General Corp., Southboro, Massachusetts.

Davies, D. W. and Barber, D. L. A. (1973). *Communication networks for computers.* Wiley, Chichester.

Davies, P. M. (1972). Readings in microprogramming. *IBM Systems J.,* **11** (1), 16–40.

Davis, G. M. (1960). The English Electric KDF9 computer system. *Comput. Bull.,* **4** (3), 119–20.

Davis, S. (1969). *Computer data displays.* Prentice-Hall, Englewood Cliffs, New Jersey.

DEC (1972a). *PDP8/e and PDP8/m small computer handbook.* Digital Equipment Corp., Maynard, Massachusetts.

—— (1972b). *PDP11/45 processor handbook.* Digital Equipment Corp., Maynard, Massachusetts.

—— (1972c). *DEC system 10 assembly language handbook.* Digital Equipment Corp., Maynard, Massachusetts.

DENNING, P. J. (1968a). The working set model for program behaviour. *Commun. Ass. Comput. Mach.*, **11** (5), 323–33.

—— (1968b). Thrashing: its causes and prevention. *AFIPS Conference Proceedings,* **33,** Pt. 1, 915–22. [Fall Joint Computer Conference 1968.]

—— (1970). Virtual memory. *Comput. Surv.*, **2** (3), 153–89.

DENNIS, J. B. (1965). Segmentation and the design of multiprogrammed computer systems. *J. Ass. Comput. Mach.*, **12** (4), 589–602.

—— AND VAN HORN, E. C. (1966). Programming semantics for multiprogrammed computations. *Commun. Ass. Comput. Mach.*, **9** (3), 143–55.

DICKINSON, M. M., JACKSON, J. B., AND RANDA, G. C. (1964). Saturn V launch vehicle digital computer and data adapter. *AFIPS Conference Proceedings,* **26,** Pt. 1, 501–16. [Fall Joint Computer Conference 1964.]

DIJKSTRA, E. W. (1968). Co-operating sequential processes. In F. Genuys (ed.) (1968). *Programming languages,* pp. 43–112. Academic Press, London.

—— (1971). Hierarchical ordering of sequential processes. *Acta Informatica,* **1,** 115–38.

DREYFUS, P. (1958a). System design of the Gamma 60. *Proc. Western Joint Computer Conference* (Los Angeles: 6–8th May 1958), pp. 130–2.

—— (1958b). Programming design features of the Gamma 60 computer. *Proc. Eastern Joint Computer Conference* (3–5th December 1958), pp. 174–81.

ECKERT, J. P., WEINER, J. R., WELSH, H. F., AND MITCHELL, H. F. (1951). The UNIVAC system. AIEE–IRE Conference (6–16th December 1951). [Reprinted in Bell and Newell (1971), pp. 157–69.]

ELLIOTT, W. S., OWEN, C. E., DEVONALD, C. H., AND MAUDSLEY, B. G. (1956). The design philosophy of Pegasus, a quantity-production computer. *Proc. Inst. Elect. Engrs,* Part B, Vol. 103, Suppl. 2, pp. 188–96. [Reprinted in Bell and Newell (1971), pp. 171–83.]

ENSLOW, P. H. (ed.) (1974). *Multiprocessors and parallel processing.* Wiley, New York.

FABRY, R. S. (1974). Capability-based addressing. *Commun. Ass. Comput. Mach.*, **17** (7), 403–12.

FALKOFF, A. D. (1962). Algorithms for parallel-search memories. *J. Ass. Comput. Mach.*, **9,** 488–511.

——, IVERSON, K. E., AND SUSSENGUTH, E. H. (1964). A formal description of System /360. *IBM Systems J.*, **3** (3), 198–262.

FEUSTEL, E. A. (1972). The Rice research computer—a tagged architecture. *AFIPS Conference Proceedings,* **40,** 369–77. [Spring Joint Computer Conference 1972.]

—— (1973). On the advantages of tagged architecture. *IEEE Trans. Comput.*, **C-22** (7), 644–56.

FLORES, I. (1963). *The logic of computer arithmetic.* Prentice-Hall, Englewood Cliffs, New Jersey.

—— (1969). *Computer organization.* Prentice-Hall, Englewood Cliffs, New Jersey.

FLYNN, M. J. (1966). Very high-speed computing systems. *Proc. Inst. elect. electron. Engrs,* **54** (12), 1901–9.

FOSTER, C. C. (1976a). *Computer architecture.* Van Nostrand Reinhold, New York.

—— (1976b). *Content addressable parallel processors.* Van Nostrand Reinhold, New York.

FOTHERINGHAM, J. (1961). Dynamic storage allocation in the Atlas computer, including an automatic use of a backing store. *Commun. Ass. Comput. Mach.,* **4** (10), 435–6.

FRIEDMAN, A. R. AND MENON, P. R. (1971). *Fault detection in digital circuits.* Prentice-Hall, Englewood Cliffs, New Jersey.

GARDNER, M. (1970). Mathematical games. *Scient. Amer.,* **223** (4), 120–3.

—— (1971). Mathematical games. *Scient. Amer.,* **224** (2), 112–7.

GIRLING, B. (1967). Introducing hybrid computation for commercial users. *Comput. Bull.,* **10** (4), 38–42.

GLUSKIN, R. S., JACOBY, M., AND READER, T. D. (1964). FLODAC—a pure fluid digital computer. *AFIPS Conference Proceedings,* **26,** Pt. 1, 631–41. [Fall Joint Computer Conference 1964.]

GOLDSTINE, H. H. AND GOLDSTINE, A. (1946). The electronic numerical integrator and computer (ENIAC). *M.T.A.C.,* **2** (15), 97–110. [Reprinted in Randell (1975), pp. 333–47.]

—— AND VON NEUMANN, J. (1947). Planning and coding of problems for an electronic computing instrument, Part 2, Vol. 1. Report prepared for U.S. Army Ordnance Department. [Reprinted in Von Neumann (1963), pp. 80–151.]

——, —— (1948). Planning and coding of problems for an electronic computing instrument, Part 2, Vol. 2. Report prepared for U.S. Army Ordnance Department. [Reprinted in Von Neumann (1963), pp. 152–214.]

GRAHAM, R. M. (1968). Protection in an information processing utility. *Commun. Ass. Comput. Mach.,* **11** (5), 365–9.

HALEY, A. C. D. (1956). DEUCE: a high-speed general-purpose computer. *Proc. Inst. Elect. Engrs,* Part B, Vol. 103, Suppl. 2, pp. 165–73.

—— (1962). The KDF9 computer system. *AFIPS Conference Proceedings,* **22,** 108–20. [Fall Joint Computer Conference 1962.]

HALTON, D. (1972). Hardware of the system 250 for communication control. International Switching Symposium. (M.I.T., Cambridge, Mass.: 6–9th June 1972).

HAMER-HODGES, K. J. (1972). Fault-resistance and recovery within system 250. International Conference on Computer Communication. (Washington, D.C.: 24–6th October 1972.)

HAMILTON, F. E. AND KUBIE, E. C. (1954). The IBM magnetic drum calculator type 650. *J. Ass. Comput. Mach.,* **1** (1), 13–20.

HANSEN, P. B. (1973). *Operating system principles*. Prentice-Hall, Englewood Cliffs, New Jersey.

HASSITT, A., LAGESCHULTE, J. W., AND LYON, L. E. (1973). Implementation of a high level language machine. *Commun. Ass. Comput. Mach.*, **16** (4), 199–212.

HAUCK, E. A. AND DENT, B. A. (1968). Burroughs' B6500/B7500 stack mechanism. *AFIPS Conference Proceedings*, **32**, 245–51. [Spring Joint Computer Conference 1968.]

HEART, F. E., KAHN, R. E., ORNSTEIN, S. M., CROWTHER, W. R., AND WALDEN, D. C. (1970). The interface message processor for the ARPA computer network, *AFIPS Conference Proceedings*, **36**, 551–67. [Spring Joint Computer Conference 1970.]

——, ORNSTEIN, S. M., CROWTHER, W. R., AND BARKER, W. B. (1973). A new minicomputer/multiprocessor for the ARPA network. *AFIPS Conference Proceedings*, **42**, 529–37. [National Computer Conference 1973.]

HELLERMAN, H. (1973). *Digital computer system principles*. McGraw-Hill, New York.

HELLERMAN, L. AND HOERNES, G. E. (1968). Control storage use in implementing an associative memory for a time-shared computer. *IEEE Trans. Comput.*, **C-17** (12), 1144–51.

HIGMAN, B. (1966). Codewords and floating point addresses. *Proc. British Joint Computer Conference* (3–5th May 1966: Eastbourne, Sussex), pp. 196–203.

HILL, F. J. AND PETERSON, G. R. (1973), *Digital systems: hardware organization and design*. Wiley, New York.

HOBBS, L. C., THEIS, D. J., TRIMBLE, J., TITUS, H., AND HIGHBERG, G. I. (1970). *Parallel processor systems, technologies and applications*. Spartan Books, New York.

HOLLAND, J. (1959). A universal computer capable of executing an arbitrary number of sub-programs simultaneously. *Proc. Eastern Joint Computer Conference 1959*, pp. 108–13.

—— (1960). Iterative circuit computers. *Proc. Western Joint Computer Conference 1960*, pp. 259–65.

HONEYWELL (1965). *Honeywell series 200 programmers' reference manual*. Honeywell Inc., Wellesley Hills, Massachusetts.

HUSSON, S. S. (1970). *Microprogramming: principles and practices*. Prentice-Hall, Englewood Cliffs, New Jersey.

HUXTABLE, D. H. R. AND PINKERTON, J. M. M. (1977). The hardware/software interface of the ICL 2900 range of computers. *Comput. J.*, **20** (4), 290–5.

HYNDMAN, D. E. (1970). *Analog and hybrid computing*. Pergamon Press, Oxford.

IBBETT, R. N. (1972). The MU5 instruction pipeline. *Comput. J.*, **15** (1), 42–50.

—— AND CAPON, P. C. (1978). The development of the MU5 computer system. *Commun. Ass. Comput. Mach.*, **21** (1), 13–24.

—— AND HUSBAND, M. A. (1977). The MU5 name store. *Comput. J.*, **20** (3), 227–31.

IBM (1964). *IBM system /360 principles of operation.* Form Number A22–6821–1, IBM Corp.

—— (1970). *IBM system /370 principles of operation.* Form Number GA22–7000–3, IBM Corp.

ICL (1968). *KDF9 programming.* Technical Publication 1003 mm (R), International Computers Ltd., London.

ILIFFE, J. K. (1968). *Basic machine principles.* MacDonald and American Elsevier, London and New York.

—— AND JODEIT, J. G. (1962). A dynamic storage allocation scheme. *Comput. J.*, **5** (3), 200–9.

IVERSON, K. E. (1962). *A programming language.* Wiley, New York.

JODEIT, J. G. (1968). Storage organization in programming systems. *Commun. Ass. Comput. Mach.*, **11** (11), 741–6.

KAPLAN, A. (1963). A search memory subsystem for a general-purpose computer. *AFIPS Conference Proceedings*, **24**, 193–200. [Fall Joint Computer Conference 1963.]

KAPLAN, K. R. AND WINDER, R. O. (1973). Cache-based computer systems. *Computer* (March 1973), 30–6.

KATZAN, H. (1971a). *Computer organization and the system /370.* Van Nostrand Reinhold, New York.

—— (1971b). Storage hierarchy systems. *AFIPS Conference Proceedings*, **38**, 325–36. [Spring Joint Computer Conference 1971.]

KILBURN, T., EDWARDS, D. B. G., LANIGAN, M. J., AND SUMNER, F. H. (1962). One-level storage system. *Inst. Radio Engrs. Trans. Electron. Comput.*, **EC-11** (2), 223–35. [Reprinted in Bell and Newell (1971), pp. 276–90.]

——, MORRIS, D., ROHL, J. S., AND SUMNER, F. H. (1968). A system design proposal. In *Information processing 68: Proceedings of IFIP Congress 1968* (ed. A. J. H. Morrell), Vol. 2, pp. 806–11. North-Holland, Amsterdam.

——, TOOTHILL, G. C., EDWARDS, D. B. G., AND POLLARD, D. B. W. (1953). Digital computers at Manchester University. *Proc. Inst. elect. Engrs*, Part 2, **100** (77), 487–500.

KIRSTEIN, P. T. (1975). Distributed computer networks. *Nature*, **257** (5527), 549–54.

KNUTH, D. E. (1968). *The art of computer programming vol. I: fundamental algorithms.* Addison-Wesley, Reading, Massachusetts.

—— (1969). *The art of computer programming vol. II: Semi-numerical algorithms.* Addison-Wesley, Reading, Massachusetts.

—— (1970). Von Neumann's first computer program. *Comput. Surv.*, **2** (4), 247–60.

LAVINGTON, S. H. (1975). *A history of Manchester computers.* NCC Publications, Manchester.

LEAMAN, R. J., LLOYD, M. H., AND REPTON, C. S. (1973). The Development and testing of a processor self-test program. *Comput. J.*, **16** (4), 308–14.

LEINER, A. L., NOTZ, W. A., SMITH, J. L., AND WEINBERGER, A. (1958). PILOT, the NBS multicomputer system. *Proc. Eastern Joint Computer Conference 1958*, pp. 71–5. [Reprinted in Bell and Newell (1971), pp. 440–5.]

——, ——, ——, —— A new multiple computer system. *J. Ass. Comput. Mach.*, **6,** 313–35.

LIPTAY, J. S. (1968). Structural aspects of the system/360 model 85 Part II: The cache. *IBM Systems J.*, **7** (1), 15–21.

LISKOV, B. H. (1972). The design of the Venus operating system. *Commun. Ass. Comput. Mach.*, **15** (3), 144–9.

LISTER, A. M. (1975). *Fundamentals of operating systems.* MacMillan, London.

LORIN, H. (1972). *Parallelism in hardware and software: real and apparent concurrency.* Prentice-Hall, Englewood Cliffs, New Jersey.

LOURIE, N., SCHRIMPF, H., REACH, R., AND KAHN, W. (1959). Arithmetic and control techniques in a multiprogram computer. *Proc. Eastern Joint Computer Conference 1959*, pp. 75–81.

LUCAS, H. C. (1971). Performance evaluation and monitoring. *Comput. Surv.*, **3** (3), 79–91.

MCATEER, J. E., CAPOBIANCO, J. A., AND KOPPEL, R. L. (1964). Associative memory system implementation and characteristics. *AFIPS Conference Proceedings*, **26,** Pt. 1, 81-92. [Fall Joint Computer Conference 1964.]

MCCRACKEN, D. D. (1962). *A guide to IBM 1401 programming.* Wiley, New York.

MCKEEVER, B. T. (1965). The associative memory structure. *AFIPS Conference proceedings*, **27,** Pt. 1, 371-88. [Fall Joint Computer Conference 1965.]

MCLAUGHLIN, R. A. (1969). The IBM 360/195. *Datamation*, **15** (10), 119–22.

MADNICK, S. E. AND DONOVAN, J. J. (1974). *Operating systems.* McGraw-Hill, New York.

MARILL, T. AND STERN, D. (1975). The datacomputer—a network data utility. *AFIPS Conference Proceedings*, **44,** 389–95. [National Computer Conference 1975.]

MATHUR, F. P. AND AVIZIENIS, A. (1970). Reliability analysis and architecture of a hybrid-redundant digital system: generalized triple modular redundancy with self-repair. *AFIPS Conference Proceedings*, **36,** 375–83. [Spring Joint Computer Conference 1970.]

MELBOURNE, A. J. AND PUGMIRE, J. M. (1965). A small computer for the direct processing of FORTRAN statements. *Comput. J.*, **8** (1), 24–7.

MIDDLEHOEK, S., GEORGE, P. K., AND DEKKER, P. (1976). *Physics of computer memory devices.* Academic Press, London.

MINSKY, M. L. (1967). *Computation: finite and infinite machines.* Prentice-Hall, Englewood Cliffs, New Jersey.

MORRIS, J. B. (1972). Demand paging through utilization of working sets on the MANIAC II. *Commun. Ass. Comput. Mach.*, **15** (10), 867–72.

MURPHEY, J. O. AND WADE, R. M. (1970). The IBM 360/195. *Datamation,* **16** (4), 72–9.

MYER, T. H. AND SUTHERLAND, I. E. (1968). On the design of display processors. *Commun. Ass. Comput. Mach.*, **11** (6), 410–4.

NEEDHAM, R. M. (1972). Protection systems and protection implementations. *AFIPS Conference Proceedings,* **41,** Pt. 1, 571–8. [Fall Joint Computer Conference 1972.]

NEWMAN, W. M. AND SPROULL, R. F. (1973). *Principles of interactive computer graphics.* McGraw-Hill, New York.

NICKEL, K. (1968). Error-bounds and computer arithmetic. In *Information processing 68: Proceedings of IFIP Congress 1968* (ed. A. J. H. Morrell) Vol. 1 pp. 54–9. North-Holland, Amsterdam.

NISENOFF, N. (1966). Hardware for information processing systems: today and in the future. *Proc. Inst. Elect. Electron. Engrs,* **54** (12), 1820–35.

ORGANICK, E. I. (1972). *The Multics system: an examination of its structure.* M. I. T. Press, Cambridge, Massachusetts.

—— (1973). *Computer system organization: the B5700/B6700 series.* Academic Press, New York.

PARMELEE, R. P., PETERSON, T. I., TILLMAN, C. C., AND HATFIELD, D. J. (1972). Virtual storage and virtual machine concepts. *IBM Systems J.,* **11** (2), 99–130.

PETERSON, W. W. (1961). *Error-correcting codes.* M. I. T. Press and Wiley, Cambridge, Massachusetts and New York.

PHILLIPS, E. W. (1936). Binary calculation. *J. Inst. Actuaries,* **67** 187–221. [Extracts reprinted in Randell (1975), pp. 293–304.]

VAN DER POEL, W. L. (1956). The essential types of operations in an automatic computer. *Nachrichtentechnische Fachberichte,* Vol. 4 [Proceedings of Conference on Electronic Digital Computing and Information Processing: Darmstadt: October 1955], pp. 144–5.

—— AND MAARSSEN, L. A. (eds.) (1974). *Machine oriented higher level languages.* North-Holland, Amsterdam.

RAMAMOORTHY, C. V. AND LI, H. F. (1977). Pipeline architecture. *Comput. Surv.,* **9** (1), 61-102.

RANDELL, B. (1975). *The origins of digital computers.* Springer-Verlag, Berlin.

—— AND KUEHNER, C. J. (1968). Dynamic storage allocation systems. *Commun. Ass. Comput. Mach.*, **11** (5), 297–306.

—— AND RUSSELL, L. J. (1964). *Algol 60 implementation.* Academic Press, London.

RENWICK, W. AND COLE, A. J. (1971). *Digital storage systems.* Chapman and Hall, London.

RICE, R. AND SMITH, W. R. (1971). SYMBOL—A major departure from classic software dominated Von Neumann computing systems. *AFIPS Conference Proceedings,* **38,** 575–87. [Spring Joint Computer Conference 1971.]

RICHARDS, M. (1969). BCPL: A tool for compiler writing and system programming. *AFIPS Conference Proceedings,* **34,** 557–66. [Spring Joint Computer Conference 1969.]

RICHARDS, R. K. (1955), *Arithmetic operations in digital computers.* Van Nostrand Reinhold, New York.

ROBERTS, L. G. AND WESSLER, B. D. (1970). Computer network development to achieve resource sharing. *AFIPS Conference Proceedings,* **36,** 543–9. [Spring Joint Computer Conference 1970.]

ROSEN, S. (1969). Electronic computers: A historical survey. *Comput. Surv.,* **1** (1), 7–36.

ROSIN, R. F. (1969). Contemporary concepts of microprogramming and emulation. *Comput. Surv.,* **1** (4), 197–212.

RUGGIERO, J. F. AND CORYELL, D. A. (1969). An auxiliary processing system for array calculations. *IBM Systems J.* **8** (2), 118–35.

RUSSELL, R. M. (1978). The CRAY-1 computer system. *Commun. Ass. Comput. Mach.,* **21** (1), 63–72.

SALTZER, J. H. (1974). Protection and the control of information sharing in Multics. *Commun. Ass. Comput. Mach.,* **17** (7), 388–402.

SAVAGE, B. I. AND DRAKE, A. (1967). *AGC4 basic training manual.*M. I. T. Instrumentation Laboratory, Cambridge, Massachusetts.

SCHROEDER, M. D. (1971). Performance of the GE-645 associative memory while Multics is in operation. ACM SIGOPS Workshop on System Performance Evaluation (Harvard University: 5–7th April 1971), pp. 227–45.

—— AND SALTZER, J. H. (1972). A hardware architecture for implementing protection rings. *Commun. Ass. Comput. Mach.,* **15** (3), 157–70.

SEEBER, R. R. AND LINDQUIST, A. B. (1962). Associative memory with ordered retrieval. *IBM J. Res. Dev.,* **6** (1), 126–36.

SERRELL, R., ASTRAHAN, M. M., PATTERSON, G. W., AND PYNE, I. B. (1962). The evolution of computing machines and systems. *Proc. Inst. Radio Engrs,* **50** (5), 1039–58.

SHAW, J. C. (1964). JOSS: a designer's view of an experimental on-line computing system. *AFIPS Conference Proceedings,* **26,** Pt. 1, 455–64. [Fall Joint Computer Conference 1964.]

——, Newell, A., Simon, H. A., and Ellis, T. O. (1958). A command structure for complex information handling. *Proc. Western Joint Computer Conference 1958* pp. 119–28. [Reprinted in Bell and Newell (1971), pp. 349–62.]

Slade, A. E. and McMahon, H. O. (1956). A Cryotron Catalog memory system. *Proc. Eastern Joint Computer Conference* (New York: 10–12th December 1956), pp. 115–20.

Slotnick, D. L. (1971). The fastest computer. *Scient. Amer.,* **224** (2), 76–87.

——, Borck, W. C., and McReynolds, R. C. (1962). The SOLOMON computer. *AFIPS Conference Proceedings,* **22,** 97–107. [Fall Joint Computer Conference 1962.]

Stein, M. L. and Munro, W. D. (1971). *Introduction to machine arithmetic.* Addison-Wesley, Reading, Massachusetts.

Stone, H. S. (ed.) (1975). *Introduction to computer architecture.* Science Research Associates Inc., Chicago, Illinois.

Sumner, F. H. (1969). Instruction fetching in high speed computers. Presented at IRIA (Paris: September, 1969).

—— (1974). MU5—An assessment of the design. In *Information processing 74: Proceedings of IFIP Congress 74* (ed. J. L. Rosenfeld), pp. 133–6. North-Holland, Amsterdam.

——, Haley, G., and Chen, E. C. Y. (1962). The central control unit of the Atlas computer. In *Information processing 1962: Proceedings of IFIP Congress 62* (ed. C. M. Popplewell), pp. 657–63. North-Holland, Amsterdam.

.Tanenbaum, A. S. (1976). *Structured computer organisation.* Prentice-Hall, Eaglewood Cliffs, New Jersey.

Thornton, J. E. (1964). Parallel operation in the Control Data 6600. *AFIPS Conference Proceedings,* **26,** Pt.2, 33–40. [Fall Joint Computer Conference 1964.] [Reprinted in Bell and Newell (1971), pp. 489–96.]

—— (1970). *Design of a computer: the Control Data 6600.* Scott, Foresman & Co., Glenview, Illinois.

Tjaden, G. S. and Flynn, M. J. (1970). Detection and parallel execution of independent instructions. *IEEE Trans. Comput.,* **C-19** (10), 889–95.

Townsend, R. (1975). *Digital computer structure and design.* Newnes-Butterworths, London.

Thurber, K. J. and Wald, L. D. (1975). Associative and Parallel Processors *Comput. Surv.,***7** (4), 215–55.

Valéry, N. (1974). Calculators take the fuss out of computing. *New Scientist,* **61** (884) 326–32.

Von Neumann, J. (1963). *Collected works Vol. V: design of computers, theory of automata and numerical analysis* (ed. A. H. Taub). Pergamon Press, Oxford.

—— (1966). *Theory of self-reproducing automata.* University of Illinois Press, Urbana, Illinois.

WATSON, R. W., MYER, T. H., SUTHERLAND, I. E., AND VOSBURY, M. K. (1969). A display processor design. *AFIPS Conference Proceedings,* **35,** 209–17. [Fall Joint Computer Conference 1969.]

WEBER, H. (1967). A microprogrammed implementation of EULER on IBM system/360 model 30. *Commun. Ass. Comput. Mach.,* **10** (9), 549–58. [Reprinted in Bell and Newell (1971), pp. 382–92.]

WICHMANN, B. A. (1974). The implementation and use of stacks. In *Infotech state of the art report 17: computer design* (ed. C. Boon), pp. 469–84. Infotech Information Ltd, Maidenhead, Berkshire.

WILKES, M. V. (1951). The best way to design an automatic calculating machine. Manchester University Computer Inaugural Conference: July 1951.

—— (1965). Slave memories and dynamic storage allocation. *IEEE Trans. electron. Comput.,* **EC-14** (2), 270–1 .

—— AND RENWICK, W. (1949). The EDSAC. *Report of a Conference on High Speed Automatic Calculating Machines* (Cambridge: 22–5th June 1949), pp. 9–11. [Reprinted in Randell (1975), pp. 389–93.]

——,——, AND WHEELER, D. J. (1958). The design of the control unit of an electronic ditital computer. *Proc. Inst. Elect. Engrs,* Part B, Vol. 105 (20), pp. 121–8.

—— AND STRINGER, J. B. (1953). Micro-programming and the design of the control circuits in an electronic digital computer. *Proc. Camb. Phil. Soc.,* **49,** Pt. 2, 230–8. [Reprinted in Bell and Newell (1971), pp. 335–40.]

WILKINSON, J. H. (1953). The Pilot ACE In *Automatic digital computation,* National Physical Laboratory, pp. 5–14. [Reprinted in Bell and Newell (1971), pp. 193–9.]

WILNER, W. T. (1972a). Design of the Burroughs B1700. *AFIPS Conference Proceedings,* **41,** Pt. 1, 489–97. [Fall Joint Computer Conference 1972.].

—— (1972b). Burroughs B1700 memory utilization. *AFIPS Conference Proceedings,* **41,** Pt. 1, 579–86. [Fall Joint Computer Conference 1972.]

WIRTH, N. (1968). PL360, A programming language for the 360 computers. *J. Ass. Comput. Mach.,* **15** (1), 37–74.

—— (1969). On multiprogramming, machine coding, and computer organization. *Commun. Ass. Comput. Mach.,* **12** (9), 489–98.

—— (1972). *On Pascal code generation, and the CDC 6000 computer.* Stanford University Computer Science Report, STAN-CS-72-257.

YAU, S. S. AND FUNG, H. S. (1977). Associative Processor Architecture —a survey. *Comput. Surv.,* **9** (1), 3–27.

YUVAL, G. (1977). Cray-l for 6000/7000 Hackers. *Software Practice and Experience,* **7** (3), 427–8.

# Index